Dictionary
of Law

Dictionary of Law

W.J. STEWART

Collins

HarperCollins*Publishers*
Westerhill Road, Glasgow G64 2QT

www.collins.co.uk

First published 1996
Second edition published 2001

Reprint 5

© First edition 1996 W. J. Stewart and Robert Burgess

© Second edition 2001 W. J. Stewart

ISBN 0 00 710294 1

A catalogue record for this book is available from the British Library.

Typeset by Davidson Pre-Press Graphics Limited, Glasgow.

Printed in Great Britain by Clays Ltd, St Ives plc

Foreword to Second Edition

IN MEMORIAM

Professor R. A. ('Bob') Burgess 1946–99

Co-author of the First Edition

Most work has gone towards meeting the original mission, which was to have a modern contemporary work that would be useful in the ordinary working life of most users. The introduction of European human rights law and devolution within the UK has spawned a considerable addition to the lexicon. I have also tried to ensure that other legislative and judicial developments over the last five years have been reflected in the text. While the dictionary is not intended to state the law, in defining legal concepts this is inevitable, and when these concepts are changed by decision or legislation, the definitions have had to change too. I have taken the opportunity to add some words omitted from the last edition where I have seen that they still appear in current materials or in materials people are still required to read. Notwithstanding a recent judicial pronouncement that Latin should not be used, it still is. All the law's 'hard words' remain in the texts of the law, which live as long as the law itself.

One technical issue has arisen. That is the matter of the use of the letter 'J' in Latin words. Here we encounter the well-known division between Latin as a language and Latin as a legal language. Even the classical periods of Latin and Roman law do not coincide. The medieval epoch spawned some curious Latin and much legal Latin. 'J' is used as a consonant and 'i' for the vowel.

The vast improvement in the content of the Internet has allowed me to read very many more legal texts from abroad, so permitting some enhancement to entries and the presence of some new ones. The downside is that I had no excuse with this edition for a trip to the Bodelian, as I did the last time. Not everything about progress is good.

Finally, thanks to Professor Rebecca Wallace of the School of Law at Napier University, Cowan Ervine at Dundee University and P. B. Mathews of Withers, Solicitors, London, for reading the text and proposing amendments and saving me from many errors and omissions. I am solely responsible for those that remain.

W. J. Stewart, Tollcross, March 2001

Preface to First Edition

The law has been well served by 'dictionaries'. Well before Dr Johnson started on his English Dictionary, words used by lawyers had been set out as an aid to comprehension: Rastell, The Exposicions of the Terms of the Laws of England (1526) and for Scotland in Skene, De Verborum Significatione: The Exposition of the Terms and Difficill Wordes etc (1597). This reflects the fact that the law has its own vocabulary and uses ordinary words of the English language in special senses.

The early dictionaries were dictionaries of 'hard words'. (Note that old 'books of entries' were in fact alphabetically arranged collections of precedents or styles and not dictionaries in the ordinary sense.) Many of the words used by lawyers today still fall into the category of 'hard words'. This dictionary therefore meets the same need today as that of the oldest dictionaries: of making these peculiar legal words intelligible to the ordinary reader. However, there are words other than hard words in this dictionary. Modern legislation uses ordinary English words, which acquire additional meanings from this very special context. A selection of such words is included. Ordinary words and phrases of the English language as judicially considered are not generally collected here – they are collected in a special kind of dictionary sometimes called a 'judicial dictionary', e.g. in England, Stroud (Sweet and Maxwell) and in Scotland, Stewart (Green).

In modern times different types of legal tables arranged alphabetically that are not dictionaries have appeared, so it is important to say what this book is not. It is not an 'Everyman's own lawyer' – a compendium of legal advice set out alphabetically. Thus, the book should not, under any circumstances be used as a substitute for legal advice, although it will be most helpful in assisting the layman to understand letters written by the few lawyers who are not yet able to appreciate the change of register required when writing to clients. It is not always a mere glossary that simply sets out the denotation of the terms alphabetically listed. However, it is *at least* a glossary of most of the significant words likely to be found by students who are studying law as part of their general degree studies. It is also *at least* a glossary of very many of the core terms encountered by law degree students in their first years of study. It is not an encyclopedia: the encyclopedia tells all there is to know. That cannot be done in a book this size. In any event, modern lexicography prefers dictionaries to avoid the encyclopedic entry. For reasons stated below, we have deviated from this counsel of perfection in respect of a small number of entries.

Having said what the book is not, what is it? It is a concise dictionary incorporating a glossary of selected important terms. It is defined by its readers. The book is written to be of use to the person who buys it. Primarily the dictionary is written for the person studying law as part of another degree, the term most often used in the UK for such studies being Business Law. The orientation and selection of terms is directed primarily towards those needs – European law and institutions, company law and legal aspects of finance are deliberately more prominently represented here than in other similar texts. The attempt to satisfy this category of reader explains the more encyclopedic entry and explains the table of cases and statutes.

The secondary audience, an audience at the front of our minds in the course of writing, is the general lay public. Television reports of famous (and infamous!) trials, proceedings in the House of Commons, the law report pages of the quality press and the need to decipher and decode communications from banks, building societies and 'the authorities' all require a tool to translate the terminology, or jargon, of the law into something more meaningful. This we have tried to do. We hope our text should be easily understood by readers who are not university or college undergraduates.

The senior legal secretary and the paralegal, the accountant, doctor, nurse and the surveyor are examples of readers who fall between the two foregoing categories of reader. In their own field they will know many more terms than appear in this book, but inevitably there will be an overlap with the unfamiliar, and this book should be a useful companion in that regard.

Much of the talk in lexicography, linguistics and literary theory is of exclusion. We have been keenly aware of the issue of the use of gender-specific language and have gone some considerable way to take account of this. The law itself is inter-textual and for centuries has been what would now be called by some phallocentric. As our task is merely to explain rather than proselytise, we have left a number of gender-specific references that reflect the law we seek to explain. We hope our female readers will not feel as excluded as they might with other similar books. As has been made clear, this is a book that is a subset of the class 'English dictionary'. The people who live in England no longer have a monopoly over the language that fermented in their land. Nonetheless, English law has rather followed the English language in its travels around the world. Thus, in many countries where English is the main language it will be found that English law is at the heart of the legal system. As a result, the dictionary should be useful well beyond the shores of the UK, the USA, Canada, Australia and New Zealand being obvious examples. To meet the issue of exclusion, we have tried to incorporate points from these jurisdictions where they have made their own contribution to English legal terminology, although we have not attempted to note every local divergence. Even within the UK, it would have been easy to exclude about a tenth of the population by ignoring Scots law, an independent system founded upon Roman rather than English law. We have not done so, making this perhaps the only dictionary of its kind to ensure this particular local difference is extensively noted. However, unless otherwise stated, the law is the law of England. The Republic of Ireland is a separate state with its own legal system. Obviously, it is not dealt with under UK entries. As the UK's only contiguous neighbour it merits some entries not accorded to other countries.

We hope the book will satisfy most of the users most of the time.

Finally, this is a new and original dictionary. It was created by reading leading legal textbooks and texts with an eye to spotting the 'hard words' or words used in an unusual sense. Having established the word list, we defined the words by reference to leading legal texts, cases and statutes and our own understanding of the meaning of the words.

We are grateful to Rebecca Wallace for reading drafts of the European Union entries; to Professor John Blackie and Dennis Edwards for development work on the first draft; and to Cowan Ervine who, as a reader of the MS, made very many valuable comments as well as writing the Irish entries.

A

ABA abbreviation for American Bar Association.

abandonment 1. surrender of something, whether a CHATTEL or right, with the intention of never reclaiming it.

2. a High Court action is *abandoned* when the procedure under the CIVIL PROCEDURE RULES is followed.

3. in Scotland an action can be abandoned by a *minute of abandonment*.

4. appeals that are withdrawn are said to be abandoned.

5. a CHILD is abandoned by its parents when they leave it without making provision for its care and welfare.

6. the giving up of a PATENT, COPYRIGHT or TRADEMARK.

7. the surrender of insured property to the insurer on payment to the insured.

8. (USA) withdrawal by a criminal from the course of an offence by change of heart as opposed to force of circumstances.

abatement interruption of legal proceedings on a plea from the defendant to a matter that prevented the plaintiff from proceeding at that time or in that form (e.g. objections to the mode and time of the plaintiff's claim).

   Civil proceedings are not *abated* by reasons of the marriage, death or bankruptcy of a party if the cause of action survives or continues. Criminal proceedings are not abated by the death of the prosecutor (or the sovereign) but they are by the death of the accused or, if the accused is a COMPANY, by the winding up of the company.

   A NUISANCE is abated when it is stopped. By statute, *abatement notices* may be served in respect of certain nuisances by local authorities: Environmental Protection Act 1990.

abatement of legacies in both the English and the Scots law of SUCCESSION, upon there being insufficient funds to pay general legacies, e.g. a legacy of a sum of money, legacies are *abated*, that is, reduced PARI PASSU ('in proportion').

abdication the giving up of a position that is not held from another. In the CONSTITUTIONAL LAW of the UK, a process of voluntary surrender of the throne by a reigning monarch. It has happened only once, in the 1930s, and that was itself without precedent.

Edward VIII *abdicated* by virtue of the His Majesty's Declaration of Abdication Act 1936. If it were to occur again, however, the procedure would be similar, involving consultation with the Commonwealth, culminating in an Abdication Act and, if appropriate, alteration of the succession.

abduction the wrongful taking away (usually by force) of a person. In respect of the taking away of a girl under the age of 16, it is a statutory offence in terms of the Sexual Offences Act 1956.

In Scotland the abduction of a girl under 18 is an offence under the Sexual Offences (Scotland) Act 1976. There is also a common law crime of *abduction with intent to ravish*.

The problem of separated parents removing children from one country to another is now regulated in many states by the application of the 1980 Hague Convention on Civil Aspects of International Child Abduction. The child should normally be returned to its country of habitual residence unless there is a grave risk of physical or psychological harm or an otherwise intolerable situation. See, for example, *in re C* (a minor) [1999] TLR 371.

abet see AID OR ABET.

abeyance suspended. When there is no person in whom an estate can VEST, (see VESTING), it is said to be *in abeyance*. Often used of titles.

ab initio 'from the beginning'.

ab intestato 'from an intestate'. See INTESTACY.

abjuration renunciation by an OATH.

abjuration of the realm a renunciation on OATH of a person's country; now in the USA a departure from a state with no intention to return.

able legally entitled. See DISABILITIES.

abode see RIGHT OF ABODE.

abolish to terminate the legal effect of some provision or doctrine.

abominable crime a phrase used in older law reports to denote SODOMY, BUGGERY and BESTIALITY.

abortion termination of a pregnancy before it is complete, with the purpose of destroying the foetus.

In English criminal law, procuring an abortion was a FELONY and indeed it is still subject to the provisions of the Abortion Act 1967 (as amended by the Human Fertilisation and Embryology Act 1990).

In the criminal law of Scotland it is the crime of procuring an early termination of a pregnancy and disposal of the foetus with felonious intent. Either or both the woman and the abortionist may be charged.

Under the 1967 Act, which applies in both jurisdictions, no offence is committed where the pregnancy is terminated by a registered medical practitioner if two medical practitioners are of the BONA FIDE opinion that allowing the pregnancy to continue would involve risk to the woman's life or result in injury to the physical or mental health of the woman or her family. If the foetus were to be born seriously handicapped, this too is a ground. A husband cannot prevent a wife having an abortion: *Paton* v. *Trustees of British Pregnancy Advisory Service* [1978] 2 All ER 987. *Kelly* v. *Kelly* [1997] SCT 816. Medical practitioners have a 'conscience clause' in the Act, which means that they do not have to be involved in performing abortions.

In the USA there was a famous decision allowing abortion, *Roe* v. *Wade*, 410 US 113 (1973), and despite subsequent retrenchment at a practical level in *Webster* v. *Reproductive Health Services* (1989) 492 US 490, the constitutional right remains: *Planned Parenthood of Southeastern Pennsylvania* v. *Casey*, 505 US 833 (1992).

abridge to reduce the effect (of a law, privilege or power).

abrogate to repeal or annul.

abscond to run away, especially from the jurisdiction of a court. It is an offence under the Bail Act 1976 to fail to surrender to custody and an offence under the Insolvency Act 1978 to avoid proceedings.

absent parent a parent of a CHILD not living in the same household as the child when the child has his home with a parent with care. The phrase is relevant in the law relating to CHILD SUPPORT. Each absent parent of a qualifying child is responsible for maintaining the child. This is done by making PERIODICAL PAYMENT ORDERS. The amount is fixed at a MAINTENANCE ASSESSMENT.

absolute discharge after conviction for an offence that is not punished by a fixed sentence, a court may decide punishment is not required and allow the convicted person to go free of penalty.

absolute insolvency see INSOLVENCY.

absolute liability a phrase to describe a case where liability attaches to a person on the happening of a given condition and despite any care that that person may have taken and despite any facts suggesting the happening was outside human foresight. It appears in some statutory crimes and civil duties. See FAULT, STRICT LIABILITY.

absolute privilege see DEFAMATION.

absolution the absolving or formal setting free from guilt, sentence or obligation; the remission of sin or penance.

abstention (USA) the staying of a federal case because that court considers the issue can better be dealt with by a state court.

abstract of title in unregistered land, a statement, in chronological order and beginning with a GOOD ROOT, of all the instruments and events over the period of the title, showing how the vendor came to acquire the land and, where appropriate, what has happened to it between the acquisition and the current transaction. The period of title is currently 15 years. See Schedule 6, Law of Property Act 1925.

abuse of a dominant position see COMPETITION POLICY.

abuse of process TORT or DELICT of using procedures of courts and the like other than to litigate, an example being where a person raises actions to annoy another rather than to try to recover money.

ACAS see ADVISORY CONCILIATION AND ARBITRATION SERVICE.

ACC abbreviation for ACCIDENT COMPENSATION Commission.

acceptance 1. (of a BILL OF EXCHANGE) the acknowledgement by the person on whom the bill is drawn (the *drawee*) that he will accept the order of the person who drew it (the *drawer*). An acceptance must be written on the bill and be signed by the drawee. An acceptance is either general or qualified. In the case of a *general acceptance*, the assent is without qualification to the order of the drawer. A *qualified acceptance* in express terms varies the effect of the bill as drawn.
2. (of service) procedure in both England and Scotland by which a solicitor can legally take the proceedings served on his client, avoiding the cost involved in having it done otherwise.
3. (of a CONTRACT offer) an acceptance is an unqualified assent to the terms of an *offerer* (the original person making the offer). If qualifications are made, the so-called acceptance becomes a counter-offer that itself would have to be accepted by the original offer: *Hyde* v. *Wrench* (1840) 49 ER 132. Difficulties arise in many cases; see POSTAL ACCEPTANCE RULE, BATTLE OF THE FORMS. The general rule is that the acceptance must be communicated to the offerer: *Entores* v. *Miles Far East Corporation* [1955] 2 QB 327. Conduct may imply acceptance: *Carlill* v. *Carbolic Smoke Ball Co.* [1893] 1 QB 256. It is not possible to stipulate silence as a way of acceptance: *Felthouse* v. *Bindley* (1863) 1 New Rep. 401.
4. (of GOODS) in the law of sale, in terms of the Sale of Goods Act 1979 as amended by the Sale and Supply of Goods Act 1994, the buyer has *not* accepted goods until he has had his limited right to examine them. This negative formulation is important because, once accepted, there can be no rejection. Where goods are delivered

to the buyer, and he has not previously examined them, he is not deemed to have accepted them until he has had a reasonable opportunity of examining them for the purpose of ascertaining whether they are in conformity with the contract. Such an opportunity must be granted on request. The Act sets down various ways in which acceptance can take place or be deemed to take place. The buyer is deemed to have accepted the goods: (i) when he intimates to the seller that he has accepted them so long as there has been a reasonable opportunity to examine the goods; or (ii) when the goods have been delivered to him and he does any act in relation to them that is inconsistent with the ownership of the seller (but not where the seller repairs or because of a subsale); or (iii) when, after the lapse of a reasonable time (which includes at least the time for a reasonable opportunity to inspect the goods), he retains the goods without intimating to the seller that he is rejecting them. A consumer cannot lose the right to reject by agreement waiver or otherwise.

access 1. the opportunity to see and visit a CHILD in cases where spouses have separated or divorced and care and custody of a child has been awarded to one spouse. The granting of access and the terms on which it is granted are within the discretion of the court. In both England and Scotland the appropriate order would be a *contact order*. See SECTION 8 ORDER.

2. this term when used in deeds signifies the right to go into property and, often combined with *egress*, the right to go out of it.

accession 1. a doctrine of English law by which a person is held to be responsible for a crime even although he is not the principal actor. An *accessory before the fact* is someone who procures, counsels, commands or abets it. An *accessory after the fact* assists the principal by harbouring him or assisting him to get away. A person who actually is present but does not commit the act is not an accessory but a *principal in the second degree*. Accession after the fact is not generally accepted in Scotland, although it has been imposed by statute in cases of TREASON.

2. the doctrine of the Roman and Scots law of property that declares that the owner of a thing becomes the owner of any subsidiary thing that becomes attached to it. A door stuck to a house becomes the property of the house owner.

3. succeeding to the throne as monarch.

See also ACCESSION AGREEMENTS.

accession agreements in the law of the EUROPEAN UNION agreements concluded between the communities and states that are not MEMBER STATES, usually, in their terms, 'with a view to membership'. They are not legally different from other agreements; it is the definition of their scope that gives them their significance. In some cases, such as those of Spain and Portugal, they were a means of gearing the applicant state as far as possible to the economic and infrastructure levels of the Communities. Some accession agreements have been moribund for a time but have later been resurrected, such as was the case of the agreement with the Hellenic Republic when democracy was considered as suspended in that state. Sometimes described as 'an antechamber to membership', they are a useful way of dealing with the Communities' legal mechanism for accession. See also ACQUIS COMMUNAUTAIRE.

accessory see ACCESSION.

accessory after the fact see ACCESSION.

accessory before the fact see ACCESSION.

accident an undesired or unintended happening. While the lay person uses the term with implications of blame, the lawyer tends to use it in a neutral sense to describe the phenomenon. *Inevitable accident* falls within the concept of ACT OF GOD, or *damnum fatale*.

accident compensation (New Zealand) payment in respect of most accidents in New Zealand. While in the UK accident compensation is generally decided upon the basis of the TORT or DELICT systems and generally requires proof of FAULT, New Zealand introduced a different scheme under the Accident Compensation Act 1982. The concept is one of no-fault compensation, and the principles upon which it is founded are community responsibility, comprehensive entitlement, complete rehabilitation, real compensation and administrative efficiency, so the injured person is compensated without the difficulties inherent in proving fault and will be sure of receiving payment. The payment may be much less than the 'windfall' damages often paid under the UK system. The right to raise a civil action for matter covered by the scheme is withdrawn. The trigger for a claim is 'personal injury accident'. This includes physical and mental consequences, medical misadventure, industrial injuries and incapacity, actual bodily harm, including pregnancy and mental or NERVOUS SHOCK. It does exclude what might be called some of the vicissitudes of life, so does not include damage from heart attacks and brain episodes unless these result from the effort of abnormal or excessive stress or strain arising out of, and in the course of, EMPLOYMENT. Disease, infection and the ageing process are excluded. The scheme is funded by earnings from a motor vehicle account and from a government-funded supplementary account. The scheme is presently administered by the Accident Compensation Commission (ACC), owned by the government. The Accident Insurance Act 1998 remains the principal Act under which ACC operates. The Accident Insurance Amendment Act 2000 and the Accident Insurance (Transitional Provisions) Act 2000, both passed in March 2000, mainly provide for workplace accident insurance to return to ACC.

accommodation bill a BILL OF EXCHANGE accepted by an accommodation party, that is, a person signing without receiving value and for the purpose of lending his name (and his credit) to someone else. An accommodation party is liable on the bill to a HOLDER for value.

accomplice a person who participates in a crime, either by ACCESSION or as a perpetrator, before or after the fact, by committing, procuring or aiding and abetting. Some degree of guilty knowledge is necessary.

accord and satisfaction the purchase of a release from an obligation, whether arising under CONTRACT or TORT, by means of any valuable consideration, not being the actual performance of the obligation itself. The *accord* is the agreement by which the obligation is discharged. The *satisfaction* is the consideration that makes the agreement operative.

accountability of partners see PARTNERSHIP.

accountancy in bankruptcy the process by which an AUTHORISED INSOLVENCY PRACTITIONER is required to maintain accountancy records covering his activities during the bankruptcy administration for submission to the creditors and to the Secretary of State.

Accountant in Bankruptcy in Scotland, an official who may become interim or permanent TRUSTEE and who will do so in many small assets cases.

Accountant of Court an official in the Scottish legal system charged with overseeing aspects of INSOLVENCY practice, TRUSTEES and JUDICIAL FACTORS. As a result of the Bankruptcy (Scotland) Act 1993, the Accountant of Court has been given a new function. He may become an interim or permanent trustee and will act as such in small assets cases.

account payee a crossing or direction on a BILL OF EXCHANGE that the drawee should credit funds only to the bank account of the payee. Under the Bills of Exchange Act 1882 this had no effect upon the ability of the instrument to be negotiated, but the law has been changed by the Cheques Act 1992, making it impossible for the cheque to be transferred when the words 'account payee' are used.

accounts (of limited companies) annual accounts for circulation to members. Such accounts should be sufficient to show and explain the COMPANY's transactions and be such as to disclose with reasonable accuracy at any time the financial position of the company at that time and to enable the directors to ensure that the BALANCE SHEET and PROFIT AND LOSS ACCOUNT comply with the requirements of the Companies Acts. The directors are required in respect of each financial year to lay before the company in general meeting copies of the company's annual accounts, the directors' report and the auditor's report on those accounts.

accretion 1. the natural increase in the area of land by accumulation of soil and the like. In Scotland the Roman term ALLUVIO is used for the same concept.

2. in Scotland, the term used in CONVEYANCING to denote the fortification of a title by subsequent acquisition of ownership.

accusatorial procedure a procedure that resolves a dispute between the parties by having one bring the other to court and challenging the other over the issues. The role of the judge is to maintain fair play – it is an umpiring role rather than a participating role. This is the form of procedure, both civil and criminal, that is prevalent in the Anglo-American world. It contrasts with INQUISITORIAL PROCEDURE.

accused the person charged with a CRIME. In Scotland the accused in serious cases is often called the *panel*.

a coelo usque ad centrum 'from the heavens to the centre of the earth'.

acquiescence the tacit approval of conduct that might otherwise have provided grounds for an action but which cannot be objected to if undertaken with the CONSENT of the party affected. Consent may be express or implied, and one circumstance where consent may be implied is where the party affected, in full knowledge of his rights, takes no action.

acquis communautaire (literally 'community achievement') the accumulated legal regime of the EUROPEAN UNION. Applicants for admission to the European Union must accept the achievements to date. If they cannot, what tends to happen is that a transitional period can be provided to allow the new member to catch up. See also ACCESSION AGREEMENTS.

acquisitive prescription gaining a right over land (especially an EASEMENT or profit) by passage of time. At common law a right could only be acquired prescriptively if use, enjoyment or benefit (user) as of right could be shown to have been enjoyed from 'time immemorial'. For this purpose, the year 1189 was fixed as the limit of legal memory, so that any right enjoyed at that date was unchallengeable. In practice, however, it was impossible to demonstrate this, so by the middle of the 19th century 20 years' uninterrupted use was sufficient to found a claim at common law (see also LOST MODERN GRANT).

acquittal a decision of a court that a defendant prosecuted for a criminal offence is not guilty. Also describes the Scottish verdict of NOT PROVEN.

acte claire see PRELIMINARY RULING.

actio de effusis vel dejectis in Roman law the action against an occupier for double damages where a person suffered as a result of things poured or thrown from a building, no matter who expelled them. In Scotland, it is argued that this represents a special head of recovery of damages, as opposed to a penalty. The courts have preferred to treat such cases on the basis of negligence: *Gray* v. *Dunlop*, 1954 SLT (Sh. Ct) 75.

actio de in rem verso a Roman law form of action in respect of something turned to the benefit of another's estate. In some modern civilian systems it is a recognised head of claim in the law of RESTITUTION.

actio de positis vel suspensis in Roman law the action against an occupier for a penalty at the instance of anyone who complained in respect of things suspended that would do damage if they fell. In Scotland it is argued that this represents a special head of recovery of damages, as opposed to a penalty. The courts have preferred to treat such cases on the basis of negligence: *MacColl* v. *Hoo*, 1983 SLT (Sh. Ct) 23.

action on the case a writ for wrongs and injuries causing indirect damage where similar cases gave a PRECEDENT. The STATUTE OF WESTMINSTER 1285 permitted the courts of Chancery to give such a remedy. This increased the number of remedies available to the litigant at a time when causes of action could only proceed if there was a form of action. A famous example is ASSUMPSIT.

actio personalis moritur cum persona 'a personal action dies with the person.'

actio quanti minoris originally a remedy in Roman law granted to the *aedile* (a magistrate with jurisdiction over markets) when a latent defect appeared that had not been revealed to the buyer, allowing the buyer (within a year) to seek the difference between the price paid and the value. Liability was strict. In late Roman law it applied even to land. It is still discussed in civilian jurisdictions to this day. The Sale of Goods Act 1979 (amended in 1994) prevailing in the UK provides a general right to retain the property and claim damages for the difference in value in respect of goods that disconform to the contract, including its statutorily implied terms.

The position in Scotland in relation to land has been clarified by the Contracts (Scotland) Act 1997, which provides that it is not necessary to rescind before being able to claim damages.

act of God an accident or event that cannot be prevented by ordinary human foresight. The occurrence should normally be a natural one, like flood or earthquake. It exempts a party from STRICT LIABILITY in common law and, by definition, from NEGLIGENCE.

act of indemnity legislation passed to relieve persons of the penal consequences of particular conduct.

Act of Parliament in the CONSTITUTIONAL LAW of the UK, a *Bill* that has passed through all its stages and received the ROYAL ASSENT, thus becoming *statute* and LAW. Bills are introduced in PARLIAMENT either by a government minister or an unofficial (or private) Member presenting it at the Clerks' table. It has a *first reading*, which is purely formal, and the Bill is only a dummy – a sheet of paper with the Bill's title on it and the Member's name. The *second reading* is a discussion on the principles of the bill. At this stage it can be sent to a second reading committee for this discussion. If it is an opposed bill, it has to go before the House of Commons on one of the days set down for that sort of business. The next stage is the *committee stage*. It is at this stage that details and amendments are discussed. The Bill then proceeds to its *report stage*, when the Bill is reported to the House. At this stage or at the committee stage the *kangaroo procedure* can be adopted. This is a power vested in the Speaker, or chairman, to select which clauses are debated and to select the others for a simple vote, and it is done to save time. The Bill then has a *third reading*, at which point its principles may be debated and sent to the House of Lords. A similar procedure to that in the House of Commons is followed in the Lords. See ACT OF THE SCOTTISH PARLIAMENT.

act of state see ROYAL PREROGATIVE.

Act of the Scottish Parliament legislation of the Scottish Parliament, which must, however, be within the competence of that body or it may be struck down: Scotland Act 1998, Section 29; see also Section 57(2) with respect to secondary legislation.

Acts of Union the Acts that gave effect to the treaties that forged the UK, especially the Act of the English PARLIAMENT, the Union with Scotland Act 1706. The constitutional result is not clear because the two former nations ceased to exist, as did the parliaments, becoming a new body, the Parliament of Great Britain. Some argue that the Act of Union is fundamental law in the UK and that Parliament is not sovereign in relation to this matter, which is at the heart of its very foundation. The difficulty is in finding a tribunal to deal with infringements: see *MacCormick* v. *Lord Advocate* 1953 SC 396.

About 1494, Poyning's law conceded that laws for Ireland had to be approved by the English Council. The Irish Parliament remained until the Act of Union in 1800. In 1920 Ireland was partitioned (Government of Ireland Act 1920) and the north remained part of the UK, the south becoming the Irish Free State, emphasised when the new Republic of Ireland left the Dominions (Ireland Act 1949).

There is a devolved SCOTTISH PARLIAMENT, but the Union holds, as the Westminster Parliament remains the sovereign parliament of the Scottish people.

actual authority the express power granted to an agent (see AGENCY) by his principal. It appears also in PARTNERSHIP. Where it has been agreed between the partners that any restriction is to be placed on the power of any one or more of them to bind the firm, no act done in contravention of the agreement is binding on the firm with respect to persons having notice of the agreement.

actual grant presumed in the English law of PRESCRIPTION, if long enjoyment of a right is shown, the court will uphold the right by presuming that it had a lawful origin; in other words, that there was some actual grant of the right although it is, at the time of the action, impossible to show any evidence of such a grant.

actual knowledge the state of knowing the material facts at issue.

actus reus see CRIME.

ad colligenda bona 'to collect the goods', a form of GRANT OF ADMINISTRATION.

ademption (of legacies) in both the English and the Scots law of succession, a special legacy that specifies that the gift (e.g. 'my treasured dictionary') will be cancelled or reduced (*adeemed*) if the object is no longer part of the estate at the date of death, as where the TESTATOR has sold the dictionary to a book collector. A specific legacy of £1,000 sterling may be reduced if, before the testator's death, he has given the legatee a portion of the money. Furthermore, if a specific legacy changes its nature, the legacy will adeem, as the description of the legacy will no longer match the object.

adherence in Scots family law, parties to a marriage are obliged to *adhere*, or live one with the other, but since 1984 the court will no longer compel parties to do this.

ad hoc 'for this purpose' ('only' sometimes implied).

ad idem 'to the same things', an important phrase when considered in relation to a contract that requires *consensus ad idem* – 'agreement to the same things'.

adjectival law the law relating to procedure.

adjournment the postponement of the hearing of a case until some future date. The adjournment may be to a specified date or for an indefinite period (*sine die*).

adjudication 1. in immigration law, an *adjudicator* is an officer with the function of dealing with immigration appeals. The post of adjudicator was created by the Immigration Appeals Act 1969. Adjudicators take appeals from decisions of the immigration authorities; they may examine the factual basis of an immigration official's decisions and review any conclusions of fact on which the decision was based. An appeal must be allowed if the adjudicator considers that the decision made was not in accordance with law or with an immigration rule, or, if discretion is involved, if the adjudicator feels the discretion should have been exercised differently. If the adjudicator allows the appeal, he is empowered to give such directions for giving effect to that determination as he thinks proper. An appeal from a decision of an adjudicator lies with the Immigration Appeals Tribunal.

2. in the Scots law of DILIGENCE or legal enforcement, the process used against debtors to take away their heritable property. The action is raised in court and the decree registered. When this is done, the property thenceforward belongs to the creditor but is subject to a right of redemption in 10 years, known as the *legal*.

3. the new procedure for resolving disputes in building contracts in the UK. It is intended to be speedy and relatively informal; an independent person is appointed – an adjudicator who is obliged to come to a decision in 28 days.

adjudicator see ADJUDICATION.

adjustment 1. the computation of the amount due to an insured and the fixing of the proportion to be borne by the underwriters.

2. in Scottish civil procedure, the changing of the writ or defences before the RECORD is closed.

adjustment of prior transactions where an individual has at a relevant time entered into a transaction at an undervalue, application may be made by the trustee of the bankrupt's estate for a court order restoring the position to what it would have been had the transaction not been entered into, thereby requiring the repayment of some part or property transferred by the bankrupt.

ad litem 'for the case'.

administration order see ADMINISTRATOR, COMPANY INSOLVENCY PROCEEDINGS.

Administrative Court the name since October 2000 for the old CROWN OFFICE list in the Queen's Bench Division of the High Court.

administrative law the body of rules and procedures that organises government and provides mechanisms for redress of grievances as a result of decisions or actions of government. For lawyers its main practical manifestation is seen in cases of JUDICIAL REVIEW of administrative action.

administrator 1. in the law of succession an administrator is a person appointed by the court to represent and administer the estate of a person who has died intestate or without having appointed executors who are willing to act. The appointment is made via a grant of LETTERS OF ADMINISTRATION; where the deceased has left a will the grant will be of *letters of administration with will annexed*.

2. under the Insolvency Act 1986, provision is made as an alternative (or as a precursor) to liquidation or receivership for a company in financial difficulties to go into *administration* under the management of an administrator. Essentially, the rights of creditors are suspended for a period to enable the administrator to ascertain if the company can be reorganised so that its business(es) may be sold as a going concern, thereby protecting the interests of employees and, in the longer run, the creditors themselves. This is distinct from the function of an *administrative receiver* appointed under a debenture.

administrator-in-law in the family law of Scotland, the guardian of a child under 16. The title confers no extra powers, nor does it constitute an office separate from that of GUARDIAN.

Admiralty Court a section of the Queen's Bench Division made up of PUISNE judges assisted by a nautical assessor.

admissibility the concept in the law of evidence that determines whether or not evidence can be received by the court. The evidence must first be RELEVANT, but even relevant evidence will be tested for its admissibility. Thus, that a suspect has confessed is relevant but, in modern times, if the confession has been obtained other than voluntarily it will, in many jurisdictions, be excluded as inadmissible. See eg. HEARSAY.

admission a statement by a party to litigation that is adverse to that party's case. Admissions must be made voluntarily if they are to be admissible in evidence. Admissions may be informal (i.e. made in a pleading or in reply to an interrogatory). See EXCLUSIONARY RULE, HEARSAY.

Adopted Children's Register the register that records ADOPTION proceedings and their outcome.

adoption the legal process by which the rights and obligations of a child's natural parents are extinguished and equivalent rights and obligations are vested in the adoptive parents. In English family law, a statutory procedure under the Adoption Act 1976. The effect of an order is to have the child treated as if it had been born as a child of the marriage. Adoption prevents a child from being illegitimate thenceforth. Any person under 18 who has not been married can be *adopted*. A person adopting children (not already a parent) must be over 21. The consent of a father of an illegitimate child is not required. The court can dispense with a parent's consent. A husband and wife may adopt the legitimate children from the wife's former marriage. A local authority or approved adoption agency can apply for an order freeing a child for adoption that renders unnecessary the need later for difficult petition procedure. The effect is to extinguish parental rights and vest them in the adopters. The child succeeds to the new parents and does not succeed to the former parents.

In Scots family law, there is a similar statutory procedure under the Adoption of Children (Scotland) Act 1978.

A child adopted under an adoption order made in the UK will become a British citizen if the adopter (or, if more than one, one adopter) is a British citizen. An adoption order made outwith the UK in favour of a British citizen will not give the adopted child automatic British citizenship; this may be gained by registration or naturalisation.

ADR abbreviation for ALTERNATIVE DISPUTE RESOLUTION.

adultery voluntary sexual intercourse during the subsistence of a marriage between one spouse and a person of the opposite sex who is not the other spouse. It is sufficient in both England and Scotland to constitute the ground of divorce: IRRETRIEVABLE BREAKDOWN. Proof need not involve an eyewitness of the act in question. It is sufficient if evidence is led of circumstances from which the necessary inferences can be made, such as use of overnight accommodation in a hotel.

ad valorem 'according to the value', often used in the context of taxes and duties.

advance 1. to lend money to someone; a loan of money.

2. to make a payment before it is lawfully due; in the law of TRUSTS, trustees make advance capital under an express power or under Section 32 of the Trustee Act 1925 to a beneficiary who has a vested or contingent interest in the capital of the trust. *Advancements* under Section 32 may be up to half the beneficiary's expectant share and are subject to the consent of the holder of any prior interest.

advance corporation tax a sum payable to the revenue when a company pays a dividend to its shareholders, abolished for distributions made after April 1999.

advance directive a declaration by a person in relation to medical treatment (usually to instruct that it stop) to provide for a situation in which he might himself be unable to comment, e.g. the so-called *living will*. The US Supreme Court established the right for a person to refuse medical treatment, which in the case of a comatose patient can be difficult to establish: *Cruzan* v. *Missouri Department of Health*, 497 US 261 (1990). This is an issue that is troubling most legal systems because it raises moral, philosophical and practical questions.

advance freight see FREIGHT.

advancement see ADVANCE.

advisement (USA) deliberation. Where the judge takes the matter *under advisement* he is considering his decision. See also AVIZANDUM, CUR AD VULT.

Advisory Conciliation and Arbitration Service (ACAS) a body established under an Act of Parliament of 1975 to facilitate the resolution of industrial strife. Apart from its important role in resolving major strikes, it is involved in trying to achieve settlements in every case before an EMPLOYMENT TRIBUNAL.

advisory opinion (USA) a judicial opinion issued in response to a government request. The concept is not known to the UK courts.

ad vitam aut culpam 'for life or until blame'. Many office holders are appointed on this basis, but the modern trend is to fix retirement ages; for example, judges are now appointed subject to a retirement age.

advocate in Scotland, a general term for a BARRISTER, a member of the FACULTY OF ADVOCATES. (Note, however, that in Aberdeen solicitors call themselves advocates.) They have the exclusive right to represent parties in the higher courts, subject since the passing of the Law Reform (Miscellaneous Provisions) (Scotland) Act 1990 to the provision that SOLICITOR ADVOCATES are allowed to appear in these courts as well. The Faculty is a self-regulating body dating from the early 16th century. Its head is the elected Dean of Faculty. He is assisted by a Council. Training and education are generally similar to those of SOLICITORS, both doing the diploma in legal practice after their LLB degree, with the principal exceptions being (i) that the Roman law of obligations is compulsory for the Bar and conveyancing is not, the situation in respect of solicitors being vice-versa; (ii) the aspiring advocate breaks off the period of traineeship in a solicitor's office and then spends a period of *pupillage*, assisting and learning from his *pupil master*. The entrant has to be elected at the end of the process.

The professional code of the advocate is similar to that of the barrister, involving an obligation to act for any client willing to pay the necessary fee. The barrister's immunity for negligence having been departed from it may reasonably be assumed that advocates will now be liable for their negligence in Scotland.

Advocates do not practise in chambers; rather they are independent. They do arrange to have one clerk act for a number of advocates. Although the advocate's fee is legally an honorarium and not recoverable through the courts, the Faculty established Faculty Services Ltd, which acts as a debt collector for members and provides them with general office services.

advocate depute in Scotland, an advocate who acts for the LORD ADVOCATE in the prosecution of crime in the High Court.

Advocate-General an officer who assists the COURT OF JUSTICE OF THE EUROPEAN UNION. Advocate-Generals are not members of the Court but are selected in much the same way and have to be equally qualified. It is a peculiarly European office, so does not have an obvious analogue in UK procedure. The Advocates-General investigate the case, as the judges cannot express personal opinions in a report to the Court. As the Court does not sometimes express detailed judgements, again in the continental tradition, the opinion, if followed, is a useful indication of the possible reasoning of the Court and is accordingly published along with the decision in the official reports.

Advocate General for Scotland the newly created UK law officer who advises the UK government in relation to Scots law. The Advocate General may intervene in court proceedings dealing with a devolution issue or refer a Scottish bill considered to be outside the Scottish parliament's competence to the PRIVY COUNCIL.

aemulationem vicini 'in a spiteful way towards one's neighbours', a basis of liability in some civil law systems, including that of Scotland, but not in English law, although such conduct may indicate an unreasonable use of land and attract liability in NUISANCE.

aequitas 'uniformity' or 'evenness', in a legal context the idea of EQUITY or fairness.

affiant another word for a DEPONENT.

affidavit a written statement sworn or affirmed before a commissioner for oaths (or notary public in Scotland), used in some circumstances as evidence in court.

affinity the relationship or connection between one spouse and the blood relatives of the other. *Consanguinity* is the relationship of persons descended from the same ancestor. Thus sons are *consanguine* with their fathers, brothers with each other.

affray in English criminal law, the use or threat of the use of unlawful violence, causing a person to fear for his safety; defined in the Public Order Act 1986 in terms of the fear caused to a person of reasonable firmness fearing for his safety. Mere words are sufficient, and the offence may be committed in public or private with no other person actually being about.

affreightment a contract by a shipowner to carry goods for the freighter. The contract will be found in a BILL OF LADING or CHARTERPARTY.

aforethought see HOMICIDE.

agency a legal arrangement (which is not a trust), utilised especially in business, under which one person acts on behalf of another. An agency may be expressly created or be implied from a course of dealing or conduct; it may be limited to a particular transaction or cover a whole course of dealing; it may be limited as to time, or not. Thus, an *agent* is a person appointed by another (the *principal*) to represent that other or to act on his behalf. Often an agent will negotiate contractual arrangements on behalf of his principal with third parties.

In the law of PARTNERSHIP, every partner is an agent of the firm and of his other partners for the purposes of the business of the partnership.

Under the rules of COMPANY law, directors are agents of the company for which they act, and as such the general principles of the law of agency in many respects regulate the relationship of the company and its directors.

Agents are obliged to keep proper accounts of money and assets passing through their hands in the course of their agency and to render such accounts to their principals. An agent is under a strict duty to make full disclosure of any interests he may have in the transaction he is to perform. An agency may be terminated by operation of law: (i) by the death of either party; (ii) by the insanity of either party; (iii) by the bankruptcy of either party; (iv) by frustration of the agency agreement.

Where a person signs a bill as drawer, indorser or acceptor and adds words to his signature indicating that he signs for or on behalf of a principal, he will not be personally liable thereon. However, merely designating himself as agent without intimating for whom he is signing will not be sufficient to confer this immunity.

There is a special European regime for commercial agents, which requires, among other things, that such contracts be in writing, that reasonable payment is presumed and that compensation is paid on termination.

See DEL CREDERE AGENCY, FACTOR, FOREIGN PRINCIPAL, IRREVOCABLE AUTHORITY, MANDATE, APPARENT AUTHORITY, OSTENSIBLE AUTHORITY, COMMERCIAL AGENT.

agent see AGENCY.

age of majority see MAJORITY.

aggravated damages in England, in certain cases, the court can consider the defendant's conduct in fixing the damages to take into account the injury to the plaintiff's dignity and pride.

aggravated trespass see COLLECTIVE TRESPASS.

agistment 1. grazing people's animals for reward.

2. an Irish term for the right to graze livestock on land.

AGM abbreviation for ANNUAL GENERAL MEETING.

agnates relatives on the father's side. Compare COGNATES.

agreement to sell an agreement by which the time when property is to pass to the person who has agreed to buy is to take place at some future time or subject to a condition. See SALE.

agricultural holding a tenancy of agricultural land. A statutory system of protected leasehold tenure for agricultural land is provided by the Agricultural Holdings Act 1986 and in Scotland by the Agricultural Holdings (Scotland) Act 1949 (as amended). Tenants have a limited security of tenure, and there is a procedure to fix rents by arbitration if the parties cannot agree. The landlord normally has to give at least one year's notice to quit, and the tenant can usually appeal to the Agricultural Lands Tribunal to determine whether the notice should operate. On the death or retirement of the tenant, his spouse or other close relative can, in certain defined circumstances, succeed to the tenancy.

AI abbreviation for ARTIFICIAL INSEMINATION.

aid or abet in English law, *aiding and abetting* is the helping in some way of the principal offender. It is in itself a crime but depends upon some earlier communication between the parties. See for Scotland, ART AND PART.

AKA abbreviation for 'also known as', which in Scottish practice is inserted in complaints to show the accused's use of another name. See ALIAS.

aleatory contract a betting CONTRACT.

alias 'another name', particularly used to describe the use of another name by criminals. This practice makes it more difficult for them to be detected by the police. See AKA.

alias writ where a WRIT OF EXECUTION has been issued and returned, and the judgment or order is still unsatisfied, another writ of the same kind may be issued in the same country. If it is returned, another writ can be issued and is known as a *pluries writ*.

alibi 'elsewhere', the defence in a criminal trial in the UK (and, indeed, the USA) that the accused was somewhere else at the time the alleged crime was committed.

In both England and Scotland, the defence must give the prosecution notice of such a defence.

alien a person who is not a British citizen, a Commonwealth citizen, a British protected person or a citizen of the Republic of Ireland. At common law, a distinction is drawn between *friendly aliens* and *enemy aliens*, with the latter comprising not only citizens of hostile states but also all others voluntarily living in enemy territory or carrying on business there; enemy aliens are subject to additional disabilities. The law is set out mainly in the British Nationality Act 1981.

aliment in Scots family law, the obligation to maintain a member of one's family. It is now generally regulated by the Family Law (Scotland) Act 1985. Spouses have a mutual duty of aliment. The obligation is to provide such support as is reasonable in the circumstances. It is possible to bring an action although the spouses are living together, as where the spouse earning money keeps the other short of money. The amount is related to need and ability to pay. It may be obtained on an interim basis. See also CHILD SUPPORT.

alimony in English family law, the payment due to a spouse on separation and a term that is now no longer a technical term. In the USA it is sometimes called *spousal support*. See ALIMENT, MAINTENANCE pending suit. See also CHILD SUPPORT.

allegiance the obligation owed to the head of state in return for protection. See TREASON.

allocation of feu duties see FEU DUTY.

allonge an extra piece of paper added to a BILL OF EXCHANGE to allow INDORSEMENTS to be made.

allotment of shares the process by which members take shares from a company is the *issue of shares*; this ends with allotment, when individual shares are assigned to particular holders. A previously unissued share is *allotted* when a person acquires an unconditional right to be entered in the register of members in respect of that share.

alluvio a form of ACCRETION whereby the sea or a river retreats, enlarging one's property. The owner of the land acquires the new land. In Scots law, the rule does not apply where there is a sudden transfer, called *avulsio*, such as the flooding of a river.

alteration a change that, when made in a legal document, may affect its validity.

Where a BILL OF EXCHANGE or ACCEPTANCE is materially altered without the assent of all parties liable on the bill, the bill is avoided except against the party who made, authorised or assented to the alteration (and subsequent indorsers). However, where a bill has been materially altered but the alteration is not apparent and the bill is in the hands of a HOLDER IN DUE COURSE, such a holder may treat the bill as if it had not been altered and may enforce payment of it according to its original tenor. Alterations of the date, sum payable and time and place of payment are material alterations. See ALTERATION OF ARTICLES, ALTERATION OF CAPITAL.

alteration of articles a company's ARTICLES OF ASSOCIATION, or any part of them, may, subject to the provisions of the Companies Acts and to the conditions in the MEMORANDUM OF ASSOCIATION, at any time be altered or deleted by special resolution, others being substituted as necessary. Likewise, the application to the company of clauses of Table A adopted by the company may be similarly varied; this is a power of which the company cannot deprive itself by a statement in the articles. The company has the power to adopt any new article that could lawfully have been included in the original articles.

alteration of capital a LIMITED COMPANY may not issue more shares than are authorised by its MEMORANDUM OF ASSOCIATION. However, members of such a company may agree, by a provision in the articles, that the company's authorised capital may be increased; such an increase may be made if power to do so is provided by its articles.

alternative dispute resolution (ADR) a relatively new area of activity by which disputes are resolved other than by the ordinary courts. ARBITRATION is a form of ADR, but it is only one of many. Most examples have their own procedures and rules, and usually the parties will have to agree to abide by the decision. CONCILIATION and *mediation* are the newer forms and are already employed in everything from construction disputes to family law problems.

alterum non laedere 'not to harm anyone', the second of the three precepts upon which the Roman emperor Justinian said the law was based. The other two are not nearly so often seen in modern writing. They are *honestere vivere*, 'to live honestly'; and *suum cuique tribuere*, 'to give each his due'.

altius non tollendi see LIGHT or PROSPECT.

ambiguity uncertainty in meaning. In legal documents an ambiguity may be *patent* (i.e. apparent from a perusal of the document) or *latent* (i.e. one that becomes apparent in the light of facts that become known from sources outside the document). The general rule is that extrinsic evidence can be used to resolve latent ambiguity but not patent ambiguities.

Since the decision in *Pepper* v. *Hart* [1992] 3 WLR 1032, an ambiguity in a dispute over a statute will allow the court to hear not only the terms of LAW COMMISSION reports but also of the debates in Parliament as recorded in HANSARD.

ambulatory revocable for the time being.

amendment the alteration of a writ, pleading, indictment or other document for the purpose of correcting some error or defect in the original or to raise some new matter, claim or allegation.

a mensa et thoro literally 'from bed and board', a form of DIVORCE by way of separation that does not, however, free the parties from the bonds of marriage. In England, before the Matrimonial Causes Act 1857, a decree in these terms from the ecclesiastical courts was equivalent to a decree of judicial SEPARATION.

In Scotland, prior to the Reformation, this was the only form of divorce known. It is still used in the context of judicial separation.

American realism see REALISM.

amicus curiae 'friend of the court', a person who is not actually involved in a case as a party but who brings a matter to the attention of the court. Usually the issue involves the public interest. It is not a universally applicable procedure.

amnesty an act of a sovereign power waiving liability for a past offence. The term is also used for similar orders of inferior bodies.

amotio see THEFT.

Amsterdam Treaty (EU) the treaty signed in Amsterdam in 1997 that did not come into effect until 1999, making further alterations in the treaties setting up the EUROPEAN UNION.

ancient documents deeds and other documents that are more than 30 years old and that are probative (i.e. they prove themselves and do not require proof of their execution when coming from proper custody).

Anglo-Irish Agreement an international treaty concluded in 1985 between the Republic of Ireland and the UK. It recognised the requirement for majority consent within Northern Ireland for any change in its status, established an intergovernmental ministerial conference, serviced by a secretariat, that provided an opportunity for ministers from Ireland and the UK to discuss security, policing, prison policy, law enforcement and extradition, and set up an intergovernmental parliamentary council that permitted members of the British and Irish parliaments to meet to discuss matters of mutual interest. It moved on to such an extent that a GOOD FRIDAY AGREEMENT was reached, intended to establish a power-sharing devolved government in Northern Ireland. Its first meeting failed to comply with the necessary requirements for its continued function and it was suspended. At the time of writing the Northern Ireland government was reactivated, so there is a power-sharing executive in operation in the province.

animals, liability for the special area of law dealing with civil liability of people for the behaviour of animals.

In England, prior to the Animals Act 1971, the owner was liable for an animal of a dangerous species – FERAE NATURAE – or for one that was not of such a species if, but only if, the owner was aware of the animal's dangerous propensities.

Under the Animals Act 1971 it is a matter of law whether an animal is of a dangerous species or not. Liability in respect of such animals is STRICT LIABILITY. Liability is fixed on the keeper. Liability for non-dangerous species depends upon knowledge of the particular beast being likely to cause severe damage. See *Curtis* v. *Betts* [1990] 1 All ER 769. Defences include contributory negligence and assumption of risk. Notably, it is not a defence to strict liability under the Act to show ACT OF GOD or the act of a third party.

In Scotland dogs are deemed to be within the category of animals likely to cause physical injury. The knowledge aspect is not part of the Scots statute: the Animals (Scotland) Act 1987. That Act imposes liability according to the zoological category of the animal (using the schedule to the Dangerous Wild Animals Act 1976) and according to the damage likely to be caused. Liability is upon the keeper, and the defences of assumption of risk and contributory negligence are available. In both Scotland and England the ordinary law of negligence applies.

animus donandi 'the intention of making a gift'. Where a document conferring rights to property has been prima facie validly executed, a presumption exists that the maker intended it to have effect. This presumption may be negatived if it can be shown that the execution of the document was procured by fraud, under duress, by the undue influence of another or as a result of some material mistake.

animus gerendi 'the intention to administer' (for another). The issue arises in relation to the (questionably) restitutionary remedy in civilian jurisdiction's NEGOTIORUM GESTIO.

animus testandi 'the intention of making a WILL'.

annual general meeting (AGM) a compulsory general meeting of a COMPANY required under the Companies Acts; this is in addition to any other meetings in that year. The annual general meeting must be designated as such in the notices calling it.

It is at the annual general meeting that dividends are decided. The company's accounts are considered and the directors' and auditor's reports are put before the shareholders. It is the occasion when directors are appointed in place of those retiring and where their remuneration and conditions are fixed. The annual general meeting is an important safeguard for shareholders since it is the one occasion when they can be sure of having an opportunity to question directors on the accounts, on their report and on the company's condition and prospects.

annual payment a payment made annually. INCOME TAX is chargeable under Case III of SCHEDULE D on annual payments. Since the Finance Act 1989 the charge effectively covers interest and payments under annuities.

annual return a return made once a year by a COMPANY. Every company is required under the Companies Acts to make an annual return to the registrar made up to a date not later than its 'return date'. The return must specify: (i) the address of the registered office; (ii) the whereabouts of the register of members and debenture holders; (iii) a summary of the share capital and debentures; (iv) debts secured by mortgage or charge; (v) the identity of members; (vi) particulars of the company's directors and secretary.

annuitant a person who receives an ANNUITY.

annuity an entitlement to a specified sum of money that lasts for the duration of the life of the beneficiary or annuitant. Annuities may be created under a TRUST or they may be purchased from a life insurance company (in which case no trust is needed).

annul to render VOID.

antecedent negotiations a term in relation to CONSUMER CREDIT legislation referring to negotiations by or on behalf of the owner or creditor prior to contract.

antedating 'dating before'. The date on a BILL OF EXCHANGE, acceptance or indorsement is deemed to be the true date of the drawing, acceptance or indorsement unless the contrary is proved. The date is relevant only in that it regulates the term of payment that bears reference to the date of the bill. A bill, therefore, is not invalid by reason only of the fact that it is antedated or postdated.

ante litem motam 'before the case began'.

ante-nuptial agreement an agreement entered into before marriage by which one or both potential spouses exclude, so far as the law allows, his or her property at the time or to follow from falling within the scope of the law of DIVORCE. Such agreements are clearly more important in jurisdictions that have a COMMUNITY PROPERTY rule and less important in jurisdictions that have a separate property rule. They were very common in previous centuries when great landowners were anxious to preserve estates against unfortunate marriages. States that allow such agreements are likely to require them to be at least fair and reasonable when entered into.

antichresis in Roman law the agreement whereby the creditor in a pawn or mortgage-type transaction was permitted to have the fruits of the property pledged in lieu of interest.

anticipatory breach of contract where a party to a CONTRACT intimates, or it becomes clear, that he is not going to perform on the due date, then there is said to be anticipatory breach: *Hochster* v. *de la Tour* (1853) 2 E&B 678. The difficulty is that the innocent party could, in many cases, in the time available mitigate his loss by finding another to perform. The unfortunate thing about that would be that the contract-breaker would escape liability. It is accepted that the innocent party may decline to accept the repudiation and instead sue on the due date, when, of course, the losses may be higher than at the anticipatory date: *Tai Hing Cotton Mill* v. *Kamsing Knitting Factory* [1979] AC 91. The most dangerous thing about the doctrine for a contract-breaker is the rule that a party may completely ignore the breach and himself perform on the due date, assuming he does not require the contract-breaker's assistance in so doing, and then sue for the obligations under the contract. The benefit of this course is that the claim is one for a due debt, not for damages, and there is therefore no need to mitigate loss: *White & Carter (Councils)* v. *McGregor*, 1962 SC (HL) 1. See also CANCELLATION.

antidumping see COMPETITION POLICY.

antisocial behaviour order an order that can be made by a court, where necessary, preventing alarming or distressing conduct to protect the neighbourhood. Breach is a criminal offence: Crime and Disorder Act 1998.

antitrust law (USA) the law applying to issues of attack on free competition by businesses or other organisations. See SHERMAN ACT.

Anton Piller orders in English procedure, an order of the High Court that orders the defendant to allow the plaintiff to inspect, remove or copy documents, granted on the plaintiff's showing there is danger to the evidence: see *Anton Piller KG* v. *Manufacturing Processes Ltd* [1976] Ch. 55, the case after which the orders are informally named.

apparent authority the situation where, objectively looked at, it seems that an agent does have the authority of his principal. Where an agent has apparent authority to enter into a transaction, the fact that he lacks real authority will not necessarily render the transaction void; the appearance of authority will operate to create an ESTOPPEL preventing the principal from denying the existence of such authority. See AGENCY.

apparent insolvency see INSOLVENCY.

appeal the process of taking a case to a court with power to alter the decision of the court that has made the decision complained of. A court with power to hear appeals is called an *appellate court*, and a person appealing is usually called an *appellant* and his opponent the *respondent*. (In Scotland, a person appealing to the Inner House of the COURT OF SESSION is called a *reclaimer*, the process a *reclaiming motion*.) Some courts hear appeals completely anew, but usually an appeal is argued with a view to correcting a legal error in the court below. As witnesses are not usually heard, the facts are normally taken as found in the court below, but if a transcript is available, the reasonableness of a decision or inferences taken from primary facts established may often be challenged on appeal. Sometimes a court has power to order a new trial or to deal with a case again if new evidence that could not have been put before the lower court comes to hand. See also IMMIGRATION APPEAL.

appellant see APPEAL.

appellate court see APPEAL.

apprentice a person bound under an *apprenticeship*, a special and ancient contract binding the apprentice to serve and learn and the master to instruct. The deed recording the contract is sometimes called an *indenture*.

approbate and reprobate see ELECTION.

approval see PROPERTY.

appurtenance an incorporeal interest added to a corporeal hereditament by grant or prescription.

aquaeduct in Scots property law, the SERVITUDE right to lay pipes to take water and access for the purpose of maintaining the pipes.

aquaehaustus in Scots property law, the SERVITUDE right to enter ground belonging to another to take water from a well there.

arbiter see ARBITRATION.

arbitration a form of ALTERNATIVE DISPUTE RESOLUTION by which the determination of a dispute is entrusted to one or more independent third parties rather than the court. While an *arbitrator* is bound to apply the law accurately, he may adopt a form of procedure that appears to him to be appropriate and is not bound by exclusionary rules of evidence. In Scotland, the arbitrator is known as an *arbiter*.

arbitrator see ARBITRATION.

arguendo 'by way of argument'.

arra in ROMAN LAW, a payment that could be forfeit to escape from a contract before it was concluded in writing or that, on another view of the law, could be paid to escape from any sale. Arra was often more than half the value of the property in question. The modern Anglo-American equivalent is payment of a non-returnable DEPOSIT. See also EARNEST.

arraign in English and American legal process, to call the accused to the bar of the court to answer an INDICTMENT. The hearing is called an *arraignment*.

arrest the seizure or touching of a person's body with a view to his detention. In England, the law is set out in statute and in some detail in the Police and Criminal Evidence Act 1984. In many common law jurisdictions the fact of arrest triggers various legal protections of the person arrested. See ARRESTMENT.

arrestable offence in English criminal law an offence for which the sentence is fixed by law or for which the sentence is five years' imprisonment. The significance is that any person may arrest anyone committing such an offence or anyone whom he reasonably suspects to be committing such an offence without a warrant. There is a category of *serious arrestable offences* that includes TREASON, murder and manslaughter (see HOMICIDE), RAPE and specified offences such as causing death by reckless driving. There is a general provision that makes an arrestable offence a serious arrestable offence if it involves serious harm to state security, serious injury or death.

arrestment in the Scots law of DILIGENCE or legal enforcement, the attachment of a debtor's moveable property – like GOODS – that is in the hands of a third party. The situation is thus: A sues B, C owes money to B, A can arrest the debt owed by C to B until his own action against B is concluded (called *arrestment on the dependence*) or, if the arrestment is after the action between A and B, until A actually gets an order to have C make the money over, which is done by FURTHCOMING. Arrestment prohibits the party in whose hands it is laid from parting with the property but does not affect the property. It does not operate IN REM. It can be used to keep the property available in case the debtor does not pay. There is a special diligence for attaching ships, called *arrestment of a ship*, that generally can only be done if the claim is a maritime claim. If it is feared the ship will leave, a warrant can be granted to dismantle the ship. Arrestment can be extinguished by the court by recall. Loosing frees the subject of arrestment but preserves another security for the creditor. Arrestment can take place before an action is served on the defender (called *arrestment on the dependence*).

arrestment on the dependence see ARRESTMENT.

arrest of ship in English procedure, the process of securing maritime claims against the owner. The ADMIRALTY writ is affixed to the mast. See ARRESTMENT.

arson in English criminal law, the crime of maliciously burning down the dwelling of another, now covered by and extended in the Criminal Damage Act 1971. See WILFUL FIRE-RAISING.

art and part Scottish form of guilt by association. For an accused to be guilty on this basis, the Crown must establish *concert*, that is, an agreement or harmony of purpose to commit the crime – whether long-standing or spontaneous, it matters not. See AID OR ABET.

articles of association regulations governing the mode of conduct of business of an incorporated COMPANY and its internal organisation. They constitute, together with the MEMORANDUM OF ASSOCIATION, the contract between company members and the company. In the case of a company limited by shares, Table A of the Companies Act 1985 may be taken as the company's articles if not otherwise expressly provided.

articles of impeachment see IMPEACHMENT.

articles of partnership the agreement between the partners establishing the partnership. The matters normally dealt with in articles of partnership are the firm's name, the duration of the partnership, capital and provision for dissolution. Many provisions of the Partnership Act 1890 apply only in the absence of any agreement to the contrary, with the consequence that the articles may supersede provisions of the statute. In Scotland the term *partnership agreement* is usually used. See PARTNERSHIP.

artificial insemination (AI) the introduction of semen into the female genital tract artificially (i.e. not by sexual intercourse) by the use of a syringe or other instrument. Where the semen is from someone other than the woman's husband and the husband has not consented to the insemination, the husband is in law to be treated as the father of the resulting child and the donor is not to be treated as the child's father. See generally Human and Fertilisation and Embryology Act 1990.

ascertained goods identified existing GOODS at the time a contract is made.

as of right in the law of prescription, use as of right is use *nec vi* ('without force'), *nec clam* ('without secrecy'), *nec precario* ('without request'). To be able to establish an EASEMENT or profit by prescription at common law or under the doctrine of LOST MODERN GRANT (or, indeed, under the Prescription Act 1832 except insofar as it otherwise provides) the claimant must be able to show user as of right.

asportation carrying away to steal. See, for Scotland, THEFT.

assault 1. in the law of TORT, an assault is an act that causes another person to apprehend the infliction of immediate unlawful force on his person; a *battery* is the actual infliction of unlawful force on another person (*Collins* v. *Wilcock* [1984] 3 All ER 374). There can be *assault without battery*, as where the wrongdoer is restrained, but if a battery is immediately impossible then there is not assault, as where a man behind bars threatens violence. There is a conflict of authority concerning the degree to which there must be an actual gesture rather than simple words. There can be *battery without an assault* in any situation where there is no preceding cause of apprehension, such as a blow to a sleeping person. There does not need to be a direct blow – pulling a chair from under a person is sufficient. Any contact with a person is sufficient to be an assault in law subject to the defence of consent. The Court of Appeal is flirting with a necessity for hostility (*Wilson* v. *Pringle* [1986] 2 All ER 440), but that might not become the law: Lord Goff in *F.* v. *West Berkshire Health Authority* [1989] 2 All ER 545.

2. in English criminal law, the crime constituted broadly as stated above. When included with battery it is an offence in terms of the Offences Against the Person Act 1861: see *Fagan* v. *Metropolitan Police Commissioner* [1969] 1 QB 439. The concept of 'informed consent' has been held to have no place in English criminal law. A dentist who having been suspended from practice treated patients without telling them this fact had his conviction quashed – the patients agreed to be treated by a dentist and were so treated: *R* v. *Richardson* [1998] TLR 221.

3. in Scots civil law, the DELICT of unlawful touching or an attack likely to touch, like spitting.

4. in Scots criminal law, a deliberate attack on another person. Intention to injure is essential, although it does not matter that a person other than the person aimed at is injured. There is no need to connect with the blow. Arranging for another to do the act is the same as doing it. The offence may be aggravated by using weapons or by the nature of the victim – for example, the assault of a police officer. SELF-DEFENCE is a defence but CONSENT is a very limited defence, most likely to succeed in cases of medical treatment, sport played within the rules and sexual contact: *Smart* v. *HMA* 1975 JC 30.

assembly gathering or associating with others. *Freedom of assembly* is a European Human Right under Article 11, applicable in the UK. See UNLAWFUL ASSEMBLY, RIOT, EUROPEAN CONVENTION ON HUMAN RIGHTS.

Assembly Secretary see NATIONAL ASSEMBLY FOR WALES.

assets 1. property available for the payment of debts of a person or company in the event of insolvency or, in the case of a person, on death. Such property includes real estate and personal estate and property over which a person has a general power of appointment.

2. within the context of company and business accounts assets may be categorised as fixed assets or current assets. *Fixed assets* are those acquired with the intention that they should be held and used without change over a long period for the purpose of earning income. Fixed assets may comprise *tangible assets* (such as buildings, plant and machinery), *fixed intangible assets* (such as goodwill) and *deferred assets* (such as long-term loans). *Current assets* comprise *liquid assets* (cash or property that can quickly be converted into cash with little or no risk of loss) and *circulating assets* (goods and rights acquired in the ordinary course of business with the intention that they be held temporarily until resale). Also within the category of current assets are *prepaid expenses* and *accrued revenue*. Company accounts are required to differentiate between fixed and current assets (Companies Act 1985, Schedule 4).

assignation in Scots law, the mode of transferring ownership of INCORPOREAL PROPERTY. The grantor is known as the *cedent* and the person to whom the property is assigned is the *assignee* or *cessionary*. No form is required, but one is provided in the Transmission of Moveable Property (Scotland) Act 1862. The general rule in Scotland is that anyone may assign to anyone else. The cedent impliedly warrants that the debt is subsisting and that any foundation deeds cannot be subject to reduction. To perfect the right it must be intimated to the debtor. This prevents the debtor paying the cedent instead of the cessionary. There are many special rules relating to intimation and many equivalents to intimation. The effect is to place the assignee in the shoes of the cedent and subject to all rights of the debtor: *assignatus utitur jure auctoris*, 'the assignee may use the rights of his author'. See ASSIGNATION OF WRITS, ASSIGNMENT.

assignation of writs transfer of the deeds. As a matter of statutory implication in Scottish CONVEYANCING, the person obtaining land under a disposition or original grant is *assigned the writs*, the purpose being to fortify his *ex facie* valid title if challenged, a purpose now not so important as extracts photocopied from the record are held to be as good as originals.

assignatus utitur jure auctoris see ASSIGNATION.

assignment the transfer of property, especially terms of leases, CHATTELS personal and CHOSES in action. Assignments may be legal or equitable. *Legal assignments* of terms of years must be by deed (even where the creation of the right assigned did not require a deed, as, for example, in the case of a lease of not more than three years); *equitable assignments* need not be by deed but must usually be in writing. Legal assignments of choses in action do not, as a rule, require to be by deed. In the case of life and marine insurance policies, notice of assignment must be given to the company. See ASSIGNATION.

associated company a company is associated with another if both companies are controlled by the same (or substantially the same) individuals. In common parlance the term 'associated company' is used to denote a subsidiary or other company that is part of the same group of companies.

assumpsit a voluntary promise made by words, an old form of action abolished by the Judicature Act 1925. Modern theoretical writings refer to one of its grounds, *indebitatus assumpsit*, an action for breach of an undertaking, either to do or pay something. The leading case is still discussed: *Slade's Case* (1602) 4 Co. Rep. 91.

assumption of risk the defence to a TORT claim that what happened to the plaintiff is what he could reasonably expect. In the USA there is sometimes a distinction between *primary assumption*, which is where there is no duty, and *secondary assumption*, where there is a duty but it is waived by the plaintiff. In the UK this is dealt with under the head of *volenti non fit injuria*, but some statutes are now written in terms of assumption of risk.

assured tenancy a private-sector tenancy under which a dwelling house is let as a separate dwelling but which is not subject to the Rent Acts. A tenancy will be an assured tenancy if: (i) since its creation the landlord's interest has belonged to an 'approved body' (i.e. a body specified by the Secretary of State); (ii) construction work on the building first began after 8 August 1980; (iii) no part of the dwelling had been occupied as a residence (except under an assured tenancy) before the tenant first occupied it; (iv) the landlord had not, before granting the tenancy, given the tenant valid notice stating that it was to be a protected or housing association tenancy and not an assured tenancy.

asylum 1. a place of safety or retreat.
2. a place where the mentally ill stay or are detailed. *Mental hospital* is the modern equivalent.
3. a country other than that of a person unable to stay in his own. The applicant has to have a well-founded fear of persecution if returned (the Asylum and Immigration Appeals Act 1993, the Asylum and Immigration Act 1996 and the Immigration and Asylum Act 1999). There has therefore to be a reasonable degree of likelihood that he will be prosecuted for a conventional reason. There has to be a NEXUS demonstrated between persecution and one of, or a combination of, the five enumerated grounds as stated in the 1951 Convention Relating to the Status of Refugees and the 1967 Protocol. The five enumerated grounds are race, religion, nationality, membership of a particular social group and political opinion. In the UK, *political asylum* is often granted whereas *economic asylum*, the seeking of an economically more secure place, is not.

attachment 1. the legal process for the holding of a debtor's property until the debt is paid; *attachment of earnings* is a common remedy by which some or all of a person's wages or salary is withheld from him and used towards the discharge of a judgment debt.

2. a writ of attachment in a writ of enforcement.

attainder an obsolete procedure not unlike IMPEACHMENT.

attempt an *attempted crime* is one that is not completed. Because the criminal law focuses so much on the mental state of the offender, it has long been established that a mere failure to carry through the act intended by the wrongdoer will not allow him to escape criminal liability. To be criminal, matters must have progressed from preparation to perpetration: thus, the purchase of a mask and a glass-cutting tool may be insufficient whereas wandering the streets at night, mask on face and cutter in hand, might be enough. A hand in a pocket, which never reaches the wallet, is an *attempted theft*.

In England, the common law has been supplemented by the Criminal Attempts Act 1981, which creates a statutory offence of attempt. This applies to any act that is done with intent to commit an indictable offence and is more than merely preparatory: *Anderson* v. *Ryan* [1985] AC 560. See also *R* v. *Pearman* (1984) 80 Cr. App. R 259. It is a crime even to attempt the impossible in terms of the Act and as a result of the decision in *R* v. *Shirpuri* [1987] AC 1.

In Scotland, in terms of the Criminal Justice (Scotland) Act 1975, all attempts to commit a crime are criminal offences. It is attempted theft even if there is nothing in the pocket to steal: *Lamont* v. *Strathern* 1933 JC 33, although it was held not possible to attempt to procure an abortion by supplying the necessary materials where the woman was not in fact pregnant: *HMA* v. *Semple* 1937 JC 41.

attestation the signature of witnesses to the making of a will or execution of a deed. In English law, it is now a requirement that wills and deeds be attested by two witnesses. Such witnesses are called *attesting witnesses*. Where a deed, will or other instrument is executed in the presence of another and that other records the fact by signing his name on it, he is said to be an attesting witness. It should be emphasised that what is being witnessed is the signature rather than the document itself. For Scotland, see REQUIREMENTS OF WRITING.

Attorney General chief law officer of the Crown and leader of the English bar. He represents the public interest in many matters. He regularly represents the government or government departments in litigation. He may also refer matters of law to the Court of Appeal after an acquittal. The same term is used for a senior law officer in many other jurisdictions, notably the USA, where the Attorney General is head of the Department of Justice, and also in the BAILIWICK of Jersey.

attornment 1. in sale of GOODS, the acknowledgement that goods are held on another's behalf.

2. agreement by a tenant to hold his land from the owner of the FEE.

auction a (normally public) sale of property usually conducted by competitive bidding where the item auctioned is sold to the person who makes the highest bid. It is conducted by an *auctioneer*, who is deemed to be the agent of the seller until the hammer falls and he announces the completion of the sale in favour of the highest bidder. See MOCK AUCTION.

audi alteram partem see NATURAL JUSTICE.

auditor an accountant who verifies the books of a COMPANY. Every company is required to appoint at each general meeting at which accounts are laid an auditor or auditors to hold office from the conclusion of the meeting until the conclusion of the next such general meeting. Except in the case of a continuation of an appointment of auditors whose appointment was approved at the previous general meeting held to consider the accounts, special notice is required of a resolution concerning the appointment of auditors. To be eligible for appointment as a company auditor, a person, either an individual or a firm, must be a member of a recognised supervisory body and eligible for appointment under the rules of that body.

authorised insolvency practitioner a person legally permitted to carry through certain duties in relation to an INSOLVENCY. The Insolvency Act 1986 introduced a system of licensing to ensure the professional competence and skill of insolvency practitioners in individual and corporate insolvencies. Authorisation is granted only if certain statutory requirements are met; these include membership of an approved professional body (such as the Institute of Chartered Accountants or the Insolvency Practitioners Association).

authorised lay representative in Scots law a person, other than a solicitor or advocate, who is permitted to represent a litigant in all aspects of a SMALL CLAIM and some parts of SUMMARY CAUSE procedure.

authority to issue shares the shares of a COMPANY, apart from those taken by the subscribers of the memorandum, are issued by the board of directors (subject to the condition that they may not issue shares beyond the amount fixed as the authorised capital of the company). The directors may issue shares only for an authorised purpose and in the best interests of the company. The authority that the directors require has to be given by an ordinary resolution of the general meeting or in the articles. Authority may be given for a particular issue or generally, and it may be unconditional or subject to conditions; the authority must state the maximum amount of the relevant securities that may be allotted thereunder and the date on which it is to expire. Except in the case of a private company, the authority of the directors to issue relevant securities is limited to five years; this authority may be renewed from time to time by an ordinary resolution of the general meeting for further periods not exceeding five years.

automatism see INSANITY.

autopsy see POST-MORTEM.

autrefois convict 'formerly acquitted'. If a defendant has been previously acquitted of the same offence or could have been acquitted of the offence at a previous trial, then this is a plea in bar of the second trial. The same concept applies in Scotland: see RES JUDICATA.

average damage. See GENERAL AVERAGE.

averment an allegation in pleadings, used frequently in Scottish pleadings.

avizandum in Scottish procedure, a judge makes avizandum or takes a case to avizandum ('advising') when he wants to think about it. The same terms are used of a court made up of more than a single judge. It is similar to the English CUR. ADV. VUL.

avulsio see ALLUVIO.

award of sequestration in the law of BANKRUPTCY in England, the award is in the form of a writ directed to commissioners ordering them to enter the properties and take rents and profits and the goods of the person against whom the award has been made.

In the law of bankruptcy in Scotland, the award is made and an interim trustee appointed to report the state of affairs of the bankrupt estate before a permanent trustee is appointed.

B

B baron, judge of the COURT OF EXCHEQUER.

Babanaft proviso see MAREVA INJUNCTION.

backed for bail in England, when a magistrate grants a WARRANT it can show that, when arrested, the person shall be released on BAIL.

bail the release of an accused person pending further process, a procedure known in England since the time of Richard III. The court may seek security, in terms of money, or impose conditions. In England bail is governed by the Bail Act 1976 and the Supreme Court Act 1981. There is a presumption in favour of bail: Bail (Scotland) Act 1980. Money bail is no longer required. The standard conditions in Scotland require the accused not to commit offences and to keep the authorities appraised of his address and to turn up for the callings of the case. Special conditions may restrict the accused from approaching the complainer in the case. In both jurisdictions, refusal may be appealed. Bail need not be granted if there are substantial grounds for believing that the accused would re-offend, interfere with witnesses or abscond. In both England and Wales and Scotland, there are no longer any automatic refusals of bail as a result of a decision of the EUROPEAN COURT OF HUMAN RIGHTS: *Caballero* v. *UK* [2000] TLR 144. In some US states there is a *bail schedule* setting out the amount of bail for each crime.

bailee see BAILMENT.

bailiff 1. a person employed by the court to seize property in satisfaction of a court order and to ensure the due service of documents.

2. the Chief Magistrate, President and first citizen of both the BAILIWICKS – Jersey and Guernsey.

bailiwick one of the two jurisdictions in the Channel Islands. The bailiwick of Jersey comprises the island of Jersey and the two groups of islets known as Les Minquiers and Les Ecréhous. The bailiwick of Guernsey comprises the islands of Guernsey, Sark, Alderney, Brechou and associated islets.

bailment a delivery of goods by one person (the *bailor*) to another person (the *bailee*) for a certain purpose, upon an express or implied promise by the bailee to return them to the bailor or to deliver them to someone designated by him, after the purpose has been fulfilled. While not a trustee, the bailee is bound to exercise a reasonable level of care in respect of the thing bailed during the period of the bailment. Bailments are of six kinds:

(1) *depositum*, where goods are delivered by one person to another to keep for the use of the bailor;

(2) *commodatum*, where goods are 'lent' gratis to be used by the bailee and returned to the bailor after such use;

(3) *locatio et conductio*, where goods are hired by the bailee for use by him;

(4) *vadium* (pawn or PLEDGE), where goods or chattels are delivered to another as security for money borrowed by the bailor;

(5) *locatio operis faciendi*, where goods are delivered to another for transportation or for the bailee to carry out some work on them;

(6) *mandatum*, as in (5) but where the transportation or work is to be undertaken gratis and without any reward.

balance of probabilities the standard of proof in civil cases, demanding that the case that is the more probable should succeed. This is the kind of decision represented by the scales of justice. The court weighs up the evidence and decides which version is most probably true. Thus, the actual truth may never be known. All that is done in the Anglo-American system is to choose which of the combatants has presented the most probable version. If both seem equally balanced, then the person pursuing the case loses on the basis of the maxim *melior est conditio defendentis*, 'better is the position of the defender'. For the standard in criminal cases see BEYOND A REASONABLE DOUBT.

balance sheet a statutory account required by the Companies Acts. The function of a balance sheet (sometimes called a *position statement*) is to show the financial position of a business at a given date. This is done by showing the assets of the business, its debts and liabilities, and the equity of the owners. The balance sheet is verified by the AUDITOR.

balance sheet test the process of ascertaining, from a COMPANY's BALANCE SHEET, what would be available to members of the company were it to be immediately wound up, with the assets being sold and the liabilities discharged. If, on examination, the company is found to be insolvent (i.e. liabilities exceed its assets), it is an offence for the directors to permit it to continue trading. Any debts incurred by the company by continued trading after the directors are aware that the company is insolvent becomes the personal liability of the directors.

banking the business of receiving deposits from the public or via the financial markets, with the object of on-lending at a higher rate of interest. Sums deposited by customers with *bankers* become the property of the *bank*, over which the customer has no further control: *Foley* v. *Hill* (1840) 2 HL Cas 28. In return, the customer obtains a personal right to repayment of the sum deposited on demand, although it has been held in Scotland (somewhat doubtfully) that demand is not necessary: *Macdonald* v. *North of Scotland Bank* 1942 SC 369. The banker owes a number of duties to his customer, including the duty to encash cheques drawn on the account while in credit or within agreed overdraft limits and the duty to maintain confidentiality. To carry on the business of banking in the UK, authorisation is required from the BANK OF ENGLAND.

Bank of England established in 1694, the Bank of England is the CENTRAL BANK of the UK. It was nationalised by the Bank of England Act 1946 and acts as competent authority for the banking sector under regulatory powers conferred by the Banking Act 1987. It now sets interest rates independent of government and in this respect resembles a central bank.

bankruptcy the process taken to have a person declared *bankrupt* and to have his property administered for the benefit of his creditors. A bankruptcy consists of an act of bankruptcy followed by an ADJUDICATION. The property of the bankrupt becomes vested in a TRUSTEE IN BANKRUPTCY whose function is to identify and gather in assets belonging to the bankrupt; these are subsequently distributed among the creditors towards satisfaction of their claims, with the debtor being released from future liability in respect of his debts upon giving all the assistance in his power towards the realisation and distribution of his estate and fulfilling any other conditions required by the law for his discharge. The distribution is so many pennies for each pound of debt. A PARTNERSHIP may become bankrupt without any of the partners becoming bankrupt; conversely, individual partners may become bankrupt while the firm remains solvent. However, since individual partners are ultimately liable without any limitation of liability for the debts of the firm, concurrent bankruptcies of the firm and the individual partners are common. A *bankruptcy notice* may be issued against a partnership in the firm's name; if it is served on one partner only and at an address that is not the business premises of the firm, a *receiving order* may be made against the partner alone. Similar provisions apply in Scotland, but there are significant differences. See Bankruptcy (Scotland) Act 1985 (as amended). See INSOLVENCY, LIQUIDATION, RECEIVER.

banns of marriage in England and Wales, the public pronouncement in church of an intended marriage. Banns are necessary only if the marriage is to take place in the Church of England other than by religious licence or a superintendent registrar's certificate. In 1977 banns were abolished in Scotland, notice to the registrar being submitted in all cases.

Bar see BARRISTER.

barratry 1. wrongs committed by the crew of a ship that prejudice the ship owner or the charterer.

2. formerly, the wrong of persistently taking out court actions.

barrister a member of the *Bar*, the professional body of barristers, also known as *counsel*, or if the counsel has taken silk to become a QC – Queen's Counsel (or KC, King's Counsel when the monarch is male) – *Senior Counsel*. The barrister becomes such by virtue of being called to one of the *Inns of Court* (Lincoln's Inn, Inner Temple, Middle Temple and Gray's Inn). The barrister's liability for mistakes is now the same as that of other professional persons (*Rondel* v. *Worsley* [1969] 1 AC 191) having been departed from by a seven-judge decision in the House of Lords: *Hall & Co.* v. *Summons* [2000] TLR 554. The barrister is bound by the *cab rank principle* by which any barrister in practice must accept any instructions to appear before a court on a subject that he professes to practise and at a proper fee. He has a duty to the court that is paramount, so is not in any sense a 'mouthpiece'. His fees are an honorarium, not a contractually due payment, so he cannot sue for them but may refer a defaulting solicitor to the LAW SOCIETY. Similar terminology is used in the Republic of Ireland. There, however, a Senior Counsel is a person called to the Inner Bar by the Chief Justice with the approval of the government and is designated SC. For Scotland, see ADVOCATE.

barter exchanging one thing for another. If there is money involved (a *part exchange*) then the transaction is probably one of sale. The incidents of the contract in England in relation to goods are governed by the Supply of Goods and Services Act 1982, as amended by the Sale and Supply of Goods Act 1994. In Scotland, by virtue of the 1994 Act, the 1982 Act is broadly applied. The position in both jurisdictions is that barter is now governed by the same kind of implied terms as a sale. See QUALITY, DESCRIPTION, TITLE.

bastard an illegitimate child born out of wedlock. See ILLEGITIMACY.

battery see ASSAULT.

battle, trial by an ancient form of ALTERNATIVE DISPUTE RESOLUTION by which parties fought each other to the death. Champions could be substituted. It was abolished in England after the case of *Ashford* v. *Thornton* (1818) 1 B. & Ald. 405. In Scotland, it took longer for a final determination on competency, a ruling on the point being sought only in 1985.

battle of the forms in the law of CONTRACT, cases where the parties on their business forms include terms saying that the contract must be governed by their own, and not the other party's, terms and conditions. The courts usually resolve these matters by accepting that there is a contract and deciding which terms apply by seeing who, in the exchange of offers and acceptances, fired the last shot: see *Butler Machine Tool Co.* v. *Ex-Cell-O Corp.* [1979] 1 All ER 965; *Uniroyal Ltd* v. *Miller & Co.* 1985 SLT 101.

bearer the person holding. Where a BILL OF EXCHANGE or a security is made payable 'to bearer', anyone who presents the bill or security may claim payment; in the case of a transfer, indorsement is not necessary. A *bearer bill* (of exchange) is therefore one made out to bearer.

Beddoe order (from the case *Re Beddoe* [1893] 1 Ch. 547) an order permitting trustees to sue or defend using the TRUST fund to meet the costs.

behaviour (establishing the ground of divorce) the ground of divorce, IRRETRIEVABLE BREAKDOWN, is established by this mode, in English and in Scots law, if the defender has at any time during the marriage behaved (whether or not as a result of mental abnormality and whether such behaviour has been active or passive) so that the pursuer cannot reasonably be expected to cohabit with the defender. The way in which the mode is set out makes it evident that the focus is at the time of the petition, and accordingly there is always the argument that aged incidents have ceased to have effect, for the pursuer has subsequently found it reasonable to live with the defender despite the incident. Thus, courts look at the whole circumstances and often seek a pattern of behaviour in which older incidents are highly relevant. A single incident, however, can constitute behaviour if it strikes at the heart of the marital bond.

Belfast Agreement see GOOD FRIDAY AGREEMENT.

belligerency the state of carrying on war.

bench trial (USA) a trial before a judge without a jury.

beneficiary a person who has or is entitled to a *beneficial interest* in property. The term is most frequently encountered in relation to gifts by WILL or entitlements under a TRUST. In English law, a beneficiary is sometimes called a *cestui que trust*. Beneficial interest is a right of enjoyment of property, as opposed to merely nominal ownership. For example, if property is held in trust, the trustees have the nominal ownership (or *legal interest*) in the trust property that they hold for the benefit of others. The entitlement of those others is called the beneficial (or *equitable*) interest.

benefits in kind income from employment is taxed under SCHEDULE E and includes not only wages and salaries but also 'perquisites', that is, benefits in kind as opposed to payment in money. At the time of writing, relevant employees are charged on the basis of the cost to the employer of providing the benefit rather than the value of the benefit to the employee.

Benjamin order (from the case *Re Benjamin* [1902] 1 Ch. 723) an order allowing an estate to be wound up on the assumption that a BENEFICIARY who cannot be found is dead.

bequest a gift in a WILL.

best evidence rule the rule that evidence will be admitted provided it is the best the nature of the case will allow and, conversely, that it will be excluded, whatever its other merits, if it is shown not to be the best. There are many exceptions to the rule. See COMPUTER EVIDENCE, HEARSAY.

bestiality the offence of having sex with an animal.

Beth Din a Jewish court. The London Beth Din is the court of the Chief Rabbi. Aside from dealing with matters of Jewish law for Jewish people, it offers its services in dispute resolution to Gentiles. So far as Jewish matters are concerned, it has jurisdiction in respect of adoptions, circumcision, conversion to the faith, Kashrut (in relation to kosher food and Gittin) and Jewish divorces. See GET.

betterment the increase in value of land resulting from adjacent public works.

beyond a reasonable doubt the standard of proof in criminal cases in the UK, higher than the civil standard of the BALANCE OF PROBABILITIES. Contrasted with the balance of probabilities, it is not a matter of weighing up both sides and deciding who has won. Thus, if matters are evenly balanced, the accused must be acquitted. Juries when charged are often reminded that they are allowed to have doubts. The doubt must be a real doubt before they acquit – it must not be a fanciful doubt.

bicameral see UNICAMERAL.

bigamy the crime of entering what would be – if it were not for a valid and subsisting marriage – a second marriage. A reasonable belief in the death of a spouse even without a court order may exculpate, for then the MENS REA would be lacking.

Bill see ACT OF PARLIAMENT.

bill of exchange a form of documentary credit that requires one person to pay money to another. Section 1 of the Bills of Exchange Act 1882 defines a bill of exchange as 'an unconditional order in writing, addressed by one person to another, signed by the person giving it, requiring the person to whom it is addressed to pay, on demand or at a fixed or determinable future time, a sum certain in money to, or to the order of, a specified person or to bearer.'

bill of lading an instrument that authenticates the transfer of property in goods sent by ship; in form, it is a receipt given by the captain to the shipper or consignor, undertaking to deliver the goods, on payment of the freight, to some person whose name is stated in it or indorsed on it by the consignor. A bill of lading is used both as a contract for carriage and a document of title. It is not, however, a NEGOTIABLE INSTRUMENT, and a bona fide purchaser for value obtains no better title to the consigned goods than that enjoyed by the consignor (though it is possible for him to defeat the right of stoppage of an UNPAID SELLER). Nevertheless, it has similarities to a negotiable instrument in that if it is drawn 'to the order' of a person it may be endorsed and transferred by delivery. See the Carriage of Goods by Sea Act 1992.

bill of rights a document, frequently but not essentially, of high standing in CONSTITUTIONAL LAW, which sets out protections for the citizen, usually from the state itself. Three notable examples now follow:

In the UK, an Act of the English parliament in 1689 on the assumption of the throne by William and Mary. It was a reaction to the excesses of the Stuart kings and declared the pre-eminence of Parliament and the constitutional restraints on the monarch. Parliament's right to levy money and free speech in Parliament were expressly provided for. Excessive bail and cruel and unusual punishments were forbidden. It went on to provide for the

Protestant succession. In Scotland the CLAIM OF RIGHT was to the same effect. It is not, however, like the two more modern documents now considered.

In the USA, the first ten amendments of the Constitution of the USA. They protect, *inter alia*, the freedom of expression, freedom of the press, freedom of religion, the right to assembly and procedural rules in criminal matters. Although they would appear to relate only to federal matters, the Fourteenth Amendment, enacted to protect Blacks after the Civil War, provides two clauses that have enabled the US Bill of Rights to extend to the states. The 'due process' clause has been treated as allowing the basic rights to be treated as applying to states, thus in *Roe* v. *Wade* 410 US 113 (1973) the Supreme Court struck at state abortion legislation. The 'equal protection' clause is directed towards discrimination and has allowed the court to interfere with state education policy: *Brown* v. *Board of Education* 347 US 483; 349 US 294 (1955).

In Canada, the Canadian Bill of Rights, properly so called, was enacted in 1960. It was, and is, a code of conduct to be followed in the creation of federal legislation – it is similar to the US Bill of Rights and protects traditional freedoms. Subsequently there has been enacted the Charter of Rights and Freedoms, which is entrenched in the constitution in Part I of the Constitution Act 1982 (Canada). The Bill of Rights remains law, and there are matters in the Bill that are not in the Charter, and vice versa. The Charter is founded on a categorisation of civil liberties into 'egalitarian liberties', relating to equality under law; 'legal liberties', covering protection under the criminal code; and 'political liberties', like freedom of speech, assembly, etc. New categories of rights were included: 'mobility rights' and 'linguistic rights', which protect people's right to use their language if it is French or English. The Charter goes further and provides for education in the first language learned and understood; it provides aboriginal rights. The 'reasonable limits' upon the Charter rights have been explored by the Supreme Court in *R* v. *Oakes* [1986] 1 SCR 103 and *R* v. *Edwards Books* [1986] 2 SCR 713. See also HUMAN RIGHTS.

bind over an order made in English criminal cases to have a person enter into a bond to do or not to do something.

blackmail in English law, under the Theft Act 1968, a person is guilty of blackmail if, with a view to gain for himself or another or with intent to cause loss to another, he makes any unwarranted demand with menaces and for this purpose menaces are unwarranted unless the person making it does so in the belief that he had reasonable grounds for making the demand and that the use of menaces is a proper means of reinforcing the demand: *R* v. *Garwood* [1987] 1 WLR 319. For Scotland, see EXTORTION.

blank acceptance an ACCEPTANCE written on blank stamped paper and acting as prima facie authority by the acceptor to complete a BILL OF EXCHANGE for any amount the stamp will cover.

blasphemy statements, oral or written, that, in an offensive or insulting manner, impugn the doctrines of Christianity, the Bible, the Book of Common Prayer or the existence of God. The crime does not strike at similar conduct in relation to non-Christian religions. Blasphemy is a crime at common law. There is one old English case that suggests the doctrine applies only to the Anglican denomination. In Scotland there has been modern academic scepticism as to its continued existence.

blight notice in planning law, a notice served on an authority proposing a development indicating that it has been attempting to sell the property with no success and requiring the authority to purchase it because its value has been affected by the plan.

block exemption see COMPETITION POLICY.

Blue Europe see FISHERIES POLICY.

board meeting a meeting of the board of DIRECTORS of a COMPANY at which the policy of the company and major decisions as to its future actions are discussed. It is decisions of the board that decide or ratify action taken or to be taken on behalf of the company. The powers of the board are usually set out in the company's ARTICLES OF ASSOCIATION. At meetings of the board of directors, the proceedings are governed by the company's articles and by any rules made by the directors themselves by virtue of any powers conferred on them by the articles. The presence of all the directors at a meeting is not essential if, as is usually the case, the articles provide that a specified number will constitute a quorum. If a quorum is not so prescribed a majority of the board is required to attend.

boilerplate (USA) a form or document with blanks that can be used as a template, precedent or style.

bona fide percepta et consumpta 'acquired and consumed in good faith', a defence in Scotland to some claims, particularly those based on equitable remedies or restitution.

bona fides 'good faith'.

bona vacantia property to which no one has a claim; included within the term are the property of dissolved corporations and the residuary estate of persons who have died intestate without relatives entitled to succeed. Bona vacantia goes to the Crown. See OCCUPATION.

bonus shares shares allotted free to existing members of the company, usually in proportion to their existing shareholdings, and paid up by an accounting transfer to share capital account from profit and loss account, revaluation reserve, share premium account or capital redemption reserve.

Books of Council and Session a public register in Scotland. Its main function is to provide a record of documents. Important deeds, including wills (although usually recorded only after death), are kept in the register. Interested parties can obtain an official copy of the document, called an *extract*.

borrowing the process by which money is received subject to a condition for repayment, either on demand or at some ascertainable future time.

borrowing powers the power of a public or corporate body to borrow. Most public bodies are invested by statute with power to borrow; the extent of any power in a particular case will depend on the precise language of the statute concerned (see *Att. Gen.* v. *De Winton* [1906] 2 Ch. 106).

A UK-registered COMPANY has no inherent power to borrow. However, a company that carries on a business has an implied power to borrow money and give security for the purpose of its business (see *General Auction Estate Co.* v. *Smith* [1891] 3 Ch. 432). Borrowing powers may be expressly conferred by provision in the company's MEMORANDUM OF ASSOCIATION; a company whose object is to carry on business as a general commercial company is endowed with the power to do all such things as are incidental or conducive (including borrowing) to that end in terms of the Companies Act 1985.

borstal a form of custodial sentence for young offenders, now superseded by YOUNG OFFENDER INSTITUTIONS.

bottomry a contract in the maritime law, recognised by many nations, concluded in a foreign port for repayment of advances made to supply necessaries, secured on the keel, or bottom, of the ship. The contract is recorded in a bond of bottomry. See HYPOTHEC, RESPONDENTIA.

brain death see DEATH.

breach of arrestment in the Scots law of DELICT, the wrong of paying money away or giving goods over when one has been served with a lawful ARRESTMENT.

breach of confidence an act or omission that infringes the obligation of *confidence*. This obligation is difficult to classify. Many obligations of this kind arise from contract, express or implied. It may be a tortious or delictual obligation or it may be completely SUI GENERIS, founded on equity. It was clearly accepted in the 'Spycatcher' case (*Att. Gen.* v. *Guardian Newspapers Ltd* (No. 2) [1988] 3 WLR 776) and again approved in the House of Lords in the Scottish case involving yet another security services' case: *Lord Advocate* v. *The Scotsman Publications Ltd* 1989 SLT 705. The general rule is that anyone is entitled to communicate anything he pleases to anyone else, by speech or in writing or in any other way. That rule is limited by law of DEFAMATION and other restrictions similar to these, mentioned in Article 10 of the Convention for the Protection of Human Rights and Fundamental Freedoms (1953) (Cmd 8969). On the widest view, however, if information is imparted in circumstances from which it is clear it was confidential, the recipient comes under an obligation not to impart it. Others receiving the information from this primary confidant may come under a similar obligation. The wrongfulness in the conduct may make it possible for a claim RESTITUTION to succeed, making the person revealing the information liable to account for profits. This was certainly the case where the House of Lords held that the publication was a breach of confidence, even although at the time of publication the information was not confidential! The decision was, however, against a notorious spy: *Att. Gen.* v. *Blake* (2000) TLR 595.

breach of contract in the law of CONTRACT a breach of contract occurs when at least one party does not perform his obligations under the contract. A statement or a clear intention that there will be no performance is often known as *repudiation*. Breach results in an award of DAMAGES or SPECIFIC PERFORMANCE (in England) or SPECIFIC IMPLEMENT (in Scotland). See also ANTICIPATORY BREACH, REMOTENESS OF DAMAGE.

breach of the peace in England, conduct causing harm or likely to cause harm or generally disturb the peace. The preservation of the peace is an ancient Crown prerogative. It is an especially important offence in relation to civil liberties, for if conduct is likely to occasion a breach of the peace that will justify ARREST.

In Scots criminal law, disorderly conduct that is likely to occasion a public disturbance. It is a very widely construed crime and often causes concern in relation to civil liberties. It encompasses looking in at a lighted window: *Raffaelli* v. *Heatly* 1949 SLT 284; statements made to another in the absence of witness in private: *Young* v. *Heatly* 1959 JC 66; and even an exuberant blow to the chest of a fellow footballer: *Butcher* v. *Jessop* 1989 SCCR 119.

breach of trust a failure by a TRUSTEE to discharge the duties imposed on him by the terms of the TRUST or by the general law in relation to the trust property or the beneficiaries.

breach of warranty of authority conduct contrary to the representation that one is an agent for a principal (see AGENCY). Where an agent has contracted as agent (rather than personally), in general he cannot be made personally liable on the contract. An exception to this rule exists, however, where he has made some representation that he has authority when in reality he does not and where that representation is relied on by the other party to the contract. In such a case the agent may be made personally liable for any loss suffered by the other party arising out of the contract.

breaking and entering see BURGLARY.

brehon laws early Irish laws under the control of *brehons*, an hereditary caste of lawyers. They survived the Danish and Anglo-Norman invasions, but in the Case of Tanistry in 1607 were declared to be incompatible with English common law, which henceforth should apply throughout Ireland.

brief 1. in England, the papers given to a BARRISTER to conduct a case. **2.** colloquially, a barrister.
3. (USA) a document submitted to a court in support of a case. It usually involves a history of the case in question and presents arguments and authority.

bright line a legal rule that makes it possible to say that a given argument or set of facts falls on one side or the other rather than leaving the decision to the facts and circumstances of the case.

British citizen a person who was a citizen of the UK and its colonies and had the right of abode before the coming into force of the British Nationality Act 1981 automatically became a British citizen when it came into force. This rule is subject to two exceptions: an illegitimate and formerly stateless person who became a citizen by registration under the British Nationality (No. 2) Act 1964; and a

British subject who became a citizen by REGISTRATION outside the UK by reason of an ancestral connection with the UK. After 1 January 1983, British citizenship is acquired by birth only if one parent (or both) is a British citizen or is settled in the UK. An illegitimate child can trace entitlement only through its mother.

British nationality for the purposes of international law, British nations include citizens of British Dependent Territories, BRITISH OVERSEAS CITIZENS, BRITISH SUBJECTS and BRITISH-PROTECTED PERSONS.

British overseas citizens those persons who are citizens of the UK and its colonies who are not either BRITISH CITIZENS or British Dependent Territories' citizens. This category encompasses those who did not, when the colony in which they lived became independent, acquire the citizenship of that new country but retained their citizenship of the UK and colonies; they are not citizens of the country in which they live, but yet they have no right to enter and stay in the UK.

British-protected person one of a class of persons defined as such by an order made under the British Nationality Act 1981 because of a connection with former protectorates, protected states and trust territories. A British-protected person may become entitled to REGISTRATION as a BRITISH CITIZEN by reason of residence in the UK.

British subject under the British Nationality Act 1981 the status of British subject was confined to those who enjoyed it under the British Nationality Act 1948. These were persons who were citizens of the UK and colonies under that Act but who failed to acquire citizenship when the country in which they lived adopted its nationality laws; unlike BRITISH OVERSEAS CITIZENS, persons within this category cannot possess any other citizenship. They are entitled to British passports but have no right to enter and remain in the UK. If admitted to the UK, they may acquire British citizenship by REGISTRATION.

brothel-keeping it is an offence to keep or manage a brothel or knowingly to permit premises or part thereof to be used for such purposes, viz. habitual prostitution: Sexual Offences Act 1956. Similar provisions exist in Scotland under the Sexual Offences (Scotland) Act 1976.

brutum fulmen 'empty thunder', an ineffective order.

buggery the insertion of the male member into the anus of another person or animal (or an animal's vagina) and an offence in English law. There is a defence in the UK if the parties were consenting male adults over the age of 21 and the act was committed in private, but European human rights law has now extended that to 'group sex'. For Scotland, see SODOMY and BESTIALITY.

building consent in England, a certificate granted by a local authority or an approved inspector confirming that building control regulations have been complied with. For Scotland, see BUILDING WARRANT.

building society a financial institution whose purpose or principal purpose is that of raising, primarily through the subscription of its members, a stock or fund for the making of loans secured on land for residential use governed by the Building Societies Act 1986. The 1986 Act allowed building societies to act more like retail banks (see BANKING) – for example, by making unsecured loans and providing money transference facilities.

building warrant a document authorising certain building work. Under the Building (Scotland) Act 1959, 1970, almost all building work requires to be approved by the appropriate authority and a building warrant obtained. Failure to have such a warrant can mean the building is demolished; those involved in CONVEYANCING are thus often concerned to see that any work has been so authorised.

bundle the papers in the case in good order. English practice has now reached a stage where bundles are used very frequently. Practice varies and in some cases is subject to detailed rules, as, for example, family cases in the Family Division of the High Court where the bundle should normally be in a ring binder or arch lever file and limited to 350 pages per file. The great advantage is that there is only one set of papers instead of as in, for example, Scotland where there is an applicant's and respondent's set, often duplicating the same papers. Pagination and indexing allow hearings to proceed very quickly and facilitate the writing of judgments.

burden of proof the task of making out a case. In adversarial proceedings, the onus, or burden, of proof begins with the plaintiff, pursuer or prosecutor who has set the action in motion. The burden may shift in civil cases if the party establishes a prima facie case that is in all respects sufficient. There are two main standards, viz. proof on BALANCE OF PROBABILITIES and proof BEYOND A REASONABLE DOUBT.

burglary in English criminal law, the CRIME of entering any building or part of a building or inhabited vehicle or vessel as a trespasser with the intent to steal or rape or commit grievous bodily harm or doing unlawful damage. It is still burglary if, having entered as a trespasser, the accused attempts to steal or inflict personal injury. It is an aggravation to carry additional weapons, particularly firearms, whether real or artificial, or explosives. For Scotland, see HOUSEBREAKING.

but-for test see CAUSATION.

buyer a person who buys or agrees to buy GOODS.

buyer in possession, sale by see NEMO DAT QUOD NON HABET.

bye-law a rule promulgated by some body other than Parliament that has effect if done in pursuance and within the limits of some higher authorisation such as an Act of Parliament.

bypass trust (USA) see TRUST.

C abbreviation for Chancellor.

Cabinet in the CONSTITUTIONAL LAW of the UK, as a result of various CONVENTIONS, the executive part of the British government. Beginning as a group of special advisers to the CROWN, the lack of interest shown by monarchs in the 18th century meant that the Crown took little part in their deliberations. Parliament was concerned about this practice, and as early as the Act of Settlement of 1700 had tried to restrain the practice. Nonetheless, the REFORM ACT of 1832, extending the franchise, meant that the support of the HOUSE OF COMMONS was ever more important. Accordingly, whoever had support there could have the direct link to the Crown, which was the essence of the Cabinet. The acceptance of the limited role of monarchy and the increase in representation have increased the status of the Cabinet so that it is now effectively the executive branch of government answerable to PARLIAMENT and requiring to legislate through Parliament with the Crown but in practical day-to-day matters being able to carry through all business subject to the duty of doing so in accordance with the policy of Parliament. It is entirely distinct from the PRIVY COUNCIL, whose meetings take precedence, but naturally many of the same individuals sit on both. Members of the Cabinet are usually ministers and are appointed by the Crown on the recommendation of the PRIME MINISTER. There are usually about 20 members, and the existence of the Cabinet, although a matter of convention, has been noticed in legislation and judicial decision. It has a secretariat, and in modern times it keeps records, including minutes. Even Cabinet ministers do not have unrestricted access to previous Cabinet papers. A narrative of events by an ex-Cabinet minister was published despite the government's opposition: *Att. Gen.* v. *Jonathan Cape* [1976] QB 752, resulting in a report by Privy Councillors giving guidelines for future publications. Members subscribe to a doctrine of *collective responsibility* under which dissension in Cabinet is silenced after a decision, and all abide and promote that course. The Cabinet is responsible as a whole to Parliament under this doctrine.

cab rank rule see BARRISTER.

calendar a listing of cases that are ready to be heard.

call 1. a demand by a COMPANY on shareholders to pay all or part of the subscription price of the shares not already paid.

2. to admit, in the sense of a BARRISTER being called to the Bar.

call in the right in planning law of a superior body, such as the relevant government minister, to take over the consideration of a planning application from the local planning authority.

CALR abbreviation for computer-assisted legal research. See LEXIS, WESTLAW.

cancellation 1. where a BILL OF EXCHANGE is intentionally cancelled and the cancellation is apparent thereon, the bill is discharged, as is any party liable on it. Intentional cancellation may be manifested by the cancellation of the signature. A cancellation made unintentionally or under a mistake or without the authority of the holder is inoperative.

2. at common law, an attempt to terminate a CONTRACT that can succeed only on terms agreed. A cancellation that is not agreed would result in an award of DAMAGES for BREACH OF CONTRACT. See also ANTICIPATORY BREACH OF CONTRACT. Under the law of CONSUMER CREDIT, a CONSUMER CREDIT AGREEMENT is cancellable if oral representations are made by the negotiator in the presence of the debtor or hirer and the agreement was not signed by the debtor on trade premises. Non-commercial agreements and certain small debtor-creditor supplier agreements are excluded. The protection allowed is for a five-day cooling-off period. Overlapping protection is given by the Consumer Protection (Cancellation of Contracts Concluded away from Business Premises) Regulations 1987. These apply to unsolicited visitors or a solicited visit where different goods are sold. They do not apply to land transactions, sale of food and drink for consumption, or insurance and investment contracts. The regulations offer a seven-day cooling-off period.

Candlemas see QUARTER DAY.

canon law the law of the church, particularly the Roman Catholic Church but also used of the law of the Church of England. The *Codex Juris Canonici* ('Body of the Canon Law') was until 1983 authoritative only in Latin. It is called canon law because each of the rules is called a *canon*. The present English translation is approved in Australia, Canada, England and Wales, India, Ireland, New Zealand, Scotland and South Africa.

canvassing the attempt made, off trade premises, to get another person to enter into a regulated CONSUMER CREDIT AGREEMENT. Canvassing for debtor-creditor agreements off trade premises is an offence.

CAP abbreviation for COMMON AGRICULTURAL POLICY.

capacity strictly, the ability of a person to effect a legal transaction. Questions of capacity differ according to whether the person is a *natural* or a *juristic person*. If the latter, capacity will be governed by the document or statute creating the person. Thus, in the case of a public corporation, the relevant founding statute (as amended) will set out what the corporation can or cannot do. Likewise, the capacity of local authorities to enter into transactions is set out in the Local Government Acts; the capacity of companies is governed by their memorandum and ARTICLES OF ASSOCIATION. (In Australia and New Zealand, in the absence of provisions to the contrary in the memorandum and articles, companies are endowed with the powers of natural persons.) Traditionally, in English law three categories of natural persons lacked full capacity, namely, infants, lunatics and married women. The Married Women's Property Act 1882 removed the remaining disabilities for married women. So far as persons under 18 years are concerned, the position is regulated by the Minors' Contracts Act 1987.

In Scots law, women have equal capacity to contract as men. So far as those under 18 years are concerned, the position is regulated by the Age of Legal Capacity (Scotland) Act 1991.

capital allowance a set-off for tax in relation to expenditure on capital rather than revenue. Under the Capital Allowances Act 1990, the cost of capital assets acquired by a trader for the purposes of his business may be deducted from his total profit. The nature and extent of the deduction vary according to the nature of the business; however, for most purposes, capital allowances are now largely 'writing-down allowances', where the cost of the asset is written down at 5 per cent per annum over 20 years.

capital clause a clause in a company's MEMORANDUM OF ASSOCIATION stating the amount of share capital with which the company proposes to be registered and the division of it into shares of fixed amount.

capital gains tax a tax charged on gains of a capital nature. More specifically, the charge to capital gains tax is on chargeable gains; these are gains accruing from the chargeable disposal of chargeable assets by chargeable persons. It follows from this that some disposals are chargeable disposals while others (such as a disposal on death by a testator to his executors) are not; likewise, some assets are chargeable and others are not (e.g. cash), and some persons are chargeable persons and others not (e.g. charitable trustees). Chargeable gains made by companies otherwise than in a fiduciary capacity are charged to CORPORATION TAX rather than capital gains tax. The current law has been consolidated into the Taxation of Chargeable Gains Act 1992.

capital issues the further issue of securities, a common method by a COMPANY of raising additional capital for companies. Such issues are made by the directors if properly authorised under the articles or the Act.

capital punishment punishment that consists of killing the offender. Methods vary around the world and include, or have included, hanging, garrotting, use of the guillotine, shooting, gassing, lethal injection and electrocution. In the UK, general capital punishment for murder was abolished by the Murder (Abolition of Death Penalty) Act 1965 and was replaced by life imprisonment. Capital punishment for TREASON and PIRACY was abolished by the Crime and Disorder Act 1998. See CORPORAL PUNISHMENT, DEATH PENALTY.

capital transfer tax see INHERITANCE TAX.

caption 1. seizure of a thing or a person.
2. the heading of a legal instrument.

care order a court order committing the care of a CHILD to a local authority. The authority has the same powers and duties as a parent or guardian, except that it cannot alter the child's religion or consent to an adoption. While a care order is in force, the rights and powers of the parents or guardian are overridden: Children Act 1989.

In Scotland a different system applies whereby a report investigates matters and, if appropriate, brings the case before a CHILDREN'S HEARING where, if matters are established, the court can order supervision of the child or order it to reside in a residential establishment: Social Work (Scotland) Act 1968, Children Act 1975.

cargo goods and merchandise, other than the personal luggage of passengers, carried by a ship or aircraft.

carnal knowledge illegal sexual intercourse. Originally used in English law and now found in the USA, the phrase sometimes denotes an offence in itself or may be part of a wider definition.

carriage by air a contract to carry goods or passengers by air. Carriage of goods by air is effected under a CONTRACT between the consignor and the carrier, with the rights and liabilities of the parties being governed by contract law. In the case of international carriage by air, however, certain international conventions (e.g. Warsaw, 1929) to which the UK is a party impose limits on the nature and extent of carriers' liability. These conventions also deal with such matters as who can sue and be sued, rights to stops in transit, the documentation of air carriage and time limits for complaints. The effect of the Warsaw Convention on ordinary claims in the UK was extensively considered in the House of Lords: *Abnett* v. *British Airways Plc* 1997 SLT 492; and in the Scottish Inner House: *Herd* v. *Clyde Helicopters* 1996 SLT 976.

carriage by rail a contract to carry goods or passengers on the permanent way, or railway. Essentially the same law applies as in CARRIAGE BY ROAD. After the Transport Act 1962, British Rail ceased to be a COMMON CARRIER of goods, and carriage was by CONTRACT. International carriage of goods is governed by international convention: the Berne Convention of 1980.

carriage by road a contract to carry goods or passengers by road. COMMON CARRIERS of passengers must carry any passenger who offers and is willing to pay the fare (and is not otherwise objectionable), provided that the vehicle is not overloaded; PRIVATE CARRIERS carry under special contract only. In either case, however, liability will follow a damage or injury resulting from failure to take reasonable care for the passengers' safety. A common carrier of goods must carry goods of a type that he holds himself out as carrying to a place that he holds himself out as travelling to. The common carrier of goods is strictly liable for damage to the goods carried, subject to: the defences of ACT OF GOD; act of the Queen's enemies; the inherent value of the goods; the fault of the consignor. The Carriers Act 1830 protects against the STRICT LIABILITY exceeding £10 where the value of certain goods beyond that sum is not stated. The goods that must be declared are gold and silver coin, gold and silver, precious stones, jewellery, watches, clocks, trinkets, bills of exchange, bank notes, securities for the payment of money, stamps, maps, title deeds, paintings, engravings and pictures, gold and silver plate, glass, china, silk and furs. Carriers may exclude liability by contract but subject to the UNFAIR CONTRACT TERMS Act 1977. A private carrier of goods need only take reasonable care of the goods. International carriage by road is governed by the Carriage of Goods by Road Act 1965 as amended by the Carriage by Air and Road Act 1979.

carriage by sea a CONTRACT to carry goods or passengers by sea. Carriage of passengers or goods by sea depends on the individual contracts involved; such contract may exclude or limit liability for damage to goods, or death or injury to passengers. However, international contracts are governed by international conventions. The Carriage of Goods by Sea Act 1971 gave force of law to the Hague-Visy rules, which overrode any particular terms of a BILL OF LADING. The Carriage of Goods by Sea Act 1992 improved certain aspects of the law under which goods are shipped, reforming and replacing the Bills of Lading Act 1855.

carrier see COMMON CARRIER, CARRIAGE BY ROAD.

carrier's lien see LIEN.

cartel see COMPETITION, COMPETITION POLICY.

CAS abbreviation for COURT OF ARBITRATION FOR SPORT.

Case of Proclamations (1610) 12 Co. Rep. 74 in the CONSTITUTIONAL LAW of the UK, the case that laid down the principle that the Crown could not simply by declaring acts to be offences in criminal law make them so.

casus belli 'cause of war', the event that is said to justify a war.

cattle-trespass the wrong of allowing cattle to go on to another's land, an ancient TORT repealed by the Animals Act 1971, which does, however, make new provisions for the same facts. See ANIMALS, LIABILITY FOR.

causa causans 'real, or the effect of, damage'. The concept is a legal one based on common sense. See CAUSATION.

causation a philosophical notion deeply rooted in Western (but not necessarily Eastern) philosophy that has become absorbed into the legal system, by which two events are said to be connected, the one later in time having been brought about by the earlier. Clearly, this has implications for the ascription of liability or responsibility. In CRIME and in TORT and DELICT, many cases become issues of causation, especially where there is competition between causative factors. The concept of *intervening cause* is often encapsulated in the phrase *nova causa interveniens* ('new intervening cause'). Thus, the person charged with murder may try to show that the simple punch landed on the victim was not the cause of the death but the incompetence of the medical team who treated the victim for his bruise. The general attitude of the courts is to treat the first cause as subsisting and to ignore the intervention unless it very clearly breaks a chain of causation. Quantum physics, synchronicity and chaos theory, if valid and if appreciated by lawyers, might one day render causation less important. In any event, actual decisions show that the courts refuse to take a scientific view of the concept and apply the common man's view of causes. See *R* v. *Blaue* [1975] 1 WLR 1411; *Finlayson* v. *HMA* 1979 JC 33; *McGhee* v. *NCB* 1973 SC (HL) 37.

caution see GUARANTEE.

caveat emptor 'let the buyer beware', no longer an accurate statement of the law unless very fully qualified. In relation to immoveable or heritable property, it is still a guiding general principle, the terms of the CONTRACT between the parties tending to resolve many common problems. In relation to the sale of moveable corporeal property or goods, there are implied terms that in some cases cannot be excluded even by the agreement of the parties and others that may be excluded only if it is fair and reasonable to do so. See QUALITY.

CB abbreviation for Chief Baron of the now defunct COURT OF EXCHEQUER.

CDS abbreviation for CRIMINAL DEFENCE SERVICE.

cedent see ASSIGNATION.

Cententier a member of the 'honorary police' in the BAILIWICK of Jersey, who presents and often prosecutes minor criminal cases.

central bank a national bank that does business mainly with a government and with other banks; it regulates the volume and cost of credit. See also EUROPEAN CENTRAL BANK.

Central Criminal Court formerly an assize court for greater London, it was abolished by the Courts Act 1971. It was always known as the *Old Bailey* and still is, for the CROWN COURT when it sits in London is still known as the Central Criminal Court or the Old Bailey.

certificate of entitlement a proof of right of abode for persons seeking to enter the UK if they cannot prove they are BRITISH CITIZENS or produce British passports.

certificate of incorporation a document signed by the Registrar of Companies showing that the COMPANY to which it relates has been formed. In the case of a PUBLIC COMPANY, the certificate of incorporation must contain a statement that the company is a public company.

certificate of insolvency a document that states that a company is insolvent. An administrator, on forming the opinion that the relevant circumstances in which a company is deemed to exist, must forthwith issue a certificate of INSOLVENCY. Notice of the certificate is to be given to all the company's unsecured creditors.

certificate of registration (limited partnerships) a document indicating that a LIMITED PARTNERSHIP has registered. The Registrar of Companies is required to keep a register and index of all limited partnerships and of all statements registered in relation to them. If a limited partnership is not registered, it is deemed to be a general partnership. The point is that general partners are personally liable for the debts of the firm, whereas limited partners are liable only to the extent of their stake, hence the desirability of publishing (by means of registration) that a particular partnership is a limited one.

Certification Officer see TRADE UNION.

certified copy a copy of a document signed and certified that it is a true copy of the original by the official who has custody of the original.

certiorari formerly a writ, now a statutory order made to transfer a cause from a lower court to a higher court. It is used as a means of allowing the High Court to regulate lower courts and tribunals.

cessante ratione legis cessat ipsa lex 'the law itself ceases if the reason of the law ceases,' a controversial doctrine that has, on the face of it, reason on its side. The difficulty, especially in a case-based system, is to agree upon what is the rationale of the law. The application of the doctrine runs contrary to the fundamental doctrine of the English common law, STARE DECISIS. See *Milangos* v. *George Frank Ltd* [1976] AC 443.

cessio bonorum in the Scots law of INSOLVENCY, an older form of BANKRUPTCY that did not give the debtor a discharge but allowed him to be released from civil imprisonment on giving up all his property

cessionary see ASSIGNATION.

cestui que trust an archaic term in English law for the BENEFICIARY under a TRUST.

chambers a judge's room or the offices of a barrister.

champerty see MAINTENANCE AND CHAMPERTY.

Chancellor see LORD CHANCELLOR.

change of position in the law of RESTITUTION, the defence to a claim that the defendant has changed his position as a result of receiving the money value that is said to be an unjust enrichment in his hands. It has to be a genuine alteration of position as opposed to a simple spending of money; for example, spending a mistaken payment received on a yacht as opposed to using the payment for ordinary routine bills. It is only now emerging in English jurisprudence: see *Lipkin Gorman* v. *Karpnale* [1991] 2 AC 548. For Scotland, see *Credit Lyonnais* v. *George Stevenson & Co. Ltd* (1901) 9 SLT 93.

Chapter 11 (USA) part of the Bankruptcy Reform Act of 1978 that allows an alternative to liquidation under Chapter 7. The business is preserved as a going concern. There is usually no trustee, and the business may be conducted by a committee of creditors. The debtor is given 120 days to submit a plan for liquidation or reorganisation. For the UK process of administration, see ADMINISTRATOR.

character evidence evidence of the character of a witness. In criminal proceedings, evidence as to the accused's bad character may only be adduced if it has been sought to establish good character. In civil proceedings, character evidence of the parties is largely irrelevant except in DEFAMATION cases where the plaintiff's general bad reputation may be proved in mitigation of damages, subject to rebuttal by general evidence of good character. Evidence as to the truthfulness of witness may be given in both civil and criminal cases.

charge 1. a formal accusation by the authorities that the accused has committed a specified offence.

2. the price to be paid for GOODS or services.

3. a form of SECURITY over property. In the case of a MORTGAGE, an interest in the mortgaged property is conferred on the mortgagee, providing him with certain rights and powers to enable him to protect his investment: in contrast, in the case of a charge, the *chargee* acquires rights and powers but not interest. In the case of a *charge by way of legal mortgage*, the chargee has the same protection, powers and remedies as if a mortgage term by DEMISE or sub-demise were vested in him (see Law of Property Act 1925). A charge may be fixed or floating: a *fixed charge* is a charge over a particular asset or property; a FLOATING CHARGE is a charge over the entire assets (from time to time changing) and undertaking of a company. Property subject to a fixed charge may not be disposed of without the consent of the chargee, whereas such consent is not required in the case of a floating charge. A charge may be legal or equitable: a *legal charge* (which must be created in due form, i.e. by deed) confers legal rights on the chargee that will prevail over all-comers, including a bona fide purchaser of a legal estate for value without notice; an *equitable charge* (which may be created informally, as, for example, by the deposit of documents of title) confers rights that prevail over all subsequent interests in the property charged except those of a bona fide purchaser for value of a legal estate for value without notice. See CHARGE FOR PAYMENT.

4. the instruction given by a judge to a jury of the law that he considers is applicable to the case. This is so fundamentally important that it is a frequent source of appeals, and as a result judges in many jurisdictions resort to (or are assisted by) standard charges covering the essentials of many common crimes and typical evidential points.

charge for payment in the Scots law of DILIGENCE or legal enforcement, the warning given to a debtor that another form of diligence is soon to be used. An example would be (and usually is) POINDING.

charges having equivalent effect (to customs duties) levies having effect as duty payable on a cross-border transfer of goods. The legal regime of the EUROPEAN UNION in attempting to establish a CUSTOMS UNION prohibits not only customs duties but those charges that, if they were allowed, might seriously distort the market. A charge will be treated as subject to these rules if it is a levy imposed by a MEMBER STATE on goods when they cross a border, even if the charge is not formally called a customs duty but which does actually have the same blocking effect on the goods in question: see *United Foods and Van den Abeele* v. *Belgium* [1981] ECR 995. Compare MEASURES HAVING EQUIVALENT EFFECT, QUANTITATIVE RESTRICTIONS.

charging order an order of the court granting the applicant a charge over property belonging to a debtor of the applicant.

charity the giving of money to help the needy or a body that is established to administer such donations. The concept of charity dates from a permission given by the Emperor Constantine allowing subjects to make bequests to the church. This facility came to be so abused that it was severely restricted by the Emperor Valentinian; this restraint was, however, gradually relaxed so that by the time of Justinian it had become a fixed maxim of the civil law that bequests to pious uses were entitled to privileged treatment.

In English law, the State of Charitable Uses Act of 1601 codified the received law up to that point, and the PREAMBLE to that statute still provides the starting point for the definition of charity in modern law. This, according to the House of Lords in *Pemsel's Case* [1891] AC 531, comprises gifts for the relief of poverty, for the advancement of religion, for the advancement of education, and for other purposes beneficial to the community not falling under any of the preceding heads but within the words or spirit of the Act of 1601. A *charitable* TRUST is treated more favourably than others, in that it is not subject to the RULE AGAINST PERPETUITIES, it is not subject to the beneficiary principle that requires that trusts be for the benefit of persons rather than of purposes, and it attracts favourable tax treatment. To qualify as *charitable*, however, a gift must be exclusively charitable, that is, it must be so conditioned that no part of it can be devoted to any non-charitable purpose. If a charitable gift fails because the object no longer exists or the purpose has been satisfied, the gift may be applied CY PRES to the satisfaction of similar charitable purposes. Charities are under the general jurisdiction of the Charity Commissioners in England and Wales and the Lord Advocate in Scotland.

In Scotland, for tax purposes, charity and charitable purposes are to be interpreted according to English law: *Scottish Burial Reform and Cremation Society* v. *Glasgow Corp.* 1967 SC (HL) 116.

charter company a company incorporated by royal charter.

Charter of Rights and Freedoms (Canada) see BILL OF RIGHTS (Canada); CONSTITUTIONAL LAW.

charterparty a contract in writing under which a person, the *charterer*, hires or leases a vessel from a shipowner where the intended use is carriage of goods by sea and the consideration is known as *freight*.

chattel in English law, any property other than freehold land. Interests in land that are not freehold may be called *chattels real*. Moveable corporeal articles of property are *chattels personal*. See GOODS.

cheque a BILL OF EXCHANGE drawn on a banker, payable on demand. A cheque operates as a mandate or authority to the drawee's bank to pay the party named as drawer and debit the account of its customer, the drawer. Cheques are essentially NEGOTIABLE INSTRUMENTS and may be negotiated by indorsement. The Bills of Exchange Act 1882, however, provides that a cheque may be crossed. In this case the cheque should be presented for payment by a bank (rather than the person named as drawee). If accompanied by the words 'not negotiable', this has the effect that the cheque cannot be negotiated, and the words 'ACCOUNT PAYEE' or 'account payee only' mean that the cheque cannot be passed on to another: Cheques Act 1992.

child 1. a young person. The law in either England and Scotland cannot be said to offer any single definition of the word. Various ages are defined as *childhood*, but all are under the age of MAJORITY, which is 18: Children Act 1989. In relation to CRIME, a child is a person under 14: Children and Young Persons Act 1969.

In Scotland, majority is attained at 18: Age of Majority (Scotland) Act 1969. However, the Age of Legal Capacity (Scotland) Act 1991 establishes the age of 16 as generally conferring full legal CAPACITY, subject to some provisos, until majority. For the purposes of crime, a child of under eight years cannot be prosecuted. The position in relation to DELICT is uncertain. The Social Work (Scotland) Act 1968 refers and applies to children who have not reached the age of 16. See CHILDREN'S HEARING. The law on parental rights and responsibilities in Scotland under the Children (Scotland) Act 1995 applies largely to children under 16 with a few provisions for those under 18.
2. in wills and deeds, 'child' can refer to persons of any age. Normally 'child' will refer to issue in the first generation only, excluding grandchildren or remoter issue, but if the testator's intention can be interpreted as including descendants then the position may be different: *Morgan* v. *Thomas* 51 LJQB 55. The practice is the same in Scotland: *Adam's Executrix* v. *Maxwell* 1921 SC 418.
3. throughout the UK for the purposes of CHILD SUPPORT, a qualifying child is a person under the age of 16 or under 19 and in full-time (but not advanced) education or under 18 in certain circumstances and a person who has not contracted a valid, void or annulled marriage. A qualifying child is one for which one or both parents is an ABSENT PARENT.

Child Care Index a list, maintained by the Department of Health, of people thought to be unsuitable to work with children that has been held to be legal and reasonable. The list is not published and contains material other than criminal convictions, such as referrals from employers, although the person listed has the opportunity to make representations at the time of his inclusion. Statutory provisions for a similar scheme under the Protection of Children Act 1999 are expected to be brought into force soon.

children's hearing in Scotland, children under 16 years of age are not dealt with through the courts except in the most exceptional circumstances but are dealt with by a *panel* at a private hearing. Assuming that grounds for referral are accepted or proved, the child is sent to a *Children's Panel* made up of citizens. A *reporter* presents the case, and the Panel decides what to do with the child, including the option of compulsory measures of care. Not only criminal matters are dealt with. The reporter can initiate proceedings on the basis of other information and on the basis that the child needs help.

Children's Panel see CHILDREN'S HEARING.

child support the statutory regime devised to make parents of children pay maintenance: Child Support Act 1991. It is based upon payments for a qualifying CHILD by an ABSENT PARENT. It is channelled through a CHILD SUPPORT OFFICER.

The ordinary courts are not involved. Appeals are possible to the Child Support Appeal Tribunal and the Child Support Commissioner. The ultimate appeal (for Scotland as well as England) is the English Court of Appeal. See also MAINTENANCE ASSESSMENT.

Child Support Agency (CSA) the body charged by the Secretary of State to apply the Child Support Act 1991, answerable to the Department of Social Security. It is headed by a chief executive. There is a separate agency for Northern Ireland. It has been given financial targets. It employs CHILD SUPPORT OFFICERS and inspectors. There are complaints procedures. In some cases, fees are payable. Essentially it works out how much people owe for CHILD SUPPORT and collects it according to the statutory formula. See also MAINTENANCE ASSESSMENT.

child support officer an official who makes a MAINTENANCE ASSESSMENT in applications for CHILD SUPPORT under the Child Support Act 1991. In certain simple cases the officer may determine the paternity of the child, although the officer may have to apply to the court in the usual way in more difficult cases.

Chiltern Hundreds the short form of name for an officer under the Crown, 'Steward or Bailiff of Her Majesty's three Chiltern Hundreds of Stoke, Desborough and Burnham'. A Member of Parliament is not allowed to resign, but if a Member wants to give up a seat then the Member can apply to accept this office, which has virtually no duties. As it is an office under the Crown, acceptance of the office disqualifies the Member under the House of Commons Disqualification Act 1975.

chose 'a thing'.

chose in action a cause of action to recover money or damages.

chose in possession a thing that a person has the right to enjoy and of which he has actual enjoyment or possession.

Christmas Day see QUARTER DAY.

CICA abbreviation for CRIMINAL INJURIES COMPENSATION Authority.

cif abbreviation for 'cost, insurance, freight', a special type of sale of GOODS. The quoted price includes the cost of the goods, the cost of insurance while the goods are in transit and the cost of the freight to the destination. It clearly eases the buying of goods across national boundaries, especially so where distance is involved. The seller is in the best position to obtain a good price for insurance and freight, so the utility of the standard contract is evident. The seller delivers the goods to the carrier and sends the invoice, insurance policy and BILL OF LADING to the buyer. Its incidents are well known, but any tampering with the arrangement can have unfortunate legal consequences: see *Leigh and Sillivan* v. *Aliakmon Shipping* [1986] AC 785.

Circuit Court the court in the Republic of Ireland above the District Court, which has both civil and criminal jurisdiction. The country is divided into seven circuits, in each of which there are several towns in which the court sits. In civil matters the judge hears cases without a jury and can award compensation of up to £30,000 and deal with issues relating to land where the rateable value of the land does not exceed £200. As a criminal court, it can deal with indictable offences referred to it by the District Court, when a judge sits with a jury. Certain serious criminal cases, of which the most common are murder and rape, may only be tried in the Central Criminal Court in Dublin. The Circuit Court hears appeals in both criminal and civil cases from the District Court, which take the form of a rehearing of the case. Appeals from the decisions of a circuit judge in a civil case are to the High Court and from it to the Supreme Court. In a criminal case, appeal is to the Court of Criminal Appeal and then the Supreme Court.

circuit judge see CROWN COURT.

circumstantial evidence in the law of EVIDENCE, indirect evidence of a fact in issue. An inference of the fact in issue can be made from a consideration of a number of other facts. It is sometimes spoken of as a chain but better considered as a cable: the more strands, the stronger, and the absence of one of the strands does not break the connection. The lay person often considers it in some way inferior, but not the lawyer, who appreciates the difficulties inherent in direct eyewitness evidence. Nonetheless, it is only as good as the strands that comprise it. These may have to be evaluated in their own right, otherwise a sound inference may be based on a defective premise, as where Othello, asking for proof of Desdemona's infidelity, was answered by Iago:

> 'It is impossible you should see this,
> Were they as prime as goats, as hot as monkeys,
> As salt as wolves in pride, and fools as gross
> As ignorance made drunk: but yet I say,
> If imputation and strong circumstances,
> Which lead directly to the door of truth,
> Will give you satisfaction, you might have it.'
> (Act 3, Scene 3, line 400)

citation 1. the procedure of serving notice of court proceedings on a person, instructing them to attend.
2. reference to a PRECEDENT or other authority in a court or legal writing.

citator a book that lists CITATIONS of one authority in a later authority. This allows the legal researcher to discover whether a case has been approved or if it has been decided to overrule it. In the UK, 'Current Law' is the primary source and is available on CD-Rom, a form of CALR. In the USA, one of the biggest services is provided by Shepherd's, thus the process is called *Shepherdising*.

citizen's arrest an apprehending of a person by a member of the public. It is assumed in the UK that a private citizen (including a police constable) may arrest another without warrant if the citizen has witnessed the commission of a serious crime. Any force used must be reasonable (or in certain limited circumstances where there has been no unlawful conduct but there is a real threat of a breach of the peace interfering with the rights of another that would involve unreasonable violence: *Bibby* v. *Chief Constable* [2000] TLR 323).

citizenship the legal link between an individual and a state or territory as a result of which the individual is entitled to certain protection, rights and privileges, and subject to certain obligations and allegiance.

City Code on Takeovers and Mergers a body of principles and rules regulating the conduct of takeovers and mergers of public companies. While its provisions are not legally binding, contravention may result in the imposition of sanctions by the Stock Exchange. The Panel on Takeovers and Mergers (The City Panel) is responsible for the operation of the Code.

City Panel see CITY CODE ON TAKEOVERS AND MERGERS.

Civil Bill in Ireland, a legal document by which civil cases are begun in the Northern Ireland county courts and in the CIRCUIT COURTS in the Republic of Ireland.

civilian 1. a person learned in the civil or Roman law.

2. as an adjective, pertaining to the civil or Roman law.

3. a person not in the armed forces.

civil imprisonment in the Scots law of DILIGENCE or legal enforcement, a remedy now considerably restricted, by which the debtor was placed in prison until the debt was discharged. It is still competent for failure to pay fines for CONTEMPT OF COURT and for wilful failure to pay ALIMENT. Failure to perform a decree that orders specific performance (called a *decree ad factum praestandum*) may result in imprisonment if the court is satisfied that the non-performance is wilful.

civil law 1. the domestic law of any particular nation.

2. the law of ancient Rome. See ROMAN LAW.

3. law or legal systems based on Roman law.

4. law that is not criminal law.

5. law that is not military law.

civil legal aid see LEGAL AID.

civil list in the CONSTITUTIONAL LAW of the UK, money paid to certain members of the royal family. The monarch surrenders for life all hereditary revenues, with the exception of those of the duchies of Cornwall and Lancaster, to form part of the CONSOLIDATED FUND. In exchange, the Crown is paid the civil list, being sums required for the royal household and the privy purse, which pays employees' pensions and the expenses of Sandringham and Balmoral.

civil procedure the rules of law regulating the forms, pleading and operation of the civil, as opposed to the criminal, courts.

Civil Procedure Rules the name given to the new rules on CIVIL PROCEDURE introduced in England and Wales in April 1999 to implement the WOOLF REFORMS.

civil proceedings proceedings brought for the purpose of enforcing or declaring a right, or for recovery of money or property.

civil service in the CONSTITUTIONAL LAW of the UK, servants of the Crown who are permanent and do not change with a political change of government. There is no definition of a *Crown servant*. A subordinate who is employed by a *civil servant* is a servant of the Crown and not of the person employing him. Recruitment and examination, for many the insignia of a mature and independent civil service, have for over one hundred years been carried out by the Civil Service Commission, a body established not by statute but by ORDER IN COUNCIL. Independence is supported by having pay decided by the Civil Service National Whitley Council. In *Council of Civil Service Unions* v. *Minister for the Civil Service* [1985] AC 374, the HOUSE OF LORDS considered the right of certain civil servants to be members of a trade union, but the House of Lords did not disturb an order in council that withdrew the right of membership on the basis of national security. Civil servants have no special constitutional status separate from the minister they serve and have no right to reveal confidential information in the public interest, an issue discussed in relation to OFFICIAL SECRETS. There is a sliding scale of permission to take part in politics, the higher the official, the lesser the activity permitted.

CJ abbreviation for Chief Justice.

claim form the form in which one starts CIVIL PROCEEDINGS in England and Wales under the CIVIL PROCEDURE RULES. It is worth saying in a dictionary that this represents a deliberate attempt to introduce plain English into legal usage and has accordingly done away with a good number of 'hard words'.

Claim of Right the Scottish counterpart of the English Declaration of Right of 1689, to the effect that James VII of Scotland (and II of England) had forfeited his right to the throne (which was then offered to William and Mary). See BILL OF RIGHTS.

clam secretly.

Clandestine Outlawries, Suppression of see PARLIAMENT.

class action 1. in company law, an action by or on behalf of shareholders of a company.
2. generally, an action by one or more nominal plaintiffs for others. The idea is long established in the USA but is not yet widespread in the UK, where often a case is selected as a test case or a lead case and other similar cases are settled on the same basis. The practice of the LEGAL AID Board facilitates a group approach in certain cases, such as disaster cases or pharmaceutical cases.

class rights rights that attach to a particular class of shares but not to another class or to shareholders generally; such rights may be created by a COMPANY'S MEMORANDUM OF ASSOCIATION or ARTICLES OF ASSOCIATION and may relate to such matters as the right to a dividend, the right to share in surplus assets if the company is wound up, and the right to attend and vote at company meetings.

The particular relevance relates to occasions when the company in general meeting wants to alter its capital (or take other action) that will affect the rights of particular classes of shareholders differently from others.

clause 1. part of a document.

2. part of a Bill that, if it becomes an ACT OF PARLIAMENT, will become a SECTION.

Clayton Act a US statute that prohibits certain practices like price discrimination and exclusive dealing where goods are sold for use, consumption or resale in the USA. Mergers are restricted under the Act.

Clayton's case, the rule in payments towards a running account, such as a bank account, are applied to the earliest debt first. Thus, the most recently incurred charge is the last charge that will be paid off. See the case after which the rule is named. See *Devaynes* v. *Noble* (1816) 1 Merivale 529, the case after which the rule is named.

clean break principle the principle that upon DIVORCE the former spouses should settle their financial affairs in such a way that financial relations between them come to an end. This may be achieved by either a property adjustment order, an order for PERIODICAL PAYMENTS for a specified limited time or a lump sum order.

clean hands see EX TURPI CAUSA.

clear days the number of days available without counting the starting day or the finishing day.

clearing the process by which the cheques drawn on CLEARING BANKS are exchanged and the differences between what is due from and to each bank are settled daily by transfers between the accounts of such banks with the BANK OF ENGLAND: *Barclays Bank plc* v. *Bank of England* [1985] 1 All ER 385.

clearing bank a bank that is a member of the Committee of London and Scottish Clearing Bankers.

close company a UK resident company that is controlled by five or fewer participators, by participators who are directors or by five or fewer persons to whom over 50 per cent of the assets could be distributed on a notional winding up. The consequences of close company status are now that for CORPORATION TAX purposes a wider definition of distribution (e.g. loans to directors) applies. Until the Finance Act 1989 such companies were required to make distributions up to 'the required standard', with any shortfall being treated as having been distributed and, as such, taxable as if it were income in the hands of the shareholders.

closing speeches the speeches made at the end of a court case before the judge's summing up. The defence usually has the last word. See OPENING SPEECHES.

CLS abbreviation for COMMUNITY LEGAL SERVICE.

co-accused in Scotland, a person appearing on the same COMPLAINT or INDICTMENT as another.

COD abbreviation for 'cash on delivery'.

code see CODIFICATION.

Code Napoléon see NAPOLEONIC CODE.

codicil a document executed in testamentary form that acts as an amendment and supplement to a WILL.

codification the process of stating laws in a *code*. This is the mode of lawmaking in continental Europe among the CIVILIAN systems. The model is no doubt that of the codes of the ancient world, pre-eminently the Digest of Justinian (see CORPUS JURIS CIVILIS). The idea is that all the law is in the code, making it known to all the people and not just a trained elite, which made the idea appealing to the revolutionaries of the 18th century. The courts merely interpret the code, which can be altered by the legislature. Codes have spread for intellectual reasons, but Napoleon's imposition, on conquered countries, of codes modelled on his NAPOLEONIC CODE assisted the spread of codification. Many codes are periodically revised.

The English legal system, which has resisted codification, may have been tempted in the Victorian era to put together a code of commercial law. This explains the well-drafted, intelligent and rational Sale of Goods Act 1893, Partnership Act 1890, Bills of Exchange Act 1882 and Marine Insurance Act of the latter part of the 19th century. English lawyers are still resistant to the idea. Law commissioners in Scotland and England are more likely to favour it. Some regularly consolidated statutory areas of law come close to being very complicated codes, an example perhaps being the Companies Acts. To be a proper codification, an Act must consolidate previous statutory enactments and take into account precedents in point.

cognates relatives through the mother's side of the family. See AGNATE.

cohabitants persons living together as husband and wife, whether or not legally married.

cohabitation (with habit and repute) in Scots family law, the last form of IRREGULAR MARRIAGE to survive. The court must declare the marriage but can date the marriage from the initial cohabitation. The parties must have lived as husband and wife, both factually and intentionally. They must cohabit in Scotland. They must cohabit long enough for the court to accept they were meaning to live together as husband and wife, a period of eleven months being sufficient in one case. People generally must believe them to be married, even if a few friends and acquaintances know it is not so. Finally, the parties must have CAPACITY to marry.

collateral 1. something that is independent of another but relates to the same subject matter, thus, the phrases *collateral agreement* or *collateral guarantee*.

2. of the same family line although not in the direct descent.

collatio inter haeredes the doctrine in the Scots law of succession, now abolished, whereby an heir-at-law who sought to claim on the LEGITIM fund had to bring into account the heritable property to which he was heir to the fund. See COLLATIO INTER LIBEROS, HOTCHPOT.

collatio inter liberos in the Scots law of succession the doctrine that requires sums advanced to children other than for ALIMENT or under natural duty or as a loan to be repaid, notionally, before the LEGITIM fund is distributed. See COLLATIO INTER HAEREDES, HOTCHPOT.

collective bargaining the process by which a TRADE UNION negotiates terms and conditions with an employer. The agreement, known as a *collective agreement*, is not intended to be legally binding unless expressed to be so in writing.

collective responsibility see CABINET.

collective trespass a series of crimes created by the Criminal Justice and Public Order Act 1994 with a view to controlling the activities of New Age travellers, hunt saboteurs and protesters. Police officers can ask two or more persons reasonably believed to be trespassing for the purposes of residing there to leave if any person has caused damage to land or property or used threatening, abusive or insulting words or behaviour towards the occupier; or they have between them six or more vehicles on the land. Failure to move, or returning within three months, is an offence. The vehicles can be seized. *Aggravated trespass* is committed where a person trespasses on land in the open and does anything that is intended to have the effect of intimidating those engaged in lawful activities on the land or adjoining land, or obstructing or disrupting such activities. It is possible to obtain prohibition orders against *trespassory assemblies* (unauthorised assemblies of 20 or more persons that could cause serious disruption).

collusion a deceitful or unlawful agreement. In England it is not a bar to an action of DIVORCE. In Scotland it is still a defence to an action of divorce.

colourable justifiable on the face of it. So lawyers speak of a *colourable argument, case* or *warrant*.

combat, trial by see BATTLE, TRIAL BY.

comfort letter a letter in business matters written to assure another party of the writer's intentions. It is essentially not supposed to be binding in law but can allow negotiations or commerce to continue. Examples are in relation to contract negotiations and in relation to the absence of permissions from local authorities.

A special instance is a communication from the COMMISSION OF THE EUROPEAN UNION to the effect that an agreement submitted for an exemption under Article 81 (formerly Article 85) of the COMPETITION LAW does not infringe Article 81 or that if it does infringe Article 81 it still qualifies for an exemption. Following such a communication, the Commission will normally close its dossier. However, the letters are only administrative letters, so are not binding on national courts. Neither are they open to challenge in annulment proceedings before the COURT OF JUSTICE OF THE EUROPEAN UNION.

command theory or **imperative theory** (associated with Jeremy Bentham and John Austin) is based on the notion of commands issued by a sovereign. Bentham did not insist that the sovereign power be single, indivisible and answerable to no one. The habit of obedience to the commands of the sovereign is an important aspect of the theory. The basic idea involves the incorporation of *sanctions*, which are penalties laid down in a law for the contravention of its provisions. While explaining criminal law reasonably adequately, it is much more difficult to incorporate aspects of civil law. See HARTIAN JURISPRUDENCE, KELSINIAN JURISPRUDENCE, REALISM.

commercial agent as a result of EUROPEAN UNION (EU) legislation certain agents are given special indemnity or compensation when the contract is terminated. Heretofore, in the UK at least, there would have been no liability. The EU law is applied in the UK by the Commercial Agents (Council Directive) Regulations 1993 (No. 3053), which came into force on 1 January 1994. The Regulations apply to agents trading as individuals, partnerships or companies.

They cover selling agents and buying agents. However, they apply to agents for the sale or purchase of goods, not services. In Scotland, compensation was awarded in one case by a capital sum representing two years' commission following French law: *King* v. *T. Tunnock Ltd* [2000] TLR 372; and in an English case those who marketed gas as self-employed intermediaries were held to be entitled to the protection of the legislation; they were not 'secondary agents', who are excluded from protection: *Tamarind International Ltd* v. *Eastern Natural Gas Ltd* [2000] TLR 499.

commercial court part of the HIGH COURT that deals with actions arising out of the transactions of merchants and traders, especially actions relating to mercantile documents, export and import matters and cases arising from agency banking and insurance.

commercial unit separate things that in the market place are treated as a whole. In US commercial law and in the UK law of sale of GOODS, it is recognised that, for example, a damaged chair in a three-piece suite of furniture affects the whole suite and not just the chair, so if there is a right to reject the chair as being unsatisfactory, there is a right to reject the whole suite.

commissariat see COMMISSARY COURTS.

commissary courts in the Scottish legal system, the courts that deal with succession matters. The jurisdiction and function are now part of the SHERIFF COURT. The territory is still known as the *commissariat*.

commissioner 1. a member of the COMMISSION OF THE EUROPEAN UNION.

1. a lawyer in Scotland appointed to take evidence out of court.

commissioner of oaths a solicitor authorised to authenticate oaths on sworn statements. For Scotland, see NOTARY PUBLIC.

Commission of the European Union technically the civil service of the EUROPEAN UNION (EU). As the EUROPEAN PARLIAMENT has not yet assumed its predominant role, however, the Commission is the dynamo of development of the EUROPEAN COMMUNITIES. It is charged with upholding European law and does so by gathering information and instigating action before the COURT OF JUSTICE OF THE EUROPEAN UNION, but before doing so reminds the MEMBER STATE governments of their obligations and issues a reasoned opinion on the matter. It can impose fines on undertakings and natural persons, and those fines are enforceable in the member states. It is use of this power that has made the Communities' COMPETITION LAW of significance to international commerce. It issues recommendations and opinions. It makes executive decisions, and the Commission is specially entrusted with the functioning and development of the COMMON MARKET. It legislates by virtue of powers delegated by the COUNCIL OF THE EUROPEAN UNION. The Commission's legislative input is derived from the fact that frequently the Council can act only after receiving an opinion from the Commission. The Council can, however, ask the Commission to submit proposals, and on the basis of the cooperation that is at the core of Community organisation, these will be treated with respect. The Commission prepares a preliminary draft budget and sets the non-compulsory expenditures' maximum level. Once the budget is determined, the Commission implements it, following the rules laid down by the Council. It then submits its accounts to Council and the Parliament. Finally, the Commission is responsible for external relations.

The Commission is made up of 20 Commissioners. It must have one national of each member state and has two from Germany and Spain. They are, however, appointed as independent members of a SUPRANATIONAL body. They are appointed by the member states for a period of five years. As a result of recent treaties, the President of the Commission is chosen by EU heads of state or government meeting in the European Council. This choice has to be approved by the European Parliament. The other members of the Commission are nominated by the governments of the member states in agreement with the new Commission President.

The whole Commission is subject to a collective vote of approval by the European Parliament. The Commission may be removed by the Parliament and once was. In 1994 the Parliament actually exercised its constitutional power to dismiss the Commission, thereby demonstrating the founders' intention that eventually the Parliament would drive Europe and the Commission would revert to its intended role as the civil service.

Most of the Commission's work is carried out through a hierarchical system. Its functions are carried out by *directorates-general* commanded by *directors-general* and referred to by name. These are further subdivided into *units* commanded by *heads of unit*. The Commission also has a secretariat-general and a legal service.

See also COUNCIL OF EUROPE.

committal the sending of a person to court or to prison.

Committee of Ministers see COUNCIL OF EUROPE.

committee stage see ACT OF PARLIAMENT.

commixtio 'the mixture of things', a doctrine in the Roman law of property. If the items could be separated, then there was no problem; if they could not, ownership was in common unless the nature of the mixing were such that one thing was clearly an accessory to the other, in which case the rules on ACCESSION applied.

commodatum in Roman law and in Scots law, a proper loan, that is, loan of a thing to be returned in exactly the form in which it was lent. It is a gratuitous contract, the obligation being to return the goods, fair wear and tear excepted. See MUTUUM.

Common Agricultural Policy (CAP) in the law of the EUROPEAN UNION, one of the very foundations, being the legal regime supporting the coordination of agriculture in Europe. Although included in the COMMON MARKET, it was necessary to make special provision for agriculture because of the contradictory nature of the policies of some founding MEMBER STATES, made none the easier by the ACCESSION of others. The essence of it is that the market is unified, allowing FREE MOVEMENT OF GOODS throughout the community. There is a Community preference protecting the market against imports from outside and the CAP is to be financially secure: the European Agricultural Guidance and Guarantee Fund was set up to this end. Market organisations have been set up for most products, which have the effect of stopping member states from setting up competing systems. The principal effect of the CAP differs in relation to different products: wheat and related produce are protected by intervention purchases made to support producers; beef and related produce are supported by excluding outside competition; and fruit and vegetables and wine are controlled by quality.

The *intervention price* is set as that at which the national authorities must buy certain crops – some farmers may be tempted to grow crops for the intervention price rather than any real market. The more member states become involved in the Union, the more interested they become in reforming the CAP rather than using it as an excuse for complaining.

The *target price* is part of the cereal market scheme. It is the price at which it is expected that sales can be made in the next year in the Community. It is not a fixed price. It is established annually by the Council with a qualified majority on a proposal from the Commission after consulting the Parliament.

The *threshold price* is the price fixed for certain imports from outside countries. It protects Community farmers from outside cheap competition. It is fixed by taking the cost of imports through Rotterdam sold on the Duisburg market and making sure that it does not exceed the set internal target price for the Duisburg area. By deducting the transport costs of cereals from Rotterdam to Duisburg from the target price in Duisburg, the threshold price can be ascertained.

The CAP is always under reconsideration and the object of proposals for reform.

common assault an ASSAULT that is not aggravated.

common carrier a person who publicly undertakes to carry any goods or persons for payment on the routes operated. A common carrier is under duties to carry everyone who offers to pay his charges and to answer as an insurer for everything carried. However, a carrier is not a common carrier if he holds himself out as ready to carry for the public at large only in connection with some other business to which the carriage of goods is merely ancillary.

common customs tariff the charge upon GOODS from outside the EUROPEAN COMMUNITIES to enter the COMMON MARKET. Along with the elimination of CUSTOMS DUTIES, this is the other major plank of the CUSTOMS UNION that itself was, and is, a crucial part of the Common Market of the EUROPEAN UNION. Accordingly, MEMBER STATES cannot fix the duties levied on goods entering their territories. The revenue from the duties they do charge accrues to the Community. The effect was to make trade within the Union cheaper and imports from outside more expensive. When goods from an external country enter the Community they are then treated as European goods and can move freely.

common error see MISTAKE.

common interest in Scots property law, the right in a piece of property with others, not amounting to a form of ownership. It is to be distinguished from COMMON PROPERTY.

common law 1. the law developed by the common law courts as being common to all the Crown's subjects, as distinct from EQUITY. **2.** a general name for Anglo-American case-based systems, as opposed to civilian code-based systems.

common law marriage in the USA, some states still accept that marriage can take place without statutory formalities. To operate, there must be a present agreement to marry, cohabitation in fact and representation by the parties to the community that they are married and a correlative acceptance by the community that the parties are married. There is no such form in England. For Scotland, see COHABITATION (WITH HABIT AND REPUTE).

common market a market where obstacles to free movement of the important sectors of the economy have been removed. Although a general term in economics, it is of special significance to lawyers as one of the foundations of the EUROPEAN UNION. In the EUROPEAN ECONOMIC COMMUNITY Treaty, the essential part of the Common Market was expressed as involving four freedoms: FREE MOVEMENT OF GOODS, FREE MOVEMENT OF PERSONS, FREE MOVEMENT OF SERVICES and OF ESTABLISHMENT and FREE MOVEMENT OF CAPITAL. It also requires more positive steps, and these are reflected in policies: the COMMON AGRICULTURAL POLICY, the TRANSPORT POLICY and COMPETITION POLICY. The SINGLE EUROPEAN ACT prescribed a timetable for the single internal market. In the UK, in common parlance, the term Common Market is still erroneously or mischievously used of the European Union itself.

common property in Scots property law, the right of ownership of a number of people over the one thing. In case of dispute, the thing or land may be divided or sold and the proceeds of the sale divided. Compare COMMON INTEREST.

Commons see HOUSE OF COMMONS.

commonty a form of COMMON PROPERTY once found in Scotland. It is very similar in effect to a servitude right of PASTURAGE.

Commonwealth citizen any person who is either a BRITISH CITIZEN, a British dependent territories' citizen, a British national (overseas), a BRITISH OVERSEAS CITIZEN, a BRITISH SUBJECT (in the sense of the Immigration Act 1981) or a citizen of one of the independent countries mentioned in Schedule 3 to the 1981 Act. Under the British Nationality Act 1948, Commonwealth citizen was a status synonymous with British subject. Under the 1981 Act Commonwealth citizen was redefined.

Community law the law of the EUROPEAN UNION and its associated bodies. It is superior to the law of MEMBER STATES, taking precedence over the law of the member states and yet actually is law in the states. It has many different sources, but legislation is chiefly passed through the COMMISSION OF THE EUROPEAN UNION and the COUNCIL OF THE EUROPEAN UNION. Legislation is carried through in many forms, principally the DIRECTIVE and REGULATION. The JURISPRUDENCE of the

COURT OF JUSTICE OF THE EUROPEAN UNION is a very important source of law, especially as it has assumed the power to strike down the legislation of member states and, indeed, the organs of the Union itself. See ACQUIS COMMUNAUTAIRE.

Community Legal Service (CLS) a part of the system for provision of LEGAL AID in non-criminal matters in England and Wales. The service is essentially delivered by, among others, solicitors, Citizens' Advice Bureaux, law centres, local authority services (including libraries) and community centres. Partnerships are to be established to arrange for the most efficient delivery. Insofar as the services are not actually free, there is a Community Legal Service Fund (the old Legal Aid Fund) to help people who cannot pay. It is intended to establish meaningful quality standards, mainly by means of contracts. There is a funding code. The Legal Aid Franchise Quality Standard (LAFQAS) provides the quality assurance framework within which the main suppliers operate. The *quality mark* is the quality standard that will underpin all the services provided by the wider CLS. There are three quality mark standards; information, general help and specialist help.

community property in some of the states of the USA and elsewhere in the world, there is a form of implied partnership in the profits resulting from a marriage. Premarital property remains the individual property of each party, but property acquired during the marriage is common property.

community protection (Australia) incarceration for the protection of the state, as opposed, for example, for a crime or mental illness. It has entered the legal lexicon courtesy of the state of Victoria, which passed the Community Protection Act 1990 with a view to continuing the incarceration of a very dangerous prisoner whose sentence had come to an end. The prisoner was named in the Act and the Act was designed to expire in a year to give the authorities some time to decide how to deal with someone who was not mad but likely to be very bad; even in prison he had committed 15 assaults and mutilated his body.

community-service order a form of disposal in UK criminal justice by which an offender may be ordered to do work in the community without payment if the offence was one that could have been punished by imprisonment. The work is to be done within 12 months and the maximum number of hours is 240. Its availability depends upon local authorities having schemes available.

Companies Acts the Acts that provide the statutory framework within which companies operate in the UK. The principal Acts are now the Companies Act 1985, the Business Names Act 1985, the Company Securities (Insider Dealing) Act 1985, the Companies Consolidation (Consequential Provisions) Act 1985, the Insolvency Act 1986, the Company Directors' Disqualification Act 1986, the Financial Services Act 1986 and the Companies Act 1989.

company an association of persons formed for the purpose of some business or undertaking, which has a legal personality separate from that of its members. A company may be formed by charter, by special Act of Parliament or by registration under the Companies Acts. The liability of members is usually (but not always) limited by the charter, Act of Parliament or MEMORANDUM OF ASSOCIATION. A company may be a *public limited company* (PLC or plc), in which event its shares may be transferred freely among, and owned by, members of the public. All *limited liability companies* that are not public limited companies are *private companies*, denoted by the term Ltd. While companies are owned by their members (i.e. shareholders), they are managed by a BOARD OF DIRECTORS. Historically, the duties owned by the board are fiduciary in nature and owed to the company rather than the shareholders. Companies are the major instrument for economic and financial growth and development in the Western world.

A company may be limited by shares or, in the case of a private company, by guarantee. Since the Companies Act 1980, it is no longer possible to create a *company limited by guarantee* and having a share capital in the UK. A company limited by guarantee is a company that has the liability of its members limited by the memorandum of association to such an amount as the members may undertake to contribute to the assets of the company upon its being wound up.

A *company limited by share* is a company having the liability of its members limited by the memorandum of association to the amount, if any, unpaid on the shares respectively held by them.

company insolvency proceedings there are four types of INSOLVENCY proceedings that govern the affairs of insolvent companies: *voluntary arrangements* under Part I of the Insolvency Act 1986; *administration orders* under Part II; *receivership* under Part III; and *winding up* under Parts IV-VI. Under the Insolvency Act 1986 no company registered under the Companies Acts may be liable to

BANKRUPTCY proceedings.

company limited by guarantee see COMPANY.

company limited by shares see COMPANY.

comparative negligence (USA) see CONTRIBUTORY NEGLIGENCE.

compellability in the law of EVIDENCE, the power to make a WITNESS come to court to testify. The general rule is that a competent witness is *compellable*. The sovereign and certain diplomats are competent but not compellable. Parliamentary privilege probably has the same effect as regards Members of Parliament. Jurors are not compellable in regard to the discussions in the jury room. Parties, their spouses and their lawyers are compellable in civil cases. The rules in regard to criminal matters vary from jurisdiction to jurisdiction, but the accused is not a competent witness if tried alone. If the accused gives evidence for the defence, he loses the privilege against self-incrimination in respect of the offence charged. Spouses are generally not compellable.

compensation 1. a monetary payment for loss or damage.
2. in Scotland, the right to set off one debt against another with the effect of reducing the one by the amount of the other. The right is not available after decree. It applies only to liquid debts or, at the discretion of the court, debts easily made liquid. There must be *concursus debiti et crediti*, meaning that each party must be the other's debtor and creditor. An executor sued for a private debt has been held unable to plead compensation in respect of a debt owed to him as executor. The rules operate differently in INSOLVENCY. See CRIMINAL INJURIES COMPENSATION.

compensation recovery the clawback by a government agency of a proportion or all of the DAMAGES awarded or agreed to be paid to a person in respect of certain state benefits obtained by that person in consequence of an accident, injury or disease. In principle, this is a reasonable scheme. It was introduced in the UK by the Social Security Act 1989. It stops *double compensation*, with the state and insurers, their shareholders and premium-payers overpaying. For a time the state took recovery even from damages for pain and suffering, but the position now is that there is no recovery from such damages. Recovery is effected by the Compensation Recovery Unit (CRU) and is governed by complex rules. Recovery is made from the *compensator* (the person making the compensation) but the compensator takes account of this in negotiating any settlement.

compensator see COMPENSATION RECOVERY.

competency 1. with respect to evidence, competency is equivalent to ADMISSIBILITY.

2. in relation to a witness, competency refers to his legal CAPACITY to be a witness.

3. in relation to proceedings that have no legal foundation, these are said to be *incompetent*.

Competition Commission a body charged with controlling cartels, monopolies and mergers and hearing appeals against the Director General of Fair Trading in such matters. Its decisions may be challenged in the High Court or the Court of Session in Scotland. It is modelled partly on the COMMISSION OF THE EUROPEAN UNION's function in competition matters (see COMPETITION POLICY).

competition law the law that restrains excesses in the market, such as cartels, MERGERS, monopolies and price-fixing. See ANTIDUMPING, CLAYTON ACT, COMPETITION POLICY, SHERMAN ACT, STATE AIDS.

competition policy (EU) the competition policy of the EUROPEAN UNION (EU). It is no different in principle from national measures. The ideas and issues are the same – to allow everyone the benefits of larger markets without the disadvantage of monopolies and the like. The legal regime is unique and is a major contribution to commercial law. It focuses on rules in relation to undertakings and rules applying to STATE AIDS. The rules relating to undertakings are divided into two sets of provisions – those relating to cartels under Article 81 (formerly 85) and those to what is called abuse of a dominant position under Article 82 (formerly 86).

In relation to *cartels*, in strict law the treaties apply to agreements between undertakings and concerted practices principally under Article 81. Cartels are automatically void if they can affect inter-MEMBER STATE trade and have as their object or effect distortion of competition. If the agreement is a binding legal obligation, then it need not actually affect trade and may yet be void. If there is no legally binding agreement, then the cartel can be restricted only if there is established a concerted practice and one that is not the ordinary coincidental operation of the market, as where all prices of a product tend to go up at the same time: see *Hoffman-La Roche* v. *Commission* [1972] ECR 619. Agreements can be given individual exemptions from these rules if production or distribution or technical and economic progress is made; consumers obtain a fair share of the resulting benefit; no extra obligations are imposed; and the agreement does not allow the parties to eliminate competition.

Certain categories of agreements are given a block exemption, an example being exclusive dealing agreements.

Abuse of a dominant position exists under Article 82 of the EUROPEAN COMMUNITIES when an undertaking can hinder the maintenance of effective competition on the relevant market by allowing it to behave to an appreciable extent independently of its competitors and customers and ultimately of consumers: see *Michelin* v. *Commission* [1983] ECR 3461. However, it is the abuse of this position that is controlled. Abuse is an objectively determined criterion and relates to the effect on the market. The essence of it is that there are actings to diminish or distort competition: *Hoffman-La Roche* v. *Commission* [1979] ECR 461.

MERGERS were not clearly controlled by either of the foregoing concepts, although they have been considered under Article 81 and Article 82. A new regulation, which came into force in 1990, controls mergers and concentrations. It requires referral to the COMMISSION OF THE EUROPEAN UNION if there is a Community dimension.

By virtue of the Competition Act 1998, UK competition law now closely follows EU competition policy, striking at cartels and concerted practices and prohibiting the abuse of a dominant position. See also ANTIDUMPING, STATE AIDS.

complainant the person who makes a criminal complaint in England. See COMPLAINER.

complainer the person who instigates a criminal investigation in Scotland. The prosecution itself is initiated by the Crown.

complaint 1. the start of a civil action in a magistrate's court.
2. an allegation against another.
3. the name of the papers used by the court and served on the accused in Scottish summary criminal proceedings.

completion a non-technical term used to describe the last stage of a sale of land when the land and its title are exchanged for the price. For Scotland, see SETTLEMENT.

composition a sum paid and accepted by creditors to ward off BANKRUPTCY.

compos mentis 'having one's right mind', usually used in the context of saying that the person concerned is not intoxicated or insane.

Comptroller and Auditor General head of the Exchequer and Audit Department and a parliamentary officer. The Comptroller's main function is to scrutinise public accounts to ensure that money is being spent as Parliament authorised. The holder of the office is paid from the CONSOLIDATED FUND. An annual report to the Committee on Public Accounts has to be made.

compulsion see NECESSITY.

compulsory purchase the process by which land is legally acquired for public use, irrespective of the wishes of the owners. There are two procedures under which this may be achieved: the first involves the service of a *notice to treat* (compensation is determined on the basis of the market value of the land at the date of the notice) or through a *general vesting declaration* by the acquiring authority, as a result of which the land vests in the authority from the date of the declaration.

compulsory winding up a procedure for the dissolution of a COMPANY involving a petition presented to the court, usually by a creditor. The petition must be based on one of the grounds specified in the Companies Act 1985. The most usual ground is that the company is unable to pay its debts.

compurgation the medieval procedure by which a person could defend a claim or charge by giving his OATH and being supported by *compurgators*, usually 12 in number. They testified that they believed the person who called them and did not speak to the facts of the case, as is the modern procedure.

computer-assisted legal research see CALR.

computerised records records held in a computer. The lawyer's preference for papers made it essential that special provision should be made for computer records. The Civil Evidence Act 1968 and the Police and Criminal Evidence Act 1984 allow such evidence to be admissible subject to certain specific provisions. Similar rules apply in Scotland.

conacre an arrangement common in Ireland under which a farmer has the right to till land, sow crops on it and to harvest them. It usually lasts for eleven months but does not create the relationship of landlord and tenant.

concealment of pregnancy in the criminal law of Scotland, the statutory crime of not calling for help during the period leading up to and including childbirth if the child is later missing or dead. Nondisclosure is sufficient.

concert see ART AND PART.

concerted practice see COMPETITION POLICY.

conciliation settlement out of court, usually by the assistance of a neutral third party. There is a current trend to use this method in family matters relating to children. It is already well established in EMPLOYMENT matters. See ADVISORY CONCILIATION AND ARBITRATION SERVICE.

conclusions in Scottish civil procedure, that part of a SUMMONS that sets out what the PURSUER seeks.

conclusive evidence evidence that cannot be disputed and that, as a matter of law, must be taken to establish some fact in issue.

concubinage a slightly old-fashioned word for COHABITATION.

concurrent sentence a sentence of imprisonment that runs at the same time as another. Two sentences of three years served *concurrently* are over in three years. The practice is not completely redundant because one of the sentences may be restricted or quashed on appeal and then the other remains in force. See CONSECUTIVE SENTENCE.

condescendence in Scottish civil procedure, that part of either a SUMMONS or an INITIAL WRIT that sets out the fact founded on.

condictio in ROMAN LAW, the action for debt – to have the defender make over something that belonged to the defender. It became a more general claim, many instances being enrichment actions.

condictio causa data causa non secuta in ROMAN LAW, the personal action for non-materialisation of one side of a bilateral agreement. Originally its scope was narrower, applying to cases where one side of innominate real contract had been performed and the other person pulled out. This action allowed for a claim to be made for a return. The terminology is much used in Scots law. It is known in many modern civilian systems.

condictio indebiti in ROMAN LAW, a personal action to require a defender to make over a sum of money or a thing given to the defender in the belief that the pursuer was legally obliged to give it to the defender when legally the payment was not due. By analogy, a ground for recovery of certain unjust enrichments in Scots law. The remedy is widely known in modern civilian systems and appears in many CODIFICATIONS.

condictio sine causa in ROMAN LAW, a personal action for the restitution of something, there, in fact or in law, having been no cause for the transfer in the first place. The action was known in Roman law, is known in South African and other civilian systems and appears in Scottish writings and a few cases.

condition a term, usually in a CONTRACT or a unilateral deed like a will, that of itself does nothing but that limits or suspends or provides for the resolution of other terms. A *condition precedent* is one that must be satisfied before an obligation takes effect. (In Scotland *suspensive condition* is the term used.) A *condition subsequent* destroys the obligation (called a *resolutive condition* in Scotland).

In English law there is a technical distinction between terms of a contract: conditions, warranties and 'intermediate or innominate terms'. Conditions, if breached, give the right to RESCISSION of the contract and damages; warranties, if breached, give a right to damages only; and conditions in the third category are remedied according to the factual consequences following the breach.

In Scotland there is no such distinction and the remedies depend upon the materiality of the breach in relation to the contract.

In New Zealand, courts have developed a different structure from that of the English common law in relation to conditional contracts. In England the distinction is between conditions precedent or subsequent; in New Zealand no particular categorisation is adopted, but commentators have suggested the cases fall into three classes: conditions affecting formation of an agreement; conditions required for an agreement to become a contract; and conditions relating to the performance of contractual obligations.

conditional fee agreement see CONTINGENCY FEE.

conditional sale agreement an agreement under which the sale is suspended until the price is paid. The term is important in relation to CONSUMER CREDIT law.

conditio si testator sine liberis decesserit in the Scots law of succession, a WILL that does not make provision for children yet to be born is presumed to be revoked by the subsequent birth of a child to the testator, whether or not the child is legitimate. The presumption can be revoked.

condominium joint ownership. The term has come to describe a flat held in this way, especially in the USA.

condonation see ADULTERY.

confession and avoidance a defence pleading that admits certain material facts for attempts to avoid the legal consequence of those facts by alleging further facts to establish some defence to the claim. The facts relied on as constituting the avoidance must be specifically pleaded and the BURDEN OF PROOF is on the party relying on the plea.

confessions see EXCLUSIONARY RULE, HEARSAY.

confidence see BREACH OF CONFIDENCE.

confirmation in the Scots law of succession, the official document that allows the executor to administer the estate. It reproduces the inventory of the estate submitted by the executor. The confirmation includes HERITAGE and is effective throughout the whole of the UK. It affects property outside Scotland if the deceased had been domiciled in Scotland. A simpler form is available for small estates in terms of the Small Estates (Scotland) Act 1979. See EIK.

confiscation the taking away of the property of another, usually by the state. In relation to the acquisition of land and the like for state projects, most systems have procedures allowing for appeal and always with compensation. Customs and Excise authorities can confiscate certain goods where the proper duty has not been paid. In criminal cases, confiscation or forfeiture is now much more common than once was the case, with statutory powers being available to penalise serious criminals in a much more effective way than handing out sentences of imprisonment. So it is now possible in the UK for drug dealers to lose the houses bought with the proceeds of their trade and for the getaway car in a bank robbery to be taken and sold. There is, of course, no compensation in such cases, but there is usually a right of appeal as with any sentence. The right to property under European human rights law (see EUROPEAN COURT OF HUMAN RIGHTS) means that confiscation measures cannot operate against the presumption of innocence nor by perhaps confiscating the property of another person in a process in which he is not involved.

conflict of laws see PRIVATE INTERNATIONAL LAW.

confusio the mixing of liquids, the property in which is governed by rules in the law of Scotland. If the liquids are of the same kind, e.g. wine and wine, there is common property in proportion to quantity and value. If of different substances that cannot be separated, e.g. water and wine, this is but a form of SPECIFICATIO.

confusion 1. in the law of CONTRACT, in Scotland, a party cannot be under an obligation to himself. Thus, if a person becomes his own creditor the debt is extinguished.

2. an anglicisation of CONFUSIO.

congenital disabilities in English law, injuries in respect of which action may be raised for a child born disabled in respect of a tortious act done to his parent before birth causing injuries: Congenital Disabilities (Civil Liability) Act 1976.

The Act does not apply in Scotland, but the same result is achieved at common law: *Cohen* v. *Shaw* 1992 SLT 1022; *Jones* v. *Lanarkshire Health Authority* 1990 SLT 19.

Congress the federal legislature of the USA comprising two chambers: the Senate, made up of Senators, and the House of Representatives, made up of representatives, or Congressmen and Congresswomen. The Congress represents the states. The Senators are elected on a state-wide basis and the representatives on a district-wide basis. Legislative powers cover *inter alia* interstate and foreign commerce, federal tax, currency, the post, declarations of war, much commercial law and the establishment of the armed forces. So-called general clauses have allowed Congress, with the decisions of the SUPREME COURT, to be active in other areas. Statutes are passed by simple majority of both houses.

conjoined arrestment order in the Scots law of DILIGENCE or legal enforcement, the process used where a debtor owes more than one creditor. Certain statutory sums are deducted by his employer from his earnings and distributed by the court among his creditors.

connected persons persons who deal with each other otherwise than at arm's length. Examples include members of the same family, companies within the same group, trusts and trustees, companies and their shareholders, partners and their families. The relevance of the concept is primarily in the field of insolvency and taxation.

consanguinity see AFFINITY.

consecutive sentence a sentence that runs at the end of another. Two sentences of three years served *consecutively* equate to a six-year sentence. See CONCURRENT SENTENCE.

consent agreement with another on the same matter.

1. a defence to a civil action for ASSAULT.

2. a defence to some criminal charges but not murder.

3. an essential element in the formation of a CONTRACT.

4. an essential element in the formation of a MARRIAGE.

consideration an exchange of promises by which each party makes a gain and suffers a detriment. The requirement for there to be consideration before there will be a legally binding CONTRACT in English law emphasises the theory held by many legal commentators and theorists that contract is based upon a bargain – something for something else. The consideration must be sufficient but need not be adequate: *Chappell* v. *Nestlé* [1960] AC 87 – i.e. it is still possible to make a bad bargain. The avoidance of a disbenefit might be sufficient, assuming there is no DURESS or FRAUD: *Williams* v. *Roffey* [1990] 1 All ER 512. Past consideration is not sufficient unless the original act was done by the promisor's request. Part payment of a debt in English law can only be discharged by full ACCORD AND SATISFACTION under the rule in *Pinnel's Case* (1602). The absence of consideration is fatal (*Foakes* v. *Beer* (1884) 9 AC 605), but the common law permits satisfaction if the creditor has requested payment of a smaller sum before the due date, requested payment at a different place or requested payment by different means. The doctrine of promissory ESTOPPEL in equity has been accepted as providing a basis for holding parties to agreements in the absence of consideration: see *Central London Property Trust* v. *High Trees House* [1947] 1 KB 130. See CONTRACT.

consignment the sending of goods. The person sending them is the *consignor* and the person to whom they are sent the *consignee*. The consignor is generally responsible for the payment of any charges. The rights and liabilities of the consignor and consignee on the one hand and the carrier of the goods on the other will usually be based on the terms of the contract of carriage. See BILL OF LADING, CARRIAGE BY AIR, CARRIAGE BY RAIL, CARRIAGE BY ROAD, CARRIAGE BY SEA.

consistorial in Scots legal practice, cases to do with status, such as divorce. It is no longer a technical term, but many practitioners still use it.

Consistory Court the ecclesiastical courts of the diocese of the Church of England.

consolidated accounts accounts used in relation to the activities of a group of companies to the effect that duplications in items are eliminated so that the combined figures do not show more assets and equity than actually exist.

consolidated fund a government-maintained account with the BANK OF ENGLAND to receive the public income of the state and to meet annual public expenditure. It pays the interest on the national debt.

conspiracy 1. the DELICT or TORT of agreeing with others to cause damage to another by committing a lawful act by unlawful means or committing an unlawful act. Its scope is not determined, and the courts are at pains to exclude legitimate business agreements from its scope. TRADE UNIONS have immunity from action in many instances. Despite the fact that the effect of the tort is to allow two people to be made liable for an act that, if done by one, would not be actionable, the courts have allowed it to develop. See *Crofter Co. Ltd* v. *Veitch* [1942] AC 435.

2. a statutory offence in England under the Criminal Law Act 1977 as amended. It is committed by an agreement to a course of conduct that, if carried out, will necessarily involve the commission of an offence, or would do but for the impossibility of committing the planned offence. See *R* v. *Cooke* [1986] AC 909. It was an offence at common law.

3. in the criminal law of Scotland, it is itself a crime where two or more persons agree to commit an act that, if attempted or achieved, would be a crime in Scots law. The agreement itself is a crime. See *Maxwell* v. *HMA* 1980 JC 40. See ART AND PART.

constable 1. a person who has undertaken to serve the Crown as an officer of the peace. Now in the UK a police officer.

2. an elected position, similar to mayor, in the parishes of the BAILIWICKS of Jersey and Guernsey, bringing with it the right to a seat in the local legislative assembly.

constitutional law the law that determines the relationship of the citizen to the state and that controls the operation of the various branches of the state. Some examples are now discussed.

In the UK there is no single fundamental document in which the constitutional law can be found. The law is found in certain important Acts of Parliament (like the ACTS OF UNION), in the law and custom of PARLIAMENT and in conventions. The supreme law-making body is the Queen in Parliament. The House of Lords is not a constitutional court and cannot generally strike down legislation. Membership of the EUROPEAN COMMUNITIES has affected the constitutional law of the UK in ways not fully appreciated. There is a devolved SCOTTISH PARLIAMENT and a NATIONAL ASSEMBLY FOR WALES. See ACT OF PARLIAMENT, CABINET, CONVENTIONS, HOUSE OF COMMONS, HOUSE OF LORDS, PRIVY COUNCIL.

In the USA, the Constitution, ratified by 13 states in 1788, is the heart of the American legal system. In seven articles and 26 amendments it lays down the political and legal structure of the federal government. The first ten amendments are known as the BILL OF RIGHTS. Changes are seldom effected, but the SUPREME COURT creatively interprets the intention of the first founding fathers of the Constitution. Each state has its own constitutional documents. The federal government is delegated specific powers involving regulating interstate trade, taxation and war treaties. CONGRESS enacts laws. The executive function lies with the President of the USA. The Constitution provides the checks and balances to allow the three divisions of government to cooperate.

In Australia, the Commonwealth of Australia Constitution Act

1900 is an Act of the imperial UK Parliament. It can be amended only by a referendum procedure. The states themselves have constitutions also derived from the UK and antedating the federal constitution. Much more radical independence from the UK came with the Australia Act of 1986, which removed the right of appeal to the privy council. The Parliament consists of the Queen, Senate and a House of Representatives. Executive power is in the hands of the Queen, exercisable by the Governor General. Judicial power is in the hands of the HIGH COURT OF AUSTRALIA, headed by a Chief Justice. There is a division of powers between the states and the federal government, which, as in the USA, has been a source of much jurisdictional legislation and controversy. Many important powers are held concurrently. UK law no longer applies to Australia – indeed, no longer can apply; state parliaments can repeal any previous imperial legislation.

The Canadian Constitution has three major written parts: the Constitution Acts of 1867 (formerly the British North America Act) and 1982 and the Charter of Rights and Freedoms. The Meech Lake Constitutional Accord of 1987 was expected to come into force in 1992 but did not actually do so. By implication, the 1867 Act was held to imply the freedoms of the British Constitution. Executive authority in federal Canada resides in the Crown in the form of the Governor General, in the provinces in the Lieutenant Governors. Under conventions of the constitution, their powers are exercised only after consultation. The UK enacted the Canada Act 1982, which set up a new constitution and one that bound Quebec, despite its having rejected the package. The Meech Lake Constitutional Accord recognised the distinctiveness of Quebec. The Accord also gave the provinces increased power, allowing them to nominate persons for the Senate and the Supreme Court. It made constitutional certain practices, such as consultation of the provinces and the federal government. The procedure for amendment was changed. The Act provides that UK legislation should no longer apply to Canada and provides for a Charter of Rights and Freedoms – a Canadian BILL OF RIGHTS.

In New Zealand the main constitutional provision is the Constitution Act of 1852, which gave responsible government to the Crown colony; also important is the New Zealand Constitution Amendment Act 1947. Dominion status was granted in 1907. The Parliament of New Zealand can, like the UK Parliament, alter any previous laws, including all or any of the provisions of the Constitution Act. Parliaments are summoned and dissolved by proclamation of the Governor General – in dissolutions he acts on the advice of the prime minister – and a session lasts three years. It is a UNICAMERAL parliament. The government is led by a prime minister who has a cabinet and an administration – the executive council, including the non-cabinet ministers. The council is legally government and includes the Governor General.

In Ireland, under the Constitution of the Republic, the head of state is directly elected by the people and may hold office for up to two seven-year terms. The President, on the nomination of DAIL EIREANN, appoints the TAOISEACH, or prime minister, and, with the approval of the Taoiseach, the other members of the government. The Dail is summoned and dissolved by the President on the advice of the Taoiseach, and it is the President who must sign legislation before it can become law. The President may, after consultation with the COUNCIL OF STATE, refer the bill to the SUPREME COURT for a decision on whether it is repugnant to the Constitution. The President's Commission exercises the functions of the President should that person be unable to do so through absence from the state, incapacity, resignation, removal or death. It comprises the Chief Justice, the Chairman of Dail Eireann and the Chairman of SEANAD EIREANN.

construction the process of interpreting a document or statute.

constructive dismissal see UNFAIR DISMISSAL.

constructive knowledge or **constructive notice** knowledge that a person is deemed to have of facts that he would have discovered had he made the usual and proper inquiries. In the law of property, if a person omits to investigate some fact that has been brought to his notice, suggesting the existence of an adverse claim or title, or if he deliberately refrains from making due inquiry in order to avoid obtaining actual knowledge, he will be fixed with constructive knowledge of it.

constructive trust a TRUST imposed by operation of law rather than by the expression of the parties.

Consultative Committee see EUROPEAN ECONOMIC AREA.

consumer normally (but not always) a customer who buys for personal use and not business purposes and who is accordingly treated differently in the law. See CONSUMER CREDIT, CONSUMER CREDIT AGREEMENT, UNFAIR CONTRACT TERMS.

consumer contract see UNFAIR CONTRACT TERMS.

consumer credit lending to a CONSUMER, as opposed to a commercial enterprise. The words have a special significance because of the Consumer Credit Act 1974: 'An Act to establish for the protection of consumers a new system, administered by the Director General of Fair Trading, of licensing and other control of traders concerned with the provision of credit, or the supply of goods on hire or hire-purchase, and their transactions and related matters.' While 'consumer' is defined for the purposes of a consumer contract under the unfair contract terms legislation, there is no such definition on the 1974 Act. It provides controls where the debtor is a natural person or is an individual, including a partnership or unincorporated body of persons not consisting of bodies corporate.

The Act is primarily concerned with:

(a) the control and regulation of the consumer credit industry by means of a licensing system, together with restriction on the ways of seeking business; and

(b) the greater regulation of the rights of the parties under a consumer credit agreement. See CANCELLATION.

consumer credit agreement a consumer credit agreement is an agreement under which credit is extended to an individual. Those agreements that are *regulated agreements* cover extensions of credit up to a statutory limit. These include credit sales, hire-purchase, secured and unsecured loans; they may be *bipartite debtor-creditor agreements* or *tripartite debtor-creditor-supplier agreements*.

consummation of marriage full sexual intercourse between married persons after their marriage by the insertion of the penis into the vagina. Inability to consummate because of impotence or refusal to consummate is a ground for nullity of the marriage.

contact order see SECTION 8 ORDER.

contemporanea exposito 'contemporaneous interpretation'. In interpreting a document or statute this rule of CONSTRUCTION requires that the reader should try to read the document as it would have been read by someone at the time when it was written.

contempt of court the offence of showing disrespect for a court. Contempt may be criminal or civil. *Criminal contempt* is conduct (whether words or actions) that obstructs or tends to obstruct the administration of justice; *civil contempt* is deliberate disobedience of an order of the court or breach of an undertaking given to the court; either is punishable by committal or a fine.

In Scots criminal law, an offence against the dignity of the court (not the judge) that can be committed inside or outside the court. Drunkenness can be sufficient but strange dress is not.

contingency fee a fee for legal services that depends upon success and is related to that success. Such charging schemes are permitted in (among other places) the USA, Canada, Spain and Germany. A contingency fee proper is a fixed fee that is paid only on success. A fee that is a share of the litigation in the event of success might be treated differently.

In England, a *conditional fee agreement* is permitted in English law in terms of the Courts and Legal Services Act 1990, providing the case does not relate to criminal, family or children cases. Such an agreement allows that fees are payable only if the action is won.

'*No win, no fee*' is a marketing slogan that can be used by lawyers. It can equally be used by unqualified claims handlers who may or may not refer the cases to solicitors. What the phrase conceals is that the claimant may face the costs of his opponent if the claimant is unsuccessful – indeed, normally the claimant may have to pay disbursements or outlays such as for medical reports. Recently, the more generous '*no win, no cost*' has been seen, which means that the claims handler or lawyer will cover disbursements and cover the costs of the opponent, albeit perhaps by funding an insurance premium. Both of these, however, do not mention the consequences of winning. A claims' handler may take a percentage of the damages regardless of the fact that very little work has been done. The *uplift* (or increased fee) when a case is won on a 'no win, no fee' basis is called a *success fee*, and it is a fee because it is related to the work done, albeit uplifted. Some solicitors may take a substantially uplifted success fee or take a contracted work rate. In both cases the claimant has to pay money for the claims service from his damages. Where a lawyer charges a normal fee, both in England and Wales and in Scotland, it is not uncommon for the claimant to recover all or most of his legal costs and be able to keep his damages.

In Scotland, a *pactum de quota litis* ('a promise of a share of the action') is ex facie illegal and unenforceable so far as lawyers are concerned. Curiously, it has been held in Scotland that unqualified unregistered claims' handlers are free to take a share of the action: *Quantum Claims Compensation Specialists Ltd* v. *Powell* [1998] TLR 108. However, the Law Reform (Miscellaneous Provisions) (Scotland) Act 1990, amending the Solicitors (Scotland) Act 1980 and effected by Act of Sederunt, permits the charging of an increased fee of up to 100 per cent if the action is successful. These fees are known as *speculative fees*.

In the USA it is possible for any share of the proceeds of the litigation to be the subject of agreement on condition that no charge is made if the action is not successful. Note, however, that in the USA there is no basic rule that the loser pays the winner's costs. The client must generally remain liable for the costs and expenses of the action for such an agreement to be valid.

continuous employment to be entitled to many (but not all) of the remedies of modern EMPLOYMENT law it is necessary to have achieved a given period of continuous employment. These periods are not immutable and can be, and have been, changed and are subject to detailed computational rules.

continuous user uninterrupted use. The claimant to an easement or profit by prescription must show that his *user as of right* has been continuous, that is, without interruption. In the Prescription Act 1832, user is not deemed to have been interrupted unless the interruption has continued for twelve months or more.

contra 'against'.

contra bonos mores 'against the best customs or morals or a good way of life'.

contract the branch of the law of obligations that deals with obligations voluntarily assumed. CIVIL LAW jurisdictions share the inheritance of Roman law, but the CANON LAW idea of *pacta sunt servanda* ('promises ought to be obeyed') has had a considerable influence. The main development since classical Roman law has been the movement away from having a law of mainly specific contracts like hire, service or sale and accepting that CONSENT underlies them all.

There is a difference between the civil law tradition and the Anglo-American law. The requirements for a contract in Anglo-American law are that there be an OFFER, an ACCEPTANCE, CONSIDERATION and an intention to effect legal obligations. Scots law, because of its civilian origins, does not require the consideration. Contractual consent is generally discovered by objectively, rather than subjectively, investigating the parties' positions. The possibility that they have not actually reached agreement on the same thing – *consensus ad idem* – is treated under the law relating to MISTAKE or error. See also UNFAIR CONTRACT TERMS.

contra proferentem rule a rule of interpretation that demands that the words to be construed should be construed against the party seeking to utilise them. Thus, in the law of CONTRACT an *exemption clause* is construed against the party founding on it, as are contracts in restraint of trade.

contravention see CRIME.

contributory negligence lack of care by a plaintiff for his own safety. (In the USA the term *comparative negligence* is sometimes used.) Before the Law Reform (Contributory Negligence) Act 1945, NEGLIGENCE on the part of the party suing was a complete defence, however insignificant it was in the whole picture. The Act allowed a proportion of the damages to be reduced to reflect the plaintiff's fault.

In England it applies to certain contractual claims: *Forsikringsaktieselskapet Vesta* v. *Butcher* [1986] 2 All ER 488.

In Canada it has been accepted as a defence to a negligent misstatement case: *Grand Restaurants of Canada Ltd* v. *Toronto* (1981) 123 DLR (3d) 349. Children can be held to be contributorily negligent.

contumelia contumely, or spitely comment.

conventions (of the British constitution) discernible rules of conduct that are considered binding by the Crown and those involved in government. They are not laws in the sense of legally binding people in such a way that they could be compelled to perform or be sanctioned for failure to do so in a court. Neither are conventions, strictly speaking, customs because custom is a source of actual law and a convention is not law. It was Dicey who insisted that the CONSTITUTIONAL LAW of the UK could not be understood without understanding the conventions. The nature of conventions as extra-legal was confirmed by the Supreme Court of Canada in *Re Amendment of the Constitution of Canada* (1981) 125 DLR 3d 1, leading some to believe that the existence of a convention may be a justiciable issue.

The bulk of conventions regulate the following: the ROYAL PREROGATIVE and the CABINET; the workings of PARLIAMENT, particularly the relationship of the HOUSE OF COMMONS and the HOUSE OF LORDS; the organisation of the Commonwealth; the making of war; the dissolution of government; the refusing of the ROYAL ASSENT to Bills; ministers being collectively responsible; the business of the House of Commons being arranged behind the SPEAKER's chair by the leader of the government and the leader of the opposition; the restriction on the UK Parliament legislating for a former dependent territory now an independent member of the Commonwealth unless it is asked to do so; the appointment of the governor general of an independent Commonwealth country. All involve the conventions.

conversion the wrong committed by a dealing with the goods of a person that constitutes an unjustifiable denial of his rights in them or his assertion of rights inconsistent with them. Conversion and TRESPASS overlap. To take away the goods of another will be trespass but also may be conversion. If the taking is temporary, however, and not done to exercise rights over the goods, then there is no conversion. Taking to use the goods is sufficient, it not being necessary to assert ownership over the goods. In English law, it holds that the voluntary receipt by the defendant of the goods from a wrongfully interfering third party is conversion. Abuse of an authorised possession may be conversion – where goods are pawned, for example. Allowing the goods to be stolen through lack of care, being an omission, is not conversion: *Ashby* v. *Tolhurst* [1937] 2 KB 242; *Tinsley* v. *Dudley* [1951] 2 KB 18. Destruction of the goods or alteration of the goods to another species is conversion. It is not known in Scotland although sometimes similar issues arise: *Leitch* v. *Leydon* 1931 SC (HL) 1. The closest analogue is SPUILZIE.

It is also a CRIME in English law, if fraudulent, under the Theft Act 1968.

conveyancing the practice (some would say art) of transferring ownership in PROPERTY. In some cases the law takes care of the transfer – this is so in many everyday transactions for the sale of GOODS where the property is transferred according to the Sale of Goods Act 1979 (as amended) if the parties have not sought to regulate matters for themselves. In many other cases difficult issues usually involve the writing of some instrument. Thus, some incorporeal moveables have to be transferred by ASSIGNATION, and real or heritable property may often have to be conveyed by a formal written document, usually one recorded in a register.

In England and Scotland the conveyancing of land is largely the domain of SOLICITORS, although often members of the Bar specialise in resolving problems that are contractual or relate to land law. In both jurisdictions there are practices that grow up to facilitate what is often, but not always, a piece of non-contentious business – it is this practical part of the business that conveyancers consider their art.

In England there is a body of people who are *licensed conveyancers* but not solicitors or barristers. The same system exists in Scotland, but the necessary regulatory body was only recently activated, so conveyancing is still done at the time of writing by solicitors.

convicium in Scots law, the verbal injury of bringing a person into public hatred and ridicule, even (according to some, but not all, commentators) by saying something that is true.

conviction a person is *convicted* of an offence if he pleads or is found guilty of that offence.

cooling-off period a time during which a person can withdraw from a binding contract without any serious penalty. A cooling-off period is not normally available. It applies in terms of the Consumer Credit Act 1974 where contracts such as hire-purchase contracts are concluded off trade premises and in the Timeshare Act 1992 and in ever more areas of activity to protect those easily pressured into contracts without seeking time to consider or take advice.

cooperation procedure in the law of the EUROPEAN UNION, instead of issuing a DECISION, as in the past, where this procedure operates the COUNCIL OF THE EUROPEAN UNION adopts a common position that is then communicated to the EUROPEAN PARLIAMENT. The Parliament can then adopt the position and propose amendments, which the Council must then take into consideration, or the Parliament can reject the common position, in which case, if the Council wishes to press on regardless, it must do so unanimously.

copyright the law concerned to prevent the copying of physical material existing in the field of literature and the arts and creation generally. A copyright is a legal right (that endures during the lifetime of, and for 70 years after the death of, a person whose work has been published) not to have such work copied or reproduced or adapted without the author's authorisation and without the payment of royalties (subject to some complex transitional rules). It is concerned only with the copying of physical material and not with the reproduction of ideas, and it does not confer a monopoly to any particular form of words or design. In this it may be distinguished from rights conferred by a PATENT or TRADEMARK.

Besides books and works of art, copyright also subsists in artistic works, sound and television broadcasts, sound recordings, cinematograph films and computer programs. A work generated by a computer, which is not created by a human, is protected for only 50 years. There are various defences and most notable is that of *fair dealing* for research or private study or for criticism, review or news reporting.

Coreper abbreviation for Comité des Representant Permanents, 'Committee of Permanent Representatives'. The COUNCIL OF THE EUROPEAN UNION meets on only a few days a month, so others must handle the business. This body comprises civil servants of the MEMBER STATES. It is a subordinate body in that it cannot decide; it carries through the discussion and negotiation phases. As a matter of practice, what it decides goes on to the A part of the Council's agenda and is passed 'on the nod' when it next meets. If anyone did want to reopen the matter, he could, in which case it is put on the B agenda of the next Council meeting.

co-respondent in English practice, the alleged adulterer (see ADULTERY) who is designated on the SUMMONS and served with the papers as well as the spouse.

coroner a quasi-judicial figure in the English legal system. A lawyer or a doctor, his principal jurisdiction is to inquire, sometimes with a jury, into the cause of death of persons dying within his territorial jurisdiction and to pronounce on whether, for example, the death was homicide, by misadventure, accidental cause or suicide. Since the Lord Lucan affair (where the 'suspect' vanished) coroners have not been permitted to name the person suspected of causing the death by homicide. The coroner also holds inquiries into matters of TREASURE TROVE.

In the Isle of Man a similar function is carried out by the *coroner of inquests*. There the *coroner* is an officer of the court who enforces judgments.

corporal punishment punishment to the body, no longer imposed by the state in the UK. See CAPITAL PUNISHMENT.

corporation (aggregate) a group of persons who are deemed in law to be a single legal entity. The *corporate entity* is legally distinct from its members; it has legal personality and can hold property, sue and be sued in its own name as if it were a NATURAL PERSON.

In the USA, corporation is a plain term for all incorporated bodies. The legal form is the same whether or not the body trades for profit and whether or not it is public or close (like a family company).

See COMPANY.

corporation sole a series of holders of a single office (e.g. the King or Queen or a bishop).

corporation tax a tax on the profit or gains of a COMPANY other than profits or gains made by it in a fiduciary capacity. Corporation tax is charged on both income and capital profits. Income profits are calculated on income tax principles while capital profits are calculated on CAPITAL GAINS TAX principles.

corporeal having a physical body, tangible.

corpus delicti 'the body of an offence', the essential facts that constitute the CRIME. Thus, it is *not* the corpse in a murder trial although a dead body is one of the facts that constitute the *corpus delicti*.

Corpus Juris Civilis Justinian's compilation of the ROMAN LAW for his empire. It is in four parts: the *Institutes* (a student introduction); the *Digest* or *Pandects* (a collation in four sections of the Roman law from the jurists, which was, however, heavily interpolated by the compilers); the *Codex* or *Code* (a compilation of legislative measures); and the *Novels* (some later supplementary laws). Both the Digest and the Institutes were to form the basis of the later revival of Roman law throughout the continental European world. They are still the object of intense study and debate today.

corroboration the doctrine in the law of evidence that material facts require to be proved by evidence from two independent sources as, for example, two eyewitnesses or one witness and facts and circumstances. It is often said to be very important in preventing miscarriages of justice, but the fact is often overlooked that the effect of a rule on corroboration may be to produce two lying witnesses instead of just one. Then, if the lies are not exposed, the effect on a jury is all the stronger. Its benefit is that if two witnesses are lying it should be easier to catch them out. The story of Susanna and the Elders in the Book of Daniel in the Bible has entrenched the idea in the Judaeo-Christian world. Even in Scots criminal law, which holds the doctrine in high esteem, the rigour of the rule is relaxed in relation to confessions that show a special knowledge of the crime that only the perpetrator would know. There are many statutory relaxations of the rule both in England and Scotland. It is seldom required in either jurisdiction in civil cases. See also MOOROV DOCTRINE.

costs the expenses incurred in relation to a legal action that may be awarded by the court, usually (although not always) to the party who wins.

Council of Europe an intergovernmental body set up in 1949 to promote European political, economic, social and cultural integration. It is distinct from the EUROPEAN UNION. There were originally ten signatory states, including the UK. There are currently 41 member states. The Council's principal work has been in the area of HUMAN RIGHTS. The EUROPEAN CONVENTION ON HUMAN RIGHTS and Fundamental Freedoms was drawn up under the auspices of the Council. The economic and social counterpart of the Convention on Human Rights, the European Social Charter, was promulgated in 1961. Although lacking an equivalent enforcement mechanism, the European Social Charter is intended to protect the rights of the individual in such areas as employment, social security and discrimination. The Charter also promotes social cohesion and cooperation amongst member states in relation to migration. Considerable discretion is left to member states in the realisation of these rights. Other work of the Council of Europe includes the Convention for the Prevention of Torture and Inhuman or Degrading Treatment or Punishment (1987) and the Convention on Human Rights and Biomedicine (1997).

Council of State in the Republic of Ireland, the body set up under the 1937 Constitution to advise the President on the exercise of his or her powers. Its ex-officio members are the TAOISEACH, the TANAISTE, the Chief Justice, the Chairman of DAIL EIREANN, the Chairman of SEANAD EIREANN and the Attorney General. In addition, the President may appoint up to seven members, and every former President, Taoiseach and Chief Justice willing and able to serve is a member.

Council of the European Union the body that represents the interests of MEMBER STATES in the EUROPEAN UNION (EU). While instructed by and representing the home states, the members of Council act as a Community institution and not as delegates to intergovernmental conferences, although this theoretical position is not always easily observed in practice. Sometimes more than one representative actually attends and different representatives attend at different meetings. Practically, two types of meeting take place: *general council meetings*, which are attended by foreign ministers, and *special councils*, which are attended by ministers from the member state with responsibility for the area of activity. Because the same person need not be in attendance, it is possible that a number of 'councils' meet at the same time.

It is the Union's legislative body; for a wide range of EU issues, it exercises that legislative power with the EUROPEAN PARLIAMENT. It coordinates the broad economic policies of the member states.

It concludes international agreements with one or more states or international organisations. It shares budgetary authority with the Parliament. It takes the decisions necessary for framing and implementing the common foreign and security policy, on the basis of general guidelines established by the EUROPEAN COUNCIL, and coordinates the activities of member states and adopts measures in the field of police and judicial cooperation in criminal matters. Depending on what powers it exercises, it requires to vote unanimously or sometimes by qualified majority. The system at the time of writing is that Germany, France, Italy and the United Kingdom have ten votes, Spain has eight votes, Belgium, Greece, Netherlands and Portugal five votes, Austria and Sweden four votes, Denmark, Finland and the Republic of Ireland have three votes, and Luxembourg has two votes. In qualified majority voting, Commission proposals must receive 62 votes out of a total of 87 in order to be approved. To amend a Commission proposal without the Commission's consent, unanimity among Council members is required. The Presidency is held on a rota for six months in alphabetic rotation – each member state assuming its position in the alphabet by virtue of its own language name. Thus Greece appears under H (Hellenic Republic) and Spain under E (España).

Council on Tribunals in the CONSTITUTIONAL LAW of the UK, a supervisory body set up as a result of the Franks Report. It has a Scottish Committee. There are 2,000 tribunals under its remit. It is not a court of appeal but a focus for complaint and information.

counsel another name for a BARRISTER or ADVOCATE.

counterclaim a cross-claim brought by a defendant in civil proceedings that is not a defence to the claim made by the plaintiff but that asserts an independent cause of action against him. In Scotland, it is available to a defender. See SET-OFF.

counterfeiting the crime of illegally copying currency, whether coin or note, intending to pass it or tender it as genuine: Forgery and Counterfeit Act 1981.

County Court an English court. The workhorse of the English CIVIL court system, it deals with civil matters subject to financial limits. It is peopled by judges of the Supreme Court, circuit judges and recorders. Most cases are heard by a district judge but more valuable cases may be heard by a circuit judge.

Cour de Cassation a French court. The only French court with a jurisdiction that covers the whole country but quite different from the British and American notion of a supreme court. There must be a *violation de la loi* before it can interfere with the lower court. It only 'breaks' the lower court's decision – the case is then remitted back to the court at the same level as the original court (although not the same one). The court is divided into five chambers for civil cases and one for criminal cases. If a case comes back again after having been reversed, it is sent to the *Assemblée plenière* on which all the chambers are represented. It will make a final decision if the issues are the same. There is the possibility of a third remit if matters are not the same or further information is required. It has over a hundred members, and it hears well over a hundred times more cases than the House of Lords. Judgments are given as a college, much like the COURT OF JUSTICE OF THE EUROPEAN UNION. While there are no dissents, the *rapport* produced by one of the judges to the court is published.

course of employment see VICARIOUS LIABILITY.

court martial a court held to try matters of MILITARY LAW. Made up of serving officers advised by a judge advocate, its sentences are subject to confirmation by higher military authority. There is an appeal tribunal headed up by the Lord Chief Justice.

Court of Appeal an English court. It comprises a Civil Division and a Criminal Division and hears most appeals in England. It is a central court, and cases come from all over the country. The Master of the Rolls heads up the Civil Division; the Lord Chief Justice the Criminal Division. Its influence in civil matters is so significant that Lord Denning left the House of Lords to become Master of the Rolls. Its importance lies in the fact that unless the House of Lords itself grants leave, there is no appeal beyond the Court of Appeal without leave of that court itself.

In civil courts it receives appeals from the High Court (all divisions) and from the County Court. In criminal cases appeals lie primarily for the Crown Court.

Court of Arbitration for Sport (CAS) an extrajudicial forum for the adjudication of sporting disputes. Established in 1984, it sits in Switzerland It operates under Swiss law unless the parties agree to the contrary. Financing of the court is arranged through the International Council of Arbitration for Sport, which is designed to act as an independent buffer between the Court and the International Olympic Committee, which set it up.

Court of Auditors a body of the EUROPEAN COMMUNITIES. It was created by the MERGER TREATY. It considers the accounts of the Community and related bodies, not only to monitor the legality but also to determine the quality of the financial management. Checks are made in the institutions but also in MEMBER STATES, usually in cooperation with the national audit bodies. It produces an annual report.

Court of Criminal Appeal in Scotland, the High Court of Justiciary sitting as an APPEAL court. There is not appeal to the House of Lords, but devolution issues can in some cases be sent to the PRIVY COUNCIL.

Court of First Instance (of the European Communities) a court created by the SINGLE EUROPEAN ACT that has a jurisdiction to hear and determine at first instance certain actions brought by natural or legal persons. There is a right of appeal to the COURT OF JUSTICE OF THE EUROPEAN COMMUNITIES. It has 15 members, any of whom may carry out the function of ADVOCATE GENERAL of the Court. It deals with: disputes between the institutions and their employees; actions against the Commission by undertakings in relation to EUROPEAN COAL AND STEEL COMMUNITY (ECSC) charges; actions in relation to COMPETITION POLICY rules; actions for damages caused by an institution in respect of a matter over which the Court of First Instance has jurisdiction; by Council Decision 94/194 (7/3/94), a further transfer of jurisdiction was accomplished. The Court of First Instance now considers actions brought by persons for annulment and failure to act under the ECSC Treaty (relating to Article 74) and under the EUROPEAN ECONOMIC COMMUNITY Treaty in the case of ANTIDUMPING and subsidies. Soon it is expected to take most cases other than preliminary hearings.

Court of Justice of the European Union the principal court of the EUROPEAN UNION, charged with ensuring that in the interpretation and application of the treaties the law is observed. It is a collegiate body and elects its own President. It is made up of independent members and can act only by judgment. The system of PRELIMINARY RULING allowed the court much more material with which to state the law.

It consists of 15 judges and nine ADVOCATES GENERAL. It sits in six chambers of three or five judges, but when it hears a case brought by a MEMBER STATE or one of the other institutions, or when it has to give a preliminary ruling, it must sit in plenary session. It does not issue dissenting judgments. It has the following jurisdiction: to discover whether a member state has failed to fulfil an obligation under the treaty; to determine penalties in actions by natural or legal persons; to review the legality of the acts or failures to act by the Council and Commission at the request of a member state, to give preliminary rulings; to grant damages to persons complaining of damage caused by the institutions; to resolve disputes between the Communities and their employees; to act as court of appeal for the relatively new COURT OF FIRST INSTANCES. It has had a pivotal effect in European Community law.

Court of Session Scotland's supreme civil court located *in* Scotland. It is divided into an *Outer House*, which deals with important cases at first instances, and an *Inner House*, which (except for a few unusual matters) acts as a court of appeal. The decisions of the Inner House can be appealed to the House of Lords (save for a few special cases). Thus the court is not the supreme court *of* Scotland. The PRIVY COUNCIL has a jurisdiction in relation to devolution issues.

Court of the Arches an appellate court in the English ecclesiastical system.

Coutume de Normandie the customary law of the ancient Duchy of Normandy, one of the several customary legal systems of northern France (distinguished from the written systems of the south) that underlie the legal systems in Jersey and Guernsey, especially in relation to land law, succession and contract.

covenant a promise contained in a deed. The word is used more generally, however, to denote an agreement or undertaking in a CONTRACT or instrument of transfer. So, *to covenant* to do something (e.g. pay £10 per annum to a charity) is to undertake to do that thing. The point about the requirement for a deed is that a promise contained in a deed is prima facie enforceable with anything further (such as CONSIDERATION).

A covenant may be *express*, in that its terms are created by the parties themselves, or *implied* by law. For example, on a conveyance on sale of freehold land by a person expressed to convey as beneficial owner, the Law of Property (Miscellaneous Provisions) Act 1994 implies four covenants by the transferor, namely:

(1) that the transferor has the power to convey the subject matter of the conveyance;

(2) that the purchaser will not be disturbed in his physical occupation (known as the *covenant for quiet enjoyment*);

(3) that the property is free from encumbrances other than those expressly mentioned;

(4) that the vendor will, at the request and expense of the purchaser,

execute all such documents and do all such acts and things as may be necessary to give effect to the transfer.

Where the land is leasehold, a further covenant is implied, namely, that the transferor (assignee) has paid all rent due and observed all covenants contained in the lease.

Covenants may be *positive* or *negative*. For negative covenants, see FURTHER RESTRICTIVE COVENANT.

crave in Scottish civil procedure, that part of an INITIAL WRIT that states what the pursuer requires.

credibility in the law of evidence, the aspect of evidence, usually the testimony of a witness, such that the fact-finder tells that the evidence can be believed. See also RELIABILITY.

credit 1. to put money into a person's account, in contrast to DEBIT, which is the taking of money from an account.

2. a period given to someone before he has to make payment.

3. in the law of evidence, credit is synonymous with CREDIBILITY; objections that were formerly sufficient to make a witness incompetent are now, in general, only available as affecting his credit or worthiness to be believed.

creditor 1. the person to whom a debt is owed by a debtor.

2. in relation to a bankrupt, a person to whom any of the bankruptcy debts are owed (as specified in the bankruptcy order).

3. an individual who would be a creditor in the bankruptcy if a bankruptcy order were made on that petition.

crime an *offence* against the state that is punishable. The act or omission may also be civilly actionable. Prevailing legal thinking takes the positivist view (see POSITIVISM) that any conduct can be declared criminal, so everything from murder to a failure to renew a television licence can be a crime. Most legal systems require that the accused person should exhibit MENS REA ('a guilty mind') as well as having carried out the *actus reus*, being the physical requirement. Thus, in THEFT the accused must have taken the thing (although this is interpreted differently in different systems) and have intended to deprive the true owner of his ownership (although this too can be formulated differently in different systems). Motive is generally irrelevant. A crime is sometimes distinguished from DELICTS and contraventions, especially in the CIVIL LAW jurisdictions: a *crime* is a serious crime, a *delict* a major offence and a *contravention* a trivial breach of the law. Crimes are also distinguished from offences, the latter being considered more trivial.

Criminal Cases Review Commission an investigative body for England and Wales with power to review alleged miscarriages of justice. It cannot itself quash convictions but may remit cases to the COURT OF APPEAL. There is a Scottish equivalent – the Scottish Criminal Cases Review commission.

Criminal Defence Service (CDS) a part of the system for provision of LEGAL AID in criminal matters in England and Wales set out in the Access to Justice Act 1999. At the time of writing the details were the subject of consultation by the Lord Chancellor's Department. The model is that of a publicly salaried public defender.

criminal injuries compensation in the UK, a state-funded scheme by which payments are made to a person who is injured as a result of crime. It was originally ex gratia but is now statutory by virtue of the Criminal Injuries Compensation Act 1995. The scheme is administered by the Criminal Injuries Compensation Board, which is a body corporate. There is a right of appeal on point of law. There is a list of qualifying offences including, among others, rape, assault and arson. Attempts are included. Generally included are offences that require proof of intent (or recklessness) to cause death or personal injury. Injuries sustained in apprehending or attempting to apprehend offenders are included. Applications are made by the injured party or his relative, if deceased. Compensation for pain and suffering is calculated according to a tariff. Future wage loss and other heads of damage are recoverable. If the injured person later recovers TORT damages, he must repay the Board. The Board may refuse or reduce an award in light of the applicant's criminal record or his conduct in relation to the incident in question. Certain cases of domestic violence are excluded, as are incidents covered by compulsory insurance or by the MOTOR INSURERS' BUREAU. See also MALICIOUS INJURIES LEGISLATION.

criminal legal aid see LEGAL AID.

cross-examination in court practice, the part of a case, whether civil or criminal, where evidence is elicited from the other side's witness. Thus, the defence will *cross-examine* the investigating police officers after the prosecutor has conducted the EXAMINATION IN CHIEF. It serves two functions:

(1) to test the veracity of the witness and the accuracy of the evidence;

(2) to obtain evidence on points on which he has not been questioned in chief and which may support the cross-examiner's

case. Failure to cross-examine on any matter generally implies acceptance of evidence on that point.

Crown the monarch.

Crown Agent see CROWN OFFICE.

Crown Court an English court, a part of the SUPREME COURT and a single court, although it sits in many places all over England and Wales. It is the workhorse of the English criminal system (along with the MAGISTRATE'S COURT). Its decisions and sentences may be appealed to the Court of Appeal.

Crown Office 1. in England, formerly the office that dealt with Crown and ministerial business for the Court of King's Bench. It is now part of the Central Office of the Supreme Court. It has recently been renamed the Administrative Court.
2. in Scotland, a department under the authority of the LORD ADVOCATE that organises the prosecution of crime, not only by assisting the Lord Advocate, Solicitor-General and ADVOCATES DEPUTE but also by administering and supporting the PROCURATOR FISCAL's service. The senior official is called the Crown Agent.

Crown proceedings actions by and against the Crown. Prior to the Crown Proceedings Act 1947 (now amended by the Crown Proceedings Act 1987), special procedures had to be used against the Crown. They were difficult for the claimant. Contractual actions had to proceed by way of PETITION OF RIGHT and in TORT, and because of the doctrine that the king could do no wrong, there was no liability unless admitted ex gratia on a case-by-case basis. Now proceedings may be brought by ordinary civil action. The Crown is liable for torts and delicts committed by its servants or agents acting in the general course of their functions and for breach of duties owed as employers or occupiers. The Crown will not be held liable for damages unless expressly bound or bound by necessary implication. Under the 1987 amendment, the Crown became liable to members of the armed forces.

An action must be raised against the authorised department, failing which the ATTORNEY GENERAL. In Scotland all proceedings are raised against the LORD ADVOCATE.

Although the Act allows applications to be made against the Crown for recovery of documents, this is subject to Crown privilege, which is itself subject to judicial control: *Conway* v. *Rimmer* [1968] 1 All ER 874. More recently, the head of protection has extended beyond the Crown, in the narrow sense, and instead lawyers speak of privilege on the ground of public interest: *D.* v. *NSPCC* [1977] 1 All ER 589.

European law has created independent heads of action against the Crown, permitting injunctions against the Crown: *Factortame Ltd* v. *Secretary of State for Transport* (No. 2) [1991] 1 All ER 70; and a general right to claim for damages for a failure to comply with European law: *Francovich* v. *Italian Republic* [1992] ECR 143.

Crown Prosecution Service (CPS) a government agency set up to prosecute crime in England. It is headed by the Director of Public Prosecutions. It takes over all prosecutions instigated by the police. It closely corresponds to the Scottish PROCURATOR FISCAL service.

CRU abbreviation for COMPENSATION RECOVERY Unit.

crystallisation the fixing of a FLOATING CHARGE on assets. Where money borrowed by a COMPANY is secured by a floating charge over the company's assets and undertaking, the company may continue trading and dispose of any assets in the course of that business. If the company defaults on its obligations under the terms of the loan agreement, the charge will *crystallise*, that is, immediately attach to the assets owned by the company at that time. Crystallisation is therefore the process by which a floating charge becomes fixed on to particular assets.

CSA abbreviation for CHILD SUPPORT AGENCY.

culpable homicide in the criminal law of Scotland, any HOMICIDE that is not by misadventure, justifiable or murder. It covers cases of DIMINISHED RESPONSIBILITY, e.g. defective reason short of INSANITY or PROVOCATION. It also covers cases where an accused has been grossly careless or reckless in a legal activity and caused death. See, for England, HOMICIDE.

culpa tenet suos auctores 'fault adheres to its authors', a maxim that can be extended in its meaning to establish a general rule that only the person at fault is liable and thus militate against VICARIOUS LIABILITY.

cur. adv. vult abbreviation for *curia advisari vult*, 'the court wishes to be advised'. It can be seen in the law reports and signifies that the court is thinking about its decision. In Scotland, the court makes AVIZANDUM.

curator in the family law of Scotland, usually a parent who has responsibility to act with a minor in his affairs. The Age of Legal Capacity (Scotland) Act 1991 has practically replaced the term with the GUARDIAN, who has responsibility for children under 16 who, under the Act, cannot contract without his consent save in exceptional circumstances set out in the Act.

curator ad litem in Scottish procedure, a person appointed by the court to look after the interests of a minor or an adult who cannot look after his or her own interests – usually for a minor or a person INCAPAX until a CURATOR BONIS can be appointed.

curator bonis in Scots law, an ADMINISTRATOR appointed by the court to look after the affairs of a person mentally or physically incapable of representing himself or herself.

current maintenance arrestment in the Scots law of DILIGENCE or legal enforcement, this process enforces payment of ALIMENT or PERIODICAL ALLOWANCE. A notice is served on the defender's employer who deducts instalment payments according to a statutory chart.

custody a concept broader than mere care and control (but encompassing them) involving control over long-term decisions affecting a CHILD's future. It is replaced now by the idea of a residence order as part of parental responsibility: Children Act 1989; Children (Scotland) Act 1995.

custom or usage a residual source of law.

customs duties the duties payable on the importation into a country of GOODS purchased abroad. In the UK, VALUE-ADDED TAX on imported goods is payable on a sum comprising the price of the imported goods plus any customs duty payable thereon.

customs union one of the main ways in which the EUROPEAN UNION seeks to achieve a COMMON MARKET. It involves two major steps:

(1) the prohibition of CUSTOMS DUTIES and MEASURES HAVING EQUIVALENT EFFECT;

(2) the adoption of a common external tariff against the rest of the world.

Cynulliad Cenedlasthol Cymru the Welsh name for the NATIONAL ASSEMBLY OF WALES.

cy pres 'so near', the term used in relation to TRUSTS when the court applies the trust property to a charitable purpose very like the one originally intended where that original has become impossible to meet.

D

Dail Eireann the lower house of the Parliament, or OIREACHTAS, of the Republic of Ireland, elected by a single transferable vote method or proportional representation. It consists of 166 members.

daily every day, including Sundays.

damages a monetary sum, awarded by a court, or the subject of an advance agreement between parties, payable for breach of a legal obligation. In a case of breach of contract, the innocent parties may want the goods they bought or hired – in Scotland they may be able to claim this as of right by way of SPECIFIC IMPLEMENT. In England, SPECIFIC PERFORMANCE is discretionary. For this reason, an award of damages is sometimes described as substitutional redress – instead of getting exactly what one wants a substitute is given. In the case of personal injuries this is seen clearly – the accidentally amputated leg is gone and a new one cannot be given; instead, the courts try to compensate as best as money can. Much depends, however, on why damages are being awarded. In contract, the attempt is to make up for the disappointed expectation of the contractual performance, in tort or delict it is to put matters back as they were before the wrong was done. In some cases, and they are very few, damages are to punish the wrongdoer, when they are called penal. Exemplary damages are awarded, in England, to show that tort does not pay and to make an example of the tortfeasor. Since *Rookes* v. *Barnard* [1964] AC 1129, it is clear that they cannot be awarded generally but only in two types of case:

(1) oppressive and unconstitutional action by government servants. This could include local government and police officers (*Bradford City Metropolitan Council* v. *Arora* [1991] 3 All ER 545);

(2) where the defendant proceeds in the knowledge that he is wrong and is calculated to make a profit that he calculates will exceed the compensation payable (*Broome* v. *Cassell & Co. Ltd* [1972] AC 1027).

damnum absque injuria 'damage without legal wrong'.

damnum fatale see ACT OF GOD.

damnum injuria datam 'loss wrongfully caused'. See LEX AQUILA.

dangerous driving the offences of driving dangerously or causing death by dangerous driving: Road Traffic Act 1991. This replaces the former offence of reckless driving, and the definition of this new offence is very similar to the approach taken by the Scottish courts to reckless driving: *Allan* v. *Patterson* 1980 RTR 97. A person is driving dangerously if: (a) the way he drives falls far below what would be expected of a competent and careful driver; and (b) it would be obvious to a competent and careful driver that driving that way would be dangerous. 'Dangerous' refers to damage to person or property. Regard is to be had to circumstances of which the driver could be expected to be aware and also to those of which he can be shown to have been actually aware.

dangerous things see ESCAPE OF DANGEROUS THINGS.

dangerous wild animals a category laid down in the Dangerous Wild Animals Act 1976 that deals with licensing and criminal liability. The Act lays down a list of species that are thus deemed to be dangerous no matter how nice any particular member of the species may be. The definition is incorporated in the Animals (Scotland) Act 1987 as the main definition of dangerousness for the purposes of civil liability in Scotland. See ANIMALS.

data protection the law applicable to the control of the use of information about people by those into whose hands it has come. It derives from the COMMUNITY LAW of the EUROPEAN UNION (EU), which provides that member states must protect the fundamental rights and freedoms of natural persons, in particular their right to privacy with respect to the processing of personal data. The law is not restricted to information on a computer. The system in the UK works through a Data Protection Register and the supervision of a Data Protection Commissioner, all under and in terms of the Data Protection Act 1998 (replacing the 1984 Act). Those who are to use the information must register – data controllers and data processors. Even those who do not are obliged to deal properly with data as laid down in eight principles: data must be fairly and lawfully processed; be processed for limited purposes; the processing must be adequate, relevant and not excessive; the data must be accurate; data should not be kept longer than necessary; data must be processed in accordance with the data subject's rights; data should be kept secure; data cannot be transferred to countries without adequate protection, generally, intra-EU transfer is permitted, as is transfer to so-called safe havens like the USA. The person about whom data is held – the *data subject* – has certain rights: a right of access; a right to prevent processing likely to cause damage or distress; a right to prevent certain processing for the purpose of direct marketing; rights in relation to automated decision-taking; and in certain circumstances a right to compensation. There are many detailed exemptions for the security services and other lawful authorities.

Data Protection Commissioner see DATA PROTECTION.

day 24 hours, from midnight to midnight. See TIME OF DAY.

dayan a judge in the BETH DIN.

dead's part in the Scots law of succession, the part of a person's estate that can be left to persons other than the deceased's wife and children, i.e. the part left over after legal rights have been satisfied.

Deasy's Act the Landlord and Tenant Law Amendment (Ireland) Act 1860, commonly known as Deasy's Act as it was Sergeant Deasy, the then Attorney General for Ireland, who piloted it through parliament. The Act is the basis of the law of landlord and tenant in both parts of Ireland. It is largely a consolidating Act, but it introduced the notion of contract as the basis of the relationship of landlord and tenant in Ireland.

death the cessation of life. There is no statutory definition, nor, indeed, a fixed definition at common law. In relation to medical treatment, the court may consider that a person's being in a persistent vegetative state is sufficient to indicate that his or her life need no longer be preserved by artificial means, while not accepting the concept of euthanasia. See *Airedale NHS Trust* v. *Bland* [1993] TLR 47; *Frenchay Healthcare NHS Trust* v. *S* [1994] TLR 29. It is important in many different legal contexts. Absence of brain-stem activity is coming to be recognised as a sound practical test: *Re Baby A* (1992) 3 Med. LR 303.

Wills take effect on death. For many legal purposes it is possible to obtain a court order declaring that a person died on a certain date by virtue of a presumption of death, which comes into effect in both England and Scotland if a person has not been known to be alive for seven years.

death penalty punishment by way of killing the offender. The various modes through time and space have been hanging (Anglo-American), guillotine (France) and electrocution and lethal injection (USA). It is extremely popular with the public and the families of victims, but because it is so easy to make a mistake in any judicial process and this particular legal cock-up cannot be corrected by more paper shuffling, it is going out of fashion. While the framers of the US Constitution could not outlaw it by preventing cruel and unusual punishment (if everybody does it, it is usual and if you do it quickly it's not cruel) modern human rights lawyers have rather started to eliminate it. The penalty no longer exists for any offence in the UK. The UK-ratified Protocol 6 of the European Convention in May 1999. Protocol 6 commits contracting parties to permanently abolishing the death penalty. In December 1999 the UK ratified the Second Optional Protocol to the International Covenant on Civil and Political Rights, which also abolishes the death penalty. The death penalty for treason and piracy was abolished by the Crime and Disorder Act 1998.

debate in Scottish civil procedure, that part of an action where legal argument takes place only on the PLEAS IN LAW. It can take place before any proof if the plea is preliminary, such as a plea to the RELEVANCY or SPECIFICATION or after the case if it was impossible to answer the plea in law until evidence had been heard, for example, in ordinary NEGLIGENCE cases where, until the facts have been heard, it is not possible to say that the defender has or has not been legally negligent.

debenture a document, almost invariably by or on behalf of a COMPANY, that creates or acknowledges a debt owed by the company. The term includes debenture stock, bonds and other debt securities issued by a company. Companies usually keep a register of debenture holders. It is a word without precise definite signification. Normally, debentures are issued in connection with secured borrowings and incorporate a fixed or floating CHARGE; but this is not strictly necessary, and debentures can be used in connection with unsecured borrowings.

de bonis asportatis 'of goods carried away'. This is the name of a writ of TRESPASS in respect of goods wrongfully taken away. Forms of writ have long been abolished.

debt a sum of money owed by one person to another. Debts are of various kinds, according to their origin; thus, for example, *judgment debts* or *contract debts*.

Contract debts may be either speciality debts or simple contract debts: *speciality debts* are those created by deed (e.g. in a covenant), while *simple contract debts* are all debts not secured by record (e.g. a judgment debt) or deed. The importance of the distinction is that the limitation period for the former is 12 years while actions on simple contracts must be brought within six years: Limitation Act 1980

Sections 5 and 8. Debts may be secured or unsecured: *secured debts* are those over which the creditor has some SECURITY in addition to the personal liability of the debtor (as in a MORTGAGE, CHARGE or LIEN). So, a secured creditor may proceed against the assets or promises (in the case of a GUARANTEE) that constitute his security; an unsecured creditor must prove with the general creditors in the debtor's insolvency.

Debts provable in BANKRUPTCY are *preferential debts* when they are payable in full before all other debts. These include employees' wages and salaries, rates and taxes, and employer's national insurance contributions.

After the making of a bankruptcy order, no person who is a creditor of the bankrupt in respect of a debt provable in the bankruptcy has any remedy against the property or person of the bankrupt in respect of that debt, or may, before the discharge of the bankrupt, commence any action or other legal proceedings against the bankrupt except with the leave of the court and on such terms as the court may impose. In place of these rights, the creditors acquire a right to share proportionally in the distribution by the trustee of the bankrupt's estate of the bankrupt's assets that became vested in the trustee.

debtor someone who owes a debt to a creditor.

deceit the tort of making a fraudulent statement committed where the defendant knowingly or recklessly makes a false representation intending that the plaintiff should act upon it where the plaintiff does act and to his detriment: *Derry* v. *Peek* (1889) 14 App. Cas. 337. In Scotland similar facts would be litigated as FRAUD.

deception in English criminal law it is an offence to obtain property by deception. It is committed by deceiving, whether deliberately or recklessly, by words or conduct as to fact or law, including the person's present intentions. It is also an offence to obtain services in this way. For Scotland, see PRACTICAL CHEATING.

decision an act of the EUROPEAN UNION that (unless it comes from the EUROPEAN COAL AND STEEL COMMUNITY (ECSC)) is binding in its entirety on the person or persons to whom it is addressed whether MEMBER STATE, person or undertaking. It can be imposed by the COUNCIL OF THE EUROPEAN UNION or the COMMISSION OF THE EUROPEAN UNION. It tends to be administrative in character. It can have DIRECT EFFECT. A decision of the ECSC is binding in its entirety and thus corresponds to a REGULATION under the EUROPEAN COMMUNITIES (EC) and EURATOM treaties. See COMMUNITY LAW.

declaration against interest as an exception to the rule against the ADMISSIBILITY of HEARSAY evidence, a declaration by a person who has subsequently died that he knew, when he made it, that it would be against his pecuniary or proprietary interest, may be admitted.

declarator in Scotland, an order of court declaring a party's rights. It cannot be sought as an academic exercise – there must be some real dispute. It is frequently sought as a preliminary to INTERDICT.

declaratory power an inherent power in the Scottish HIGH COURT OF JUSTICIARY to punish any crime even if not known as such at the time it was committed. Although an exception to the maxim NULLA POENA SINGE LEGE, it has been restricted by the court to cover cases only of the commission of an existing offence in a new way.

declinature the renunciation of an office, used most frequently of trustees and judges.

decree an order of a court.

decree absolute see DECREE NISI AND ABSOLUTE.

decree nisi and absolute an order of the court in two stages:

1. terminating a MARRIAGE.

2. granting foreclosure in respect of a MORTGAGE where the mortgagor has defaulted.

decree of irritancy see IRRITANCY.

deduction of tax at source the process whereby the payer of, e.g. interest, deducts income tax at the basic rate from the payment and accounts for it to the Inland Revenue. It can be compared with the system of Pay-As-You-Earn (PAYE), whereby employers are required to deduct INCOME TAX from payments of wages or salaries.

deed a written instrument whereby an interest, right or property passes, or an obligation binding on some person is created that affirms some prior act as a result of which some interest, right or property has passed. In English law, prior to the Law of Property (Miscellaneous Provisions) Act 1989, execution of a document as a deed required that the document be signed, sealed and delivered. Since that Act, sealing is no longer required, although the document must make it clear that the parties to it intended that it should take effect as a deed; indeed, the usual formula presently employed is 'executed as a deed'. Prior to the 1989 Act, it was not strictly necessary to a deed's validity that it be witnessed; since 1989 such an attestation is mandatory.

In Scotland there is no specific definition, but it has been held that jottings on an envelope did not constitute a deed: *Lennie* v. *Lennie's Trs* 1914 1 SLT 250.

deed of grant an express grant of an easement or profit, being an incorporeal hereditament, would always be by deed.

deed poll a deed in one part and signed only by the granter. The 'poll' part refers to the fact that originally the edges of the deed were shaven, or 'polled'. The phrase is seen mostly in the expression 'change one's name by deed poll', which refers to a declaration needed in England and Wales for a person to change his or her name.

deemster judge of the High Court of the Isle of Man.

defamation a form of wrong done by words. A *defamatory* statement is one that tends to lower the plaintiff in the minds of right-thinking people: *Sim* v. *Stretch* (1936) 52 TLR 669.

In England there is a technical distinction in the law of defamation between libel and slander. *Libel* refers to a permanent form such as print and *slander* to a transient form such as speech. Some Australian states have abolished the distinction between slander and libel. In England, but not in Scotland, the statement complained of must be communicated to a person other than the plaintiff. The essence, however, is that the statement must be defamatory, as above defined. If it has this special quality, then it is not essential that the plaintiff should prove malice, making the effective onus fall on the defendant. To allege a person is a criminal or behaves immorally is defamatory. To be actionable, the statement must be false, and this is resolved in court by the defendant pleading *justification* (or *veritas* in Scotland). The Defamation Act 1952 makes it unnecessary for the defendant to show that every charge is true so long as those that remain false do not materially injure the plaintiff's reputation. Communication has been established by many means, including film and effigy or by the Internet (see *Godfrey* v. *Demon Internet Ltd* [1999] TLR 301).

The statement need not always be a bald assertion. It is open to the plaintiff to *innuendo* a statement, that is, to show that a statement is not, on the face of it, defamatory, actually has a defamatory meaning. The plaintiff must state in words in his pleadings what this meaning is. A statement in a foreign language always requires an innuendo.

Of practical importance are the other defences. *Absolute privilege* protects certain communications – parliamentary proceedings, judicial proceedings and official communications. The Defamation

Act 1996 allows absolute privilege to fair and accurate contemporaneous reports of judicial proceedings in newspapers and in broadcasts. *Qualified privilege* is more subtle. It protects (subject to the qualification discussed later) statements made in certain circumstances. The categories are not closed, but among those that have been recognised are included statements in pursuance of a duty, in protection of an interest, and fair and accurate reports by any means of proceedings of public and semi-public bodies. Some categories of statement are given qualified privilege and others qualified privilege subject to explanation or contradictions. The qualified nature of qualified privilege is that the maker of the false defamatory statement is protected only if there is not actual malice – in other words, the defence really only takes away the presumption of malice inherent in a defamatory statement.

Fair comment is another frequently used defence, but it depends upon the matter being shown to be a comment on facts truly stated. People are allowed to be most vehement in such comment. It has recently been called *honest comment* in the House of Lords. It does not forgive false statements. The matter must be one of some public interest.

The Defamation Act 1996 gives a publisher, including, for example, an Internet service provider, a defence where it neither knew nor had reason to know that a statement was defamatory of the person complaining. However, there must be an offer of amends, that is, to publish a correction and apology and to pay such compensation as may be agreed.

In Scotland defamation is only one form of VERBAL INJURY, the others being a narrow form of verbal injury CONVICIUM and malicious falsehood.

See also ROLLED-UP PLEA.

default the failure to do that which ought to be done. Thus, failure to make payment under a contract is a default; more specifically, failure to repay or otherwise comply with the terms of a loan agreement are acts of default.

When a defendant fails to take certain necessary steps in a court action, the court may give judgment by default. See DEFAULT OF PLEADINGS.

default of pleadings failure by either party to complete a step required of him in the prescribed time limits. So, where the plaintiff is required to serve a statement of claim on a defendant and fails to do so, the defendant, after the expiration of the period prescribed for service of the statement of claim, may apply to the court for an order to dismiss the action; the court may dismiss the action or make such other order on such terms as it thinks just. Also, if a defendant fails to serve a defence the plaintiff, after the expiration of the period prescribed for service of a defence, he may (subject to the nature of the claim) obtain a final or interlocutory judgment in default. The court may, on such terms as it thinks just, set aside or vary any default judgment thus obtained.

defeasance see VESTING.

defect in the law of TORT or DELICT, a defect exists if the safety of the product is not such as persons generally are entitled to expect. In terms of the Consumer Protection Act 1987, defect is further explained as involving an examination of all the circumstances, including: the manner in which, and purposes for which, the product has been marketed; its get-up; the use of any mark in relation to the product and any instructions for, or warnings with respect to, doing or refraining from doing anything with or in relation to the product; what might reasonably be expected to be done with or in relation to the product; and the time when the product was supplied by its producer to another. Even if a product is *defective*, that is not enough to establish liability, particularly in light of the defences available. See EMPLOYERS' LIABILITY, PRODUCT LIABILITY.

defective equipment see EMPLOYERS' LIABILITY.

defence in CIVIL PROCEEDINGS a defence may be one of the following: (i) a *traverse*, i.e. a formal denial of an alleged fact; (ii) a denial of the plaintiff's claim; (iii) an allegation of COUNTERCLAIM; (iv) a CONFESSION AND AVOIDANCE; (v) a *statement of defence* raising an objection in point of law to the effect that the facts alleged, even if established, do not disclose a good cause of action. In Scottish written civil pleadings, a defender lodges written defences. In the SHERIFF court there is an intermediate pleading, called a NOTICE OF INTENTION TO DEFEND.

In criminal matters there is no written defence; a defence is raised by the plea of not guilty. In Scottish solemn criminal procedure, there are certain special defences that require to be lodged timeously in writing: ALIBI, incrimination (see INCRIMINATE), INSANITY and SELF-DEFENCE.

deferred sentence in Scotland a court can put off sentencing an offender, either for a short time to obtain reports to assist in disposal or often for a longer time on conditions, the most common being a deferred sentence for the accused to be of good behaviour or, less often, to allow repayment of sums embezzled or stolen. For England, see SUSPENDED SENTENCE.

deferred shares see SHARES.

de jure 'by law'.

delay failure to perform on time.

del credere agency an agent who, in selling goods on credit, guarantees to his principal the solvency of the purchaser and that the purchaser will duly perform his part of the contract. This guarantee attracts an extra commission (known as a *del credere commission*). See AGENCY.

delegate see DELEGATION.

delegated legislation laws made under a higher authority. Usually the power to make such legislation is delegated to a minister of the government or to a local authority. The names under which such legislation appears are many and various, including ORDERS IN COUNCIL, rules, REGULATIONS, STATUTORY INSTRUMENTS or BYE-LAWS.

delegation the assignment of a duty to another person or the grant of authority to another person to act on behalf of one or more others for agreed purposes. In general, an agent may not *delegate* (although delegation is permitted in certain limited circumstances).

delegatus non potest delegare 'a delegate himself cannot delegate'. See DELEGATION.

delict the name used for civil liability for wrongs in Roman law and in Scots law and in the law of most of the civilian legal systems, such as those of France, Germany and South Africa. It is a much more universal concept than torts but clearly much the same sort of issues are considered. Again, in civilian systems, delict is seen within the overall picture of the law of obligations. See ANIMALS, DUTY, ECONOMIC LOSS, ECONOMIC TORTS, FAULT, NEGLIGENCE, NUISANCE, OCCUPIER'S LIABILITY, PRODUCT LIABILITY, STRICT LIABILITY, TORT, TRESPASS.

deliverable state GOODS are only in a deliverable state if they are in the state required by the actual contract between the parties. This does not ncessarily coincide with the apparent meaning of the phrase and is dictated by the terms of the Sale of Goods Act 1979. Thus, goods would only need to be parcelled if this was a term of the contract express or implied.

delivery 1. the transferring of possession from one person to another.

2. a method by which a BILL OF EXCHANGE (or other negotiable instrument) is transferred. If the bill is made out to 'BEARER', delivery is all that is needed to effect the transfer and confer on the transferee a valid title good against the whole world; if the bill is made out to the order of a named person, delivery must be preceded by indorsement by that person or by another as holder in due course.

3. the formal act whereby a DEED becomes effective; any act manifesting an intention that the document is to be effective as a deed will be sufficient to constitute an act of delivery.

4. in SALE, it is the duty of the seller to deliver the goods and of the buyer to accept and pay for them in accordance with the terms of the contract of sale. Unless otherwise agreed in the contract, delivery of the goods and payment of the price are concurrent conditions; the seller should be ready and willing to give possession of the goods in exchange for the price, and the buyer should be ready and willing to pay the price in exchange for the possession of the goods. The Sale of Goods Act 1979 lays down some rules as to delivery but not a complete code:

(1) whether it is for the buyer to take possession of the goods or for the seller to send them to the buyer is a question depending in each case on the contract, express or implied;

(2) apart from any such contract, express or implied, the place of delivery is the seller's place of business if he has one, and, if not, his residence; except that, if the contract is for the sale of specific goods, which to the knowledge of the parties when the contract is made are in some other place, then that place is the place of delivery;

(3) where under the contract of sale the seller is bound to send the goods to the buyer, but no time for sending them is fixed, the seller is bound to send them within a reasonable time;

(4) where the goods at the time of sale are in the possession of a third person, there is no delivery by seller to buyer unless and until the third person acknowledges that he holds the goods on his behalf;

(5) demand or tender of delivery may be treated as ineffectual unless made at a reasonable hour; and what is a reasonable hour is a question of fact;

(6) unless otherwise agreed, the expenses of, and incidental to,

putting the goods into a deliverable state must be borne by the seller.

Delivery to a carrier involves other rules. Where the seller is authorised or required to send the goods to the buyer, delivery of the goods to a carrier (whether named by the buyer or not) for the purpose of transmission to the buyer is prima facie deemed to be a delivery of the goods to the buyer.

Unless otherwise authorised by the buyer, the seller must make such contract with the carrier on behalf of the buyer as may be reasonable, having regard to the nature of the goods and the other circumstances of the case; and if the seller omits to do so, and the goods are lost or damaged in the course of transit, the buyer may decline to treat the delivery to the carrier as delivery to himself or may hold the seller responsible in damages.

Where goods are sent by the seller to the buyer by a route involving sea transit, under circumstances in which it is usual to insure, the seller must give such notice to the buyer as may enable him to insure them during their sea transit; and if the seller fails to do so, the goods are at his risk during such sea transit. These rules involving delivery via sea should be considered against a knowledge of the common contracts involved, known as EX-SHIP, CIF and F.O.B. See also NON-DELIVERY, which includes late delivery and defective delivery, and see INSTALMENT DELIVERY.

de minimus non curat lex 'the law does not concern itself with trifles.' This maxim cannot be regarded as a statement of the law. The law will frequently penalise persons who are a minute late in payment, who deliver one widget too few or who build an inch upon another's land. Nonetheless, it is sometimes relied on by parties, advocates and judges where the law does not compel a strict approach.

demise a lease.

demonstrative legacy see LEGACY.

demurrage a sum of damages agreed in the contract of charterparty in the event of the charterer delaying, to be paid to the shipowner.

de novo 'of new'.

deodand the doctrine of common law by which an article that caused death was forfeit to the Crown. It was abolished in 1846 after railway engines had been held forfeit in this way.

Department of Trade and Industry (DTI) the government department that has overall responsibility for the corporate sector of the UK economy. It has, *inter alia*, powers under Part XIV of the Companies Act 1985 to appoint inspectors to investigate the affairs of a company or to conduct its own investigations.

dependant a person who to a greater or lesser extent depends on others for the provision of maintenance and accommodation and other necessities of life. Legally, only wives and unmarried children under the age of 18 can be dependants. It has been held that a mother who looked after her disabled daughter from birth to 14 years was a dependant of the deceased daughter under and in terms of the Inheritance (Provision for Family and Dependants) Act 1975. Under this Act any person being a dependant in fact may make a claim on the estate.

For immigration purposes, dependants require entry clearance except where European COMMUNITY LAW applies.

dependent territory a territory whose government is to some extent the responsibility of another country. UK dependent territories are listed in Schedule 6 to the British Nationality Act 1981 and include Gibraltar. Hong Kong ceased to be such at the end of 1997.

de plano 'immediately', without a further hearing.

deponent a person who *depones* or gives evidence by DEPOSITION or by AFFIDAVIT.

deportation the expulsion of a person from the UK. Deportation is authorised under the Immigration Act 1971 in the case of persons not having a right of abode in the UK. Deportation from the UK may be ordered in five circumstances, namely:

(1) if the person has overstayed or broken a condition attached to his permission to stay;

(2) if another person to whose family he belongs is deported;

(3) if (the person being 17 or over) a court recommends deportation on his conviction of an offence punishable with imprisonment;

(4) if the Secretary of State thinks his deportation would be for the public good; or

(5) obtaining leave to enter by deception.

A *deportation order* is an administrative requirement by the Secretary of State (or on the recommendation of a court) that the person to whom the order is addressed leave the UK and not return. It nullifies any leave the person had to enter or remain. The person is notified of the decision, the reasons and the place to which the person is to be deported. A right of appeal exists, and during the time that appeals are pending no deportation order may be executed.

deportation order see DEPORTATION.

deposit 1. the act of placing money with a bank. Thus, a *deposit account* is a bank account that pays interest but that imposes the requirement of notice (or a penalty in terms of interest) before withdrawal can be effected; a *deposit receipt* is an acknowledgement by the bank that sums have been deposited and are being held for the account of the depositor; a *certificate of deposit* is a financial instrument providing a similar acknowledgement but where the claim of the depositor is transferable. The Banking Act 1987 provides that the acceptance of a deposit in the course of carrying on a deposit-taking business in the UK requires authorisation from the Bank of England as competent authority. (see further *SCF Finance Ltd* v. *Masri* (No. 2) [1987] 2 WLR 58.)

2. to place documents with a bank or safety deposit company for safekeeping; or the placing of property with an officer of the court for safekeeping pending litigation.

3. money paid to a person as an earnest or SECURITY for the performance of a contract or other obligation. Thus, in contracts for the sale of land, a deposit is regarded not only as part-payment of the purchase price but as a security for the purchaser's due completion of the purchase (see *Soper* v. *Arnold* (1889) 14 App. Cas. 429). In Scotland the position is that the contract is construed to determine the parties' intentions in making the payment.

4. a deposit of title deeds as security for the repayment of borrowed money has long been held to constitute an equitable MORTGAGE (see *Ex p Kensington* (1813) 2 Ves. & B 79, 84).

5. in Scotland, a contract to place something in the custody of another for reward.

deposition a statement made by a witness under OATH and reduced to writing for subsequent use in court proceedings.

de praesenti in Scots family law, a form of IRREGULAR MARRIAGE established by the exchange of consents without need for witnesses or consummation. It was abolished in 1940.

depreciation the accounting practice whereby the cost of a fixed asset is written off over the period of its expected useful life. The amount written off is a recognised deduction in computing the profits of a business, and the object of the exercise is that such amounts will provide a fund to finance the asset's replacement when the time comes. Statutory recognition of this practice is given in the Capital Allowances Act 1991, which permits the cost of most capital assets acquired by a business to be written off (*straight-line depreciation*) for income tax and corporation tax purposes over a period of 20 years.

de recenti statements see HEARSAY.

deregulation the process of revising laws and regulations to ensure that they help more than they hinder. This idea may be given force of law and power delegated to ministers based on information received from task forces to substitute cumbersome rules with clearer ones or to repeal unnecessary restraints. It is likely that the House or Houses of Parliament will control the exercise by way of a deregulation committee.

derogation in the law of the EUROPEAN COMMUNITIES, exemptions to various aspects of the FOUR FREEDOMS, particularly the FREE MOVEMENT OF PERSONS and the FREE MOVEMENT OF GOODS.

descent automatic transmission of citizenship for one generation: British Nationality Act 1981. Descent may be traced through either parent. Parents who are BRITISH CITIZENS by descent cannot normally transmit their citizenship to children born overseas, unless working for the Crown or some similar service or for a Community institution within the EUROPEAN UNION.

description that section of a deed or conveyance (sometimes referred to as the *particulars*) in which the lands being transferred are described. The description may be verbal or by reference to a plan. Where the conveyance contains both a verbal description and a plan, questions may arise as to which has precedence, especially where the two appear to conflict. In all cases this will be a question of construction of the language of the particular deed. See DESCRIPTION, IMPLIED TERMS.

description, implied term where there is a contract for the sale of goods by description, there is an implied term that the goods will correspond with the description. If the sale is by SAMPLE as well as by description, it is not sufficient that the bulk of the goods corresponds with the sample of the goods do not also correspond with the description. A sale of goods is not prevented from being a sale by description by reason only that, being exposed for sale or hire, they are selected by the buyer. The only real difficulty with this provision is the concept of description. The modern approach is to treat description as being a matter of identification under the contract – an approach that tries to avoid the metaphysical question as to what properties constitute the thing in itself: *Britain Steamship*

Co. Ltd v. *Lithgows Ltd* 1975 SC 110; *Border Harvesters* v. *Edwards Engineering (Perth) Ltd* 1985 SLT 128; *Ashington Piggeries* v. *Christopher Hill* [1972] AC 441.

desertion in both English and Scots family law, the unilateral act (usually but not necessarily by leaving the marital home) of one spouse, without the consent of the other, intended to bring cohabitation to an end. Desertion usually involves one spouse physically leaving the matrimonial home, although this is not strictly necessary if all elements of a shared life have ceased. Desertion may be *actual* or *constructive*; the latter occurs where one spouse behaves towards the other in such a way that the others is driven to leave. To constitute a ground for DIVORCE, in both jurisdictions, desertion must be followed by two years of non-cohabitation.

designs see REGISTERED DESIGNS.

destination over in Scots succession law, a clause that states to whom certain property is to transmit after the first intended recipient. See SPECIAL DESTINATION.

detention holding a person against his will. Normally this is a TORT or DELICT, but certain statutes authorise the police and other authorities to do this. For example, in the immigration law a person may be detained on arrival into the UK, for administrative removal or following a deportation decision. If an appeal has been lodged against a deportation order, the appellant may be detained pending the hearing of the appeal.

detinue a form of action in TORT, now defunct, that allowed a bailor (see BAILMENT) to sue a bailee or a person entitled to possess a thing to sue a person in actual possession of it, giving the plaintiff the right to recover the thing or, in the event of a failure, to be able to return it through lack of care by the defendant, its value. The same right of action now exists as a form of conversion, which is itself a form of INTERFERENCE WITH GOODS.

detournement de pouvoir the concept of misuse of powers adopted by European Union law from French administrative law. It is the principal ground of appeal to the EUROPEAN COURT OF JUSTICE in annulment proceedings against actions of Community institutions and the sole ground for a private individual to appeal against a general Act or regulation. The main issues considered are any fundamental lack of basis and the issue of good faith.

deviation department from the route that a carrier has expressly or impliedly agreed to follow. Deviation without reasonable justification (e.g. to save life or property) amounts to a repudiation of the contract by the carrier (see COMMON CARRIER).

devilling in England, the arrangement whereby one BARRISTER assists another. In Scotland, it has a specialised sense referring to the period of compulsory training with another ADVOCATE before call.

devolution 1. the transmission of an interest in PROPERTY from one person to another by operation of law.

2. in CONSTITUTIONAL LAW, the giving of a degree of power, functional, sectional or geographic, to an inferior body. A recent legal model appeared in the Scotland Act 1998.

dictum see OBITER DICTUM.

digest 1. a compilation of rules of law, the most famous being the Digest of Justinian, the heart of the CORPUS JURIS CIVILIS, sometimes also known as the Pandects.

2. a collection of case summaries that have the holding in the case noted briefly. Digests completely lack any attempt at synthesis but are usually very usefully cross-referenced and indexed. It is upon such digests that most legal research is based and will continue to be based until electronic information retrieval is available to all. See LEXIS, WEST LAW.

diligence the term used in Scotland for the body of law relating to the enforcement of obligations. See EXECUTION.

diminished responsibility in criminal law an aberration of mind, close to but not actually amounting to INSANITY, that is caused by mental illness. The defence in Scotland applies only to murder and attempted murder. It is construed a little wider in England where it extends to cover depression or irresistible impulse. In England, the reduced crime is manslaughter and in Scotland culpable homicide (see HOMICIDE).

Din Torah in Jewish law, a hearing of a dispute before the BETH DIN. It gains its secular authority as a result of the practice of the London Beth Din of having the parties agree to ARBITRATION.

Diplock courts the name given to courts in Northern Ireland in which certain terrorist offences are tried by a judge sitting without a jury. The name derives from that of the English law lord whose report in 1972 recommended their creation.

diplomatic immunity freedom from legal proceedings in the UK granted to members of diplomatic missions of foreign states under the Diplomatic Privileges Act 1964. Members of a mission's diplomatic staff are entitled to full criminal and civil immunity except for actions relating to certain private activities. Members of a mission's administrative or technical staff have full criminal immunity while civil immunity is restricted to acts performed in the course of his official duties. Both criminal and civil immunity for domestic staff are restricted to acts performed in the course of official duties.

direct applicability the doctrine in the law of the EUROPEAN UNION that states that a measure that has this character does not require to be implemented in a MEMBER STATE. Not only that, but the domestic authorities cannot interfere with its applicability as by passing local legislation. This doctrine is thus part and parcel of the notion of the supremacy of Community law over national law. The most common instance is the REGULATION. Direct applicability should be distinguished from DIRECT EFFECT.

directed verdict a VERDICT ordered by a court rather than waiting for a jury deliberation.

direct effect the doctrine in the law of the EUROPEAN COMMUNITIES that states that a Community Act has direct effect when those who are subject to COMMUNITY LAW are given a right. It applies to individuals and institutions. Persons who benefit from the right can sue for their protection in their national courts. These rights must be respected regardless of the domestic law, thus this is an inherent part of the notion of the supremacy of European law. The features looked for are that the measure should be clear, concise, unconditional and allow no discretion to the MEMBER STATES or Community institutions. REGULATIONS nearly always have DIRECT EFFECT. A DIRECTIVE can also have a direct effect, but this is ascertained taking each case on its merits. The COURT OF JUSTICE OF THE EUROPEAN COMMUNITIES has held that a directive can have *vertical direct effect*, which occurs where the measure in question is capable of producing rights between the addressee, which is usually the member state, and a third party: see *Nederlandse Ondernemingen* v. *Inspecteur der Inveroerrechten en Accijnzen* [1977] ECR 113. More difficult is *horizontal direct effect*, which is the situation where one third party could utilise the Act to sue another fourth party. The case law is not completely settled on the matter, although on balance it may be against horizontal direct effect: *Marshall* v. *Southampton and South-West Hampshire Area Health Authority* [1986] ECR 723; *Beets-Proper* v. *Van Lanschot Bankiers* [1986] ECR 773; and see *Colson* v. *Land*

Nordrhein-Westfallen [1984] ECR 3415.

direct evidence in the law of evidence, evidence of a fact in issue given by a witness who came to it through his own senses or evidence from a document or item produced before the court. See CIRCUMSTANTIAL EVIDENCE.

directive a legislative Act of the EUROPEAN UNION produced by the COUNCIL OF THE EUROPEAN UNION and the COMMISSION OF THE EUROPEAN UNION. It directs MEMBER STATES to produce a certain effect within a certain time. This achieves the Community goal while respecting national differences. The member state need not legislate if it can achieve the same result by administrative measures. One of the most recent to have considerable effect in PRIVATE LAW was the DIRECTIVE on PRODUCT LIABILITY. Failure to comply can result in action before the COURT OF JUSTICE OF THE EUROPEAN UNION at the instigation of the Commission. Directives are not directly applicable (see DIRECT APPLICABILITY) but they can have DIRECT EFFECT.

director a person who conducts the affairs of a COMPANY. Directors act as agents of the company, owe fiduciary duties to it and have a duty of care towards it: *Percival* v. *Wright* 1902 2 Ch. 421. Directors may have executive functions or they may be non-executive directors, their principal functions being to safeguard the interests of investors. Directors, while not servants of the company as such, have a responsibility to it not dissimilar to the responsibility owed by a TRUSTEE to his beneficiaries. Specifically, directors are under duties to exercise their powers for the purposes for which they were conferred and to exercise them bona fide for the benefit of the company as a whole; and not to put themselves in a position in which their duties to the company and their personal interests may conflict.

First directors are usually named in the ARTICLES OF ASSOCIATION; however, it is not uncommon for the articles, instead of naming directors, to contain a power for the subscribers, or a majority of them, to appoint them. Following appointment, the normal procedures is for directors to retire by rotation, although a director's office may be vacated in other circumstances. A retiring director is eligible for re-election and the members at the ANNUAL GENERAL MEETING at which a director retires may fill the vacated office by electing the same or another person to it.

The appointment of directors of a PUBLIC LIMITED COMPANY must be voted on individually unless the members who are present agree by resolution, without dissent, to a single resolution appointing two or more directors. Like trustees, directors are not entitled as of right to remuneration; accordingly, a director has no claim to payment for his services unless, as is usual, there is a provision for payment in the articles.

In INSOLVENCY proceedings, the Company Directors' Disqualification Act 1986 empowers the court to make a DISQUALIFICATION order disqualifying the persons specified in the order from being directors of companies and from otherwise being concerned with a company's affairs.

A company director may be removed by special resolution, notwithstanding anything in the articles or in any agreement between him and the company. Special notice of such a resolution must be given.

Director of Consumer Affairs a post in the Republic of Ireland created by the Consumer Information Act 1978, the holder of which is appointed by the appropriate minister to carry out certain functions independently. These include keeping under review advertising practices, controlling trade practices that might mislead consumers and encouraging the adoption of codes of practice by trade and industry. The Director has more recently acquired the powers of the Examiner of Restrictive Practices to deal with agreements restricting the supply of goods and services.

Director of Public Prosecutions (DPP) an officer who works under the ATTORNEY GENERAL and who is responsible for the prosecution of all serious CRIME. Sometimes only the consent of the DPP is required. The office is particularly important as it heads up the CROWN PROSECUTION SERVICE, which prosecutes most crimes in England.

direct rule the name given to the system of governing Northern Ireland during the suspension of the Stormont parliament from March 1972 until 1999. Executive power was exercised by the Secretary of State for Northern Ireland, and laws on matters with which the Stormont parliament could deal were made by ORDERS IN COUNCIL.

disabilities if at any time during the statutory prescriptive period the servient land was owned by an infant or a mentally incapacitated person (or, indeed, anyone other than anyone *sui juris* and holding the FEE SIMPLE) that period is excluded in relation to the acquisition of an EASEMENT or profit by PRESCRIPTION under the Prescription Act 1832 that depends, *inter alia*, on the servient owner being able to enforce his rights should he have chosen to.

disability discrimination treatment of an employee less favourably than the treatment of others for a reason that relates to a disabled person's disability and other forms of discrimination such as booking hotel accommodation: Disability Discrimination Act 1995.

discharge in any obligation, the termination of that obligation without liability on either party. In the Scots law of contract, discharge may be by performance or NOVATION, COMPENSATION, CONFUSION, ACCEPTANCE payment or DELEGATION.

discharge of an instrument in the law of NEGOTIABLE INSTRUMENTS a BILL OF EXCHANGE is discharged when all rights of action thereon are extinguished. It then ceases to be negotiable, and if it subsequently comes into the hands of a HOLDER IN DUE COURSE he acquires no right of action on the instrument. A bill is discharged by payment in due course.

disclaimer a renunciation, refusal or denial. A disclaimer, especially where a person wishes to renounce a benefit under a WILL or under the INTESTACY rules, or where a person entitled to take out a grant of PROBATE does not wish to act. The phrase is also used where a party seeks to exclude or limit liability that would otherwise attach to him. This may appear on a letter giving advice or on a notice on a wall. Such notices are controlled in a number of ways but principally by the control of UNFAIR CONTRACT TERMS in the Unfair Contract Terms Act 1977, as amended for Scotland on this point by the Law Reform (Miscellaneous Provisions) (Scotland) Act 1990 and the Unfair Terms in Consumer Contracts Regulations 1999. It is also used in the context of TRADE DESCRIPTIONS to counteract an apparently misleading indication. To have this effect the disclaimer must be as bold, clear and compelling as the description itself.

disclosed principal a principal whose identity is revealed to the person with whom his agent is contracting. Rules governing the personal liability of an agent in relation to contracts he enters into with third parties differ according to whether the principal was disclosed at the time of contracting. If the principal was so disclosed, direct contractual relations are established between the principal and the third party; this is not the case if the principal is not disclosed. See *Keighly, Maxted & Co.* v. *Durant* [1901] AC 240. See also AGENCY.

discovery see DISCLOSURE.

discrimination 1. in the law of the UK, unfavourable treatment based on some disapproved ground. See SEX DISCRIMINATION, RACE DISCRIMINATION.

2. in the COMMUNITY LAW of the EUROPEAN UNION (EU), one of the key principles enunciated under Article 7, whereby discrimination based upon the nationality of a worker within the EU is abolished. See also FREE MOVEMENT OF PERSONS.

dismantling of ships see ARRESTMENT.

dismissal see UNFAIR DISMISSAL.

dismissal of action the termination of a civil action at the motion of the defendant. While an order for dismissal may be made at the conclusion of the trial, it is usually made during interlocutory proceedings. An action may be dismissed for want of prosecution where the plaintiff has been guilty of inexcusable delay in circumstances where there has been seen to be prejudice to the defendant or where there is a risk that a FAIR TRIAL is no longer possible. In Scotland a civil action may be dismissed if it cannot be legally supported. If so, it may be raised again.

disorderly conduct see BREACH OF THE PEACE.

disorderly house a polite legal term for a brothel.

disposition in Scottish CONVEYANCING practice the name for the DEED that transfers ownership of (conveys) real or heritable property. Once it was necessary to use the word *dispone*, but this has not been the case for some time. To obtain a REAL RIGHT good against the world the title must be recorded in the REGISTER OF SASINES or the LAND REGISTRY.

disqualification I. the Company Directors' Disqualification Act 1986 contains provisions whereby directors may be *disqualified* for fraudulent or wrongful trading or for conduct that makes them unfit to be concerned in the management of companies.

2. road traffic offenders may be disqualified from holding or obtaining a driving licence. See, for example, TOTTING UP.

dissentiente dissenting by delivering a judgment contradicting the majority. Abbreviated to **diss**.

distinguish to show that a PRECEDENT is not in point. When a lawyer has distinguished a precedent, he has shown the court that it does not actually cover the facts of the case before the court.

distraint the seizing of goods or other property of another to pay debts, such as that of a landlord against a tenant.

distress the seizure of goods as security for the performance of some legal obligation (e.g. where a landlord *distrains* on his tenant's goods

and chattels for non-payment of rent). For Scotland, see
SEQUESTRATION FOR RENT.

distribution see CORPORATION TAX.

distribution (bankruptcy) after a bankruptcy order has been made,
the trustee, having gathered in the bankrupt's estate, must *distribute*
the assets available for distribution in accordance with the
prescribed order of payment. All debts proved in the bankruptcy in
the same category of priority rank PARI PASSU.

dividend the income return received by a shareholder in respect of his
investment. Unlike INTEREST, which is payable irrespective of
whether the company has made profits or not, dividends are
payable only if so declared by the directors and are payable only out
of profits (whether current profits or profits earned in previous
years) available for the purpose: Companies Act 1985. If there are no
available profits there can be no payment of a dividend. Dividends
must be declared by the ANNUAL GENERAL MEETING on the
recommendation of the directors or by the directors themselves
between such meetings.

divorce the legal termination of a MARRIAGE otherwise than by death
or the granting of a decree of nullity. The sole ground for divorce in
the UK jurisdictions is IRRETRIEVABLE BREAKDOWN of the marriage;
this may only be evidenced by ADULTERY, DESERTION, intolerable
conduct or SEPARATION for the relevant statutory period.

   The Administration of Justice Act 1982 introduced a new Section
18A in the Wills Act 1837 containing provisions bringing English
law into line with the laws of Australia and New Zealand with
regard to the effect of divorce on provisions for a spouse in a will.
The new section provides that a decree of divorce or nullity will
cause (in the absence of a contrary intention manifested in the will
– as to which see *Re Sinclair* [1985] 1 All ER 1064) any such benefits
to lapse. In Scots law divorce does not affect a will, nor does it affect
a LEGACY.

   See also BEHAVIOUR, CUSTODY, FINANCIAL OBLIGATIONS ON BREAKDOWN
OF MARRIAGE, FINANCIAL PROVISION, LUMP SUM ORDER.

DNA profiling a scientific process using samples of bodily fluid or
tissue that can establish to a very high degree of probability that two
samples are from the same person. It has obvious uses in linking
criminals to the scene of the crime and in PATERNITY testing.

D notice in the constitutional law of the UK, a notice issued by the
Defence, Press and Broadcasting Committee, which is made up of

civil servants and representatives of the press. It indicates when certain information that might be subject to the OFFICIAL SECRETS Act can safely be published. The D notice requests editors and broadcasters not to publish certain information regarded as prejudicial to national security and may well cover material that is not restrained under the Official Secrets Act.

dock brief a BARRISTER who, prior to the introduction of LEGAL AID, was instructed by an accused person directly, without a SOLICITOR, if the barrister were sitting available for selection and fully gowned.

documentary evidence evidence in written rather than oral form. The ADMISSIBILITY of such evidence depends on the authenticity of the document and the purpose for which it is being offered in evidence.

document of title any BILL OF LADING, dock warrant, warehouse keeper's certificate, warrant or order for the delivery of GOODS, or any other document used in the ordinary course of business as proof of the possession or control of goods or authorising or purporting to authorise either by endorsement or delivery the possession of the document to transfer or receive goods thereby represented.

dole in the criminal law of Scotland, in a general sense the evil intent required for conviction of a crime and more especially in relation to particular crimes, the mental element required. Statutory offences can, and often do, obviate the need for it.

domicile the country that a person treats as his permanent home and to which he has the closest legal attachment. A person cannot be without a domicile and cannot have more than one domicile at any one time; he acquires a *domicile of origin at birth* (normally, if his father is alive, his father's; if his father is not alive, his mother's). He retains this domicile until he acquires a *domicile of choice* (by making a home in a country with the intention that it should be a permanent base). Domicile is distinct from nationality; it is also distinct from 'ordinary residence' in that the latter may be acquired without any intention to reside there permanently.

dominant tenement see EASEMENT.

dominium full, complete and indivisible ownership.

domitae naturae 'domestic nature' (of an animal). See ANIMALS.

donatio mortis causa 'a gift in anticipation of death'.

donatio non praesumunitur see PRESUMPTION.

doom judgment. The word 'doom' is Old English whereas

'judgment' is a very early French import.

double jeopardy as *jeopardy* is the risk of conviction or punishment, double jeopardy refers to the rule that a person should not be tried twice for the same crime. Boasting persons who have been wrongly acquitted of murder discover that, in many jurisdictions, PERJURY is considered as a different crime from murder, so if the accused person has himself given perjured testimony he may be tried, convicted and sentenced for lying under OATH, if, of course, he chose to give evidence on his own behalf.

doubt see BEYOND A REASONABLE DOUBT.

DPP abbreviation for DIRECTOR OF PUBLIC PROSECUTIONS.

draw to write in due form. In relation to a BILL OF EXCHANGE, to draw a bill is to write it (*draw it*) in such a way that an unconditional order is addressed to another (the *drawee*).

drawdown where the provisions of a loan agreement provide for the amount of the loan to be advanced in tranches (rather than as one single ADVANCE) the process through which this is achieved is drawdown, with the relevant provisions governing the process known as *drawdown clauses*.

drawee a person on whom a BILL OF EXCHANGE is drawn. See DRAW.

drawer a person who draws a BILL OF EXCHANGE. See DRAW.

drink driving in road traffic law, a convenient term often used to describe driving or attempting to drive while unfit through drink or drugs; being in charge of a vehicle while so unfit; driving while the proportion of alcohol in breath, blood or urine is over the prescribed limit (80 milligrams blood/alcohol). It attracts a compulsory period of DISQUALIFICATION of at least one year and a second offence within ten years will result in a ban from driving lasting for at least three years.

driver in road traffic law, as well as the obvious case of a person propelling and steering a vehicle the term *driver* can include a person steering while another propels; indeed, both may be held to be driving. Someone sitting with a learner driver, who does not have control, is not driving. Pushing a car out of petrol with one hand steering has been held to be driving in Scotland but not so in a similar case in England.

droit administratif see JUDICIAL REVIEW.

drug treatment and testing order a non-custodial sentence that allows the court (with the offender's consent) to order the offender to undergo treatment, including mandatory testing, in cases of drug misuse. The order is reviewed at least monthly. See the Crime and Disorder Act 1998.

drunk driving see DRINK DRIVING.

DTI abbreviation for DEPARTMENT OF TRADE AND INDUSTRY.

dubitante 'doubting', in the law reports, signifies that the judge has doubts concerning an approach he is taking or that the majority with which he is concurring is taking.

duces tecum 'bring with you', a form of SUBPOENA.

due course see HOLDER IN DUE COURSE.

due process of law the legal mechanism. It suggests a freedom from arbitrary detention. The concept is particularly important in the USA, being enshrined in the Fourteenth Amendment preventing interference in private life without due process. See BILL OF RIGHTS (USA). See also HUMAN RIGHTS.

duress pressure to act in a certain way, in particular where there is an element of physical force. It has different effect in different branches of different legal systems.

In English criminal law, duress is a DEFENCE, albeit limited, to criminal charges: *Hudson* v. *Taylor* [1971] 2 QB 202. The fear induced by the duress must be extreme. The focus is on a reasonable person sharing the characteristics of the accused taking the defence. The phrase 'morally involuntary' may reflect the test applied by the courts. It is not available in cases of murder: *R* v. *Howe and Others* [1987] 1 AC 417.

In Scots criminal law, the defence is known under the name of *coercion*. The requirements are that there should be an inability to resist the threatened violence, the accused must not take a leading part in the crime, and the accused must do his best to disclose the crime and make amends when safe to do so: *Thomson* v. *HMA* 1983 JC 69. Whether or not the plea is available in the case of murder is not decided.

In the law of CONTRACT, its primary denotation is of actual violence or threats of violence towards the contracting party or those close to him: *Welch* v. *Cheesman* (1974) 229 Estates Gazette 99. The effect is to allow the contract to be avoided. The notion of *economic duress* has gained ground, reflecting the fact that economic pressure can affect conduct and be reprehensible. The difficulty with this, however, is that the free market capitalism that underlies many systems is rather tolerant of such conduct. See *Universal Tankships Inc. of Morovia* v. *International Transport Workers Federation* [1982] WLR 803.

It can be seen from the last-noted case that the law of RESTITUTION recognises duress as an unjust factor that may bring about a restitutionary award. See UNDUE INFLUENCE.

duty of care 1. the mechanism used in the law of TORT or DELICT to determine when a person is liable. In a way it is thus a useless fifth wheel. However, it is practically useful in separating out and explaining cases of non-liability where there is a MISTAKE or error or bungle that causes a loss to the plaintiff yet there is no liability. Normally, reasonable foreseeability of physical harm will create a duty, but the question is much more open in cases of ECONOMIC LOSS, NERVOUS SHOCK and other more unusual harms. See also CULPA, NEGLIGENCE.

2. in relation to persons who import produce, carry, keep or dump waste and waste-brokers, the obligation to take all such measures as are reasonable, among other things, to prevent the unlawful management of waste, prevent the escape of waste and to ensure waste is transferred to an authorised person: Environmental Protection Act 1990. Failure to meet the duty is a criminal offence.

dying declaration in the law of evidence, an exception to the HEARSAY rule in England whereby the oral or written statement of a dying person may be used in evidence at the trial of a person for his murder if he would have been a competent witness himself. To be effective, the maker must have been in hopeless expectation of his death. Its basis is that the person being so near death is unlikely to lie when he is so soon to come before a higher court. In more secular times, the fact that the statement cannot be contradicted should perhaps suggest the weight accorded to it might not be as great as once was the case.

E

E & OE abbreviation for 'errors and omissions excepted'.

earnest in Anglo-American law a part-payment made to seal a bargain. At times the implication has been of a token sum that is forfeitable. The Roman law tradition has a very developed equivalent - ARRA. See also DEPOSIT.

earnings arrestment in the Scots law of DILIGENCE or legal enforcement, the process whereby for ordinary debts the creditor serves notice on the debtor's employer and sums are deducted on a regular basis, calculated according to a statutory table. See CURRENT MAINTENANCE ARRESTMENT, CONJOINED ARRESTMENT ORDER.

easement an incorporeal hereditament that is enjoyed by one person in his capacity as owner of a parcel of land and that confers rights over neighbouring land belonging to another. The land benefited by the existence of this right is referred to as the *dominant tenement* while the neighbouring land burdened with this right is known as the *servient tenement*. For an easement to exist, it must be enjoyed by a fee simple owner against a fee simple owner; it cannot, for example, be enjoyed by a fee simple owner against a life tenant or a tenant for years. For an easement to exist as a legal interest, it requires to subsist 'for an interest equivalent to an estate in FEE SIMPLE ABSOLUTE IN POSSESSION or a term of years absolute', i.e. in perpetuity or for a fixed terms of years (Law of Property Act 1925, Section 12). Attempts to create easements for other periods (e.g. for the duration of someone's life) will result in the right being, at most, equitable and as such being capable of being overridden by a bona fide purchaser of the legal estate without notice.

An *easement of light* exists. Uninterrupted enjoyment of light from a window for 20 years confers an absolute and indefeasible right to continue to receive such light without obstruction; the only exception is where the enjoyment took place under some deed or written permission or agreement: Prescription Act 1832. Rights acquired in this way are often referred to as *ancient lights*.

Where an *easement other than light* has been actually enjoyed for 20 years it cannot be defeated by reason only that it can be shown that it must have commenced after 1189; however, it may be defeated in any other way possible at common law. An easement enjoyed for 40 years as of right and without interruption is deemed absolute and indefeasible unless enjoyed by written consent: Prescription Act 1832.

EC abbreviation for EUROPEAN COMMUNITIES.

ECB abbreviation for EUROPEAN CENTRAL BANK.

Economic and Monetary Union (EMU) a three-stage process for establishing economic and monetary union in the EUROPEAN COMMUNITIES, proposed by a committee of the EUROPEAN COUNCIL in 1989 (although a currency 'snake' was a clear precursor). The first stage simply involves the coordination of existing structures and preparation of consequential and necessary amendments to the Treaties. This stage began on 1 July 1990. The next two stages have not been unanimously taken forward: the establishment of the EURO, the single European currency, and the establishment of a EUROPEAN CENTRAL BANK.

economic duress see DURESS.

economic loss in the law of TORT or DELICT, certain claims for non-physical or non-proprietary damage caused negligently. Certain claims, although financial, are usually discounted from such discussion, viz. loss of wages consequent upon physical injury and loss of use following damage to property. The phrase then encompasses other cases where the plaintiff is suing because he has less money than he had before the events complained of. There are, however, two kinds of cases that can be considered under this head, and they must be distinguished. There are *primary claims*, where the loss to the plaintiff has come directly and without any intervening damage to the person or property of another. Thus, negligent financial or legal advice causes such loss. Other cases are *secondary*: the plaintiff is poorer but only as a result of the defendant having harmed the person or property of another person, as where the defendant cuts an electricity company's cable but the plaintiff who operates an amusement arcade is poorer as a result. Cases of primary economic loss have the potential to be successful, whereas secondary cases are most likely to fail. Primary cases are governed by the principle in *Hedley Byrne* v. *Heller* [1964] AC 465, based on assumption of responsibility for the potential loss. Secondary cases are governed by a long line of authority disallowing recovery based upon contractual and other relations to the primarily injured party. There are exceptions to the non-recovery rule in secondary cases, and that is where the plaintiff has some possessory title like LIEN or

HYPOTHEC; in these cases he may sue: see *Leigh and Sillivan* v. *Aliakmon Shipping* [1986] AC 785. There are some odder cases that have been allowed, notably *White* v. *Jones* [1995] 2 AC 207, in which solicitors were held liable to a disappointed beneficiary when the solicitors failed to give effect to the testator's intentions. The case is unusual because the estate had not been lost when the matter is looked at all round – it went to the wrong person.

economic theory of law the theory, often associated with Karl Marx, taking the view that law is a mere embellishment upon the exploitation of the proletariat. After revolution, the last function of the law would be to eradicate capitalism. In a technical (and non-Marxist) way, R. A. Posner is associated with analysis of legal rules from the point of view of their economic efficiency. Much work has been done in relation to accident, liability and tort. Its influence on what the courts actually do is difficult to estimate, but the general reluctance of courts to consider abstract economic data militates against it. It is of interest to legislators and law commissions.

economic torts a convenient nomenclature to bring together a number of torts or delicts with an independent line of authority that regulate economic activity. Always included are INTIMIDATION, INDUCING BREACH OF CONTRACT and CONSPIRACY. PASSING OFF and MALICIOUS FALSEHOOD are sometimes considered, and some writers have attempted to rationalise the three core categories into a single TORT of wrongful interference in trade or business.

ECSC abbreviation for EUROPEAN COAL AND STEEL COMMUNITY.

ECU abbreviation for European Currency Unit. See EURO, EUROPEAN MONETARY SYSTEM.

edictal citation in Scottish civil procedure, the SERVICE of court papers by public advertisement, usually on the walls of court where the defender cannot otherwise be found. There is a trend towards substituting intimation in newspapers circulating in the area, either as an alternative (as in the SUMMARY CAUSE) or along with posting on the walls (as is the case in many INSOLVENCY petitions).

Edinburgh Gazette see GAZETTE.

EEA abbreviation for EUROPEAN ECONOMIC AREA.

EEC abbreviation for EUROPEAN ECONOMIC COMMUNITY.

EFTA abbreviation for European Free Trade Association. See EUROPEAN ECONOMIC AREA.

egress see ACCESS.

EIB abbreviation for EUROPEAN INVESTMENT BANK.

eik (pronounced 'eek') in the Scots law of succession, the document, supplementary to a CONFIRMATION, that allows the EXECUTOR to administer an item of estate that had been overlooked or has just materialised after the original confirmation has been obtained.

ejection 1. in Scotland, the DELICT of dispossessing a person permanently from his land.

2. in Scotland, an action to remove a person from lands.

ejusdem generis rule a rule of interpretation applying to legal writings and statutes stating that a list of things should be read as the one genus and the items as a species: applying the rule to 'pansy, dandelion, daisy or others', then 'others' would have to be a flower and could not be a horse. If the rule is not held to apply, then 'other' could be a horse, which would look strange in one's buttonhole.

election both in England and Scotland the law does not allow a party to *approbate and reprobate*. A party cannot generally accept a DEED and reject it at the same time. To be operative as a choice or election, there must be free choice, the party must have CAPACITY to elect and the deed, usually a WILL, must be valid.

elective share laws that allow a spouse to take a part of an estate when the other spouse dies, regardless of the terms of any will or testament.

eleemosynary for the relief of want, alms-giving.

embezzlement in England, the CRIME of fraudulent appropriation by a clerk or servant to his own use of property delivered to or taken into possession of account of his employer. Since the Theft Act 1968 it is no longer an offence with a name of its own.

In Scotland it is the felonious appropriation without the owner's CONSENT by a person who has received a limited ownership of property subject to restoration at a future time or with an obligation to account for it to the owner. The distinction between THEFT and embezzlement is not important in Scotland.

emblements the fruit of sown lands. See GOODS.

emergency powers powers conferred on government during a state of emergency (such a state being declared by ROYAL PROCLAMATION under the Emergency Powers Acts 1920 and 1964).

emergency protection order a court order under the Children Act 1989 for the emergency protection of children at risk of significant harm. The order gives the applicant parental responsibility for the CHILD and authorises the removal of the child to accommodation supplied by the applicant.

eminent domain (USA) the power of the state to compulsorily purchase land.

emolument income from EMPLOYMENT. The term is used by the Income and Corporation Taxes Act 1988. Specifically, Section 1311 defines it as including 'all salaries, fees, wages, perquisites and profits whatsoever'. Perquisites include BENEFITS IN KIND.

emphyteusis in Roman law an agricultural lease granted for a long time or in perpetuity but requiring payment of rent.

employee see EMPLOYMENT.

employee share scheme a scheme for sharing company profits with employees with the object of conferring on them a participation in the company in the hope of engendering greater commitment from them. Schemes operate either by distributing shares already paid up by the company either directly to the employees themselves or to trustees for them or by conferring on employees options to acquire shares on favourable terms. The Income and Corporation Taxes Act 1988 provides special rules in respect of authorised schemes.

employers' association an association of employers whose principal purpose includes the regulation of relations between employers and workers or TRADE UNIONS.

employers' liability a convenient term to group together those aspects of the law, mainly the law of TORT or DELICT or CONTRACT, relating to the liability of the employer to his work force. More usually, it is applied narrowly to the liability in tort to take reasonable care for the employee's safety. At one time, for reasons that no longer apply, it was important to define this closely, and it was said to be a threefold duty comprising the provision of safe plant and equipment, a duty to provide competent fellow employees and a duty to provide a safe system of work: *English* v. *Wilsons & Clyde Coal Co.* 1937 SC (HL) 46. Now there is an overall duty to take care, even of the employee's mental health: *Walker* v. *Northumberland County Council* [1995] 1 All ER 737. The term, however, also applies quite legitimately to statutory protection by way of criminal penalties or provisions from which a case can be based upon statutory duty. Thus, beginning with the Employer's Liability Act 1880 and through to the Health and Safety at Work Act 1974, there are many provisions that provide protection for employees or an even wider class of workers. The detail of the law is increasingly set by European DIRECTIVES incorporated into UK law by regulations under the 1974 Act. Many of these regulations, unlike the Act itself, have effect to create civil liability. The standard to provide care can often be STRICT LIABILITY or even an ABSOLUTE LIABILITY: *Summers* v. *Frost* [1955] AC 740.

The employer's primary liability for failing to look after his workers is entirely different from an employer being held VICARIOUSLY LIABLE for his employees' acts.

employment the relationship formerly known as *master and servant*, a contract such as that of a chauffeur who sells his service. It can be used for the contractor who enters a contract to provide services, such as a taxi driver. Much modern employment law deals with statutory rights in relation to employment, and its focus on the 'servant' type of employment is often seen when it refers to 'worker'. Company directors are not, for example, necessarily employees but may be employed by the company. Partners are not employees of the partnership. See EMPLOYERS' LIABILITY; EMPLOYEE SHARE SCHEME.

Employment Appeal Tribunal a tribunal under the Employment Protection Consolidation Act 1978 made up of High Court judges and judges of the Court of Session and lay members. It hears appeals on points of law from EMPLOYMENT TRIBUNALS. A further appeal on a point of law can be taken to the COURT OF APPEAL or the INNER HOUSE.

employment tribunals bodies established by statute that are assigned a jurisdiction in many matters, but not all, relating to EMPLOYMENT, especially cases of UNFAIR DISMISSAL. Tribunals consist of a legal chairman and two lay members from each side of industry, and the bulk of the work relates to unfair dismissal cases, REDUNDANCY cases and terms of employment. They have jurisdiction in Wages Act cases as well as the courts. They sit all over the country and have issued their own rules of procedure that are designed to be sufficiently informal to allow parties to represent themselves effectively. Legal aid was made available in 2001 for difficult cases.

EMS abbreviation for EUROPEAN MONETARY SYSTEM.

EMU abbreviation for ECONOMIC AND MONETARY UNION.

en banc a hearing, usually of an appeal, by the full court.

encroachment unlawful interference on another's land or with their rights.

encumbrance a burden that affects land, such as a MORTGAGE.

endorsement 1. see INDORSEMENT.

2. the marking of the details of a conviction on a driving licence. It is now the penalty points rather than the endorsements themselves that are of importance. See TOTTING UP.

engagement in English law, an agreement, albeit unenforceable, to marry at some future date. The agreement is usually marked by the man giving the woman an *engagement ring*. This gift is presumed to be absolute, so that if the MARRIAGE does not take place the woman may keep the ring; this presumption may be rebutted, however, by proof that the ring was given on condition that the marriage took place.

In Scots family law, and prior to 1984, a contract, legally binding, each party promising to marry the other. Breach attracted damages, and the contract was protected by the delict of wrongful interference with contract. By virtue of the Law Reform (Husband and Wife) (Scotland) Act 1984 it cannot create legal obligations.

engross a term used in CONVEYANCING practice for preparing a final fair copy of a deed on whatever, for the time being, accepted as deed paper. *Engrossing* is the present participle and is also an obsolete term for the obsolete crime of FORESTALLING.

enjoyment the exercise of a right; *enjoyment nec vi* ('without force'), *nec clam* ('without secrecy') and *nec precario* ('not being a grant recallable at will') for the appropriate period will result in the prescriptive acquisition of the right.

enrichment a gain, or sometimes the prevention of expense, which is the focus of some parts of the law of RESTITUTION.

entail an estate tail or fee tail. In England, a settlement of land, destined to the grantee and the heirs of his body (or some more special destination; initially, such settlements rendered the land inalienable, i.e. not transferable to another owner, but after 1472 it came to be accepted that the entail could in certain circumstances be barred and the land made alienable). The whole law of entail was relaxed by the Fines and Recoveries Act 1832 and remodelled by the 1925 Property Reforms, making it possible to entail personal property and to bar an entail by will. Since the coming into force in 1997 of the Trusts of Land and Appointments of Trustees Act 1996 entailed interest cannot exist in equity, even by way of a trust.

In Scotland, entails (also known as *tailzies*, 'z' silent) were made possible by the Entail Act of 1683, provision being made for the setting up of a Register of Entails, publicising which estates were entailed. As, initially, in England, entailing land in Scotland made that land inalienable. The Entail Amendment (Scotland) Act 1848 established a procedure whereby entails could be barred, and in 1914 it was provided by the Entail (Scotland) Act that no future entails of land in Scotland would be permitted, save to implement a direction to entail combined in a will executed before the 1914 Act came into force.

enticement in the law of DELICT in Scotland, the TORT of luring a member of a person's family away from the family. The most frequent occurrence, that of defecting spouses, was taken out of the scope of the law of delict by the Law Reform (Husband and Wife) (Scotland) Act 1984.

entitled spouse in Scots family law, one of the subject of the regime established in relation to the protection of victims of domestic violence in the MATRIMONIAL HOME. An entitled spouse is generally the owner or tenant or other person entitled to live in a house. One of the major innovations of this law was to allow the non-entitled spouse to obtain an EXCLUSION ORDER against the other spouse.

entrapment encouraging a person to commit an offence to establish a prosecution. It is not a DEFENCE in English or Scots criminal law. However, the authorities should not commit crimes to trap the criminals: *R* v. *Sang* [1980] AC 402.

In the USA there has long been established a defence of entrapment where undercover police positively promote a crime that would not otherwise have occurred: *Sorells* v. *US* 287 US 435; *Sherman* v. *US* 356 US 369. The defence will not, however, be competent where policemen have merely joined an illegal practice – for example, seeking to be supplied with heroin while in the company of drug addicts with the same purpose.

entry clearance a visa, entry certificate or other document that, in accordance with the immigration rules, is to be taken as evidence of a person's eligibility, although not a BRITISH CITIZEN, for entry into the UK (Immigration Act 1971, Section 331). An entry certificate is not a work permit.

en ventre sa mère 'in his mother's womb'. The Latin phrase IN UTERO is more common in Scotland.

environmental law the body of law that governs use of the natural features, now much extended by international and national legislation. The Environment Act 1995 marked an new era in the UK. What is or is not environmental law is debatable. International Treaties, EUROPEAN UNION policies and local legislation dealing with pollution (whether of air or water), contamination of land, protection of flora and fauna (especially in relation to the food chain), disposal of waste and general nuisance are common subjects for treatments. Much of the law is enforced by the Environment Agency in England and Wales and the Scottish Environmental Protection Agency in Scotland. See ENVIRONMENTAL POLICY; HABITAT.

environment policy in the law of the EUROPEAN COMMUNITIES, a policy of the Communities added by the SEA, or SINGLE EUROPEAN ACT. The Communities are now legally enjoined to preserve, protect and improve the quality of the environment, to contribute towards health and prudently and rationally utilise natural resources. Detailed provisions exist for preventive action and a rule that environmental damage should be dealt with at source – a useful rule when the consequences of one MEMBER STATE's pollution may run down a river and harm the environment of another. The person polluting should pay in principle, not the Community taxpayers. The Community itself is empowered to act where it can do so more effectively than the member states. It is important to appreciate that even before the inclusion of the policy in the Treaties, the Community had done much in the field under other powers. The 1990 Environmental Directive permits free access to environmental information of public authorities. There is to be an environmental agency that will act as a monitoring body.

Equal Access Act (USA) a provision allowing freedom of religious worship to students in public sector schools.

equal pay see SEX DISCRIMINATION.

equal protection see BILL OF RIGHTS (USA)

equal value see SEX DISCRIMINATION.

e qui affirmat non e qui negat incumbit probatio 'he who affirms and not he who denies has the burden of proof.'

equitable compensation the remedy by which equity awarded a money sum to a claimant, similar in some respects to damages at common law.

equitable execution the appointment of a receiver as a means of enforcing a judgment or order. It is thought that, strictly speaking, this is not a means of EXECUTION but rather a form of RELIEF.

equitable interest an interest in property that can be asserted against everyone except a bona fide purchaser of the legal estate or interest for value without notice.

equity 1. fairness or balance.

2. a system of law, developed by the Court of Chancery in parallel with the common law, designed to complement it, providing remedies for situations that were unavailable at law, thereby adding a dimension of flexibility and justice that was sometimes lacking because of the common law's rigidity.

3. a right in respect of property that does not amount to an EQUITABLE INTEREST but that can be asserted against those who have notice of it. In the hierarchy of interests in property in English law, at the top come legal estates or interests. These are rights that are good against all other persons, whether or not those other persons have notice of them; next are equitable interests, which are good against all persons except a bona fide purchaser of the legal estate for value without notice; then come equities, which are rights that are good against persons other than bona fide purchasers of legal or equitable estates for value without notice.

4. that part of a COMPANY's capital that is owned by shareholders.

5. the net value of assets after taking into account any liabilities secured on them.

equity of redemption the right or interest of a mortgagor of property to redeem while the MORTGAGE subsists.

error see MISTAKE.

errore juris 'by error of law'.

escape in English law, the crime of breaking out of lawful confinement. It is also an offence to assist in the escape: Prison Act 1952; Criminal Justice Act 1961. For Scotland, see PRISON-BREAKING.

escape of dangerous things a special head of STRICT LIABILITY established in *Fletcher* v. *Rylands* (1866) LR 1 Ex. 265. That case established a rule or doctrine that states that a person who for his own purposes brings on his land and collects and keeps there anything likely to do mischief if it escapes must keep it at his peril, and, if he does not do so, is prima facie answerable for all the damage that is the natural consequence of its escape (although it must now be added that damage of an unforeseeable type may not be recoverable: *Cambridge Water Co. Ltd* v. *Eastern Counties Leather plc* [1994] 2 AC 264). In the case itself, the plaintiff's mines were flooded when the defendants (mill owners) instructed independent contractors to make them a reservoir. The fault was that of the independent contractors, but the mill owners were held liable in their own right. Although it can overlap with NUISANCE, it has been recognised as a category of liability in its own right. Cases developed the rule by requiring that the danger ought to be non-natural, something made by man. There has to be an escape from the defendant's land to harm the plaintiff. Control of the escaping thing is sufficient to establish liability. Liability is strict, although not absolute. ACT OF GOD and the act of a stranger over whom the defendant had no control are defences. STATUTORY AUTHORITY and NECESSITY are also defences. If it ever was the law in Scotland, which is not unlikely, it is no longer.

escheat in feudal law, the reversion to the immediate feudal superior where the owner of an estate in fee died without heirs. In England and Wales, the last vestiges of the law of escheat were abolished in 1925; now land that becomes ownerless on the death of its owner goes to the Crown as BONA VACANTIA. In the USA it is generally the case that land will escheat to the state or county if the owner dies intestate and no heirs are discoverable. See ULTIMUS HAERES.

escrow a DEED delivered to a third party to hold until fulfilment of a CONDITION, when it will be delivered; e.g. a conveyance executed by a vendor of property and delivered to his solicitor pending completion by the purchaser's paying the purchase price.

establishment see FREEDOM OF ESTABLISHMENT.

Establishment Clause (USA) that part of the First Amendment that prevents the government promoting a religion as part of the state.

estate agent a person who provides services for the marketing and sale of property. The extent of the authority of the agent depends on the terms of the agreement with the principal (see AGENCY). The business is now regulated by the Estate Agents Act 1979. The Director of Fair Trading has powers to enforce the Act. So far as the day-to-day conduct of their business is concerned, estate agents must comply with the provisions of the Property MISDESCRIPTIONS Act 1991, as must others who carry out similar work.

estate duty a tax formerly levied on the value of property passing on a person's death. Estate duty was abolished in the UK in respect of deaths occurring after 12 March 1975, being replaced by Capital Transfer Tax (now INHERITANCE TAX).

estoppel a rule of evidence that operates to prevent a person from denying the truth of a statement he has made or from denying facts he has alleged to exist. The statement must have been acted upon (usually to his detriment, in that he has expended resources in reliance on its truth) by the other party who wishes to take advantage of the estoppel. For Scotland, see PERSONAL BAR.

et al. an abbreviation that may represent any of the following: *et alibi* ('and elsewhere'); *et alia* ('and other things'); *et alios* or *et alii* ('and other people').

et seq. abbreviation for *et sequentes* ('and those following').

EU abbreviation for EUROPEAN UNION.

Euratom one of the first of the EUROPEAN COMMUNITIES, formed in 1957 as a result of one of the Rome Treaties and following upon the Spaak Report, itself a result of the Messina Conference. It deals with atomic energy, which, although intrinsically important, was of political importance at the time of the formation of the Treaty because of the need for uranium in the production of atomic weapons. Its institutions merged with those of the EUROPEAN COAL AND STEEL COMMUNITY and the EUROPEAN ECONOMIC COMMUNITY as a result of the MERGER TREATY.

euro the European currency unit, a single currency for certain members (not the UK at the time of writing) of the EUROPEAN UNION. It represents progress towards ECONOMIC AND MONETARY UNION. The currency is managed by the EUROPEAN CENTRAL BANK.

Euroguichets 'infocentres' set up on the initiative of the COMMISSION OF THE EUROPEAN UNION's Directorate on Consumer Protection in ten places, including London and Dublin, to provide assistance and advice to consumers on legislation and on case law at both European and national levels. They also distribute the results of comparative tests and develop cross-border studies.

European Central Bank (ECB) an independent financial institution established in 1998 to define and implement monetary policy for members of the EUROPEAN UNION (EU) that have adopted the EURO as their common currency. The ECB and the national central banks of EU MEMBER STATES together constitute the European System of Central Banks. Although all 15 EU members participate in the system, countries (i.e. UK, Denmark, Sweden and Greece) that do not use the euro have no official role in formulating monetary policy for the euro zone.

European Coal and Steel Community (ECSC) the first of the EUROPEAN COMMUNITIES, formed in 1951 as a result of the Treaty of Paris. It regulated the production of coal and steel among the MEMBER STATES (who were then only six). Apart from the economic significance of these commodities, the common control and exchange of information involved made it ever less likely that France and Germany would go to war once again. The institutions merged with those of the EURATOM community and the EUROPEAN ECONOMIC COMMUNITY itself as a result of the MERGER TREATY.

European Commission on Human Rights the now defunct body that implemented the EUROPEAN CONVENTION ON HUMAN RIGHTS.

European Communities (EC) the common term for the EUROPEAN COAL AND STEEL COMMUNITY, EURATOM and the EUROPEAN ECONOMIC COMMUNITY. They share many common bodies and institutions. The Communities are now known as the European Union as a result of the EUROPEAN UNION TREATY. See COURT OF JUSTICE, COUNCIL OF THE EUROPEAN UNION, COMMISSION OF THE EUROPEAN UNION, EUROPEAN PARLIAMENT, COREPER, EUROPEAN COUNCIL.

European Convention on Human Rights more fully, the **European Convention for the Protection of Human Rights and Fundamental Freedoms**, a charter designed to further the goals of the EUROPEAN COUNCIL. Its members accept that citizens should enjoy HUMAN RIGHTS. Civil and political freedoms are enumerated – the right to life; freedom from torture or inhuman treatment; freedom from slavery and forced labour; the right to liberty and freedom from detention save in accord with the law; the right to fair administration of justice; respect for privacy and the family; the right to peaceful ASSEMBLY; the right not to be discriminated against. Over the years protocols have added new rights – the protection of property; a parent's right to choose education; a right to free elections; liberty from prison for inability to meet a contract; free movement; the right not to be expelled from one's natural home. Many of the rights are subject to provisos on the basis of public order, public security and the need to guard the freedom of others. The Convention is upheld in the EUROPEAN COURT OF HUMAN RIGHTS. The law now applies in the UK as a result of the Scotland Act 1998 and the Human Rights Act 1998 (from October 2000). Accordingly, decisions of the Court will now be influential and in due course applicable in the UK. Recent examples involving the UK are on peaceful protest (*Steel and Others* v. *UK* [1998] TLR 575); on the right to the privacy of one's home (*McLeod* v. *UK* [1998] TLR 577); chastisement of children as an aspect of cruel or degrading punishment (*A.* v. *UK* [1998] TLR 578); on freedom of association (*Ahmed and Others* v. *UK* [1998] TLR 581); on the right to a fair hearing in court (*Osman* v. *UK* [1998] TLR 681).

European Council a body both within and outside the EUROPEAN UNION. The European Council brings together the heads of state or of government of the MEMBER STATES and the President of the COMMISSION OF THE EUROPEAN UNION. They are assisted by the Ministers for Foreign Affairs and by a member of the Commission. It meets at least twice a year.

Quite the most curious body in the EUROPEAN COMMUNITIES, its origins lie in the time when the COUNCIL OF THE EUROPEAN UNION had given up voting by qualified majority and tried to seek unanimity. Decision-making became more difficult, and momentum was sought from the extra-Community intergovernmental Conference of Heads of State or Government because the parties at this gathering were eligible to be members of the Council proper. As a result of a resolution of that body, in 1974 the parties agreed to meet three times a year and whenever necessary to constitute themselves as the Council. When they meet, the President and senior vice-president of the Commission attend. In practice, it does keep to overall policy and tries to consider issues of development and policy and the clearing of log jams. Its success has been rewarded by recognition in the SINGLE EUROPEAN ACT.

European Court of Human Rights a body charged with implementation of the EUROPEAN CONVENTION ON HUMAN RIGHTS. As a result of recent reforms, an application is now initially considered by a committee of three judges and may be declared inadmissible immediately and without a further hearing. If, however, the application does prima facie seem admissible it will be passed to a chamber of seven judges. This chamber, if it finds the application admissible, will proceed to examine the merits of the case and will seek to achieve a friendly settlement. In the absence of such a settlement, the chamber will issue a judgment. This judgment will be final unless important issues arise within three months. In such an event, the judgment will be referred to a Grand Chamber of 17 judges. The Grand Chamber's judgment is final and may not be appealed. If an alleged violation is upheld by the Court, the responsibility lies with the defendant state to take the appropriate action to make good the identified deficiency. A state at fault may be required to pay compensation.

European Currency Unit see EURO, EUROPEAN MONETARY SYSTEM.

European Economic Area (EEA) the territory covered by a series of agreements signed in 1992 between the EUROPEAN COMMUNITIES and their MEMBER STATES and the European Free Trade Association (EFTA) countries, designed to create the world's largest and most important integrated economic structure and to be a step towards the construction of a Europe based on peace, democracy and human rights. The EFTA organisation was always in trouble when the UK, Denmark and the Republic of Ireland left to join the EUROPEAN ECONOMIC COMMUNITY. Austria, Finland, Iceland, Liechtenstein, Norway and Sweden have joined this organisation, which is a mirror of the European Communities. The aim is to implement the FOUR FREEDOMS on the basis of Community achievement to date – the ACQUIS COMMUNAUTAIRE. The EFTA countries have to help pay for the poorer EUROPEAN UNION members, providing soft loans for Portugal, 'the Island of Ireland', Greece and parts of Spain. The EEA will have a Council, a Joint Committee, a Parliamentary Committee and a Consultative Committee. Matters progressed swiftly, and Austria, Finland and Sweden joined the European Union in 1995.

European Economic Community (EEC) the third of the three foundation organisations of what is now the EUROPEAN UNION. Constituted by one of the Rome Treaties of March 1957, this community drove progress towards European integration. Its 'COMMON MARKET' was the source of attraction to Europe for the UK. Its institutions merged with those of the EUROPEAN COAL AND STEEL COMMUNITY as a result of the MERGER TREATY.

European Free Trade Association see EUROPEAN ECONOMIC AREA.

European Investment Bank (EIB) a non-profit-making body that grants loans to members or to undertakings for investment in the European territories of the MEMBER STATES. Other sources of finance have to be utilised in the project as well as the EIB component. It borrows funds on the ordinary capital markets. Much of the lending is done to assist in development regions of the Community to promote economic and social integration. It can lend outwith the Community and has lent to associated states and other countries, such as Turkey, African, Caribbean and Pacific states and the Maghrehb states of northwest Africa. It is run by a Board of Governors consisting of the Ministers of Finance of the member states.

European Monetary System (EMS) a European monetary unit, an exchange rate intervention mechanism and a transfer mechanism established in 1978 under the law of the EUROPEAN COMMUNITIES. It is this system that established the European Currency Unit (ECU), a currency used to settle transactions between Community authorities and for operating the other mechanisms of the system.

MEMBER STATES have fixed interest rates, and the European Monetary Cooperation Fund (EMCF) supports intervention at levels around this figure. The EUROPEAN UNION tried but failed to move to complete economic and monetary union before the end of the 20th century.

European Parliament the democratic assembly of the EUROPEAN UNION. Each of the constituent EUROPEAN COMMUNITIES had an assembly that provided some form of democratic presence. The Assembly, by its own authority, called itself the Parliament in 1962. The SINGLE EUROPEAN ACT (SEA) regularised the practice. Nonetheless, this institution does not yet have the powers that are normally associated with parliaments. Members are elected and are known as Members of the European Parliament (MEPs). Originally sent by the MEMBER STATES, since June 1979 representatives have been directly elected. They are elected by proportional representation, and the term is for five years. The Parliament exercises an advisory and supervisory role. It has some influence as a result of the Budgetary Treaty of 1970, and the Single European Act has given it added influence by extending the COOPERATION PROCEDURE. The COMMISSION OF THE EUROPEAN UNION must reply to members' questions, and the COUNCIL OF THE EUROPEAN UNION has agreed to do so also. An elephant gun of control, existing in the power to pass a motion of censure on the Commission that, if passed, would force the Commission to resign, has been used once and improves the Parliament's influence over this body. Such a motion can be passed only after substantial procedural hurdles have been cleared. Parliament's budgetary powers allow it to modify obligatory expenditure under the Treaty and allow it to amend non-obligatory expenditure within a maximum set by the Commission. It must adopt the budget, and in 1979 exercised its power to reject it for important reasons, acting by a majority of members and two-thirds of the votes cast. Since the Inter-institutional agreement of 1 July 1988, arrangements have been made to prevent the disruption that such action can have on Community finances. Along with the COURT OF AUDITORS, the Parliament supervises the implementation of the budget. The Parliament has standing to institute action in the COURT OF JUSTICE against the Commission or the Council.

European Union (EU) the economic and political grouping that came into effect in 1993 and resulted from the European Union Treaty, an important treaty signed at Maastricht on 7 February 1992. It amended the EUROPEAN ECONOMIC COMMUNITY (EEC) Treaty, indeed, renaming it the EUROPEAN COMMUNITY. As the other two communities, EURATOM and the EUROPEAN COAL AND STEEL COMMUNITY, still exist, although affected by the MERGER TREATY, the resulting mass grouping of all three may be called the EUROPEAN COMMUNITIES or the European Union. It created a common foreign policy. It provided for judicial and police cooperation. It created a European Monetary Institute. It amended EEC Treaty to provide for Union citizenship, SUBSIDIARITY, a Community OMBUDSMAN, a Committee of the Regions and coordination of MEMBER STATES' economic policies. Other areas of new activity were agreed. One of the major aspects of the EU Treaty was to move the Community closer to ECONOMIC AND MONETARY UNION. The UK was not agreeable to this commitment and others, so a so-called opt-out was negotiated, formally recorded in Protocol 11. If it does exercise the opt-out, it will no longer be able to participate in a number of important decision-making processes. The UK also originally opted out of the Social Chapter provisions of Protocol 14. The provisions of the original Social Chapter were replaced by a new provision in the Amsterdam Treaty (effective May 1999), meaning that the UK then accepted the new Social Chapter.

euthanasia 'a happy death', the killing of another person to comply with the wishes of the victim (express or implied) where the victim is incurably ill and in pain or some miserable state. It is illegal in the UK: *Att. Gen.* v. *Able* [1984] QB 795. The House of Lords, in *Alvedale NHS Trust* v. *Bland* [1993] AC 789, held that it was not unlawful for doctors to withdraw life-supporting medical treatment from a patient in a persistent vegetative state who had no prospect of improvement, even where it was known that death would result in a matter of weeks. The patient was not brain-stem dead. Nonetheless, it was pointed out forcefully that this was not euthanasia, which is actually causing death to avoid or end suffering.

eviction the recovery of land.

evidence the body of rules that governs what can and what cannot be brought before a court in any particular cause. It determines whether and which witnesses may offer testimony and the extent to which they may testify. It is the law of evidence that regulates which writings, printouts, documents or, indeed, other items of real evidence, such as knives, dogs, cars, ships, photographs or videotapes, may be put before the court. It also determines what weight the evidence should have – whether it is conclusive, persuasive, indicative or useless. Indeed, it may be said that the known presumptions in law that may resolve a case without any real evidence or testimony are equally part of the law of evidence. See CIRCUMSTANTIAL EVIDENCE, EXCLUSIONARY RULE.

evidential burden the task to be met by proof. In civil cases facts require to be proved on the BALANCE OF PROBABILITIES; in criminal proceedings facts must be established BEYOND A REASONABLE DOUBT.

ex abundante cautela 'from an abundance of caution'.

examination in chief in court practice, the part of the case, whether civil or criminal, in which a party elicits from a witness his own case. Thus, the prosecution may examine the investigating police officers in chief to attempt to prove the case against the accused. LEADING QUESTIONS (those that suggest their own answer) should be avoided in examination in chief. In England, the court may allow leading questions if the court permits the witness to be treated as hostile. See CROSS-EXAMINATION.

examination of witness interrogation of witnesses. In court proceedings the EXAMINATION IN CHIEF is the interrogation in the first instance by the counsel calling the witness. CROSS-EXAMINATION by opposing counsel follows. Then follows the RE-EXAMINATION; this is further examination by counsel on whose side he is giving evidence on points arising out of the cross-examination.

examiner a BARRISTER appointed by the court to take evidence outside the court. For Scotland, see COMMISSIONER.

excepti doli in ROMAN LAW, a defence to a claim on account of FRAUD or DURESS. It mitigated the early Roman law under which formal promises would be enforced, no matter how or why they were granted.

excess the amount that an insured person has himself to pay towards a claim.

excess de pouvoir see JUDICIAL REVIEW.

exchange see BARTER, PERMUTATIO.

excise originally taxes charged on the retail sale within the UK of commodities such as beer, wines and spirits. Nowadays, however, licences (e.g. permitting the use of a gun or dealing in game) are classified as excise (see further the Customs and Excise Management Act 1979). One of the most commonly prosecuted excise offences is contravention of the Vehicles Excise and Registration Act 1994, which requires motorists to display a vehicle excise licence, known colloquially as a tax disc.

exclusion in terms of the Education Act 1996 as amended, schools may exclude children for disciplinary reasons, either for a fixed period or permanently. The courts will intervene where, in implementing the powers under the Act, the school does not act fairly, such as by failing to make known to the student what is being alleged against him: *R* v. *Governors of Dunraven School, ex parte B.* [2000] TLR 68. A similar system applies in Scotland under the Schools General (Scotland) Regulations 1975. See, for example, *Wallace* v. *Dundee Council* 2000 SLT (Sh. Ct) 60.

exclusionary rule in the law of evidence, the practice of allowing the court a discretion to exclude evidence technically admissible but that has a prejudicial effect out of proportion to its evidential value: see *R* v. *Sang* [1980] AC 402. The rule in its strict sense often applies to questions of ADMISSIBILITY of certain statements, particularly admissions and confessions, and thus the two issues are considered here. The same twin issues apply to REAL EVIDENCE. In England, a court may reject a statement unless it can be shown that it was not obtained by oppression or obtained in circumstances making it unreliable: *R* v. *Mason* [1988] 1 WLR 139. In determining these issues, JUDGES' RULES have given way to the Police and Criminal Evidence Act 1984, which defines oppression as including torture, inhuman or degrading treatment and the use of threat of violence (whether or not amounting to torture). The Police and Criminal Evidence Act 1984 requires the prosecution, if called upon to do so, to prove BEYOND A REASONABLE DOUBT that a confession was not obtained by oppression of the person who made it or as a result of anything that might make it unreliable.

In Scotland the issue is one of fairness – fairness to the accused and to the public interest. This requires a voluntary confession to be made by the accused while all the time understanding what was transpiring. While the police in Scotland may keep asking questions and probing, they should not bully or pressure the accused. The exclusionary rule in the strict sense mentioned above allows statements that do not exhibit any special vice, but taken as a whole seem unfair, to be excluded: Lord Advocate's Reference (No. 1 of 1983). In the landmark decision of *Chalmers* v. *HMA* 1954 JC 66, the High Court held that unfairness may be of such a degree that not only is the statement inadmissible, a whole line of evidence may be so tainted that it has to be excluded as well. This is most apparent in the case of invalid warrants or warrants that are used to recover property beyond their ambit. The vitiation of the warrant can prevent the evidence acquired being admissible.

In relation to confessions, improper procedure by the police or other investigating officials may render the evidence acquired inadmissible. The general approach was adopted by the US Supreme Court in two landmark decisions. Firstly, in *Escobedo* v. *Illinois* 378 US 478 (1964) the fruit of the poisonous tree doctrine was applied to exclude evidence that was obtained as a result of a constitutional violation. Later, in *Miranda* v. *Arizona*, 384 US 436 (1966), evidence was declared to be admissible only if the suspect was informed of certain rights: the right to remain silent; that anything he says can be used against him in court; that he has a right to consult with a lawyer and to have him present during interrogation and that if he cannot afford a lawyer, one will be provided. The rights may be waived.

exclusion clause see EXEMPTION CLAUSE.

exclusion order an order shutting out. **1.** it is used sometimes to describe orders keeping named persons out of the UK.

2. in English law, the court has the power to order the exclusion of either spouse from the MATRIMONIAL HOME if it appears to the court that the making of the order is necessary for the protection of the applicant or of any child of the family from any conduct or threatened conduct or reasonably apprehended conduct of the other spouse that is or would be injurious to the physical or mental health of the applicant or child.

In Scots family law, part of the regime established to protect the victims of domestic violence in relation to the occupation of a matrimonial home. The court can exclude on an interim or permanent basis a violent spouse, regardless of whether the person owns the house or is the tenant. The court will do so if it is necessary for the protection of the applicant or any child of the family as a result of any conduct or threatened or reasonably apprehended conduct of the other spouse that is or would be injurious to the physical or mental health of the applicant or child.

3. see EXCLUSION.

execution completion or satisfaction.

1. the signing of a DEED or will or other written instrument with the intent that it should be legally valid and effective.

2. the carrying out of a court order such as a sentence of death.

3. performance of a CONTRACT.

executor a person nominated in a WILL by the TESTATOR to ingather the estate, pay all debts enforceable against the deceased and, after payment of any INHERITANCE TAX due and of the costs of the administration, to distribute the estate according to the terms of the will.

executor-creditor in Scots law, a creditor who has constituted his debt during the lifetime of a person can petition the court to be appointed his EXECUTOR if no executor has been appointed to whom he can submit his claim. He need only obtain CONFIRMATION to enough of the estate to allow him to pay his debt.

executor-dative in the Scots law of succession, a person appointed by the court to administer the succession to an estate. It is an administrative office but is often carried through by a relative. See EXECUTOR, CONFIRMATION.

executory remaining to be done.

exemplary damages see DAMAGES.

exemption clause a term in a CONTRACT that seeks to exempt or excuse a party from his liability either under the contract to be performed or some other obligation. The clause must truly be part of the contract, and the court will, in the absence of clear ACCEPTANCE, ask whether it was reasonable to say that it has been included providing a control of sorts over clause included on tickets by reference. It must be in words that could encompass the liability sought to be included. If the interpretation is ambiguous, it will be construed under reference to the CONTRA PROFERENTEM rule. Such clauses are now regulated by the law on UNFAIR CONTRACT TERMS.

ex facie 'on the face of it'.

ex gratia 'as a favour' (and without legal obligations). However, once it is agreed that such a sum should be paid, a legal obligation may come into effect: *Edwards* v. *Skyways Ltd* [1964] 1 WLR 349.

exhibit something produced to the court or mentioned in an affidavit. For Scotland, see LABEL.

exhumation the disinterring of a corpse.

existing goods in the law of sale of goods, GOODS owned and possessed by the seller. These differ from *future goods*, which are goods to be manufactured or acquired by the seller after the contract is made. Whether goods are existing or future goods is of importance in matters such as the passing of PROPERTY and RISK and whether the bargain relating to them is a contract of sale or an agreement to sell.

ex lege 'by law'.

ex officio 'by virtue of office'.

ex parte 'on behalf of', a phrase used to indicate a hearing where the court is relying on a statement made on behalf of someone rather than after proof. In England and Wales, as a result of the CIVIL PROCEDURE RULES 1998, the phrase now used is 'without notice'.

expert witness in the law of evidence, a witness who is allowed to give opinion evidence as opposed to evidence of his perception. This is the case only if the witness is indeed skilled in some appropriate discipline. An exception to the usual rule of practice whereby witnesses are heard one after the other and do not hear the evidence of the preceding witness is made in relation to competing experts. The term *skilled witness* is favoured in Scotland.

ex post fact 'after the fact'.

expressio unius est exclusio alterius a rule of CONSTRUCTION, applying both to statute and legal writings, that states that one thing having been mentioned the other is excluded. Thus, following this rule, 'no dogs allowed' means that lions are allowed but guide dogs are excluded.

ex propriate motu 'of its own motion', referring to something done by the court without the parties asking, such as an adjournment of a case because of the lateness of the hour.

ex-ship a common form of sale of goods in commerce whereby the price includes the cost of shipping, insurance and freight. The price is payable when the goods go over the rail of the ship. See CIF, F.O.B., FAS.

extortion in English criminal law, the obtaining of a benefit by physical force. See also BLACKMAIL. In Scots law, the crime of using force to obtain money. It matters not that the money is legally due. Wheel-clamping has been held to be a form of extortion: *Black* v. *Carmichael* [1992] SLT 897.

extradition the surrender of a person by one state to another. For extradition to be possible there must be an *extradition treaty* between the UK and the state requiring the surrender. The offence alleged to be committed by the person whose surrender is required must be an offence in the UK as well as in the requesting state; it must be covered by the treaty and be within the list of extraditable offences contained in the Extradition Act 1989, and it must not be of a political nature.

extraordinary general meeting a meeting of the members of a COMPANY that is specially arranged. Such meetings can be convened by the directors whenever they think it proper and in certain circumstances by the members themselves (subject to the conditions contained in Section 368 of the Companies Act 1985, which overrides any regulations of the company). Only special business can be conducted at such meetings.

ex turpi causa non oritur actio 'an action will not arise from a disgraceful basis'. In the modern law the disgraceful element is usually considered in terms of illegality or immorality. The doctrine, once confined to contract, often appears in other areas of the law, in particular TORT. However, as the modern law has created many offences and crimes that involve little or no turpitude, the maxim is seldom applied as a strict bar to action: *Pitts* v. *Hunt* [1991] 1 QB 24; *Weir* v. *Wyper* [1992] SLT 579.

F

facility and circumvention in the Scots law of contract, the doctrine that a weak and facile person who has been taken advantage of and suffered loss can have a contract reduced.

fact an event, occurrence or state of affairs known to have happened; to be distinguished from opinion or law.

facta probantia facts that are relied on but that are not material facts in the sense that even if a party fails to prove them he will still succeed in his claim or defence; *facta probantia* should not be pleaded.

factor 1. a MERCANTILE AGENT. An agent who is in the ordinary course of business entrusted with goods or documents of title representing goods with a view to their sale. A factor has a LIEN over goods entrusted to him; this lien covers any claims he may have against his principal arising out of the AGENCY. Most factors will be mercantile agents (and have the powers of such) for the purposes of the Factors Act 1889. Under this Act, in certain circumstances a factor may pass a good title to goods entrusted to him.

2. an institution to whom a COMPANY assigns its book debts (see FACTORING).

factoring a form of asset financing based on the sale of book debts. Essentially, factoring involves the purchases from suppliers of accounts payable to them by customers to whom they have provided goods or services; such accounts are referred to as 'receivables'. For an example, see *Re Charge Card Services* [1987] Ch. 150.

factor loco tutoris in the family law of Scotland, formerly a person appointed to a pupil without a tutor until a tutor could be appointed. The post vanished with the coming into force of the Age of Legal Capacity (Scotland) Act 1991 and the role is now carried through by a JUDICIAL FACTOR.

Faculty of Advocates an ancient society and independent body, comprising the College of ADVOCATES in Scotland, that is responsible for the conduct of its members and is led by a Dean. It is broadly equivalent to the English Inns of Court. See also BARRISTER.

fair comment see DEFAMATION, ROLLED-UP PLEA.

Fair Employment Commission the body in Northern Ireland created by the Fair Employment (Northern Ireland) Act 1989 to promote equality of opportunity and eliminate unlawful discrimination on the grounds of religious belief or political opinion, and to promote affirmative action to help redress existing imbalances. It has a full-time chairman and eight part-time members, including three trade unionists and three representatives of employers, all of whom are appointed by the Secretary of State for Northern Ireland.

fair hearing a HUMAN RIGHT. See EUROPEAN CONVENTION ON HUMAN RIGHTS.

fair rent a rent fixed under the Rent Acts taking account of all the circumstances (other than personal circumstances) and, in particular, the age, character, locality and state of repair of the dwelling house and, if any furniture is provided for use under the tenancy, to its quantity, quality and condition.

fair sharing see FINANCIAL PROVISION.

fair trial a HUMAN RIGHT or constitutional right to a trial that provides certain practical protections for the citizen. Notable examples are under the US Constitution and the EUROPEAN CONVENTION ON HUMAN RIGHTS. Core concepts involve an impartial judge, effective (and sometimes free) legal representation, a lack of undue delay and freedom from self-incrimination.

fair use see COPYRIGHT.

falsa demonstratio non nocet cum corpore constat 'a false description does not vitiate a document if it is consistent with the thing intended.'

false imprisonment the TORT and CRIME of inflicting bodily restraint not otherwise authorised: *John Lewis & Co v. Tims* [1952] AC 676.

false trade description see TRADE DESCRIPTION.

Family Court of Australia a court established to administer the Family Law Act 1975. Its jurisdiction was widened by an amendment Act in 1977.

fas the abbreviation for 'free alongside', a special type of sale of goods developed by commerce. The buyer pays for the freight, the insurance and export and import duties. The seller bears the cost of delivering the goods to the ship. See CIF, F.O.B., F.O.R.

Fatal Accident Inquiry in Scotland, proceedings, instigated by the PROCURATOR FISCAL before a SHERIFF to determine the cause of death in certain designated circumstances such as accidents at work or deaths in custody. One feature of the hearing is that the evidence given is not admissible in subsequent proceedings so that people are encouraged to tell the truth to prevent further accidents.

father see PARENTAGE.

fault one of the central concepts in the law of TORT or DELICT. A legal system can look at harmful conduct in different ways. It can focus on the interest infringed and declare it a tort to occupy another's property for example. However, this produces results that certainly cause moral problems and thus eventually cause legal problems. So where a person inadvertently infringes another's interest, the law has to decide whether to penalise or not. Generally, the more advanced a legal system, the more it is likely to take this into account. Thus, Roman law achieved this result in the early years of the first millennium and English law began to do so towards the end of the second. In the 19th century especially, the proposition began to be put in reverse, it being said that there would be no liability without fault, fault being necessary but not necessarily sufficient to establish liability. Fault had the benefit of comprising most existing categories of case where the plaintiff deliberately harmed the defendant, but it also allowed cases where the defendant had been careless to be included. Fault became associated with intentional wrongdoing or recklessness, which was its equivalent, and also with certain instances of carelessness. In civilian systems, fault in this sense of exhibiting less than reasonable care would be sufficient to establish a prima facie case but would be subject to limitation in the scope of liability in the basis of the notion of remoteness. English law (and ironically) Scots law took a different course with the decision in *Donoghue* v. *Stevenson* 1932 SC (HL) 31, which established that a lack of care would constitute fault but only where there was a pre-existing duty of care. This duty could be found in PRECEDENT or arise from the relationship between the parties. Fault became much more a technical concept after that, and its moral aspect diminished. An objective approach to some aspects of the investigation into liability was a further blow to any moral approach. Fault in the later part of the 20th century fell out of favour as a mechanism for achieving many of the things that tort or delict did. Exhortation of citizens is better done through penalties inflicted through an efficient criminal justice system backed by an organised police force. The existence of an insurance industry can make it economically efficient to redirect liability in the direction of the person who is most likely to be able to acquire insurance cover at lowest cost, thus ensuring that injured persons seeking compensation are actually compensated without recourse to general taxation or charity. Statutory STRICT LIABILITY is beginning to appear in the interstices of the law so that fault may become a safety net for cases outside strict liability.

fealty fidelity, faithfulness.

federalism a system of government whereby there are at least two levels of government operating simultaneously, exercising autonomous powers. Under such a system the constitution must, and usually does, specify which level of authority has power in which areas and should provide a method of resolving jurisdictional disputes.

The central or senior body is often called the *federal government*, although any name may be used, but there are many names for the political groupings on the next level, e.g. states, provinces, *Länder* or cantons. The precise allocation of responsibilities and powers varies infinitely, but usually the higher-level body deals with matters such as foreign policy and macroeconomics. Depending upon history, the power may have developed to the lower levels or come together in the higher level (when sometimes the word *confederation* is used).

The USA, Canada, Australia, Germany and Switzerland are examples of *federal* arrangements. The UK is not a *federation*, although every so often proposals are made for varying degrees of devolution that might inevitably lead to a federal arrangement. The EUROPEAN UNION is not a federation because the Union institutions are supreme in the (limited) areas over which the MEMBER STATES irrevocably gave them jurisdiction, making the European Union a SUPRANATIONAL body. The COURT OF JUSTICE OF THE EUROPEAN UNION decides points of COMMUNITY LAW applicable in all the member states. In recent years, however, there has been discussion among commentators of the possibility that continued expansion may mean that a federal arrangement would be needed to cope with the diversity of views and cultures at national level. See also CONSTITUTIONAL LAW.

Federal Trade Commission Act a US statute that controls unfair competition and established an administrative agency, the Federal Trade Commission. While the SHERMAN ACT and the CLAYTON ACT are essentially criminal provisions, this provision allows for 'cease and desist' orders stopping a practice and injunctions and associated penalties for contempt of court.

fee in English law an interest in land that was inheritable but the term is now only relevant in the context of the phrase FEE SIMPLE ABSOLUTE IN POSSESSION. In Scots law used to denote the full and unlimited right in capital or land that is otherwise subject to the personal servitude of a LIFE RENT.

fee simple absolute in possession the freehold estate that most closely approximates to absolute OWNERSHIP in English property law.

felo de se in English law a term used to describe someone who has tried to commit suicide – *felonia de se*.

felony a now archaic term of English law for crimes that by STATUTE or by COMMON LAW carried the death sentence and forfeiture on conviction. See MISDEMEANOUR. In some US states this still denotes more serious imprisonable crimes.

feodum see FEE.

ferae naturae 'wild animal'. A distinction between such a beast and an animal *domitae naturae* was important in the common law. For the former there was STRICT LIABILITY, and for the latter there was not, unless an action based on the owner's knowledge of dangerous propensities was successful, such an action being called a *scienter action*. The law is now in the Animals Act 1971. The Scots law is in the Animals (Scotland) Act 1987 and does not use this common law term any longer. See ANIMALS.

ferry see REGALIA MINORA.

feu charter a grant of title from a feudal superior to a vassal. The superior retains the rights and power not given to the inferior. But the *dominium utile* – effective ownership – must be transferred. See FEUDAL SYSTEM.

feudal system the social and economic system operating in England from the 11th century and in Scotland from the 12th century and having as its legal manifestation the holding (rather than OWNERSHIP) of land via a hierarchical system of tenures. In England, the main incidents of feudal TENURE were abolished in 1660 with the Tenures Abolition Act, although theoretically freehold land is still regarded as being held of the Crown. In Scotland, the feudal system still operates although it has been declining in importance since the Land Tenure Reform Act 1974. The Scottish parliament intends to legislate to abolish the feudal system in Scotland. It is still relevant in the Channel Islands.

feu duties under a feudal system such as still exists in Scotland, the money that the vassal had to pay to his superior. By statute, feu duties are disappearing as they now have to be paid off by paying a sum that would produce a similar income on a transfer, this process being known as *redemption*. They are thus not all extinguished, and there is in any event no obligation to redeem an unallocated part of a *cumulo feu* duty, thus in tenement buildings feu duties may still be payable although the present vassal may apply to allocate the duty and, once allocated, redeem it.

fiat 'let it be done'.

fiat justicia ruat coelum 'let justice be done though the heavens fall.'

fiduciary relationship see TRUST.

fieri facias a writ in the prescribed form appropriate to the particular case, expressed in the form of a royal command directing the sheriff of the county in which the judgment debtor's goods are situated to seize in execution such of those goods as are authorised to be seized by law and to sell so much of them as may be sufficient to satisfy the judgment debt. The usual method of enforcement of a money judgment is by way of a *writ of fieri facias*.

filius nullius 'son of no one', a bastard.

finality clause the clause in some statutes that the decision of some delegated authority shall be final. However, the courts have developed ways of examining the decisions, particularly if they do not proceed in accord with law. See *R* v. *Medical Appeal Tribunal* [1957] 1 QB 574.

finance house a financial institution that is not a bank or building society and that provides credit to finance personal or corporate acquisitions of property. Many finance houses specialise in the financing of purchases of consumer goods on hire purchase; others specialise in equipment leasing. Authorisation for lending activities is required under the Banking Act 1987 and, for lending to individuals, under the CONSUMER CREDIT Act 1974.

financial obligations on breakdown of marriage in English family law, the process of distributing a couple's capital and income in a just and equitable way when their marriage ends in DIVORCE. The court has extensive powers to make *financial provision* for the applicant. Under the Matrimonial Causes Act 1973 and the Matrimonial and Family Proceedings Act 1984, it can make *financial provision orders*, including maintenance pending suit; PERIODIC PAYMENT ORDERS and LUMP SUM ORDERS; property adjustment orders – orders selling property. For Scotland, see FINANCIAL PROVISION.

financial provision in Scots family law, the term used for what the court does with money on DIVORCE or decree of nullity. It may involve a PERIODICAL ALLOWANCE but more regularly will involve the payment of a capital sum or the transfer of property or both. The Family Law (Scotland) Act 1985 set out five principles to be followed:

(1) the net value of matrimonial property should be shared fairly;

(2) fair account should be taken of any economic advantage derived by either party from the contributions of the other and of any economic disadvantage suffered by either in the interest of the other party or the family;

(3) any economic burden of caring after divorce for a child of the marriage under 16 should be shared fairly;

(4) a party who has been financially dependent to a substantial degree for financial support from the other party should be awarded such financial provision as is reasonable to adjust this over three years; and

(5) a party liable to suffer severe financial hardship as a result of the divorce be awarded reasonable financial provision over a reasonable period to mitigate that hardship.

These principles depend upon: the deeming of fair sharing, whether shared equally or in accordance with special circumstances, such as the terms of an agreement on ownership or sale; the source of funds if not from the parties' efforts during the marriage; the destruction of the property by the parties; the nature of the property and the ease with which it can be realised; and the cost involved in valuing and disposing of property in connection with the divorce.

Incidental orders can be made to support the foregoing. Orders can be granted but their effect delayed.

Financial Services Authority (FSA) see FINANCIAL SERVICES LAW.

financial services law the law applying to financial services such as investments and pensions. This area was thoroughly overhauled by the Financial Services Act 1986, passed to implement the recommendations of the Gower Report on Investor Protection. The regime put in place by that Act operated through the Securities and Investments Board (SIB), which authorised bodies to act as regulators. The SIB has now been replaced by the Financial Services Authority (FSA), created by the Financial Services and Markets Act 2000. This authority takes over the regulatory functions previously divided between a wide range of other organisations. For example, it will be responsible for the regulation of the Lloyds Insurance market, building societies and banks as well as companies in the investment industry. It has four objectives under the Financial Services and Markets Act 2000: maintaining market confidence; promoting public understanding of the financial system; the protection of consumers; and fighting financial crime. The range of this newly organised law is wider than often thought: it has been held that authorisation is required to market and sell a computer package that gave advice on trading equity options: In *Re Market Wizard Systems (UK) Ltd* 1998 TLR 495.

fine a monetary penalty imposed in criminal matters. It may be accepted in instalments, and in some cases, essentially based on means, the court may remit (extinguish) the fine. In the UK there are maximum levels of fines laid down for certain offences. Some levels are changed every so often in accord with the change in the value of money. There are statutory equivalent periods of imprisonment laid down for failure to pay fines.

firearm a barrelled weapon of any description from which any shot, bullet or other missile can be discharged. It includes any prohibited weapon, whether a lethal weapon or not. A certificate must be obtained to buy or possess a firearm. There are rules covering imitation firearms.

fire-raising in Scots criminal law, the crime of setting a fire with the intention so to do or with a high degree of recklessness.

firm name the name under which the partners carry on the business of the firm.

first instance first court hearing. Saying that something happened at first instance refers to the court first hearing a case. Courts may be described as being *courts of first instance* if they hear cases as opposed to appeals. See APPEAL, COURT OF FIRST INSTANCE.

First Lord of the Treasury see PRIME MINISTER.

First Minister the leader of the Scottish Executive in the SCOTTISH PARLIAMENT and of the leader of the executive in the Northern Ireland Assembly. See also GOOD FRIDAY AGREEMENT.

first reading see ACT OF PARLIAMENT.

First Secretary the leader of the NATIONAL ASSEMBLY FOR WALES.

fisheries policy in the law of the EUROPEAN COMMUNITIES, the policy regulating fishing. A recent initiative, 'Blue Europe', provides for equality of access to resources in the Community outside a 12-mile limit, a conservation regime, market support, and modernisation and development. One of the key concepts is the *total allowable catch,* or TAC. It is of the essence of the conservation measures and attempts to ensure that over-fishing does not occur. It does so by specifying fishing times and mesh sizes. There is an inspection force.

fishing speculative. In referring to INTERROGATORIES in England, or DILIGENCE in Scotland, it means that the purpose of obtaining the powers is not known; rather it is hoped that once granted something will turn up. Courts generally do not grant such orders.

fitness for purpose, implied term see QUALITY IMPLIED TERM.

fixed charge see CHARGE.

fixed penalty notice a notice that offers the alleged offender the opportunity to pay a FINE, in which case the matter is not prosecuted, thereby sparing the offender a conviction and saving time and expense. The alleged offender has the option to proceed to refuse and be charged with the offence.

fixed security a security over specific property of the company rather than over the whole assets and undertaking of the company.

fixed sum credit any facility not being a running account facility, whereby the debtor is enabled to receive credit, whether in one amount or in instalments.

fixtures the doctrine by which most legal systems (including those of England and Scotland) accept that eventually moveable property can become real or heritable by affixing the moveable thing to the realty or heritage. In Roman law, in civilian jurisdictions including Scotland, reference is often made to the maxim *inaedificatum solo, solo cedit*: 'that which is attached to the land accrues to the land.' Unfortunately, the precise rules differ from system to system and from occasion to occasion, thus what is fixed between heir and estate is not always the same as between buyer and seller or between landlord and tenant. Thus, to sell the land is to sell the buildings on it. To sell a shop is to sell the shelves on the wall. In difficult cases, two main factors are often considered:

(1) the ease of movement; thus, even heavy machinery that is not bolted to the ground may be a fixture;

(2) the damage done by removal, often making easily moveable things that are bolted to walls fixtures.

flagrante delicto see IN FLAGRANTE DELICTO.

floating charge a security created by a COMPANY by DEBENTURE (in Scotland, a floating charge) over its whole assets and undertaking for the time being. The point of this form of security is that the company may continue to conduct its business, disposing of some assets and acquiring others without having to obtain the consent of the debenture holders for each disposal. In the event of a default, the charge crystallises and becomes fixed and enforceable over the assets held at that time.

floodgates a term referring to the metaphor of the floodgates of litigation, the notion that there is potentially an ocean of potential litigants with potential claims who would, if the floodgates were opened, engulf the courts and inundate the courts of justice. It is often referred to by citing a dictum of Cardozo in *Ultrameres Corporation* v. *Touche* [1931] 225 NY 170 as a fear of creating 'liability in an indeterminate amount for an indeterminate time to an indeterminate class'. It is a legitimate worry, but Lord Fraser's suggestion in *McLoughlin* v. *O'Brian* [1983] 1 AC 410 that one should only worry about the floodgates if the instant case clearly indicates a realistic possibility of a flood of cases and otherwise deal with it, has not been rejected. On the other hand, the decisions in *Murphy* v. *Brentwood* [1990] 3 WLR 414 and *Alcock* v. *Chief Constable* [1992] 1 AC 310 show that the fear is still one to be considered. See ECONOMIC LOSS, NERVOUS SHOCK.

flotsam floating goods from a shipwreck. See JETSAM, LAGAN.

flying picket see PICKETING.

f.o.b. abbreviation for 'free on board', a special type of sale of goods developed by commerce. The buyer insures for the journey as well as paying for the goods and for the freight. The seller pays the cost of having the goods put on the ship. See CIF, FAS, F.O.R.

f.o.r. abbreviation for 'free on rail', a special type of sale of goods developed by commerce. The buyer pays insurance and freight as well as for the goods. The seller must deliver the goods to the railyard. See CIF, FAS, F.O.B.

forbidden degrees in Scots family law certain persons are not allowed to marry because of their relationship. Most relations by CONSANGUINITY are prohibited, as are a number of AFFINITY. Former spouses are affected, as are relations by adoption. ILLEGITIMACY is irrelevant, and relations of the half blood are treated the same as those of the full blood. In cases of affinity, if it is not possible to petition the court for permission to marry in certain restricted circumstances, it is possible to apply for a private Act of Parliament.

force and fear in the law of CONTRACT in Scotland, the term used for cases of EXTORTION where a party contracts as a result of some force. The *fear* aspect may reflect the need for the party to have made the choice of entering the contract instead of meeting the *force* as a result of a serious threat and preventing contracts being set aside because of vain or foolish fear: see *Hislop* v. *Dickson Motors (Forres) Ltd* 1978 SLT (Notes) 73.

force majeure an event that no human foresight could anticipate or which, if anticipated, is too strong to be controlled.

foreclosure the right to take mortgaged property in satisfaction of the amount due. Where a mortgagor has defaulted on his obligations under the terms of the MORTGAGE, the mortgagee has a number of powers available to him to protect his investment. One of these is the power to *foreclose*. Foreclosure can be effected only by an order of the court that involves, first, the granting of an order of foreclosure nisi, which effectively gives the mortgagor six months' grace within which to raise the sums due; if the mortgagor has failed to do this, the foreclosure becomes absolute, whereupon the rights of the mortgagor in the property cease and become vested in the mortgagee.

foreign bill any BILL OF EXCHANGE other than an inland bill (that is, a bill that is both drawn and payable in the British Isles or one that is drawn in the British Isles upon someone resident there). Unless the contrary appears on its face, the holder may treat a bill as an inland bill. The distinction is relevant to the steps to be taken when a bill has been dishonoured.

foreign law the law of any jurisdiction having a different system of law from that applied by the court considering the issue. In English law what is the foreign law in any given case is a matter of fact to be proved by the evidence of expert witnesses.

foreign principal a person outside the UK instructing an agent (see AGENCY) within the UK. It used to be the case that where an agent acting for a foreign principal entered into a contract with a third party, there was a strong presumption that there was no privity between the foreign principal and the third party, with the consequence that the agent might be made personally liable on the contract. This presumption has now weakened, to the extent that the existence of a foreign principal is regarded as one factor only to be taken into account in construing the parties' agreement.

forensic to do with courts. Thus a barrister has *forensic skills*, and *forensic medicine* is the application of medicine to legal issues in courts.

foreshore see REGALIA MINORA.

forestalling the now obsolete crime of buying from merchants on the way to market to sell at a better price at the market. English statutory offences were abolished in 1772, but common law equivalents were occasionally revived. The practice was outlawed in Scotland by Acts of 1535, 1540 and 1592. Sometimes also known as *engrossing,* which technically refers to the buying of dead victuals for hoarding or profiteering. An ancient crime in English law. See REGRATING.

forestry see REGALIA MINORA.

forfeiture the process by which the holder of a superior interest in property puts an end to an inferior interest in that property, usually as a result of the failure of the holder of that inferior interest to fulfil some obligation owed to the holder of the superior interest. Thus, in many leases, covenants will detail the obligations owed by the tenant to the landlord; a breach of any of these covenants will normally trigger a right on the part of the landlord to forfeit the tenant's lease. See also CONFISCATION.

forgery an offence in English law of making a false instrument so that it may be accepted as genuine: Forgery and Counterfeiting Act 1981.

Where a signature on a BILL OF EXCHANGE has been forged or placed on the bill without the authority of the person whose signature it purports to be, such signature is wholly inoperative, so that no right to retain the bill or to give a discharge therefor or to enforce payment against any party to the bill can be acquired through or under the signature unless the party against whom it is sought to retain or enforce payment is precluded from setting up the forgery or want of authority as a defence.

In the criminal law of Scotland, it is not in itself a crime. See UTTERING.

forisfamiliated 1. in English law the term was used to describe a son provided for in his father's lifetime instead of inheriting after his death.

2. in Scots law the word has a more special connotation, that of a child who has left the family home, married or set up an independent household. This had, and may still have, implications for the child's capacity: see Age of Legal Capacity (Scotland) Act 1991.

forum a court or, more specifically, the system that has jurisdiction. See FORUM NON CONVENIENS.

forum non conveniens in private international law, the doctrine that allows a court to decline its own jurisdiction because there is another jurisdiction that can more conveniently try the case.

Foss v. Harbottle, rule in the rule of law that the proper plaintiff in an action in respect of a wrong done to a COMPANY is the company itself rather than individual shareholders; as such, no individual can bring an action where the alleged wrong is a transaction that may be ratified and as such made binding on the company by its members.

foster parents persons who look after a child who is not theirs either by blood or by ADOPTION. The normal procedure involves local authorities who, under statutory powers, assume parental rights over children orphaned, abandoned, neglected or abused by parents and delegate the actual care of the child to persons whom they pay to look after it. Foster parents have no legal rights over the child they foster: Children Act 1989.

Four Courts court buildings situated by the River Liffey in Dublin, the present form of which were the work of James Gandon. They were opened in 1796 and seriously damaged in 1922 during the Civil War when many documents, some dating back to the 13th century, were destroyed. The name derives from the fact that the building originally housed the four courts of King's Bench, Exchequer Chamber, Common Pleas and Equity. The site has been extended and now houses a range of courts, including the Supreme Court, the High Court and a District Court as well as court offices and the LAW LIBRARY.

Four Freedoms see COMMON MARKET, FREEDOM OF ESTABLISHMENT, FREE MOVEMENT OF CAPITAL, FREE MOVEMENT OF GOODS, FREE MOVEMENT OF PERSONS.

franchise 1. a business arrangement whereby a trader allows another to use his business expertise and to utilise the goodwill of the business and perhaps share its intellectual property in return for fees and commissions or a single price. The legal implications and documentation differ depending on the kind of franchise, but the arrangement produces money only because of the web of contractual documentation. The self-employed businessman who is the *franchisee* pays more than the usual start-up costs but is likely to be able to succeed if the franchise is one that has proven to be successful. The franchisee does not require to have so many business skills as the usual start-up or first-time entrepreneur. **2.** in England the LEGAL AID Board introduced a system of approving certain firms to offer legal aid, said to be *franchised*. The Board benefits from being able to impose efficiency controls, as does the lawyer by having greater flexibility over the granting of legal aid and better payment terms. It is not mandatory. Thus, solicitors can still offer legal aid even if they do not hold a franchise.

fraud in criminal law, the achievement of a practical result by false pretence. Nondisclosure, where a duty to disclose exists, may be sufficient. There is no need to make pecuniary profit out of the pretence – a definite practical result is sufficient.

In Scotland, the DELICT of making a false representation of fact without belief in its truth, intending that the person to whom it is made should act in reliance thereon, causing a consequent loss. Essentially very similar to the English tort of DECEIT.

fraudulent preference a term formerly used in Scots insolvency law to describe a payment by a debtor to a favoured creditor, now replaced by the concept of UNFAIR PREFERENCE.

fraudulent trading the carrying on of business by a company for a fraudulent purpose or in defraud of creditors. If in the course of the winding up of a company it appears that a company as been so trading, the court, on the application of the liquidator, may declare that any persons who were knowingly party to such trading are to be liable to make such contributions to the company's assets as the court may think proper. See Companies Act 1985 and Insolvency Act 1986. See also *R* v. *Cox & Hedges* [1982] 75 Cr. App. Rep. 291.

free acceptance in the law of RESTITUTION, **1.** the name given by the commentators to the argument against subjective devaluation that the defender, although he does not consider the alleged value actually to be valuable, nonetheless, having the opportunity to refuse it, accepted it.
2. an argument against the defence that a given enrichment is not unjust, to the effect that it is unjust that the defender should be allowed to refrain from making restitution because he, having the opportunity to reject the enrichment, accepted it. The concept appears in the works of the leading commentators, but its scope and effect and, indeed, existence are often disputed.

freedom of assembly see ASSEMBLY.

freedom of establishment under the law of the EUROPEAN UNION a person has the right to continue his vocation or profession in another MEMBER STATE as a self-employed person rather than as a worker. He may be able to provide services there, but that falls under the FREE MOVEMENT OF SERVICES. The rules apply to firms and companies as well as individuals. The greatest difficulty is with the liberal professions, and great activity has gone into the issues of mutual recognition of diplomas: see *Reyners* v. *Belgium* [1974] ECR 631.

freehold originally an estate of free tenure. Nowadays the term is used to denote a legal estate in FEE SIMPLE ABSOLUTE IN POSSESSION, the most complete form of OWNERSHIP of land.

freeing for adoption see ADOPTION.

free movement of capital insofar as is necessary to ensure the functioning of the COMMON MARKET, the law of the EUROPEAN UNION compels the MEMBER STATES to allow capital of residents to move freely regardless of discrimination based on nationality or the place of investment of the capital. This freedom is currently being extended by DIRECTIVE and REGULATION to an extent that it is hoped that one day there will exist a European Financial Area.

free movement of goods in the law of the EUROPEAN COMMUNITIES, one body of rules designed to assist in the establishment of a COMMON MARKET. For a market to operate efficiently, there must be no barriers to the movement of goods. The legal system of the community seeks to achieve this in two ways:

(1) the establishment of a CUSTOMS UNION, and

(2) the elimination of QUANTITATIVE RESTRICTIONS and MEASURES, having EQUIVALENT EFFECT, that are sometimes called *technical barriers*.

See also GOODS.

free movement of payments under the law of the EUROPEAN COMMUNITIES, its MEMBER STATES must allow payment from a debtor in one member state to a creditor residing in another. However, it relates only to payments connected with the FREE MOVEMENT OF GOODS, FREE MOVEMENT OF SERVICES or FREE MOVEMENT OF CAPITAL. These rules have DIRECT EFFECT.

free movement of persons the right of persons to move freely within the EUROPEAN COMMUNITIES. One of the essential components of the COMMON MARKET of the European Communities. The rules on this topic are considered by the COURT OF JUSTICE OF THE EUROPEAN UNION to be of fundamental importance. The principle of non-DISCRIMINATION is fundamental to the treaties. The free movement rules have DIRECT EFFECT. There is a distinction made in the rules between workers who are employed and earn a wage and non-wage earners such as tradesmen and professionals. Wage earners' freedom is protected by rules on non-discrimination on ground of nationality. Non-wage earners are protected by provisions on FREEDOM OF ESTABLISHMENT and the right to provide services. Thus, a typist should be able to go and work in France without hindrance and a lawyer should be able to represent his client before the courts in Germany. Workers have the right to accept job offers and also have the right to free movement if they seriously want to work as an employed person. The rules protect certain part-time workers. The worker may stay in another MEMBER STATE and may take his family with him. Indeed, extensive rights are given to the worker's family to give substance to the worker's right to move. A worker may stay after having been employed. Rules have been laid down to make sure that workers do not lose social security rights. This is done by way of making sure that time periods can be fulfilled regardless of which state the worker was in: see *De Moor* v. *Caisse de Pension* [1967] ECR 197. Free movement of workers can be restricted on the basis of public policy, public security or public health (as defined by the community): see *Van Duyn* v. *Home Office* [1974] ECR 1337; *Adoui and Cornuaille* v. *Belgium* [1982] ECR 1665; *Sotgiu* v. *Deutsche Bundespost* [1974] ECR 153.

As far as non-wage earners are concerned, the rules are found under FREEDOM OF ESTABLISHMENT and under FREE MOVEMENT OF SERVICES.

free movement of services in the law of the EUROPEAN UNION these rules are provided to allow persons to provide services to persons who are in another MEMBER STATE, for example, where a Mancunian lawyer wants to advise a client in Spain. There is a right to receive services as much as to render them. The regime governs economic activities for remuneration. The right to set up business in Spain to advise the client more conveniently would be dealt with under FREEDOM OF ESTABLISHMENT. The rules apply to firms and companies as well as individuals. See *Van Binsbergen* v. *Bedrijfsvereniging Metaalnijverheid* [1974] ECR 1299.

freight the amount payable by a charterer or shipper to a shipowner for the letting of the ship or space therein for the CARRIAGE OF GOODS BY SEA.

Advance freight is payable to a shipowner on the signing of a BILL OF LADING or on shipment instead of on delivery of the goods; such freight is not normally returnable in the event of the ship or the goods being lost before the start of the voyage.

frustration the doctrine in the law of CONTRACT that allows certain events to release both parties from future performance of their contractual obligations. The events must relate to the frustration of the common object of the contract. 'Frustration of a contract takes place where there supervenes an event (without default of either party and for which the contract makes no sufficient provision) which so significantly changes the nature (not merely the expense or the onerousness) of the outstanding contractual rights and/or obligations from what the parties could have reasonably contemplated at the time of its execution that it would be unjust to hold them to the literal sense of its stipulations in the new circumstances; in such case, the law declares both parties to be discharged from further performance.' *National Carriers Ltd* v. *Panalpina (Northern) Ltd* [1981] AC 675. Three examples are:

(1) impossibility of performance, whether by the accidental burning of a building or the illness of a singer: *Taylor* v. *Caldwell* [1863] 3 B&S 826;

(2) the so-called 'coronation cases', where persons entered contracts expecting that they would see the coronation of the king, for example, from a hotel window. Such contracts were held to have been frustrated as the cancellation of the coronation was a cessation of things going to the root of and essential to the contract: *Krell* v. *Henry* [1903] 2 KB 740. The courts, however, did not extend this to cases where this fundamental or essential purpose was not so obvious from the contract: *Herne Bay Steamboat Co.* v. *Hutton* [1903] 2 KB 683;

(3) supervening illegality will frustrate the contract: *Fibrosa Spolka Akeyjina* v. *Fairbairn, Lawson, Combe, Barbour Ltd* [1943] AC 32.

In England, to regulate the difficulties involved in some situations English law has been developed by the Law Reform (Frustrated Contracts) Act 1943. The Act provides among other things:

(a) money due but not paid before frustration ceases to be payable and money paid has to be repaid;

(b) a person to whom a prepayment has been made can be allowed a sum in respect of his expenses by the court. The sum must not exceed the prepayment nor the amount actually expended.

The Act even permits a sum in respect of valuable benefits in kind rendered before the frustrating event to be recovered.

Scots law achieved and achieves similar results at common law through its much more developed law of UNJUST ENRICHMENT:

Cantiere San Rocco v. *Clyde Shipbuilding & Engineering Co.* 1923 SC (HL) 24.

fuel, feal and divot in Scots property law, the SERVITUDE right to go on to another's land and cut peat for fuel or the making of fences.

functus officio 'of no further legal effect', so it can be said that after sentencing the criminal the court is *functus*.

fundamental law some provision upon which the rest or a part of the legal system is based and which accordingly either cannot be changed or can be changed only by following special provisions. An example is the constitution of the USA.

funds flow statement a financial statement that enlarges on the traditional PROFIT AND LOSS account by identifying funds coming into a company and showing how it has deployed those resources.

funerator a person who arranges the funeral of another. Such a one may, in the absence of a better qualified candidate, be appointed as EXECUTOR DATIVE in Scotland.

fungibles goods that are dealt with in stacks, piles, quantities or lengths.

furthcoming in the Scots law of DILIGENCE or legal enforcement, the process that actually has property subject to an ARRESTMENT made over to the party who sued.

future goods see EXISTING GOODS.

G

game see POACHING.

Garda Siochana the police service in the Republic of Ireland.

garden leave an informal expression to denote the practice of employers in terminating contracts to compel the employee not to work during his notice and while being paid. Attempts have recently been made to bring such clauses under the same controls as restrictive covenants: *William Hill* v. *Tucker* [1998] TLR 230.

garnishee proceedings a process of enforcing a money judgment by the seizure or ATTACHMENT of debts due or accruing to the judgment debtor that form part of his property available in EXECUTION. As such, it is a species of execution upon debts, for which the ordinary methods of execution are unavailable. As with FORECLOSURE, garnishee orders are in two stages, namely, an order nisi followed by an order absolute.

GATT abbreviation for General Agreement on Tariffs and Trade, an international agreement concluded in 1947 that is basically oriented towards free trade. It is still current in a renegotiated form and is a major parameter of international trade. It is organised by the World Trade Organisation.

Gazette the official government publication that lists certain statutory notices such as those relating to insolvency. There are three – the London, Edinburgh and Belfast Gazettes. Its most common use is as a source of detecting firms that are potentially or actually insolvent.

General Agreement on Tariffs and Trade see GATT.

general average that part of the law merchant that provides that a loss incurred to save a vessel or cargo is distributed between all those benefiting thereby as parties to the maritime adventure. This encourages the jettisoning of cargo for the safety of all. It derives from the ancient *lex rhodia de jactu*, recorded as being adopted by Roman law in the Digest of Justinian (see CORPUS JURIS CIVILIS). Its recognition in English law may go as far back as 1285, and it is recognised by Scots law. Differences in application of the principle by the maritime nations of the world are reconciled in the YORK-ANTWERP RULES.

general damages in English law, that damage that is assumed to flow from torts actionable *per se*, like loss of reputation in a libel action, and that thus need not be specially pled. This is in opposition to *special damage*, which is damage that requires to be proved where it is essential to the tort, as in NEGLIGENCE actions. There is a secondary sense of using these two terms. *Special damages* can mean 'specific easily identified and specified losses', and *general damages*, 'an unquantified sum in respect of imponderables'.

General Medical Council (GMC) the UK body that regulates doctors. It advertises itself as 'protecting patients and guiding doctors', but doctors will realise that this guidance involves striking them off and ending their professional careers. At present there are 54 doctors elected by the doctors on the register; 25 members of the public nominated by the PRIVY COUNCIL; 25 doctors appointed by educational bodies – the universities, medical royal colleges and faculties.

The Privy Council nominees are not medically qualified. They are supposed to represent the public interest. It has four main statutory functions: keeping the register of qualified medical practitioners; fostering good medical practice; promoting high standards of education; and prosecuting and punishing rogue doctors. It is its prosecution function that is best known. Cases are heard, with the public admitted to most parts, in London. Curiously, the procedures even for Scots doctors are those of English law. There is an appeal to the Privy Council.

general meeting a meeting of the members of a COMPANY. A company exercises control and does such acts as are reserved to it by the votes of the majority at general meetings. The meetings have to be properly convened with due notice having been given. If the articles provide for a quorum, that requirement has to be met before business can be conducted. See ANNUAL GENERAL MEETING.

general partner any partner in a PARTNERSHIP other than a limited partner.

general words words in a conveyance used to describe rights and benefits incidental to the land; such express words are no longer necessary since such rights and benefits now pass under Section 62 of the Law of Property Act 1925.

Geneva Convention an international convention adopted in Geneva. There have been a number of these. The one most likely to be encountered by the general public is that on treatment of prisoners of war. As a convention it is part of international law. Other notable conventions carrying the Geneva name are those on Law of the Sea 1958 and the 1951 Law Relating to the Status of Refugees.

genocide the crime of trying to destroy a nation, ethnic, racial or religious group, committed if there has been killing or serious injury to members of the group with intent: Convention on the Prevention and Punishment of the Crime of Genocide; Genocide Act 1968. It is also committed by forcibly transferring children.

Gentleman Usher of the Black Rod see PARLIAMENT.

gentleman's agreement an agreement not intended to be legally enforceable will not be enforced if the court accepts that it is such.

genus numquam perit see RISK.

get a Jewish religious DIVORCE without which partners are not free to be properly married within the faith. It is organised through the BETH DIN. All that is required is to show that the parties consent to divorce. In the UK, however, divorce does not require consent, so a conflict can arise where a party has a civil divorce but not a religious divorce. The present authorities are taking steps to pressurise parties who do not agree to a religious divorce after a civil divorce to consent. The Beth Din does not grant a decree; it merely supervises the writing of the *get*, the deed recording the dissolution.

gift a voluntary and gratuitous transfer of property, real or personal, heritable or moveable, made with the intention of transferring OWNERSHIP from the owner to the donee. The instrument of transfer is determined by the nature of the property (i.e. a CHATTEL can be transferred by mere DELIVERY; unregistered land in England and Wales requires a DEED; registered land requires an executed land transfer plus registration).

For the purposes of INHERITANCE TAX, a gift, in relation to any transfer of value, is the benefit of any disposition or rule of law by which, on the making of the transfer, any property becomes the property of any person or applicable for any purpose (Inheritance Tax Act, Section 421).

glebe land belonging to the Church.

GMC abbreviation for GENERAL MEDICAL COUNCIL.

going-concern concept in preparing the accounts of a business it is always assumed that the business will continue to operate indefinitely. Accordingly, in accounts prepared on a *going-concern basis*, it is unnecessary to show the current sale value of fixed assets, but rather it is permissible to enter them at their historical cost. Only if the business is to be sold or closed down is the current cost figure required.

golden formulae a non-technical but convenient expression to describe the conditions required for a trade union to benefit from the limited immunities available to it under the Trade Union and Labour Relations (Consolidation) Act 1992 (as often amended). There must first be a trade dispute that relates wholly or mainly to matters such as terms and conditions of employment, sacking or suspension of workers, allocation of work, discipline, membership of a union, facilities for union officials or negotiating regime. The acts in question must be in contemplation of *furtherance* of the dispute. The House of Lords has decided that furtherance is to be measured against the state of mind of the person complained against and whether or not he had an honest belief in furthering a dispute: *Dupont Steels* v. *Sirs* [1980] ICR 161.

golden rule the rule of construction that directs the person construing a provision, usually a statute, to read it according to the ordinary sense of the words unless, however, such a reading produces some illogicality or inconsistency. If this happens then it is permissible to read it so that the illogicality is removed but no further. See STATUTORY INTERPRETATION.

good faith a requirement in the law, importing an absence of bad faith more than anything, that can be treated as equivalent to 'honestly and decently'. It is imbedded in civilian legal systems but is of lesser significance in the Anglo-American system.

Good Friday Agreement the agreement between the British and Irish governments and the political parties in Northern Ireland reached on 10 April 1998 in Belfast following lengthy talks. The purpose of the agreement is to deal with relations between the two communities in Northern Ireland; relations between the two parts of Ireland; and between Ireland north and south and the other parts of the British Isles. All parties undertook to renounce violence and to use their influence to ensure that weapons were decommissioned. A 108-member Northern Ireland Assembly was to be created, as well as a North-South Council to discuss matters of mutual interest to Northern Ireland and the Irish Republic and a British-Irish Council that would be a forum for all the jurisdictions in the British Isles. The Irish government undertook to remove the clauses in its Constitution that claimed jurisdiction over Northern Ireland, and all parties agreed that the constitutional status of Northern Ireland could be changed only by the consent of a majority of the people of Northern Ireland. It replaced the 1985 ANGLO-IRISH AGREEMENT.

good root a deed more than 15 years old that effected a transaction for valuable consideration and that casts no doubt on the title of the seller. See ABSTRACT OF TITLE.

goods 1. for the purposes of the Sales of Goods Act 1979, 'goods' include 'emblements, industrial growing crops and things attached or forming part of the land that are agreed to be severed before sale or under the contract of sale'. For the purposes of the law of Scotland, 'goods' are defined by the Act as all corporeal movables. Specifically excluded, however, is money – unless it is bought as a curiosity, as in the case of gold Jubilee pieces: *Moss* v. *Hancock* [1899] 2 QB 111.
2. in the law of the EUROPEAN UNION the word has a special definition in relation to the operation of the CUSTOMS UNION and in particular in the provisions relating to the FREE MOVEMENT OF GOODS. It covers industrial and agricultural products regardless of whether they come from MEMBER STATES or are imported from other states, and it is this inclusion of imports that makes a customs union different and more substantial than a free trade area. The important focus is upon products that can be valued in money that can be the subject of a commercial transaction: *Commission* v. *Italy* [1968] ECR 2247. See also PRODUCT.

goodwill the advantage or benefit that is acquired by the business beyond the mere value of its capital stock or property in consequence of the patronage it receives from its customers. For example, it is usual for a business to be sold on the basis of £x for the stock and £y for the goodwill. The amount by which the value of the business as a whole exceeds the assets minus the value of the company's liabilities: Companies Act 1985. In another sense, it is 'the probability that the old customers will resort to the old place', *Crutwell* v. *Lye*, 17 Ves. 335.

Governor-General the representative of the Crown in Commonwealth countries.

grand larceny a more serious version of the crime of LARCENY.

grant the creation of an interest in property and its vesting in a person (the *grantee*). In modern conditions, the word 'grant' denotes the creation of an inferior interest out of an interest retained by the *grantor*, e.g. the grant of a lease of land by the person holding the freehold.

gratuitous alienation giving things away before insolvency is struck at by rules against gratuitous alienations and property can be recovered for the estate. Naturally, if a full and fair price is paid, the estate is no worse off and the transaction is not affected on this ground.

gratuitous contract a CONTRACT where one side is not onerous. Properly speaking, this cannot cover a unilateral promise, for the nature of contract is that it is bilateral. Accordingly, a *bilateral gratuitous contract* is one where there is merely acceptance of the agreement by one of the parties. In English law it would likely be treated as outside the law of contract because of the need for CONSIDERATION. In Scotland it is valid and can be proved by any evidence unless subject to REQUIREMENTS OF WRITING.

Gray's Inn see BARRISTER.

gross negligence see NEGLIGENCE.

ground annual in Scotland, and prior to 1974, a form of pecuniary real burden. A contract of ground annual was the sale of land to be paid for by annual payments in perpetuity. Apart from the burden in the transfer, the contract provides for a reconveyance in security, allowing the creditor or his successors very powerful remedies on failure to pay. Only ground annuals created before the abolition remain valid, and they cannot be varied to increase the liability.

ground rent rent reserved under a lease, usually for a long term of years, by lessor and payable by whomsoever will be the lessee for the time being; the lessee may assign his terms subject to the ground rent. Ground rent is often reserved in respect of building leases under which the lessee will erect buildings that, at the termination of the lease, will become, together with the land, the property of the lessor.

group relief the set of rules permitting companies within the same group certain flexibility that would not be allowed if the group relationship did not exist. Thus, for example, a trading loss incurred by one group member may be set against profits of another member of the same group.

grundnorm see KELSINIAN JURISPRUDENCE.

guarantee a collateral promise to answer for the debt or obligation of another. A guarantee is a secondary obligation, becoming operative only where the principal debtor is in DEFAULT; because it is a secondary obligation, should the primary obligation be unlawful or invalid or unenforceable, the guarantor or SURETY cannot be compelled to make payment under the guarantee. A guarantee should be distinguished from an INDEMNITY, which is a primary obligation to compensate the loss of another; in the latter case the unenforceability of the principal debt will not render the indemnity unenforceable.

In Scotland, the same relationship is regulated by the institution of *caution* (pronounced 'cayshun'). *Proper caution* is the term used where the cautioner is expressly bound as guarantor to the creditor. The term *improper caution* is used when the cautioner is bound as a co-obligant with the principal debtor jointly and severally to the creditor.

The term is used colloquially in the UK for a statement by a manufacturer of goods that it will undertake some responsibility such as repair or replacement.

guardian a person who looks after the interests of an infant and is entitled to exercise parental rights over it and who is required to discharge parental responsibilities in respect of it. While still alive, parents are a CHILD's natural guardians; they may appoint guardians to look after the child after their deaths.

guardian ad litem the now obsolete term for a person appointed by the court to represent a minor in proceedings affecting his interests. See now LITIGATION FRIEND.

guillotine see ACT OF PARLIAMENT.

guilty the plea by an accused that he accepts that he committed the offence charged or the finding to that effect by a court or jury.

habeas corpus 'that you have the body', a writ older than MAGNA CARTA, originating from an order to bring a person before a court and developed by legislation in the 17th century. It has become one of the main protections of the subject from wrongful detention. It is granted as of right but may be refused if there is another remedy. It lies against the Crown. It does not extend to the colonies and does not extend to Scotland. Once discharged under habeas corpus, a person cannot be again detained or committed for the same offence.

habendum the part of a deed that demarcates the estate granted or conveyed.

habit and repute see COHABITATION (WITH HABIT AND REPUTE).

habitat the place where something or someone lives, in ENVIRONMENTAL LAW the focus of EUROPEAN UNION and UK legislation affecting conduct in relation to certain habitats. The EU Habitats DIRECTIVE requires the establishment of a series of high-quality Special Areas of Conservation (SACs) across Europe that will make a significant contribution to conserving the 169 habitat types and 623 species identified in Annexes I and II of the Directive. The Habitats Directive is implemented in the UK through the Conservation (Natural Habitats, etc) Regulations 1994 and The Conservation (Natural Habitats, etc) (Northern Ireland) Regulations 1995. It has been held that the Directive extends UK obligations beyond the 12-mile limit to the UK continental shelf: *R* v. *Secretary of State, ex parte Greenpeace Ltd* [2000] TLR 30.

Hague Convention an international convention adopted at The Hague in Holland. There have been a number of these, and lawyers often by way of shorthand refer to a 'Hague Convention'. Notable are the Hague Conventions on the conduct of hostilities. However, there are a whole connected series arising out of The Hague Conference on Private International Law, and intergovernmental organisation whose statute came into force in July 1955. The purpose of the organisation is 'to work for the progressive unification of the rules of private international law'. The method employed to achieve this is by way of a 'Hague Convention'. To date there are 35 such conventions on subjects relating to private international law. One of the most well-known Hague Conventions is that on Civil Aspects of International Child Abduction 1980. This convention has been incorporated into UK law.

handling stolen goods the crime in English law of receiving goods or undertaking or assisting in the retention, removal, disposal or realisation for another, knowing or believing them to be stolen. For Scotland, see RESET.

Hansard the official report of Parliamentary debates, known by the name of the original publisher, now published by HMSO. While it reflects verbatim what is said in Parliament, until very recently it could not be referred to for the purposes of STATUTORY INTERPRETATION. Since the decision of the House of Lords in *Pepper* v. *Hart* [1992] 3 WLR 1032, it is now permissible to refer to Hansard in cases of AMBIGUITY. See also DEFAMATION.

harassment 1. the offence in England of using threatening or abusive or insulting words within the hearing or sight of a person likely to be harassed thereby: Public Order Act 1986.

2. it is an offence in England to harass a person with demands for payment that are calculated to subject him or his household to alarm, distress or humiliation, or to pretend that criminal proceedings might be possible if payment is not made: Administration of Justice Act 1970.

3. harassment is not a tort in England: *McCall* v. *Abelesz* [1976] QB 585. See Protection from Harassment Act 1997, which also applies to Scotland. The Act does not define the term beyond including causing alarm or distress. Damages may be awarded.

4. sexual harassment of employees has become a rhetorical focus in employment law: *Porcelli* v. *SRC* [1986] ICR 564.

5. see RACIALLY AGGRAVATED HARASSMENT.

harmonisation the process of approximating the law of the MEMBER STATES of the EUROPEAN COMMUNITIES.

Hartian jurisprudence a name often given to a system of jurisprudence either directly describing the work of the late H. L. A. Hart or a follower or commentator (usually, although not necessarily, earthbound). Hart considered the typical view that the lay person might have of the sovereign's orders backed by threats (a form of thinking associated with John Austin) to be inadequate, describing such situations as *pre-legal*. His concept of law was rule-based, seeing law as the union of primary and secondary rules. *Primary rules* impose duties, and *secondary rules* confer powers, whether public or private. The secondary rules are concerned with primary rules and provide for such matters as change and adjudication. Perhaps the most important secondary rule is that which tests whether a primary rule is valid. This secondary rule is called the *rule of recognition*. This rule can take any form and may be simple or very complex. At bottom, it turns out to be a sociological fact. This analysis of law as a system of rules is often compared and contrasted with KELSINIAN JURISPRUDENCE.

heading 1. words prefixed to the start of sections of Acts of Parliament. These may be utilised in STATUTORY INTERPRETATION.
2. in Scottish civil procedure, the part of an INITIAL WRIT that specifies the particular court jurisdiction in which an action is raised.

head note a summary of points decided in a case, written by the law-reporting company and not the court, which is usually found before the judgments.

hearsay that part of the law of evidence that is concerned with evidence, usually TESTIMONY, which refers to statements made other than by a witness giving evidence in court. 'Statement' is often considered to comprise actings or writings. As a general rule it is inadmissible as establishing the fact in question but may be ADMISSIBLE where it is sought to establish that the statement was made, e.g. 'I heard a man shout, "Look out!" as the pedestrian walked in front of the car.' The rules are among the most technical and important in the law, and what follows can be only an attempt to indicate the main themes. Naturally, legal systems differ on the detail, but the general approach is broadly similar in many Anglo-American systems.

There follows an indication of the principal exceptions to the hearsay rule where it applies:
(1) a statement will be admissible if it refers to the *res gestae*, i.e. matters that are so closely linked to the alleged offence in terms of place, time and circumstances as to form a single event, e.g. 'I heard a passer-by shout, "Look out! that pedestrian is about to commit suicide."' The House of Lords in *R. Andrew* [1987] AC 281 has accepted a wider test that 'hearsay evidence may be admitted if the statement providing it is made in such conditions (always being those of approximate but not exact contemporaneity) of involvement or pressure as to exclude the possibility of concoction or distortion to the advantage of the maker or the disadvantage of the accused.'

(2) the evidence of deceased persons is admissible in Scotland unless the circumstances raise some presumption that it does not reflect what was in his mind.

(3) in Scotland a statement in the presence of the accused is admissible if it is such a statement that he should reasonably repudiate it, although the general right to remain silent suggests that the accused should have been confronted directly with the statement.

(4) in both England and Scotland statute has provided considerable inroads to the rule in civil cases. Under the Civil Evidence Act 1995 in England, hearsay may be admitted. In Scotland under the Civil Evidence (Scotland) Act 1988, evidence is not to be excluded solely on the ground that it is hearsay. Even hearsay of hearsay is admissible. It is for the court to judge what weight should be accorded to the statement.

(5) extra-judicial statements, i.e. statements made outside of judicial proceedings, are an important exception. In civil cases they are often called *admissions* and in criminal cases *confessions*. The confession or admission, even in Scotland, can be proved by one witness. In Scotland, in criminal causes, the material fact in question would require CORROBORATION. In criminal cases the circumstances of the confession are subject to scrutiny under the exclusionary rule.

(6) in Scotland, a statement made by a complainer or victim shortly after the crime to a natural confidant can be admitted to establish the credibility of the victim. A greater latitude is allowed in cases of sexual offences.

hereditament real PROPERTY whether tangible or intangible.

heritable property see HERITAGE.

heritable securities SECURITIES over HERITABLE PROPERTY or REAL PROPERTY. In Scotland the only legal form is the STANDARD SECURITY.

heritage in Scotland, property that under the law at the time when the term grew up was inherited by the heir and has come to be called *heritable property* or heritage. It describes land and buildings as well as other property and is in distinction to moveable property, which is any property corporeal or incorporeal, which in former times passed to the executor as opposed to the heir.

high seas all parts of the sea that are not included in the territorial sea or in the internal waters of a state (Geneva Convention on the High Seas 1958). The territorial sea was fixed as not exceeding 12 nautical miles by the 1982 Convention on the Law of the Sea 1982. The UK has fixed its limit at 12 miles in the Territorial Sea Act 1987.

high treason see TREASON.

High Court England's most important civil court of first instance, divided into the Queen's Bench Division, the Family Division and the Chancery Division.

High Court of Australia set up by the constitution to be guardian and interpreter of the constitution, it also has an original jurisdiction and serves as the final court of appeal, hearing appeals from the state supreme courts.

High Court of Justiciary the highest criminal court in and of Scotland. The ACT OF UNION reserved criminal law to Scotland, so there is no appeal to the HOUSE OF LORDS. It is composed of Commissioners of Justiciary. The High Court goes on circuit. For trials, it comprises one judge and one jury. Appeals can be heard by the High Court sitting as the COURT OF CRIMINAL APPEAL.

highway a road or way over which the public may pass as of right. It may be over land or water. Highways are created by statute, dedication or prescription. Preventing the public from freely, safely and conveniently passing along the highway may be a NUISANCE. Obstruction of the highway is an offence. See REGALIA MINORA.

Highway Code a publication of the Department of the Environment that gives guidance for road users. It does not have the force of law but is a relevant guide in civil and criminal proceedings as to reasonable conduct. See *Hoaxley* v. *Dartford* DC 1979 RTR 359; *White* v. *Broadbent and British Rail Services* [1950] Crim. LR 129; *Powell* v. *Phillips* [1972] 3 All ER 864.

hire the letting out of goods for a money consideration. Many such transactions are controlled by the Consumer Credit Act 1974. It can also be used of the hire of work. See also EMPLOYMENT.

hire-purchase a form of purchase under which the purchase price can be paid over an agreed period of time by instalments. During the period the goods purchased remain the property of the seller (or the hire-purchase company to whom the seller has assigned his rights of ownership); possession is granted to the purchaser (the *hirer*) by means of a BAILMENT by the seller; property passes when the last instalment has been paid and the hirer exercises the option inherent in the agreement. A hire-purchase agreement is distinguished from a CONDITIONAL SALE agreement in that in the latter property passes automatically when the last instalment has been paid (i.e. there is no exercise of any option to purchase).

HMA abbreviation for 'Her Majesty's Advocate'. Prosecutions in

Scotland on INDICTMENT are raised thus: *HMA* v. *MacPhee*. For England see R.

holder a payee or indorsee in possession of a BILL OF EXCHANGE or PROMISSORY NOTE.

holder in due course a person who has taken a BILL OF EXCHANGE in good faith and for value before it was overdue and without notice of previous dishonour or of any defect in the title of the person who negotiated or transferred the bill. A holder in due course can negotiate the bill further and stands to be recompensed if it is dishonoured by the drawer, acceptor or other endorsee: Bills of Exchange Act 1882. The original payee of a cheque is not a holder in due course: *Re Jones Ltd* v. *Waring & Gillow* [1926] AC 670; *Williams* v. *Williams* 1980 SLT (Sh. Ct) 25.

holding company a COMPANY that controls, usually through a majority shareholding, another company or companies.

holding out conduct by a person leading another to believe that he possesses an authority that in reality he does not. Such conduct in effect amounts to a representation such that he will be estopped from denying that the authority exists.

holograph handwritten.

homage see FEUDAL SYSTEM.

homelessness having no home, now the subject of legislation in England and Wales and Scotland, and having a technical signification not always congruent with the ordinary meaning of the word. The thrust of the legislation is to focus upon accommodation, and homelessness is the lack of such accommodation. The focus is wider, however, because it looks at people who normally reside together. Local authorities have to provide accommodation for the homeless but not the intentionally homeless, a critical concept around which much of the reported litigation turns. Some homeless people are legally accorded a priority need, such as pregnant women. See Housing (Homeless Persons) Act 1977, Housing (Scotland) Act 1987.

Home Office the government department responsible throughout England and Wales for law and order generally and for a variety of other matters such as immigration, nationality, extradition and deportation.

homeworker a person who works outside the control or management of the person he is contracted with and has the help of no more than two people in carrying out the contract and who works for minimum wages: Wages Act 1986.

homicide in the criminal law of England, a generic term for the killing of one human being by another. It can be *lawful* or *unlawful*, the main divisions of unlawful killing in English law being between *murder* and *manslaughter*.

In the criminal law of Scotland, an act that results in the death of a self-existent human being. It is not criminal if there is no MENS REA whatsoever, as where someone is killed during a game of rugby played according to the rules. Nor is it criminal if justified, completely excusing the executioner and the soldier. Scots law recognises two degrees of homicide: murder and CULPABLE HOMICIDE. See ABORTION.

The question has been raised in recent years, mainly as a result of tragic disasters, as to the extent to which gross carelessness by corporations can be brought home to those responsible for deaths. This is discussed as *corporate manslaughter*. It comes under the heading of manslaughter because corporations do not usually set out to kill with malice aforethought. In England the present state of the law is that evidence of a defendant's state of mind is not a prerequisite for conviction for manslaughter by gross negligence but a corporation cannot be convicted without evidence establishing the guilt of an identified human for the same crime. There is, however, a Law Commission Bill arguing for a wider doctrine based solely on the corporation's implementation of its own duties: *Attorney General's reference No. 2 of 1999* [2000] TLR 138.

homologation a form of PERSONAL BAR (estoppel) in Scots law. It focuses on the acts of the party seeking to escape an obligation as approbatory of the obligation. It is now of much less practical significance because a statutory equivalent has been introduced by the Requirement of Writing (Scotland) Act 1995. See SELF-PROVING.

honest comment see DEFAMATION.

honestere vivere 'to live honestly', one of Justinian's three precepts of justice in the Institutes, part of the CORPUS JURIS CIVILIS.

honorarium a payment made as a matter of honour and not because it is due as a legally enforceable debt.

horizontal direct effect see DIRECT EFFECT.

hornbook (USA) a student textbook, as opposed to a treatise for practitioners.

hospital order an order authorising an offender's detention in a named hospital.

hostile witness a witness expected to give testimony favourable to the examiner but who in fact begins to give testimony not only unhelpful to the case but directed against it. In general, a person called as a witness may not be CROSS-EXAMINED by the party calling him. However, where a witness in the EXAMINATION IN CHIEF demonstrates hostility to the party who called him, that witness may, with the leave of the judge, be cross-examined by the party calling him. A witness is not to be regarded as hostile by reason only of the fact that he gives evidence unfavourable to the party calling him.

This phrase has no technical meaning in Scotland, the ADVOCATE or SOLICITOR being free to challenge a witness he himself has called, without the leave of the court.

hotchpot the mixing together of property belonging to different persons with a view to dividing it equally. In English succession law it describes the bringing into account of the benefits received by a beneficiary prior to the death of an intestate. All advances to children must be taken into account: Administration of Estates Act 1925. It has been abolished for deaths after 1995. For Scotland, see COLLATIO INTER HAEREDES, COLLATIO INTER LIBEROS.

hotel 1. an establishment held out by the proprietor as offering food, drink and, if required, sleeping accommodation, without special contract, to any traveller presenting himself who appears able and willing to pay a reasonable sum for the services and facilities provided and who is in a fit state to be received: Hotel Proprietors Act 1956.

2. for the purposes of licensing, special definitions are given making a distinction between establishments in the country and those in the town, the number of apartments available as sleeping accommodation for members of the public being an essential part of the definition.

housebreaking in Scots criminal law, strictly speaking only an aggravation of THEFT and not a nominate crime. It consists in the surmounting of the security of a building or entering it in any unusual way and the 'house' part is satisfied if the building concerned has a roof. Housebreaking without intent to steal is not a crime in Scots law although it is likely to constitute a criminal offence of being in a building without permission. See BURGLARY.

House of Commons in the CONSTITUTIONAL LAW of the UK, one of the two chambers of PARLIAMENT, the other being the HOUSE OF LORDS.

Members are called simply Members of Parliament, abbreviated to MP. Many classes of people are disqualified from sitting, including those suffering from mental illness, peers, criminals, aliens and certain clergyman. Judges, civil servants and members of the armed forces and the police are all also disqualified. Day-to-day business is organised by the SPEAKER, and the party officials are known as *whips*.

House of Lords in the CONSTITUTIONAL LAW of the UK, one of the two chambers of PARLIAMENT, the other being the HOUSE OF COMMONS. It is composed of Lords Spiritual, being the Archbishops of Canterbury and York and other senior bishops. Until 1999 the rest of the membership was predominantly made up of *hereditary peers* of whom there were several hundred but very few of whom actually sat. The majority of the peers in attendance are the *life peers* and *peeresses*. There are over three hundred such peers. The Speaker of the House of Lords is the LORD CHANCELLOR. At the end of the 1998-99 session, in accordance with Section 1 of the House of Lords Act 1999, 655 hereditary peers ceased to be members of the House while, under Section 2, 90 hereditary peers, the Earl Marshal and the Lord Great Chamberlain remained as members for their lifetime or until a subsequent Act provides otherwise. This change had the effect of reducing the total membership of the House from 1,330 in October 1999 to 669 in March 2000. A Royal Commission reported in 2000, and further reform to democratise and modernise the House seems inevitable.

The House of Lords is also the highest court in the land, although not in respect of criminal matters in Scotland where there is no appeal from the HIGH COURT OF JUSTICIARY (although the same individual LAW LORDS sitting on the constitutionally different Board of the PRIVY COUNCIL now can reverse the High Court on DEVOLUTION issues). To make sure that there is an adequate number of sufficiently qualified persons to carry out this task, it has been possible since 1876 to appoint Law Lords who may speak in a personal capacity on ordinary political matters.

The House reviews legislation in often impressive debates. It can delay legislation, initiate non-controversial legislation and scrutinises legislation of the EUROPEAN UNION.

hue and cry the making of an outcry. In early English law, if the locals did not make an outcry and pursue and catch a felon or robber within forty days, they were made liable to the victim.

human rights legally enforceable rights to which people are entitled in virtue of their humanity rather than dependent on citizenship. A modern concept, at least under this name, human rights are legally significant in the UK and Europe because of the incorporation into UK law by the Scotland Act 1998 and the Human Rights Act 1998 (effective October 2000) of the EUROPEAN CONVENTION ON HUMAN RIGHTS, ratified by the members of the COUNCIL OF EUROPE. Equally important is the Universal Declaration of Human Rights, adopted by the UNITED NATIONS General Assembly in 1948.

Any provisions seeking to protect human rights usually focus on life, liberty and freedom of personality, freedom of thought and religion. The right to work (and sometimes a right to social security) often appears. See also BILL OF RIGHTS.

hybrid bill in the constitutional law of the UK, a bill that is introduced as a PUBLIC BILL but that affects a private interest in such a way that it resembles a PRIVATE BILL. It follows a procedure like that of private bill but does not include a process for allowing objectors to be heard.

hypothec a security over moveable property that permits the borrower to retain possession. A hypothec is equivalent to a charge and is employed in international trading transactions. A *letter of hypothecation* is a letter addressed to a bank giving details of a shipment of goods relating to a draft. Should the draft be dishonoured, the bank is empowered to sell the goods. See *Official Assignee of Madras* v. *Mercantile Bank of India* [1935] AC 53. Maritime liens are a form of hypothec. Seamen have a lien for wages; a salvor for any sum due on salvage; a person repairing a ship or giving supplies in a foreign port for the services; one suffering loss as a result of damage caused by the ship. Claims under bonds of BOTTOMRY and RESPONDENTIA are secured by hypothec.

In Scotland special hypothecs are known:

(1) the *landlord's hypothec* is a security over the *invecta et illata* (things brought or carried into the premises) subject to recognised exceptions in respect of one year's rent and not for prior arrears. The security will attach goods on hire or hire purchase;

(2) the *feudal superior's hypothec* for FEU DUTY (analogous to the landlord's hypothec) is of less significance now that very many (but not all) feu duties have been statutorily redeemed;

(3) a solicitor has a hypothec over any expenses to which his client is entitled;

(4) the maritime hypothecs mentioned in respect of England are recognised in Scotland too.

hypothecation 1. a method of creating a HYPOTHEC.
2. in politics, rather than law, the assignation of an element of taxation to particular beneficiaries rather than the general coffers of the Treasury.

ICC abbreviation for INTERNATIONAL CRIMINAL COURT.

ICE abbreviation for INSTITUTE OF CHARTERED ENGINEERS.

ICJ abbreviation for INTERNATIONAL COURT OF JUSTICE.

ignorantia juris neminen excusat 'ignorance of the law will never excuse.' The maxim applies to an extent in criminal law but not always in civil law.

ILEX abbreviation for INSTITUTE OF LEGAL EXECUTIVES.

illegal contract a contract may be described as illegal if:

(1) the aim or object of the contract is criminal or immoral;

(2) some specific rule of statute or common law says that it is;

(3) the method of contracting is illegal.

At common law, contracts to commit a crime or promote sexual immorality are illegal. This latter proves difficult in an era when many people live in a state that at the time when many of the authorities were decided was considered immoral. Thus, contracts between cohabitees vary in effect across the Anglo-American world.

Trading with the enemy is contrary to public policy, another head of illegality. Restrictive covenants and contracts in restraint of trade are regarded suspiciously by the courts. There is a general assumption that such contracts are illegal but in modern times their commercial necessity means that the assumption is easily reversed.

Certain gaming contracts are made illegal by statute, and in any event wagering transactions are SPONSIONES LUDICRAE and are not enforced.

As the name suggests, the UNFAIR CONTRACT TERMS Act 1977 and other legislation make certain contract terms to have no legal effect.

In New Zealand, under the Illegal Contracts Act 1970, illegality in respect of breach of statute is now determined by the provisions of the enactment and the test is whether the enactment provides for illegality or its object requires illegality. Contracts may be illegal either on creation or on performance. The particularly interesting thing about the Act is that it allows the court very wide power of relief that can be exercised in favour of a party to an illegal contract.

illegal immigrant an illegal entrant being a person unlawfully entering, or seeking to enter, in breach of a deportation order or of the immigration laws and includes a person who has so entered: Immigration Act 1971.

illegitimacy the state of being born of parents who are not legally married. Since the Family Law Reform Act 1987, most of the disadvantages of illegitimacy affecting inheritance have been removed so that *illegitimate* children may take property under a WILL or under the INTESTACY rules as if they were legitimate. Illegitimate children cannot, however, succeed to titles of honour.

In Scots family law, formerly a distinction between children born out of wedlock and those born within (*legitimate*). The law now looks upon illegitimate children in the same way as legitimate children since the Law Reform (Parent and Child) (Scotland) Act 1986.

Existing enactments and deeds are to be interpreted without heed to the reforms. Testators may still distinguish so far as they wish. Fathers of illegitimate children do not have parental rights as of right, nor is their consent as a parent required for ADOPTION.

immigration appeal an appeal may be made against refusal to enter the UK, against conditions of leave to enter and remain, against decisions in respect of deportation orders and against directions for removal. The appeal lies in the first instance to an adjudicator and thence to an Immigration Appeals Tribunal (although, exceptionally, the appeal may go direct to the Tribunal).

immigration officer an official appointed by the Home Secretary who has powers of examination, detention, etc, and has powers under the Prevention of Terrorism (Temporary Provisions) Act 1989. Immigration officers operate the procedures for control on entry to the UK.

immoveable property property that cannot be moved, such as land or buildings.

immunity freedom from obligation or duty, especially exemption from tax, duty, legal liability, etc.

impeachment 1. in the CONSTITUTIONAL LAW of the UK, the process by which a person in some way beyond the reach of the law could be brought to justice in respect of an offence against the state. The HOUSE OF COMMONS accuses and the HOUSE OF LORDS judges both fact and law. The most famous cases are those of Francis Bacon, who was successfully impeached when he was Lord Chancellor, and of Warren Hastings, who was impeached when Governor-General of India and was acquitted.

The same term is used in the USA in relation to the President. In relation to US high officials, impeachment is the first step in a process; only after there is a vote in favour of impeachment is there a trial on the *articles of impeachment*. President Richard Milhouse Nixon resigned before impeachment could take its course. President William Jefferson Clinton was acquitted after a full impeachment process. The prosecutors did not establish that his reprehensible conduct constituted a high crime and misdemeanour.

2. more loosely, a challenge, e.g. of a witness or a judgment.

imperative theory see COMMAND THEORY.

imperitae culpae admunertur 'lack of skill is treated as fault'.

implied authority authority implied from facts or circumstances. *Actual authority* is that authority that an agent has pursuant to an agreement between him and his principal; such authority may be express or implied from the terms of the agreement. See AGENCY.

implied condition a condition in a contract that is not expressly stated or written. It may be implied by fact and deed, viz. the parties' actings; or it may be implied by law, either case law or statute. For an example, see QUALITY.

imprescriptible obligations in the Scots law of PRESCRIPTION and LIMITATION, certain rights and obligations cannot be affected by the passage of time: any real right of ownership of land, the right in land of the lessee under a recorded lease; any right to recover property *extra commercium*; the trustee's obligation to make reparation for breach of trust or to make over trust property; the obligation of a *mala fide* holder of property to restore it; the right to recover stolen property from a thief or a party to the theft; the right to be served as an heir to an ancestor; any right *res merae facultatis*.

imprisonment see PRISON, YOUNG OFFENDER INSTITUTION.

inaedificatum solo, solo cedit see FIXTURES.

in bonis 'in the goods of'. In cases concerning the disposal of property of a deceased person, the case will often be described as *in b*.

in camera 'in chambers', a most perplexing phrase for litigants who suspect they may be about to be photographed. Actually it indicates that the case, or the rest of the case, is to be heard in the judge's private chambers – excluding the public.

incapax in Scots law, a person who has not CAPACITY.

incest unlawful heterosexual intercourse between members of the same family. Consent is not a defence if the parties were aware of their familial relationship, which relationship may be of full or half blood.

In Scots law, the carnal connection of persons related one to the other in the FORBIDDEN DEGREES.

inchoate not complete.

inchoate offence a crime that can be committed even though the planned or actual crime is not completed.

incitement 1. in English criminal law it is an offence to incite another to commit an offence.

2. the Incitement to Disaffection Act 1934 is aimed at stopping people diverting members of the armed forces from their duties.

inclusio unius est exclusio alterius a rule of interpretation that states that 'including one excludes another'. The statement 'no dogs allowed' under this rule would mean that panthers were allowed.

income and expenditure account a summary account of the revenue and running costs of a non-profit-making concern such as a club or society. It serves the same function as a PROFIT AND LOSS ACCOUNT in business.

income tax a tax on income; income, however, is not defined as such but is described by reference to various schedules, as provided for in the Income and Corporation Taxes Act 1988. These relate to, for example, income from employment, trading profits, income from land and other investment income.

incommunicado without a means of communicating. By statute in England a person detained is not supposed to be kept incommunicado: Police and Criminal Evidence Act 1984.

In Scotland the position is much the same except for cases of detention under Section 2 of the Criminal Justice (Scotland) Act 1980, which allows the police to detain a person for a fixed time, without access to a solicitor. See DETENTION.

inconsistent fact a party should not in any pleading make any allegation of fact or raise any new ground of claim that is inconsistent with a previous pleading of his. However, inconsistent facts may be alleged as alternative grounds on which he is entitled to relief. 'Inconsistent' in this context does not mean 'mutually exclusive' but rather 'new or different' (see *Herbert* v. *Vaughan* [1972] 3 All ER 122). In Scotland this may be done, but the previous pleading may be put in cross-examination.

Incorporated Law Society of Ireland the representative body of solicitors in the Republic of Ireland, which has a dual role of representing the interests of its members and carrying out its statutory duties under the Solicitors Act 1954-60 of regulating the profession in such matters as legal education and discipline. See also LAW SOCIETY.

Incorporated Law Society of Northern Ireland this body performs in Northern Ireland similar functions to the INCORPORATED LAW SOCIETY OF IRELAND. See also LAW SOCIETY.

incorporation the process of forming an association that has corporate personality. See CORPORATION.

incorporeal that which has no *corpus*, or body, so cannot be touched.

incorporeal hereditament an intangible right over land in England and Wales. Examples are rights of way, rights to light and rights of pasture. See EASEMENTS, PROFITS.

incorporeal property property without a body that cannot be touched and picked up, such as a right to something. Stocks and SHARES are *incorporeal personal* or *moveable property*, as are COPYRIGHTS and PATENTS. To transfer such property ASSIGNATION is usually required.

incriminate 1. to bring into the possibility of a criminal charge.

2. in Scotland the word *incrimination* is used in a slightly different sense. Incrimination is a special DEFENCE, of which notice must be given, whereby the accused offers to show that another person committed the crime. See SELF-INCRIMINATION.

incumbrance a MORTGAGE or other SECURITY over real or personal PROPERTY.

indebitatus assumpsit see ASSUMPSIT.

indebitum solutum payment of a debt not owing. See CONDICTIO INDEBITI.

indemnity an undertaking by one person to make good losses suffered by another. Frequently confused with GUARANTEE, an indemnity is a primary obligation that is enforceable irrespective of whether the beneficiary could sue the person responsible for causing the loss. On the other hand, a guarantee is a secondary obligation to pay a specified or ascertainable sum should the primary debtor fail to do so; if the primary obligation is unenforceable, the guarantee cannot be sued upon.

An agent has the right to be indemnified by his principal against all losses and liabilities incurred by him while acting within the scope of his AGENCY.

The administrative RECEIVER of a COMPANY is personally liable on any contract entered into by him in the carrying out of his functions except in as far as the contract otherwise provides and on any contract of employment adopted by him in the carrying out of those functions, and is entitled in respect of that liability to an indemnity out of the assets of the company.

indenture see APPRENTICE.

independent contractor a person who works under a contract of EMPLOYMENT but of the type LOCATIO OPERARUM rather than LOCATIO OPERIS – the taxi driver rather than the chauffeur. See *Mersey Docks & Harbour Board* v. *Coggins & Griffiths Ltd* [1947] AC 1. See also VICARIOUS LIABILITY, LOCATIO CONDUCTIO.

independent means the ability to finance oneself without assistance from the state. A set of financial criteria that, if satisfied by a non-British citizen, will normally result in that person being admitted to the UK for an initial period of four years with a prohibition on taking up employment. At present the financial requirements are that the person has under his control and disposable in the UK a sum of not less than £200,000 or income of not less than £20,000 per year; further, the person must be willing and able to maintain himself in the UK and to support and accommodate any dependants in the UK without working, with no assistance from any other persons and without recourse to public funds. It is an advantage if such a person can show a close connection with the UK (such as relatives resident here or periods of previous residence) or that his admission would be in the UK's general interests.

indictable offence an offence is indictable if it itself may be tried on indictment or is triable either way. See SUMMARY OFFENCE.

indictment a document that sets out the charges against a person. In England they are in simple form in terms of the Indictments Act 1915. In Scotland the indictments are prepared in terms of the Criminal Procedure (Scotland) Act 1975.

indorsement or **endorsement 1.** the writing of the signature of the holder on a BILL OF EXCHANGE, this being an essential step in the process of negotiating or transferring it. The process of negotiation is completed by delivering the bill to the transferee. (For the requisites of a valid indorsement see Bills of Exchange Act 1882.) See CHEQUE.

2. a writing on the back of other documents. An *indorsement of writ* or *claim* is a writ of summons that must be indorsed with a statement of the claim made or relief or remedy sought.

inducing breach of contract a form of ECONOMIC TORT consisting in A knowingly and unjustifiably inducing B to breach his contract with

C, causing loss to C. The law generally permits considerable freedom in economic matters. In the leading case of *Mogul Steamship Co. Ltd* v. *McGregor, Gow & Co.* [1892] AC 25, the plaintiffs were put out of business by the defendants undercutting competitors by offering rebates and restricting their own agents from dealing with competitors. The necessity for a contractual relation that is being attacked was made clear in the equally important case of *Allen* v. *Flood* [1898] AC 1. The defendant must have known about a valid and subsisting contract: *British Homophone* v. *Kunz* [1935] All ER 627; *Rossleigh* v. *Leader Cars Ltd*, 1987 SLT 355, but sometimes courts take a wider view if it seems apparent that the defendant must have known there were contracts in operation: *Stratford* v. *Lindley* [1964] 3 All ER 102. Attempts have been made to classify the kind of conduct that will legally amount to interference (the most cited being that in *D. C. Thomson* v. *Deakin* [1952] 2 All ER 361) into: (i) direct persuasion; (ii) direct intervention; (iii) indirect intervention. It may be that this tort has extended to become a tort of unlawful interference in contract that would not require the need to show a breach, but it is difficult to be certain about the precise boundaries of any of the economic torts.

industrial dispute a dispute between employers and employees or more likely the organisations representing one or both groups. The dispute should relate wholly or mainly to terms and conditions of work. See GOLDEN FORMULAE.

industrial injury benefit a state benefit that pays benefit to employed earners who suffer personal injuries caused by accidents arising out of and in the course of their employment.

industrial tribunal see EMPLOYMENT TRIBUNAL.

in extenso 'in full' or 'at length'.

in extremis 'in the final illness'.

infeftment in Scottish feudal CONVEYANCING, a person is *infeft* if his title is registered in the REGISTER OF SASINES – itself a register of titles rather than a land register.

in flagrante delicto 'while the crime is flagrant'; colloquially, 'caught in the act'.

information in English criminal procedure, the statement informing a magistrate of the offence in respect of which a warrant or summons is sought.

inheritance tax a tax on property passing on death. Formerly known as *estate duty*, then as *capital transfer tax*, it became inheritance tax by the Finance Act 1986, which retrospectively allowed the Capital Transfer Tax Act 1984 to be renamed the Inheritance Tax Act 1984.

The tax applies to individuals. It is charged on the value transferred on property held at death. There are exceptions (the most significant being gifts between husband and wife and those to certain national institutions) and reliefs. Certain property is also excluded (the most significant being agricultural property).

inhibition in the context of registered land, an entry on the register prohibiting (either for a specified period or until the occurrence of a stated event or until further order) any or some specified dealing with the land.

In the Scots law of DILIGENCE or legal enforcement, a prohibition on a debtor preventing him dealing with his HERITABLE PROPERTY. It is recorded in the *Register of Inhibitions and Adjudication*, so ought to be known to the world at large. It does not prevent the carrying through of obligations established before it was effected. See DISQUALIFICATION.

initial writ the main written pleading that starts all but minor matters in the Scottish Sheriff Court.

injunction an order of the court preventing someone from doing something. See generally *Att. Gen.* v. *The Observer Ltd* [1987] 1 WLR 1248. It is a CONTEMPT OF COURT to disobey. There are various types:

(1) prohibitory;

(2) mandatory, which prohibits an omission by ordering a positive act;

(3) interlocutory, to maintain position until a full hearing;

(4) perpetual, granted after a full hearing;

(5) *ex parte*, granted in emergency after hearing only one party;

(6) interim, granted and lasting only until a given date;

(7) *quia timet*, 'because he fears'; such an application is made in respect of a wrong apprehended or threatened but not committed. The applicant must show a fear of an imminent grave danger: *Hooper* v. *Rogers* [1975] Ch. 43.

See also MAREVA ORDER.

injuria 'a legal wrong'. In Roman law it has different meanings in different contexts.

injurious falsehood see MALICIOUS FALSEHOOD.

Inland Revenue the branch of the administration responsible for collecting direct taxes from the citizen. The administration of the UK tax system is in the hands of two bodies, namely the Commissioners of Customs and Excise, who have jurisdiction over indirect taxes, and the Commissioners of Inland Revenue, who have jurisdiction over direct taxes. Thus, VALUE-ADDED TAX is dealt with by the Customs and Excise, while INCOME TAX, CAPITAL GAINS TAX, CORPORATION TAX, INHERITANCE TAX and STAMP DUTY are within the province of the Inland Revenue. The powers of the Department of Customs and Excise in relation to value-added tax derive from the Customs and Excise Management 1979 and the Value Added Tax Act 1983; the powers of the Inland Revenue derive particularly from the Taxes Management Act 1970, the Income and Corporation Tax Chargeable Gains Act 1992.

in lieu 'in place of'.

in limine 'on the threshold'. A preliminary point or plea is said to be made *in limine*.

in loco parentis 'in place of a parent', a phrase used to describe, among others, schoolteachers who have custody of a child and the responsibility for looking after the child.

in meditatione fugae 'in contemplation of flight'.

inn see HOTEL.

Inner House see COURT OF SESSION.

Inner Temple see BARRISTER.

innominate 'having no name', in Scots contract law, a contract that is both unusual and innominate, having no known name like sale or hire, for example. Now that there is no requirement for writing, the category may vanish.

Inns of Court see BARRISTER.

innuendo see DEFAMATION.

in pari delicto potior est conditio possidentis 'where both parties are equally in the wrong, the position of the possessor is the better.' Not always the law.

in pari materia 'in a like matter'.

in personam 'personal' (as opposed to REAL).

inquest an official examination of facts. In the UK (except Scotland) the inquiry presided over by a CORONER into the cause of death of an individual.

inquisitorial procedure a procedure that inquires into the facts and circumstances and the law with a view to reaching the truth. It is very common in continental Europe. The active role of the judge is perhaps the single most distinguishing feature from the ACCUSATORIAL PROCEDURE.

in re 'in the matter of'.

in rem 'against a thing' (as opposed to against a person).

in re mercatoria 'in mercantile matters'.

in rixa 'in anger', the defence, in VERBAL INJURY cases, that the words were spoken in anger or in the heat of the moment.

insanity in the criminal law of England and Scotland, a plea in relation to the mental state of the accused. It may be pled as a DEFENCE in its own right or submitted as a plea of INSANITY IN BAR OF TRIAL.

In English law, every person is presumed sane unless the contrary is proved. The burden of proving insanity rests with the accused (*Woolmington* v. *DPP* [1935] AC 462).

When insanity is pled as a defence, the criteria for determining whether or not the plea should be successful are the *McNaghten rules* (*Re McNaghten* (1843) 10 C&F, 200 8 Eng. Rep. 718). To establish such a defence the accused must show that at the time of committing the offence he was suffering from such a disease of the mind or defect of reason that he did not know the nature and quality of the act he was doing; or if he did know it that he did not know he was doing what was wrong. If the accused was aware that what he was doing was something he ought not to do and the act committed was at the time an offence, he is punishable. If the defence succeeds, the accused must be declared not guilty by reason of insanity.

In Scotland, as a defence, the state of mind must have been in existence at the time of the act in question. If sane at the time of the trial and the defence is established, then the accused will not be convicted but will be detained in the state hospital without limit of time. The accused must prove his insanity on BALANCE OF PROBABILITIES. The test is the overpowering of reason by a mental defect, leaving the person unable to control his own conduct. The McNaghten rules do not apply in Scotland: *HMA* v. *Brennan* 1977 JC 38. Scots law recognises an intermediate state between sanity and insanity, mitigating the crime of murder or attempted murder but not exculpating: the plea is called DIMINISHED RESPONSIBILITY. If successful, it results in a conviction for CULPABLE HOMICIDE (in England manslaughter – see HOMICIDE) for which there is no mandatory sentence such as life imprisonment or, as was formerly the case, death by hanging. Non-insane AUTOMATISM is recognised in Scots law as an exculpating factor: see *Sorley* v. *HMA* 1992 SLT 867.

insanity in bar of trial the plea that a person is not in a fit mental state to instruct his defence. A HOSPITAL ORDER may be made and the trial simply does not proceed. In theory, on release the proceedings may be commenced.

insider dealing the making use of price-sensitive information that is unavailable to investors at large to the extent of dealing in company securities with the object of making a profit or avoiding a loss. Under the Criminal Justice Act 1993, persons who are or have been connected with a company (e.g. directors, senior employees, professional advisers, etc) are prohibited from engaging in such dealings on or, in certain circumstances, off the Stock Exchange if they acquired the information by virtue of their connection and in confidence.

in solidum 'in whole', each for the whole amount.

insolvency 1. inability to pay debts as they fall due.

2. excess of liabilities over assets.

The Insolvency Act 1986 is essentially a legislative code governing insolvency proceedings. The practice in insolvency proceedings (insofar as it is not laid down in the Act) is governed by Insolvency Rules made under the Act.

In the Scots law, a distinction is made between absolute insolvency and apparent insolvency. *Absolute insolvency* means that the debtor's assets, if realised, would not meet his liabilities even if able to pay his way. *Apparent insolvency* means the inability to pay debts as they are demanded. The Insolvency Act 1986 regulates procedure in Scotland as much as in England. In matters of personal insolvency, however, the law in Scotland is as set out in the Bankruptcy (Scotland) Act 1985 as amended by the Bankruptcy (Scotland) Act 1993.

Insolvency Practitioners Tribunal the tribunal to which an insolvency practitioner may appeal if served with a notice that the competent authority proposes to refuse or withdraw authorisation.

insolvent company a COMPANY that is unable to pay its debts in full as they fall due.

instalment deliveries unless otherwise agreed, the buyer of goods is not bound to take DELIVERY by instalments. If there is such a CONTRACT, or if there is an express term permitting the goods to be delivered by stated instalments that are to be separately paid for, and the seller makes defective delivery in respect of one or more instalments, it is a question in each case, depending on the terms of the contract and the circumstances of the case, whether the breach of contract is a breach of the whole contract or whether it is a severable breach giving rise to a claim for compensation but not to a right to treat the whole contract as repudiated. In *Maple Flock Co. Ltd* v. *Universal Furniture Products (Wembley) Co. Ltd* [1934] 1 KB 148, it was held that factors that might usefully be considered are:

(1) the proportion the failure bears to the whole contract – one missed delivery out of twenty might not suggest repudiation whereas one out of three very well might;

(2) the likelihood of a failure recurring.

instance in Scottish civil procedure, the part of an INITIAL WRIT that specifies the names and designations of the parties to an action. See also COURT OF FIRST INSTANCE.

Institute of Chartered Engineers (ICE) the professional body of chartered engineers, which is responsible for adjusting with other users one of the standard form of building CONTRACT.

Institute of Legal Executives (ILEX) the professional body that represents LEGAL EXECUTIVES and aims to enhance their role and standing in the legal profession. ILEX is a leading provider of comprehensive legal education and endeavours to influence law reform.

Institutes 1. part of the CORPUS JURIS CIVILIS.

2. books based on the Institutes of Justinian and Gaius. In the second phase of ROMAN LAW, such systematic treatments appeared throughout Europe, attempting to state the law of the locality.

instruction another word, used mainly in the USA, for the judge's charge to a jury.

instrument a written legal document.

insurable interest a person has such an interest in property or in the life of a person if damage or destruction of the property or death of the person would expose him to pecuniary loss or liability. See INSURANCE.

insurance a contract under which one party (the *insurer*), in consideration of receipt of a premium, undertakes to pay money to another person (the *assured*) on the happening of a specified event (as, for example, on death or accident or loss or damage to property). The instrument containing the terms of the contract is known as a *policy*. Contracts of insurance are *uberrimae fidei*, requiring full disclosure by the assured of all facts material to the risk insured. See also LIFE INSURANCE, INSURABLE INTEREST.

intellectual property a convenient term to describe various parts of the law that have the effect of protecting the products of the imagination and intellect. It covers, generally, COPYRIGHT, PATENTS, designs, REGISTERED DESIGNS, TRADEMARKS, know-how and PASSING OFF.

intention to create legal relations before parties can be said to have entered into a legal contract as opposed to an agreement, they must have intended to effect a legal obligation. This can be inferred from the circumstances, and an intention to effect legal relations is readily assumed in business.

One of the purposes of the rule is to exclude social arrangements and to leave people free not to contract. One of the academic debates is the problem of whether a person who contracts as a joke or who contracts intending to default, intends to effect a legal obligation. In the USA it has been suggested that it is sufficient if the promises involved are seriously intended. In English law it is important to examine this requirement along with CONSIDERATION.

inter alia 'among other things'.

interceptive subtraction in the law of RESTITUTION, a term applied by some commentators to a taking away from the pursuer, which happens by the defender acquiring value that would otherwise have reached the pursuer. The value subtracted can thus be treated as an unjust enrichment and subject to the law of restitution.

interdict in Scotland, an order of a court prohibiting conduct. Only in certain occasions may it have a positive effect. See INJUNCTION.

interest 1. a payment made by a borrower for the use of money, calculated as a percentage of the principal sum borrowed and payable by reference to the time that the loan is outstanding. Interest may be *simple*, where the amount payable is calculated on the sum borrowed only, or *compound*, where interest is added to the capital sum borrowed and itself earns interest.

Interest on a loan taken out by a company is payable whether or not the company has earned any profits; in contrast, dividends are payable only out of profits earned. Interest on company loans is a deduction for CORPORATION TAX purposes. Dividend payments are not so deductible; indeed, such payments attract liability to advance corporation tax.

2. a right, title or estate to personal or real property. Section 1 of the Law of Property Act 1925 provides that the only estates in land capable of subsisting and of being conveyed or created at law are an estate in FEE SIMPLE ABSOLUTE IN POSSESSION and a term of years absolute. The only interests in or over land capable of subsisting or of being conveyed or created at law are an easement, right or privilege in or over land capable of existing for an interest equivalent to an estate in fee simple absolute in possession (i.e. in perpetuity) or a term of years absolute (i.e. for a fixed and determinate period) and a charge by way of legal mortgage. All other estates, interests and charges in or over land take effect as equitable interests. See INTEREST RELIEF.

In Scotland a litigant must, as well as having TITLE to sue, have an interest to sue.

interest relief payments by way of interest may be deductible in computing a taxpayer's taxable income.

interference with goods see WRONGFUL INTERFERENCE WITH GOODS.

interim interdict see INTERDICT.

interim receiver the OFFICIAL RECEIVER may be appointed as interim RECEIVER of the debtor's property until a trustee is appointed.

interim trustee see PERMANENT TRUSTEE.

interlocutor in Scots court practice, an order of the court.

interlocutory not final, while the action is still proceeding.

intermediate examination in common law, PRODUCT LIABILITY, on the basis of certain *dicta* in *Donoghue* v. *Stevenson* 1932 SC (HL) 31 as later developed, there will be no liability if the defect could have been intercepted between the manufacturer and the consumer. The requirement is not usually literally interpreted. In *Grant* v. *AKM* [1936] AC 85, it was not held to be possible where underwear was supplied to the retailer in packets. See also *Murphy* v. *Brentwood* [1990] 3 WLR 414.

International Court of Justice (ICJ) the principal judicial organ of the UNITED NATIONS (UN), the Court sits in The Hague, Netherlands. There are 15 judges elected by the General Assembly and the Security Council. No two judges may be nationals of the same state. Only states are competent to bring contentious cases to the Court. The basis of the Court's jurisdiction is consensual and is prescribed in Article 36 of the Court's statute. The Court's judgment is binding only on those states party to the case. There is no STARE DECISIS. The Court is also competent to give an advisory opinion at the request of the General Assembly or Security Council or a specialised agency at any time authorised by the General Assembly so to do. The Court's judgment is 'final and without appeal'. However, a request for construction or interpretation of the judgment may be made, as may a revision of the judgment in certain specified circumstances. Advisory opinions are of no legal binding effect but have proved to be highly persuasive. All members of the United Nations undertake to comply with the decision of the ICJ in any case to which it is a party. In the event of failure to comply, the other party may exercise recourse to the Security Council. The Security Council may make such recommendations or authorise such measures as required to give effect to the judgment (Article 94 UN Charter).

International Criminal Court (ICC) the statute of the International Criminal Court was agreed in July 1998. This permanent court will have jurisdiction over serious international crimes, namely genocide, crimes against humanity, war crimes and crimes of aggression. The Court's jurisdiction will be complementary to that of state parties. The Court will become operational only following ratification by 60 states and only in respect of crimes committed in states that are parties to the Convention or whose nationals are suspects. States that are not parties to the Convention can also choose the ICC's jurisdiction in particular cases. The ICC will have its own independent prosecutor, who will be able to institute investigations on his or her own authority as well as to investigate crimes referred by state parties or the UNITED NATION's Security Council.

international law the law applicable to the relations between nations and, to an extent, their internal conduct insofar as the subject of rules of international law. It also applies to other bodies that have international personality. The rules of law are found in treaties, conventions, rules of international customary law, and general principles of law recognised by civilised nations. Subsidiary means for the determination of rules are judicial decisions and the teachings of the most qualified publicists of the various nations. Its status as a binding form of 'real law' is still debated as a matter of legal theory. The active role of the UNITED NATIONS (UN) in the second half of the last century and the work of the INTERNATIONAL COURT OF JUSTICE provide the traditional look of a legal system. International law has expanded both in terms of the number of participants (there are now 189 members of the UN) and subject matter. Traditionally, the rules of warfare and diplomatic relations formed substantive international law, but it now covers wider aspects of international relations including, most famously, peacekeeping. Its perpetual weakness is that it can often be interpreted as the law of the strongest.

interpleader the remedy sought by a person holding property or obliged to do something who is being asked to deliver or perform by more than one person. The process has the claimants fight among themselves before involving the often innocent holder. For Scotland see MULTIPLE POINDING.

interregnum the time during which the throne is vacant.

interrogatories questions put to a person. The most usually encountered sense is of questions put in writing to a litigant or witness to be answered on oath. The purpose is to limit the scope of the inquiry.

in terrorem 'by terror'. A penalty is a term that may be said to be *in terrorem*. Often the law makes such provisions void, but there are many ways of achieving the same result without infringing the legal controls.

interruption a break in the continuity of enjoyment of a right; under the Prescription Act 1832 the break must last for 12 months or more to amount to an interruption. Where a dominant owner protests an interruption, the period of the break runs from the date(s) of the protest.

intervener a person who becomes involved in a case either for his own or for the public interest.

intervention price see COMMON AGRICULTURAL POLICY.

intestacy the state of dying, leaving property undisposed of by will. This may be because the testator has failed to make a will at all or because his will does not make any effective disposition of property (*total intestacy*) or because his will effectively disposes of some, but not all, of his property (*partial intestacy*). The distribution of the intestate estate is done according to detailed rules.

intimation see ASSIGNATION.

intimidation the tort of using unlawful pressure. There is controversy as to whether it covers the situation between two parties in a contractual relationship. It is settled, however, that it is a tort in a three-party situation, that is, where A threatens B that if he does not do something to C, A will do something unlawful to B. Thus, any court action is by C, who is injured against A who used B as his club with which to injure him. Although the common law has always 'been there' and is simply declared by judges, it was not until the case of *Rookes* v. *Barnard* [1964] AC 1129 that the House of Lords made it clear that it did exist. The Trade Dispute Act 1965 was passed to extend the immunity of trade unions to cover this tort, subject, of course, to the nature of the trade union immunity from time to time in force.

in transit in the course of travel. Under the Sales of Goods Act, an UNPAID SELLER is entitled to stop goods in transit and to recover and retain the goods until payment. There are detailed provisions stating when goods are in transit, when the transit starts and when the transit is at an end.

in utero 'in the womb'. In England, the phrase EN VENTRE SA MERE is more common.

investment the process by which funds are deployed with the object of producing gain, either in the form of income or addition to capital. The Trustee Investment Act 1961 establishes a scheme for the investment of TRUST moneys by trustees. Schedule 1 to the Financial Services Act 1986 contains a list of investments for the purposes of the Act; these include stocks and shares issued by companies, stocks and bonds issued by governments and public authorities, options and warrants.

investment relief under the Business Expansion Scheme, investment by an individual in equity capital of qualifying unquoted companies up to a maximum of £40,000 per annum may be set against his other income. See Chapter III of the Income and Corporation Taxes Act 1988 as supplemented by the Finance Act 1988.

invitation to treat see CONTRACT.

invitee a person invited on to premises and thus of significance in OCCUPIER'S LIABILITY but only specially so in English law.

IOU a corrupted abbreviated form of the words 'I owe you'. It is a written acknowledgement of a debt. It is not a NEGOTIABLE INSTRUMENT, like a cheque, but may be founded upon in court to make recovery of the sum more simple.

Iris Oifiguil the official organ of the government of Ireland in which public appointments are announced and certain matters, such as the appointment of liquidators of companies, must be advertised.

Irish law there are two legal systems in Ireland, both of which are COMMON LAW systems. From the Irish Act of Union in 1800 until 1921, Ireland was ruled as part of the UK, although it had a separate court structure from which appeals could be brought to the House of Lords. With the partition of the island, two parliaments were set up, that of Northern Ireland, which comprised the six northeastern counties, being located at Stormont on the outskirts of Belfast, and that of the Irish Free State meeting in Dublin. New court systems were also created for the two parts of the island with (as is still the case) a final appeal from Northern Ireland to the House of Lords, and, in the case of the Irish Free State, an appeal to the Privy Council, although this was abolished in 1933.

The parliament of Northern Ireland had power to make laws for the 'peace, order and good government of the province' but could not legislate on certain matters, such as the armed forces, foreign affairs, weights and measures, and copyright, which were regarded as of national significance and reserved for Westminster. The Stormont parliament was abolished in 1972, and from that time until 1999 Northern Ireland was subject to direct rule from Westminster. Since 1999 a Northern Ireland Assembly set up under the GOOD FRIDAY AGREEMENT has had powers devolved to it.

The Irish Free State, which came into existence in 1922, had a status akin to that of dominions such as Australia and Canada, with a written constitution. This constitution was replaced in 1937 with the present one, which proclaimed the complete independence of Ireland (or, in the Irish language, Eire), which by the Republic of Ireland Act 1948 formally declared itself to be a republic.

On independence, existing law continued to apply in the Irish Free State, and the 1937 Constitution also provided that existing law should continue in force insofar as it was not inconsistent with the Constitution. As a result it is not uncommon to find that legislation passed by the Westminster parliament prior to independence applies in Ireland and that rules of law laid down by UK courts prior to independence are applied. Ireland is different from the UK in that its laws can be struck down by the SUPREME COURT if found to conflict with the Constitution in a similar way to other countries with formal constitutions such as the USA.

irrebuttable cannot be controverted or argued against, usually used in the context of PRESUMPTIONS. If a presumption is irrebuttable, it is in effect a mandatory rule of law.

irregular execution an EXECUTION is irregular when any of the requirements of the rules of court have not been complied with; in such a case the proceedings may be set aside or amended or otherwise dealt with in such manner and upon such terms as the court thinks fit. An execution will be irregular where, for example, it is levied by an unauthorised officer or where there is an error in the amount ordered to be recovered or paid.

irregular marriage in Scots family law there were originally three ways of becoming married without satisfying the necessary formalities: DE PRAESENTI consent, marriage SUBSEQUENTE COPULA and marriage by HABIT AND REPUTE. Only the last of the three remains. A declarator of the court is required to constitute such a marriage, and the date of the marriage is determined by the court. See COMMON LAW MARRIAGE.

irretrievable breakdown the sole ground for DIVORCE in the UK. Irretrievable breakdown can be demonstrated only by showing at least one of the following:

(1) that the other spouse has committed ADULTERY;

(2) that the other spouse has behaved in such a way that the petitioner cannot reasonably be expected to live with him;

(3) that the other spouse has deserted the petitioner and that two years have elapsed since the act of desertion;

(4) that the spouses have lived apart for at least two years (with consent) or five years (against the wishes of one spouse). See BEHAVIOUR.

irrevocable authority certain types of AGENCY agreement are held to be irrevocable:

(1) *authority coupled with an interest*, where the underlying purpose of the agency agreement is to protect some interest of the agent;

(2) *executed authority*, where the agent has commenced performance of his agency and has incurred liabilities in connection therewith for which his principal must indemnify him;

(3) *statutory authority*, where there are certain statutory provisions designed to protect third parties against the effects of revocation of an agent's authority.

irritancy in the Scots law of property, the termination of a lease as a result of certain failures on the part of the tenant. Irritancies are either legal or conventional. *Legal irritancies* are either statutory, like that provided in the Agricultural Holdings (Scotland) Act 1949, or at common law, like the failure to pay rent for two years. Legal irritancies may be purged (satisfied) by complying with the term before a decree is extracted. *Conventional irritancies* cover matters such as non-payment of rent or prohibition of subletting. The common law was that a conventional irritancy could not be purged and a failure by some eleven days to pay rent in a commercial lease could not be escaped: *Dorchester Studios* v. *Stone*, 1975 SC (HL) 56.

However, the Law Reform (Miscellaneous Provisions) (Scotland) Act 1986 provides that even after a conventional irritancy has been committed, it may be enforced only after 14 days' written notice has been given. Other provisions may be enforced only if a fair and reasonable landlord would do so. Where an irritancy does take effect it is not an unjustified enrichment for the landlord to reap the gain of the value of the subjects when recovered: *Dollar Land (Cumbernauld) Ltd* v. *CIN Properties Ltd* [1998] TLR 523.

Islamic law broadly, legal systems that try to effect Allah's will for the Muslim. Law is here very closely related to religion. The Quran, or Koran, is at its heart. To the outsider at least, the law appears to try to serve the will of Allah every bit as much as other aspects of practice. Traditionally, the law is fixed, and it is not intended that it should shift and change according to the wishes of the citizen – in this respect not unlike Western law in times when the Churches were very closely entwined with the state. Nonetheless, its history shows all the signs of great intellectual effort, with the existence of different schools and interpretative techniques not that removed from features observable in the history and development of ROMAN LAW. Today, many aspects of the *sharia*, the body of its doctrines, in many states have been overwhelmed by Westernisation, sometimes by what traditionalists might see as illegitimate interpretative techniques but yet in others there has been fundamental reinstatement.

issue descendants.

issue of execution the sealing of a writ by an officer of the appropriate office (i.e. the district registry where the cause or matter is proceeding, the principal registry of the Family Division, the Admiralty Registry or the Central Office, as the case may be).

issue of securities securities, whether shares or debt securities, may be issued in a variety of ways, the method usually depending on the purpose of the issue and its scale. If, as will often be the case, the purpose is to raise capital, the securities may be issued via a public offer, a placement, a rights issue or an open offer.

issue of shares see ALLOTMENT OF SHARES.

J. abbreviation for JUSTICE.

jeopardy see DOUBLE JEOPARDY.

JCT abbreviation for Joint Contract Tribunal, a building industry body established in 1931 comprising all interested parties that promulgates STANDARD FORM CONTRACTS (and subcontracts) for all sorts of building work. Its interpretation is a specialist field because many disputes go to private arbitration. The latest is JCT 98.

jetsam goods, thrown into the sea from a ship, that sink and remain under water. See FLOTSAM, LAGAN.

joint and several liability liability where a person can be sued jointly with others or individually for the whole sum, leaving it to the person sued to recover from the others with whom he is jointly liable. For example, every partner is jointly liable with his co-partners and also severally liable for everything for which the firm becomes liable while he is a partner.

joint tenancy concurrent ownership of land (or other property) by two or more persons having identical interests with the quality of survivorship (i.e. if one co-owner dies the property automatically vests in the surviving joint tenant(s)).

joint tortfeasors two or more persons responsible for a tort. Courts have power to allocate responsibility among the joint tortfeasors, but each is wholly and severally liable to the victim.

joint venture an association of persons formed to carry through a single piece of business, as opposed to a PARTNERSHIP, which implies continuity of business. Nevertheless, in the absence of a specific corporate form being employed, partnership principles apply to joint ventures.

The accounting treatment of joint ventures differs according to the magnitude of the venture. The point is that if the venture is of sufficient magnitude to warrant a distinct set of books being kept, no special book-keeping treatment is necessary. However, if the books of each participant record only such transactions as affect him directly, special treatment is necessary. In such cases the practice is for each party to open one account only, that account specifically relating to the venture; in that account are recorded all payments made and all sums received by the person in connection with the venture.

JP abbreviation for JUSTICE OF THE PEACE.

judge advocate see JUDGE ADVOCATE-GENERAL.

judge advocate-general in matters of martial or MILITARY LAW, the judge advocate-general's department advises the government on matters of such law and reviews the conduct of courts martial. He will appoint BARRISTERS as judge advocates to sit in courts martial.

judges' rules in English criminal law a code of behaviour issued for the guidance of the police in the investigation phase, now replaced by a legal regime by the POLICE AND CRIMINAL EVIDENCE Act 1984. See RIGHT TO SILENCE.

judgment creditor the person who is named or ascertained in a judgment or order as being entitled to the benefit of it.

judgment debtor see EXAMINATION, JUDGMENT CREDITOR.

Judicial Committee of the Privy Council see PRIVY COUNCIL.

judicial factor in Scotland, a kind of TRUSTEE appointed by the court to administer an estate, sometimes of a person incapable or a partnership that is unable to function.

judicial knowledge in the law of evidence, that body of information that it is assumed that the court is aware of and accordingly need not be proved. It is distinct from the judge's private knowledge, which cannot be used to fill a defect in the evidence.

judicial precedent see PRECEDENT.

judicial review in the constitutional law of the UK, control by courts over certain decisions taken by administrative and other decision-making bodies. The procedure is most often used in relation to the control by the courts of the administrative actions of public bodies. The general rule is that the courts will not interfere in the normal decision-making process. One of the most commonly applied rules is that derived from the case *Associated Provincial Picture Houses* v. *Wednesbury Corporation* [1948] 1 KB 223. This 'Wednesbury' principle is that the courts may interfere where the decision that has been taken is one that no reasonable body could have reached: it is accordingly formulated to curb excess of power, a concept known to Continental jurists as *exces de pouvoir* in France, where there is a long tradition of *droit administratif*, or administrative law. Recently, the distinction between public law control and private law has been emphasised, and it has been said in the House of Lords that 'one can conveniently classify under three heads the grounds upon which administrative action is subject to control by judicial review. The first I would call illegality, the second irrationality, and the third procedural impropriety': *Council of Civil Service Unions* v. *Minister for the Civil Service* [1985] AC 374. Traditional redress had been given and still is on the basis of ULTRA VIRES. Both in England and in Scotland, special procedures have been created to allow parties to obtain swift and competent decisions. Breaches of NATURAL JUSTICE fall within the grounds of such review as a form of procedural impropriety.

For Scotland, where the availability of judicial review is different, see *West* v. *Secretary of State for Scotland* 1992 SLT 636.

judicial separation see SEPARATION.

judicial trustee a TRUSTEE appointed by and under the control of the court under the Judicial Trustees Act 1896.

junior a BARRISTER who is not a Queen's counsel. Alternatively, the barrister of two who was most recently called.

jurat 1. the part of an AFFIDAVIT in which the swearing of the OATH by the deponent is recorded.

2. a permanent lay judge of the Royal Court of Jersey or the Royal Court of Guernsey deciding questions of fact and sentence in conjunction with a professional judge of law.

jurimetrics the application of science to the law, in the sense of measuring by mathematical and statistical methods the outputs of the legal system or the system itself. It includes among its concerns data retrieval by electronic means, such as LEXIS and WESTLAW and the formulation of equations to forecast legal outcomes. Expert systems probably also fall within its ambit.

jurisdiction the power of a court or other body to hear and decide a case or make an order. In civil cases in the EUROPEAN COMMUNITIES a degree of uniformity and coherence has been achieved by the European Convention on Jurisdiction and Enforcement of Judgments in Civil and Commercial Matters 1968, adopted by the UK in the Civil Jurisdiction and Judgments Act 1982. In CARRIAGE OF GOODS BY AIR cases, the Warsaw Convention makes residence the factor in deciding questions of jurisdiction. Therefore, in an action arising from a contract of international carriage that is subject to the Warsaw Convention, English courts would have jurisdiction if the residence or main place of business of the carrier is in England. A similar principle applies in CARRIAGE OF GOODS BY ROAD cases where the Carriage of Goods by Road Act 1965 provides that an action may be brought in the courts of the country where the defendant normally resides or has his chief place of business. Alternatively, jurisdiction may lie in the country where the contract was made.

jurisprudence 1. the study of law in the philosophical sense, considering questions like 'what is law?' There are many schools of thought, the leading ones being NATURAL LAW, POSITIVISM and REALISM. Sometimes a body of thought is known by the name of a particular legal philosopher, e.g. HARTIAN and KELSINIAN JURISPRUDENCE.

2. the decisions of the courts, more often seen in civilian systems, since in Anglo-American systems the phrase 'the common law' has this meaning.

juristic person a body recognised by the law as being entitled to rights and duties in the same way as a natural or human person, the common example being a COMPANY.

jury a group of persons (in England and Wales 12, in Scotland 15) selected at random to decide the facts of a case and to deliver the verdict.

jus administrationis in old Scots law, the right of a husband to administer his wife's property, e.g. land, even although he did not acquire title to that property.

jus mariti in Scots law, the now obsolete right of a husband to his wife's moveable estate. He became vest in all moveables at the time and acquired afterwards.

jus quaesitum tertio 'the third party has acquired a right'. In the law of obligations in systems following the civilian tradition, the law will allow a third party, i.e. one who is not a party to the contract between two other parties, to receive a right under it. For the right to be conferred, the parties have to make their intentions irrevocable as by delivery or intimation to the other party or simply by making this clear from the terms of the deed: see *Carmichael* v. *Carmichael's Exx*. 1920 SC (HL) 195. See THIRD PARTY BENEFICIARY CONTRACT.

jus relecti see LEGAL RIGHTS.

jus relictae see LEGAL RIGHTS.

justice see NATURAL JUSTICE.

justifiable homicide see HOMICIDE.

justification see DEFAMATION.

kangaroo court a travesty of a court where there may be some of the paraphernalia or procedure of a court but the essence of a court hearing is absent, i.e. a *fair hearing*. See NATURAL JUSTICE, FAIR HEARING, EUROPEAN CONVENTION ON HUMAN RIGHTS.

kangaroo procedure see ACT OF PARLIAMENT.

Kashrut see BETH DIN.

KC abbreviation for King's counsel. See BARRISTER.

keeper of an animal see ANIMALS.

Kelsinian jurisprudence the school of JURISPRUDENCE based on the writings of Hans Kelsen. It is based upon a pure theory of law that attempts to explain law without the detail of any given system and without being polluted by politics or theories of justice. It is based upon an ordering of norms and relies upon the *grundnorm*, a justification for the whole system. The grundnorm justifies any 'ought' statement declaring the legal consequences of an act. An example of a grundnorm is 'the founders of the first constitution ought to be obeyed.' It provides the test of validity of other norms in the legal system. As it is the final determinant of validity it cannot itself be validated. The grundnorm is presupposed; it is a hypothesis or even a fiction. The grundnorm is not of the legal system but is a necessary postulate to support its validity. See HARTIAN JURISPRUDENCE.

kerb-crawling see IMPORTUNE.

kidnapping an offence in English common law of taking a person away against his will by force or fraud. For Scotland, see PLAGIUM.

King's Inns, The Honourable Society of the society formed in 1541, the Benchers of which are the governing body of the Bar in the Republic of Ireland. On completion of a course of education and training prescribed by the Society, a person becomes a barrister-at-law, is called to the Bar by the Chief Justice and is entitled to practise in the courts.

knock-for-knock an agreement between insurance companies that has considerable practical effects for many motorists, although not strictly speaking a legal institution. The agreement means that an insurer will, under a fully comprehensive policy, pay the losses of its own insured and will not insist upon raising an action against the other companies insured. If there are uninsured losses, the motorist may have to raise his own action in any event. The idea of insurance companies giving no-claims bonuses whereby they reduce the premium charged if there is no claim means that the issue of fault still has to be resolved, although some companies may still treat the claim as a claim destroying the bonus if they have settled knock-for-knock regardless of the issue of fault. See generally *Hobbes* v. *Marlowe* [1977] 2 All ER 241.

LAB abbreviation for Legal Aid Board. See LEGAL AID.

label in Scottish criminal law, a term used to describe a piece of REAL EVIDENCE because a signed label is attached to it. It is the equivalent of the English and American EXHIBIT.

labes realis an inherent defect in title to property. Stolen goods or goods obtained by fraud, common examples, cannot be transferred, even to an innocent third party. Sometimes also called a *vitium reale*.

laches based on the Latin maxim *vigilantibus non dormientibus jura subveniunt* ('the law serves the vigilant, not those who sleep'), a defence of an equitable claim based on the length of time the plaintiff has allowed to elapse before commencing proceedings. 'Where it would be practically unjust to give a remedy, either because the party has, by his conduct, done that which might fairly be regarded as equivalent to a waiver of it, or where by his conduct and neglect he has, though perhaps not waiving that remedy, yet put the other party in a situation in which it would not be reasonable to place him if the remedy were afterwards to be asserted; in either of these cases, lapse of time and delay are material. But in every case, if an argument against relief, which would otherwise be just, is founded upon mere delay, that delay, of course, not amounting to a bar by any statute of limitations, the validity of that defence must be tried upon principles substantially equitable. Two circumstances, always important in such cases, are the length of the delay and the nature of the acts done during the interval, which might affect either party and cause a balance of justice or injustice in taking the course or the other, so far as relates to the remedy.' – Sir Barnes Peacock in *Lindsay Petroleum Co.* v. *Hurd* (1874) LR 5 PC 221 at 239-240.

lacuna a gap, a case not provided for by a statute or in a document.

Lady Day see QUARTER DAY.

lagan goods sunk in the sea attached to a buoy. See FLOTSAM, JETSAM.

Lammas a Scottish term day, formerly 1 August, now the 28th. See QUARTER DAY.

land not only the physical surface of land but everything growing on or underneath that surface, anything permanently affixed to the surface (such as a building) and the airspace above that surface. It includes not only the soil or earth but always any water, a pond, for example, being regarded as land covered by water. Land may be divisible both horizontally and vertically; thus, ownership of the surface may be vested in one person while ownership of mines and minerals are vested in another. It is perfectly possible to have 'flying freeholds', where ownership of different storeys of the same building are vested in different persons (Scotland has a developed law of the tenement). In Australia and New Zealand the concept of strata titles has been developed to cope with the practical ramifications of this (e.g. enforcement of positive obligations in respect of freehold titles). The normal remedy of a judgment creditor against land or an interest in land of the debtor is either by application for a CHARGING ORDER on the land or for a RECEIVER by way of equitable execution, or both.

land certificate a document issued by the LAND REGISTRY to the proprietor of land, the title to which is governed by the Land Registration Acts; the certificate constitutes evidence of the proprietor's title rather than the title itself. Where title to land is subject to the Land Registration Acts, a land certificate is the document giving details of the title (i.e. a description of the land, the number of the title, the persons registered as proprietor). Although the entries on the Register constitute the actual title to the land, the land certificate is evidence thereof and is usually required to be deposited with lenders when the land is mortgaged.

A very similar system exists in respect of registered land in Scotland. Not all of Scotland is yet covered by registration. The land certificate has a title number and a plan attached based on the Ordnance Survey. The title is guaranteed by the state. It has a section that states any burdens over the land. See Land Registration (Scotland) Act 1979.

land charge third party rights affecting unregistered land that require to be registered in the Land Charges Register in order to bind purchasers for value of that land. Included in the categories of land charges are restrictive covenants, equitable easements, estate contracts, mortgages not protected by the deposit of title deeds and the right of a deserted spouse to remain in the MATRIMONIAL HOME.

Additionally, local authorities in England and Wales are required to keep a Register of Local Land Charges in which are to be entered details of local authority charges, planning charges and the like, which, when registered, bind successive owners of the land. Local land charges affect registered as well as unregistered land.

landlord one who grants a lease or tenancy to another, usually in return for a rent. See LEASE.

landlord's hypothec see HYPOTHEC.

landownership see OWNERSHIP.

Land Registry an entity established by statute to maintain registers of interests in or over land (see LAND CERTIFICATE).

Lands Tribunal a tribunal set up under the Lands Tribunal Act 1949 with jurisdiction to determine questions relating, inter alia, to: (i) compensation for the COMPULSORY PURCHASE of land; and (ii) the extinguishment or modification of restrictive covenants under Section 84 of the Law of Property Act 1925.

In Scotland, the Lands Tribunal for Scotland discharges corresponding functions.

lapse of gift the failure of a testamentary gift as a result of the death of the beneficiary in the testator's lifetime; also, in the case of a gift to a spouse, failure of the gift as a result of the annulment or dissolution of marriage. '. . . the word "lapse" is, in an appropriate context, perfectly apt to cover the happening of any event in a testator's lifetime that prevents the intended legate from being entitled to the legacy, and thus to mean nothing more than "fail".' – per Slade L. J. in *Re Sinclair (decd)* [1985] 1 All ER 1066 at 1070.

larceny another term for some kinds of THEFT, no longer in technical use in the UK.

last opportunity rule a rule that makes the person who had the last opportunity to avoid an accident liable for it. At one time it was very important when a finding of contributory negligence meant that a party failed in his action but is less so now. Indeed, it has been suggested that there is no place for it: see *Boy Andrew* v. *St Rognvald* 1974 SC (HL) 70; *Rouse* v. *Squires* [1973] QB 889.

latent damage damage that is not immediately obvious. The phenomenon is important in relation to TORT and DELICT and, indeed, CONTRACT, where a loss is suffered some time after the conduct or omission (or BREACH OF CONTRACT) that brings it about. It is important because although in theory once there is damage in breach of duty there is liability; in the case of latent damage, the period of time between the defendant's conduct and the damage may be so long that justice suggests that the plaintiff should be relieved. Accordingly, the issue becomes one of PRESCRIPTION or LIMITATION.

In relation to personal injuries in both England and Scotland, the three-year limitation does not begin to run until it can be said that the plaintiff had real and sufficient knowledge (as defined separately and in detail in both jurisdictions) that he had a legal claim for injuries. See Limitation Act 1980 (as amended); Prescription and Limitation (Scotland) Act 1973 (as amended).

So far as claims that are not for personal injuries are concerned (that is, cases for damage to property or economic losses) there are important differences between England and Scotland. In England the period is six years. The Latent Damage Act 1986 amended the principal Act to apply a time limited of six years from the date when the action accrued (perhaps the day when a chimney begins to crack) or three years from the time when the plaintiff knew or ought to have known about the damage (perhaps the day when smoke stopped coming out of the chimney or parts of the chimney began to fall into the garden), whichever is the later. There is, however, a 'long-stop' period of 15 years from the breach of duty to prevent very stale claims coming to court.

In Scotland, the general period in question is five years. Scots law does incorporate a provision for discoverability and a long-stop of 20 years.

In both England and Scotland the long-stop period in respect of claims relating to damage caused by defective products in terms of the Consumer Protection Act 1987 is only ten years.

law 'every law is the invention and gift of the gods' (Demosthenes); 'laws were made that the stronger might not in all things have his own way' (Ovid); 'it would be better to have no laws at all than it is to have so many as we have' (Montaigne); 'all law has for its object to confirm and exalt in a system the exploitation of the workers by a ruling class' (Bakunin); 'the law is reason free from passion' (Aristotle). JURISPRUDENCE is the occupation and science of trying to define law.

law agent any person entitled to practise as an agent in a court of law in Scotland. Scottish SOLICITORS are law agents.

lawburrows an ancient Scots remedy requiring an apprehended wrongdoer to find CAUTION or put up money to keep the peace. It dates back to before the 15th century but was nonetheless used a number of times in the 20th century. 'Burrow' or 'burgh' was an old Scots word for caution, so the remedy involves the court ordering a party to put up a sum of money or a bond that is forfeit should the law be broken by that party. The availability of INTERDICT and the introduction of a modern police force have rendered it less important, to the point of obsolescence.

Law Commission a body established by the Law Commissions Act 1965 to examine the law with a view to its systematic development and reform, including the codification of law, the elimination of anomalies, the repeal of obsolete and unnecessary enactments, and the modernisation of the law. Members are appointed by the LORD CHANCELLOR. See also SCOTTISH LAW COMMISSION, LAW REFORM COMMISSION.

Law Commissioner a member of a LAW COMMISSION.

law library in both the Republic of Ireland and Northern Ireland (as with Scottish ADVOCATES), BARRISTERS do not, as in England, operate from CHAMBERS but from a law library. In the Republic, this is situated in the Four Courts in Dublin and in Northern Ireland in the Law Courts in Belfast.

law lord a colloquial name for a LORD OF APPEAL IN ORDINARY or other judge who sits in the Judicial Committee of the House of Lords.

law merchant the international practice of merchants relating to commercial and maritime matters that has been judicially recognised and, as such, absorbed into the common laws of England and Scotland. 'When a general usage has been judicially ascertained and established, it becomes a part of the law merchant, which courts of justice are bound to know and recognise' – per Lord Campbell in *Brandao* v. *Barnett* (1846) 12 Cl&F 787 at 805.

Law Reform Commission an independent body set up in the Republic of Ireland by the Law Reform Commission Act 1975 to keep the law under review and to make proposals for its reform. It comprises a president and four commissioners appointed by the government and has a small staff. See also SCOTTISH LAW COMMISSION.

Law Reports the publications in which the decisions of the courts are recorded. It should, however, be appreciated that in the UK and in many other jurisdictions these are private publications rather than state-operated. The publisher makes the reports more attractive, more useful, and subject to legal protection, by adding a summary of the facts and law involved, called a RUBRIC. Indexing makes it easier to find relevant precedents for argument in court. Some series are given special weight because they are revised by the judges themselves, examples being the Law Reports in England and the Session Cases in Scotland. There is little doubt that the comprehensive reporting of judgments and the indexing of them led to the concept of STARE DECISIS, or binding force of precedent.

Law Society the body that both regulates and controls SOLICITORS in England. It was constituted by royal charter in 1845. It is responsible for the legal education of solicitors, issuing practising certificates and preserving minimum standards of behaviour. It deals with discipline. It also administers the guarantee fund for the benefit of the public. It administers a complaints system.

Law Society of Northern Ireland the body that performs in Northern Ireland the functions that the LAW SOCIETY performs in England and Wales and the LAW SOCIETY OF SCOTLAND provides in Scotland.

Law Society of Scotland the statutory body that both represents and controls SOLICITORS in Scotland, established initially by the Solicitors (Scotland) Act 1949. Its executive body is the elected Council and day-to-day business is administered by a permanent secretariat. It is not responsible for discipline as such, that being the preserve of another statutory body, the Scottish Solicitors Discipline Tribunal. The Law Society of Scotland administers a guarantee fund.

lay days the period within which, according to the terms of a charterparty, cargo must be loaded on to or unloaded from a ship. '"Lay days" are described in a charterparty in various ways; sometimes certain days are fixed for loading and unloading. . . . They may be described, and sometimes they are described, in a CHARTERPARTY as days of so many working hours.' – per Lord Escher MR in *Neilson* v. *Watt* (1885) 16 QBD 67 at 71.

LC abbreviation for LORD CHANCELLOR.

LCJ abbreviation for LORD CHIEF JUSTICE.

leading question a question that either suggests the answer expected or that assumes the existence of disputed facts to which the witness is to testify. Leading questions are not allowed except as to formal matters that are not disputed (e.g. witness's name, address, etc) and in CROSS-EXAMINATION. Even where allowed there is always the danger that the answer, thus obtained, is given less weight by the judge.

lease a grant of the use of land (or other subject matter) for a specified term. In relation to land, the grant confers a right of exclusive possession for a 'term or years', usually in return for the payment of a periodic sum (rent) or a capital sum (a premium) or both. A *lessee* may 'sublet' to a *sub-lessee*, who will then acquire the right of exclusive possession as against the lessee, who will become entitled to receive the rent stipulated for in the sublease. Leases may be *legal* or *equitable*, the latter taking effect under the rule in *Walsh* v. *Lonsdale* (1882). A legal lease is sometimes referred to as a *demise*. A legal lease for periods in excess of three years requires to be made by deed.

The term 'lease' is also used in connection with contracts for the hiring of equipment or other chattels for a specified period. In relation to equipment and plant, there are two distinct types of leasing, namely *finance leasing* and *operating leasing*. A finance lease is a lease for the bulk of the asset's economic life and from which the *lessor* expects to obtain his normal profit on the asset without being involved in further activity in respect of it; such leases are generally non-cancellable or cancellable only on payment of a major penalty. Operating leases are effectively all other leases; they are cancellable by the lessee at short notice and without major penalty; they are arrangements under which the lessor expects to release or sell the asset, obtaining significant portions of his total profit on the asset from each successive transaction. See HIRE.

leasehold see LEASE.

leasing see LEASE.

leave to enter the UK a person who is not a British citizen or a Commonwealth citizen having the right of abode requires leave to enter before entering the UK. This will normally be given by an immigration officer on production of a valid national passport or other document satisfactorily establishing the person's identity and nationality.

leave to remain in the UK a right that may be unrestricted or limited. If it is granted subject to limitations, the conditions may be varied or added to or revoked. An unrestricted leave to remain does not mean that the person concerned may not be liable to deportation in certain circumstances.

legacy a gift of personal (as opposed to real) property by will. Legacies may be specific, general or demonstrative. A *specific legacy* is a gift of some ascertained item or thing forming part of the testator's estate that, by its description, is distinguished from the mass of his personal estate. A *general legacy* is a gift that is not so separated from the general mass of the testator's personal estate; thus, a pecuniary legacy is a general legacy. A *demonstrative legacy* is a pecuniary legacy payable out of a particular fund. A gift of real property by will is referred to as a *devise*.

legal see ADJUDICATION.

legal aid assistance to litigants that they might be able to avail themselves of the usually expensive legal process. In the UK, various schemes have existed from time to time, usually inspired by the legal profession's acceptance of a duty to do work for the less fortunate. As part of the 'welfare state' provisions introduced after the Second World War, England and Wales and Scotland established legal aid schemes. As with most government-funded welfare, the rules – who gets how much for what – change according to the government of the day. The most significant recent development was the establishment of a Legal Aid Board for England and a Scottish Legal Aid Board, taking administration of the system away from lawyers. In England in 2000 the LAB was replaced by the LEGAL SERVICES COMMISSION, aimed at providing better value for money. This is being done through a franchising scheme whereby tested and audited lawyers gain certain privileges. Franchising is not yet compulsory.

There are three main forms of legal aid operated by the Scottish Legal Aid Board (SLAB):

(1) *advice and assistance* (the *pink form scheme*), which, subject to the means of the applicant, allows the solicitor to give legal advice. On some specified occasions, court appearances may be possible under the scheme called ABWOR – *assistance by way of representation*;

(2) *civil legal aid*, which allows a court action to be raised or defended. Means are assessed, and the SLAB must be satisfied that the case has merit. As well as allowing the litigant legal services (perhaps subject to a contribution) a legal aid certificate can allow the court to reduce or waive the legal expenses normally payable by a losing litigant;

(3) *criminal legal aid* is available for the defence of criminal charges. Means are less important here – the question is whether it is in the interests of justice that the accused be represented. Unless or until there are no rules of evidence or procedure, and no need to cross-examine, it is quite clear that in the majority of cases justice requires the accused to have a lawyer.

The amounts paid to lawyers by way of fees under the schemes are fixed, often at heavily discounted rates.

The availability of legal aid is an important aspect of the HUMAN RIGHT to a FAIR TRIAL.

legal aid franchise quality standard see COMMUNITY LEGAL SERVICE.

legal charge see CHARGE.

legalese the language used by the legal profession, a term now used pejoratively.

legal executive qualified lawyers who are not solicitors or barristers, who have at least five years' experience of working under the supervision of a solicitor in legal practice or the legal department of a private company or in local/national government. They have to pass INSTITUTE OF LEGAL EXECUTIVES' (ILEX) qualifying examinations in their area of legal practice. Fellows are issued with an annual practising certificate of ILEX and may describe themselves as legal executives. They specialise in a particular area of legal work. Should they so wish, their qualifications and experience allow them entry to the final stages of the solicitor's qualification scheme – the Legal Practice Course (LPC) and the Professional Skills Course (PSC).

legal interest see BENEFICIAL INTEREST.

legal rights in the succession law of Scotland, the FINANCIAL PROVISION that the law takes from a person's estate for relatives. Before this exercise takes place, statutory prior rights have to be considered – they are every bit as legal and can quite often exhaust an estate – however, prior rights operate only on INTESTACY. Legal rights apply whether there is or is not a WILL. The free moveable estate, i.e. exclusive of HERITAGE, is divided into three parts: one for the widow or widower, called *jus relictae* or *jus relicti* respectively; one for the children or, if dying before the deceased, their representative(s), called LEGITIM or the *bairn's part*; and the *dead's part*, which, as the names suggests, means that it can be willed with impunity. Clearly, these provisions can be avoided by transferring one's property into heritage or disposing of the property during life.

Legal Services Commission the body responsible for running the COMMUNITY LEGAL SERVICE Fund, which replaced civil LEGAL AID in England and Wales in 2000. It took over the work of the Legal Aid Board in this respect.

legislation the rules of the lawgiver, in the UK principally effected by ACTS OF PARLIAMENT, DELEGATED LEGISLATION and SUBORDINATE LEGISLATION. The Queen in Council (i.e. with members of the PRIVY COUNCIL), by ORDER IN COUNCIL, legislates in a restricted sphere. In Canada federal legislation is by the Queen, represented by the Governor-General, the Senate and the House of Commons. In Australia, Commonwealth legislation is by the Queen through the Governor-General, the Senate and House of Representatives.

Legislation can be used in the sense of laws made by an inferior lawgiver such as a club, society or trade union. The law governing members of an incorporated body is usually seen as contractual, but sometimes the memorandum and articles of a LIMITED COMPANY can be seen as a form of legislation for the members.

legislature as a matter of CONSTITUTIONAL LAW, a body that passes laws or LEGISLATION.

legitim in Scots succession law, the *bairn's part* – that part of the LEGAL RIGHTS in a person's movable estate that cannot be disposed of by will. The fund amounts to one third if the spouse still lives, one half if not. The children of deceased children can represent their ancestor. Advances paid to an offspring can sometimes be treated as advances of legitim. As a result, other issue are allowed to have this notionally repaid to the fund before allocation of what is now in the fund – this is called COLLATIO INTER LIBEROS. Similar legal institutions exist in other systems, for example, Jersey and Guernsey.

lenocinium connivance or furtherance by a husband of a wife's ADULTERY. It is a DEFENCE available to the wife. In Scots family law, it describes the situation where a spouse seeking a divorce is refused decree because that spouse encouraged the adultery complained of.

lesion injury or loss. In the civil law jurisdictions the word is often used in the context of an 'unfair' loss, as where an adult takes advantage of a minor or someone purchases something for much less than it's worth.

letters of administration a grant that is issued in the case where a person dies intestate or where no executor is appointed or is willing to act, permitting an estate to be dealt with (see INTESTACY). If the deceased died wholly intestate, the grant will be issued to the person entitled to take out the grant (i.e. the same person or persons who would be entitled to the intestate's estate); such a grant is often referred to as a *grant of simple administration*. If the deceased left a will but failed to make an effective appointment of an executor, or where the appointed executor refused to act and renounced probate, a *grant of letters of administration with will annexed* may be taken out, usually by the person with the greatest interest under the will.

letters of request or **letters rogatory** or **littera rogatoria** a document sent from a court in one jurisdiction to a court in another asking for some form of judicial assistance such as the obtaining of evidence.

lewd and libidinous practice in Scotland, this type of conduct (i.e. exposing of private parts to young girls) is a crime. It is not essential that the conduct is directed towards a person at the age of puberty.

lex aquilia an ancient Roman statute, probably passed in the 3rd century BC. Two provisions of it, the first and third chapters, formed the essence of the delict known as *damnum injuria datum*, 'loss wrongfully caused'. The third chapter provided that if a man caused loss to another by burning, breaking or destroying the defendant's property he would be liable for the loss caused. The Digest (see CORPUS JURIS CIVILIS) is rich in discussion of what cases would or would not attract liability. The focus on the notion of *injuria* is the origin of the requirement for fault in the law of DELICT in Scotland and the law of TORT in England. Originally it meant simply without justification but eventually it was developed to mean FAULT.

lex et consuetudo parliament 'the law and custom of parliament'. This determines the conduct of Parliament itself and its exercise of privilege. See CONVENTIONS.

lex fori in PRIVATE INTERNATIONAL LAW, the law of the court seized of the dispute.

LEXIS a private legal information retrieval system provided on a computer database that is interrogated from a dedicated terminal or from a personal computer equipped with appropriate software. It has libraries full of case reports from very many jurisdictions, including the USA and the UK, as well as very detailed references and, indeed, full texts of certain leading legal periodicals. It is the most popular such system in the UK and is ever increasing its stock of Scottish materials.

lex loci contractus in PRIVATE INTERNATIONAL LAW, 'the law of the place of the contract'.

lex loci delicti (commissi) 'the place of the DELICT or the place where the delict was committed', a term of PRIVATE INTERNATIONAL LAW. In Scotland and many continental countries, this governs the law applicable where a TORT or delict has taken place. The law applied is that of the place where the delict was committed. Both English law and Scots law used to apply a 'double delict rule' by which the conduct complained of had to be actionable under the law of the *lex loci delicti* and Scots or English law. That rule has been repealed by the Private International Law (Miscellaneous Provisions) Act 1995.

lex loci situs 'the place where the thing is', a term of PRIVATE INTERNATIONAL LAW. In a conflict of laws situation, a court may have to apply the *lex loci situs*, viz. the legal rules of the place where the property in question is situated (or in some cases where it was situated at the time of some legally relevant transaction). It is most usually applied to IMMOVEABLE PROPERTY.

lex loci solutionis in PRIVATE INTERNATIONAL LAW, 'the law of the place where the contract was performed'.

lex talionis the law of retribution in kind: 'an eye for an eye, a tooth for a tooth'.

liability of a trustee see TRUSTEE.

liability of partners see PARTNERSHIP.

liability, strict see STRICT LIABILITY.

liability, vicarious see VICARIOUS LIABILITY.

libel see DEFAMATION.

licence 1. a permission given by one person to another to do some act that, without such permission, it would be unlawful for him to do. In relation to land, a licence may arise gratuitously, or by contract, or by ESTOPPEL. Licences arising from a gratuitous act may generally be revoked at the will of the grantor unless some question of estoppel arises; licences arising from a CONTRACT are capable of specific enforcement. **2.** an official document authorising a specified activity that would be unlawful for the licensee to engage in without such document (e.g. a liquor licence authorising the manufacture or sale of intoxicating liquor; a driving licence authorising the holder to drive a motor vehicle on the public highway). See also OCCUPIER'S LIABILITY.

lien a SECURITY right permitting one person to retain possession of goods owned by another until the claims of the person retaining the goods as against the owner have been satisfied.

An agent has a lien on the goods and chattels of his principal in respect of all claims arising out of his employment as an agent. The lien entitles the agent to detain goods in his possession belonging to his principal until all the legitimate claims of the agent have been satisfied.

In connection with moveable property, a lien is the right of an agent or bailee to retain possession of a CHATTEL entrusted to him until his claim has been paid; in relation to land, a vendor has a lien over the land for unpaid purchase money. Liens are either *particular*, as, for example, a right to retain a thing for some charge or claim arising out of or in connection with the thing, like that of a garage proprietor, or *general*, as, for example, a right to retain a thing not only for such charges or claims but also for a general balance of accounts between the parties in respect of other dealings of a like nature, such as the solicitor's lien.

The UNPAID SELLER of goods who is in possession of the goods is entitled to retain possession of them until payment or tender of the price. This lien exists only where the buyer becomes insolvent. The seller may exercise his lien or right of retention notwithstanding that he is in possession of the goods as agent or bailee or custodier for the buyer. In order to exercise his lien, the seller must be in possession of the goods. He does not lose possession merely because he gives temporary or limited control of goods to the buyer, e.g. to mark them or pack them in his own containers. The unpaid seller of goods loses his lien or right of retention in respect of the goods in three situations:

(1) when he delivers the goods to a carrier or other bailee or custodier for the purpose of transmission to the buyer without reserving the right of disposal of goods;

(2) when the buyer or his agent lawfully obtains possession of the goods;

(3) a lien or right of retention may be lost by waiver.

On the dissolution of a PARTNERSHIP, each partner has a general lien on the firm's surplus assets; this lien arises out of a partner's statutory right to have the surplus assets (after payment of the firm's debts and liabilities) applied in payment of what may be due to the partners respectively (after deducting what may be due from them as partners to the firm).

In CARRIAGE OF GOOD BY AIR cases, there is no provision in the Warsaw Convention about the carrier's lien; the ordinary common law rules therefore apply. In CARRIAGE OF GOODS BY ROAD cases, the carrier has a right at common law to retain possession of goods until he is paid the freight owing to him for the carriage of the goods. In CARRIAGE OF GOODS BY SEA cases, the carrier has a lien at common law not only in respect of the freight and general average contribution due in respect of the goods upon which he exercises the lien but also for sums due for freight and general average in respect of all the goods of the same owner in the same ship of the same voyage.

Lieutenant-Governor (Canada) see CONSTITUTIONAL LAW (CANADA).

life assurance or insurance a contractual arrangement under which, in return for a stipulated premium, a life assurance company undertakes to pay, on the death of the life assured or on the occurrence of such other events as may be agreed, a specified sum of money.

life estate an estate of freehold that exists for the duration of the life of the grantee. If the grantee should assign his interest, that taken by the assignee is referred to as an *estate pur autre vie* (i.e. 'an estate for the life of someone else', namely the original grantee). Since 1925 a life estate can exist only as an equitable interest behind a trust. See INSURABLE INTEREST, INSURANCE.

life interest an interest in property, whether real or personal, conferring the right to the use of that property and the right to take the income or fruits or produce of that property for the period of the beneficiary's life. In English law, life interests, whether in realty or personalty, can exist only behind trusts. In Australia and New Zealand, while it remains technically possible to constitute legal life interests, the practice is for them to be made to take effect under a trust. The holder of a life interest is referred to as a *life tenant*; if a life tenant assigns his interest to a third party, that third party is said to have an interest *pur autre vie*.

life rent (sometimes hyphenated, always all one word in Scotland) a LIFE INTEREST in property without damaging or depleting it. It is different from an ANNUITY. It may be a *proper life rent*, where the property goes directly to the life renter, but almost always in modern times there is the interposition of a TRUST. Questions often arise as to what falls within the life rent and what is part of the right of the ultimate proprietor, the fee. The life renter pays all the usual running costs of the property. A provision of life rent for ALIMENT is known as an *alimentary life rent* and, so long as suitably drafted, it is not attachable by creditors. The Apportionment Act 1870 declares that all payments of the nature of income accrue day by day and are apportionable accordingly.

In the Scots law of property, a form of personal servitude more usually considered as an interest in land. It is the right to use and enjoy subjects during life without destroying or wasting the source. *Fee* is the full and unlimited right to the subjects, and it is the fee that is encumbered by the liferent. The liferent can be *reserved* where A transfers the fee to B, keeping the liferent to himself, or it can be *constituted*, as in the case of a will where one person may be given the liferent (such as a widow) and another the fee (such as a child). The liferenter gets the fruits of the subjects, although this principle can be quite difficult to apply in some circumstances.

life tenant see LIFE INTEREST.

lifting the (corporate) veil in company law, the court's refusal to apply the normal rule that a corporation is a different legal person from its members: *Salomon* v. *Salomon* [1897] AC 22. Instances where this has been done are:

(1) where a group of companies is an economic entity, see *DHN Food Distributors* v. *Tower Hamlets* [1976] 3 All ER 462 and *Woolfson* v. *SRC* 1978 SC (HL) 90; and

(2) where there is illegality, see *Daimler Co.* v. *Continental Tyre and Rubber Co.* [1916] 2 AC 307.

Directors who may be members are not protected by the veil in some statutory cases:

(1) where the membership of the company has fallen beneath the statutory minimum;

(2) where the company trades without having received the appropriate certificate from the registrar;

(3) where a bill of exchange is signed by an officer of the company, which does not bear the company's full name, see *Ratsanjan Pistachio Promotions Group* v. *Reis* [1990] BCC 730;

(4) where under the Insolvency Act 1986 the directors are personally liable for wrongful trading.

light or prospect in Scots property law, the urban servitude *non aedificandi* ('not to build'), *altius non tollendi* ('not to build beyond a certain height') and *non officiendi luminibus* ('not to interfere with light') combine to restrain proprietors, from their otherwise existing rights, from building, extending upwards or otherwise acting to impede the other proprietor's light. There is authority for another servitude of light that prohibits the making of windows that would interfere with the neighbour's privacy. See EASEMENT.

like work see SEX DISCRIMINATION.

limitation the body of rules that prevent actions being raised after a lapse of time. Technically they are different from PRESCRIPTION rules. Limitation does not extinguish the underlying right, whereas prescription does. In England, the Limitation Act 1980 (as amended) applies a three-year limitation period to claims for personal injury and a six-year period to most other claims.

In Scotland there is a three-year limitation period in respect of personal injuries, but most other claims are dealt with under the short negative prescription of five years: Prescription and Limitation (Scotland) Act 1973 (as amended).

limited company a COMPANY in which the liability of each shareholder is limited to the amount of the capital agreed to be invested by him in it; liability does not extend to the member's other assets.

limited liability partnership a new kind of legal entity through which business may be carried on in the UK with effect from 6 April 2001. It is a cross between the LIMITED COMPANY and the PARTNERSHIP. It will permit two or more people to combine to carry on business in partnership but will give them the benefit, which normal partnership does not, of limiting their liability to creditors. The limited liability partnership will be a separate entity from its partners and will have to be registered with the Registrar of Companies. At the time of writing, detailed regulations governing them are still being drafted, but the government has announced that they will be treated for tax purposes like conventional partnerships.

limited partnership a PARTNERSHIP under which it is possible for a person to become a partner upon terms that his liability to the creditors of the firm should be strictly limited (rather like that of a shareholder in a company). Such a person is in the position of a sleeping partner with limited liability: Limited Partnership Act 1907. See also LIMITED LIABILITY PARTNERSHIP.

Lincoln's Inn see BARRISTER.

liquid a fixed amount. *Liquidate damages* are DAMAGES set out in an agreement between the parties rather than left at large for a court or arbiter. A *liquid debt* is one that is fixed in a document of debt, such as bond, or decree of a court or arbiter.

liquidate damages see DAMAGES, LIQUID, PENALTY CLAUSES.

liquidation the procedure under which a COMPANY is dissolved (or wound up). Liquidation may be *voluntary* (where the company is solvent but where the purposes for which it was set up have been achieved or no longer exist) or *compulsory* (usually where the company is insolvent). The function of a LIQUIDATOR is to convert the assets of the company into cash, which is then distributed among the creditors to pay off (so far as possible) the debts of the company. Any surplus is then distributed among the members. See generally the Insolvency Act 1986.

liquidator a person who conducts the winding up of a company. Such a person must be a qualified insolvency practitioner (unless the winding up is done by the OFFICIAL RECEIVER). See LIQUIDATION.

lis alibi pendens a plea that the dispute is continuing in another court. It may allow the action in which it is pled to be suspended while the other action is concluded.

literal rule the rule of STATUTORY INTERPRETATION that demands that a statute be interpreted according to its very words regardless of result and regardless of any attempt that can be made to find the intention of the legislator; thus 'no dogs allowed' prohibits guide dogs and police dogs.

litigation the putting of a dispute before a court or tribunal.

litigation friend a representative in court proceedings for children who have yet to reach their majority (i.e. aged 18) who require special protection in respect of legal claims brought by or against them. The main purpose is to ensure that settlements are fair and in their interests. Normally the office will be held by a parent but not in cases where, for example, the child is a passenger in the parent's car. The person must be able to act 'fairly and competently' and have no interest that could be considered adverse to that of the child. If necessary, the court can make an appointment.

litigiosity in the Scots law of DILIGENCE or legal enforcement, the doctrine that once an action has commenced the property involved should not be dealt with in such a way that the purpose of the action is defeated. More reliable methods are often used, such as ARRESTMENT on the dependence or INTERDICT.

littera rogatoria see LETTER OF REQUEST.

livestock 1. any creature kept for the production of food, wool, skins or fur or for the purpose of its use in the farming of land or the carrying on of any agricultural activity: Agricultural Holdings Act 1986.

2. cattle, horses, asses, mules, hinnies, sheep, pigs, goats and poultry and deer not in the wild state: Animals Act 1971. See also Animals (Scotland) Act 1987, which is in different terms.

living will see ADVANCE DIRECTIVE.

LJ abbreviation for Lord Justice of Appeal.

LJC abbreviation for LORD JUSTICE CLERK.

loan a transaction whereby property is lent or given to another on condition of return or repayment. During the period of the loan the borrower is entitled to use the thing loaned for the purpose agreed between the parties. In a loan of money, the money lent becomes the property of the borrower during the period of the loan against an undertaking to return a sum of equivalent amount either on demand or on a specified date or in accordance with an agreed schedule of repayments.

loan capital that part of a COMPANY's capital that is not equity or preference capital but which has been raised by loans that are due for repayment at a future date.

loan syndication lending by a group. The size of some loans is so large that no single financial institution would possess either the resources or the inclination to lend the entire sum on its own. In such cases a syndicate of institutions is formed to provide the necessary funding. The syndication process starts when either a borrower approaches a bank and invites it to initiate arrangements for a syndication facility or when the bank itself approaches a corporate borrower that it believes is seeking funds. The bank (known as the *managing bank*) will then:

(1) settle in outline with the company the financial and other terms on the basis of which the loan is to be promoted;

(2) approach prospective lenders in the market and provide them with details of the proposed loan and information about the borrower in order to enable a judgment to be made as to whether or not to participate; and

(3) negotiate the details of the loan agreement with the borrower.

Loan syndications, therefore, comprise two distinct sets of agreements: those governing the formation of and participation in the syndicate and those governing the relationship between the syndicate and the borrower, in effect, the loan agreement itself.

locatio conductio in ROMAN LAW, the contract of HIRE. The language is still used in CIVILIAN jurisdictions. There were three main varieties: *locatio rei*, 'the hire of a thing'; *locatio operarum*, 'a worker for a wage; *locatio operis faciendi*, a contract for 'services providing a result'. Certain professions were beyond such contracts – the advocate received an honorarium rather than a fee, and a law professor received not even an honorarium.

locatio custodia in ROMAN LAW and Scots law, a form of HIRE – 'the hire of custody of a thing'. For English law, see BAILMENT.

locatio operarum the contract in Roman and civilian systems of the hire of labour in the sense of master and servant or employment as popularly understood, e.g. the chauffeur. See LOCATIO OPERIS.

locatio operis the contract in Roman and civilian systems of the hire of the services of another in the sense of an independent contractor, e.g. the taxi driver. See LOCATIO OPERARUM.

loc. cit. abbreviation for *loco citato*, 'in the place previously cited'.

locus 'place' or 'area'.

locus poenitentiae 'the right to withdraw'. Specially in Scots law, the term refers to the opportunity to treat as not binding an agreement freely entered into where the requisite formalities have not been concluded. The right to withdraw can be lost by the operation of a PERSONAL BAR, usually HOMOLOGATION or REI INTERVENTUS or in cases covered by the Requirements of Writing Act 1995.

Lomé Convention in the law of the EUROPEAN COMMUNITIES the agreement (now in its fourth version) that is the foundation for the Communities' links with the ACP (African, Caribbean and Pacific countries) and overseas territories. It is a series of bilateral agreements with more than 60 countries. Originally concluded with a view to the post-colonial situation of some of the MEMBER STATES, it is now an instrument of development and aid. The general basis of it is to allow the produce of Convention states to enter the Communities free of the common customs tariff but without reciprocity for the Communities. Member states are, however, allowed *most favoured nation* status. A system has been developed to assist states that rely on a single product – the Community evens out the good years and the bad years through the STABEX and SYSMIN systems: the downside of this may be that it does not encourage diversification in the beneficiary state.

long negative prescription see PRESCRIPTION.

loosing of arrestments see ARRESTMENT.

Lord Advocate the senior law officer for Scotland. All prosecutions run in his name, and he represents many government departments in Scotland. He is a member of the government but need not be a Member of Parliament. Actions by and against government departments are raised by and against the Lord Advocate. He is in charge of the prosecution of all crime in Scotland and all solemn prosecutions run in his name. See also ADVOCATE GENERAL FOR SCOTLAND.

Lord Chancellor head of the English judicial system and an important member of the government, remarkably contrary to any notion of separation of powers. He sits on the woolsack when in the House of Lords. He has a very heavy administrative responsibility for the whole justice system in England, including matters such as legal aid and judicial appointments.

Lord Chief Justice president of the Queen's Bench Division of the High Court and, by his office, a member of the COURT OF APPEAL.

Lord Justice Clerk Scotland's second ranking judge. In criminal matters he is second to the LORD JUSTICE GENERAL and in civil matters presides over the second division of the Inner House, the appellate division of the COURT OF SESSION.

Lord Justice General Scotland's senior judge. Apart from heading the Criminal Appeal Court, he also has heavy administrative responsibilities. He holds the office of Lord President of the civil COURT OF SESSION at the same time.

Lord Lyon King of Arms head of administration in matters heraldic in Scotland. He acts as heraldic judge in civil and criminal matters. It is an ancient office derived from the Celtic *seannachie*. The Lyon Court sits on the days of the ancient druidic feasts of Beltane and Samhain. The Lyon Court has all the powers of an ordinary court, such as to fine and imprison.

Lord of Appeal in Ordinary a person appointed to carry out the judicial function of the HOUSE OF LORDS and of the Judicial Committee of the PRIVY COUNCIL, theoretically in addition to any persons in the House of Lords who are legally qualified. The office began when it was clear there were insufficient able bodies in the Lords: Appellate Jurisdiction Act 1876. The Lord of Appeal in Ordinary, as well as sitting as a judge, is entitled to sit and vote in the Lords. Persons must have held high judicial office for two years or be BARRISTERS or ADVOCATES of 15 years' standing. Often they have sat in the COURT OF APPEAL or in the Inner House of the COURT OF SESSION. As a matter of practice there are always some Scottish Lords of Appeal in Ordinary so that in Scottish appeals an eminent Scots lawyer is available to assist the English trained judges.

Lord Ordinary a judge of the COURT OF SESSION.

Lord President of the Court of Session Scotland's senior civil judge. The Lord President chairs the first division of the Inner House, the appellate division of the COURT OF SESSION. He also holds the office of LORD JUSTICE GENERAL. He carries a heavy administrative burden, regulating many aspects of civil court business.

loss adjuster someone who specialises in investigating claims under insurance policies. The law in this area is most specialised, and adjusters do not merely check the facts but seek out such facts as are relevant to the policy or policies of the type in question. They may be employed either by way of subcontracting by insurers or by insured persons who wish to maximise their legitimate claims.

loss relief a trading loss may be set off against the total income of the taxpayer for the year in which the loss occurred. In certain circumstances the loss may be carried forward to be set against income of succeeding years; in other circumstances it may be carried back and set against the income of preceding years.

losses in partnership see PARTNERSHIP.

lost modern grant a convenient legal fiction devised to overcome the difficulty of common law PRESCRIPTION that use or enjoyment from 1189 had to be shown. Where use or enjoyment as of right for 20 years could be shown, the mere fact that use or enjoyment could not have been going on in 1189 was not allowed to stop the operation of the prescription; the courts were prepared to accept that the use or enjoyment had arisen as a result of a grant post-1189 that had subsequently been lost.

lump sum order an order for payment of a single sum. In a DIVORCE action the court has the power to make an order for the payment of a capital sum or the transfer of property. Such an order can be made at the date of the divorce or within a period specified by the court.

Maastricht Treaty see EUROPEAN UNION TREATY.

magistrate an inferior judge. In England and Scotland, they are primary lay posts filled by ordinary members of the public. *Stipendiaries* are qualified lawyers who hold the post in the busiest courts.

Magna Carta the 'Great Charter' of liberties, signed by King John at Runymede, 15 June 1215. One of the foundations of the notion of the rule of law. The barons made it clear that the king operated under legal constraints. Two clauses, 39 and 40, were developed to become a basis of the liberty of the subject to the present: 'No freeman shall be seized or imprisoned, or stripped of his rights or possession, or outlawed or exiled or deprived of his standing in any other way, nor will we proceed with force against him, or send others to do so, except by the lawful judgment of his equals or by the law of the land' (Clause 39)

'To no one will we sell, to no one deny or delay right or justice' (Clause 40).

maills and duties in the Scots law of DILIGENCE or legal enforcement, a process that allows a HERITABLE CREDITOR to attach rents due by tenants of the subjects.

maintenance money payable under an order of court by one spouse to another or, on divorce, by one ex-spouse to another or by a parent to a child for that person's living expenses. For Scotland, see ALIMENT.

maintenance and champerty two former torts and crimes striking at a third party's support of another's litigation. *Maintenance* is the stirring up of litigation by supporting a party without having a just cause or excuse for so doing: *Re Trepca Mines Ltd* (No. 2) [1963] Ch. 199. *Champerty* is where the person maintaining is to be paid out of the supported proceedings. Both were abolished as torts or crimes by the Criminal Law Act 1967.

maintenance assessment the exercise carried out by a CHILD SUPPORT OFFICER to fix the CHILD SUPPORT to be paid by an absent parent in respect of a qualifying CHILD.

The calculation is a complex one, a formula being provided in the legislation. There is, however, a protected income level to prevent the absent parent having to pay too much.

majority the age when a person attains full legal capacity, even if there may still be many things that cannot be done legally or, indeed, many things now in the UK which can be done younger, especially at 16 years. In the UK at the moment it is 18 years.

majority verdict see VERDICT.

maladministration see PARLIAMENTARY COMMISSIONER FOR ADMINISTRATION.

mala fides see BONA FIDES.

malice aforethought see HOMICIDE.

malicious injuries legislation as a result of Ireland's troubled history there has for some centuries been special provision for the payment of compensation from public funds for damage to property or personal injury in certain circumstances. In the Republic of Ireland under the Malicious Injuries Act 1981, as amended in 1986, compensation is payable by the state where damage is caused to property by two or more persons riotously assembled or as a result of an act committed by a person acting on behalf of an illegal organisation. In Northern Ireland, the Criminal Damage (Compensation) (Northern Ireland) Order 1977 provides a similar scheme for Northern Ireland under which substantial sums have been paid out in recent years. In the financial year 1992–93, for example, £76 million was paid. In addition, in both jurisdictions there are schemes under which the state provides compensation to those who have suffered physical injuries as a result of violent crimes. In the Republic, the Criminal Injury Compensation Tribunal was set up to deal on an ex gratia basis with such claims, while in Northern Ireland compensation is awarded under the Criminal Injuries (Compensation) (Northern Ireland) Order 1988. See also CRIMINAL INJURIES COMPENSATION.

malicious mischief in Scots criminal law, the crime of damaging another's property. It requires a deliberate disregard of the other's property rights, so cannot be committed accidentally. See VANDALISM.

malicious prosecution a tort of abuse of legal procedure. It consists in the defendant maliciously initiating proceedings, ending in favour of the plaintiff, where there was no reasonable cause for the prosecution, causing damage to the plaintiff. Malice for these purposes covers not only spite and ill-will but also any motive other than a desire to bring a criminal to justice: *Glinski* v. *McIver* [1962] AC 726.

malingerer in military law, a person who pretends to be ill or who deliberately injures himself, as by shooting himself in the foot, to render himself unfit for service or to delay return to service.

man Maori for 'SOVEREIGNTY'.

managing director the director appointed to deal with day-to-day management of a COMPANY.

mandamus 'we command', formerly a writ, now an order of court that commands a person, corporation or tribunal to carry out its duty. It is used to regulate the proceedings of tribunals and the like. In Scotland, the Court of Session has a general supervisory jurisdiction that allows it to achieve the same effect and, indeed, probably more: *West* v. *Secretary of State for Scotland* 1992 SLT 636. See JUDICIAL REVIEW.

mandate an authority given by one person to another to do certain things or take some course of action and accepted by the other. So, the authority given by a principal to his agent is a mandate. A mandate is commonly revocable until acted upon and is terminated by the death of the *mandator*. The gratuitous contract of mandate is recognised in Scotland.

manslaughter see HOMICIDE.

mansuetae naturae see ANIMALS.

march-fences in Scotland, in relation to lands exceeding six acres, there has been since the March Dykes Acts 1661 and 1669 an obligation for neighbouring proprietors to pay for the maintenance of division fences or dykes or to attend to the straightening of said dykes.

Mareva injunction a form of INJUNCTION named after the case in which it was first granted – *Mareva Compania Naviera SA* v. *International Bulk-carriers SA* [1975] 2 Lloyd's Rep. 509 – under which the court freezes the assets of a resident or non-resident debtor where the debtor has gone abroad but still has assets in England. A provision may be inserted to protect third parties abroad by way of preventing the order having effect until the injunction is approved by the foreign court, such a provision being known as a *Babanaft proviso* after the case in which it was first allowed: *Babanaft International Co. SA* v. *Bassatne* [1989] 1 All ER 433.

marginal notes the little notes in the margin of an ACT OF PARLIAMENT. They can be considered in a case of ambiguity as part of the process of STATUTORY INTERPRETATION: see *DPP* v. *Schildkamp* [1971] AC 1.

marketable title in CONVEYANCING in Scotland, an implied term of every contract for the sale of heritage that the seller will *inter alia* deliver a marketable title, which not only means that there will be no eviction but also that there will be no reasonable challenge that can be made. It imports an exclusive and absolute right of property and thus excludes even a long lease. It must be a title to a whole and identical property. The title must be free of all burdens and encumbrances except FEU DUTY, which in most cases will have been automatically redeemed by statute some time ago or will have to be done on sale. An unallocated part of a cummulo feu duty may still be outstanding and render a title unmarketable.

market overt see NEMO DAT QUOD NON HABET.

marriage the agreement of two persons of the opposing sex to become man and wife. In most legal systems, marriage is accepted and treated as a CONTRACT, but it is one the incidents of which the parties cannot vary. There are formalities by way of advertisement.

Part II of the Marriage Act 1949 regulates marriage according to the rites of the Church of England, whether by the publication of *banns of matrimony* or on the authority of a *special licence*, a *common licence* or the *certificate of a superintendent registrar*. Similar provisions apply in Scotland, although irregular marriage by COHABITATION (WITH HABIT AND REPUTE) is known.

There is a prohibition (in most Western countries) against marriage to other persons while the marriage subsists, this being restrained by the crime of BIGAMY. The basis of the institution is the permanent and indissoluble union of a man and woman. Relaxation of DIVORCE laws has made the permanence of the relationship de facto contingent. Attempts have been made by homosexuals to marry but these have failed.

Most systems prevent the marriage of parties related one to the other, and the scope of the restriction is usually defined by reference to PROHIBITED DEGREES.

Restriction is also usually placed on the age of parties. In Scotland and England it is 16.

In England the general rule (from Section 18 of the Wills Act 1837, as amended by the Administration of Justice Act 1982) is to the effect that marriage will operate to revoke a will unless it can be shown that the will was made in contemplation of marriage to a particular person (on whom benefits were conferred by the will). In

Scotland the will is not revoked, but see CONDITIO SI TESTATOR SINE LIBERIS DECESSERIT.

In the context of immigration where a person has been given leave to enter the UK temporarily and then marries someone settled here, that person may apply for an extension of stay as a spouse, initially for a period of 12 months and thereafter for SETTLEMENT. An extension, however, will not be granted unless the Secretary of State is satisfied with the following: (i) the marriage was not entered into primarily to obtain settlement here; (ii) the parties have met; (iii) the applicant has not remained in breach of immigration laws; (iv) the marriage is not taking place after a decision to deport or a recommendation for deportation has been made; (v) the marriage has not been terminated; (vi) each of the parties intends to live permanently with the other as his or her spouse; (vii) there will be adequate accommodation for the parties and their dependants, without recourse to public funds, in accommodation of their own or that they occupy themselves; and (viii) the parties will be able to maintain themselves and their dependants adequately without resource to public funds. See IRREGULAR MARRIAGE.

marshalling the principle that where two or more creditors seek payment from the assets of the same debtor where one creditor can claim against one source of assets and another can claim against two sources, the creditor with the two sources may be required to seek satisfaction from the source that the other creditor cannot claim against. It applies as between creditors, beneficiaries and legatees.

Martinmas see QUARTER DAY.

master a nearly obsolete term for an employer under a contract of employment in the sense of service rather than for services. The law was treated under the title 'master and servant' but is now usually collected under the title 'employment law', which includes much to do with trade unions. See EMPLOYMENT, UNFAIR DISMISSAL.

Master of the Rolls in England and Wales, the head of the civil division of the COURT OF APPEAL.

material breach in Scots law, the kind of breach of contract that allows the victim to rescind the contract as being serious, going to the essentials of the contract. The term is not used in English law as a term of art but the Sale and Supply of Goods Act 1994 has introduced the idea to cases where the victim of the breach is not a consumer.

material facts all facts that must be proved in order to establish the ground of claim or defence are material.

maternity allowance see MATERNITY RIGHTS.

maternity rights in the employment law of the UK, a series of rights given to pregnant women. Statutory *maternity pay* is payable. *Maternity allowance* is a social security benefit if she cannot get statutory maternity pay. A woman who has worked right up to the start of the eleventh week before her expected date of delivery is entitled to be kept on after her pregnancy so long as she gives her employer notice before she stops working that she intends to return to work. This notice must give the information in writing and supply medical evidence of the due date of confinement. The right is to be reinstated to a job just like the one she left – no better, no worse. If not allowed to return, the case will proceed much like one for UNFAIR DISMISSAL.

matrimonial home the residence in which a husband and wife have lived together. In England Wales (where the title is vested in one spouse only) the other spouse has certain rights of occupation that may be protected by registration. The Family Law Act 1996 confers no rights on spouses who already possess proprietary, contractual or statutory rights to occupy the matrimonial home. An innocent spouse who is joint owner of the matrimonial home has, if in occupation, a right not to be evicted or excluded from the dwelling house or any part of it by the other spouse, except by court order, and, if not in occupation, a right by court order to enter and occupy the dwelling house. If a spouse with no proprietary interest in the matrimonial home but in occupation thereof is deserted by his or her spouse, the deserted spouse has a statutory right to remain in occupation and to protect that right by registering it as a land charge, if the land is not subject to the Land Registration Acts or by an entry on the register if it is so subject.

In Scots family law, the matrimonial home is an object of protection under the Matrimonial Homes (Family Protection) (Scotland) Act 1981, as amended. A matrimonial home is any house, caravan, houseboat or other structure that has been provided or has been made available by one or both of the spouses as, or has become, a family residence, and includes any garden or other ground or building attached and usually occupied with, or otherwise required for the amenity or convenience of, the house, caravan, houseboat or other structure. A matrimonial home does not include a residence acquired by one spouse for his or her exclusive use, even if the children of the family also live there.

The degree of protection in Scotland is primarily directed towards the spouse who has no traditional legal rights over the home. This spouse is called the *non-entitled spouse*, and that spouse is granted occupancy rights under the Act, which may be enforced by the courts and are hedged in by having to be taken account of in CONVEYANCING procedures. The *entitled spouse* may be removed from the home if there is a prospect of domestic violence, which is precisely defined in the Act, by means of an *exclusion order*. Thus, the non-owner may be able to occupy the home while the owner has to perhaps obtain accommodation as a homeless person. Joint owners may not evict each other without the agreement of court.

matrimonial property see FINANCIAL PROVISIONS, MATRIMONIAL HOME.

McNaghten rules see INSANITY.

MDP abbreviation for MULTIDISCIPLINARY PRACTICE.

measures having equivalent effect (to quantitative restrictions) in the law of the EUROPEAN COMMUNITIES these measures, being non-pecuniary obstacles to the FREE MOVEMENT OF GOODS, are prohibited to bolster the COMMON MARKET. The prohibition extends to all trading rules that affect intracommunity trade, even if only potentially: see *Consten & Grundig* v. *Commission* [1966] ECR 299.

Meech Lake Constitutional Accord see CONSTITUTION (CANADA).

melior est conditio defendentis see BALANCE OF PROBABILITIES.

melior est conditio possidetis 'the possessor is in a better position' (in a dispute).

member every person who agrees to become a member of a COMPANY and whose name is entered on its register of members.

member state a state member of the EUROPEAN UNION. Each state is allocated a weighted vote when voting by qualified majority in the COUNCIL OF THE EUROPEAN UNION. The weighting follows each member state name. Initially there were six members: Belgium (5), Netherlands (5), Luxembourg (2), France (10), Germany (10) and Italy (10). Then there were nearly a few others: the UK applied to join in 1961 and was rebuffed and was refused entry again in 1967. After the Hague summit of 1969, negotiations began to admit the UK and others. The UK (10) joined with fellow European Free Trade Association (EFTA) members Norway, Denmark (3) and the Republic of Ireland (3) by virtue of the Treaty of Brussels of 1972 coming into effect in 1973. As the result of an internal referendum, Norway did not ratify its membership. The UK later had a consultative referendum to decide whether it should stay in. Thereafter, Greece (5), Spain (8) and Portugal (5) joined as at 1 January 1986. Greenland left as a result of adjusting its relationship with Denmark as at 1 February 1985. As at 1 January 1995, Austria (4), Finland (3) and Sweden (4) joined the European Union. Legally, membership is open to any European state, but (perhaps fortunately) 'European' is not defined. There is no legal procedure for leaving the Communities. The Community has always been reluctant to have classes of full membership and every member is equal. See also EUROPEAN ECONOMIC AREA.

memorandum in writing 1. formerly, a contract for the sale of land was required to be at least evidenced by some memorandum in writing, setting out the principal points of the contract. Since the Law of Property (Miscellaneous Provisions) Act 1989, this is now insufficient, the requirement being that all such contracts be in writing. However, the requirement of a written memorandum still applies to contracts of guarantee.
2. the creation of a trust of land or of an interest therein must at least be evidenced by some note or memorandum in writing.

memorandum of association the primary constitutional document of a COMPANY. It must be drawn up when a company is formed and signed by two or more founder members. It must state the company's name and registered office, the purposes for which it was formed, the amount, if any, of its authorised capital and, where appropriate, that it is a limited (or public limited) company.

mens rea 'guilty mind', the term used to describe the mental element required to constitute a crime. Generally it requires that the accused meant or intended to do wrong or at least knew he was doing wrong. The precise element varies from crime to crime.

MEP the abbreviation for Member of the European Parliament. See EUROPEAN PARLIAMENT.

mercantile agent a commercial agent, such as a factor or broker, who in the ordinary course of his business has authority to sell goods, to consign goods for sale, to buy goods or to raise money on the security of goods on behalf of his principal. See FACTOR.

merchantable quality a now obsolete implied term that applied in contacts of sale. See QUALITY.

mercy a prerogative power exercised by the Home Secretary to allow a sentence to be commuted, remitted or suspended.

merger the process whereby two or more companies come together to form a new single entity. The merger may be effected as follows: by way of a scheme for amalgamation approved by the court; in the form of a takeover whereby one company acquires the shares of the other; where a new company is set up to acquire shares in the merging companies so that the shareholders of the merging companies receive shares in the new company.

Merger Treaty effective from 1 July 1967, this treaty provided for a single COMMISSION, COURT and ASSEMBLY for all three of the EUROPEAN COMMUNITIES. See EURATOM, EUROPEAN COAL AND STEEL COMMUNITY.

MIB abbreviation for MOTOR INSURERS BUREAU.

Michaelmas see QUARTER DAY.

Middle Temple see BARRISTER.

Midsummer Day see QUARTER DAY.

military law the law that regulates the conduct of members of the armed forces; its essential concern is the maintenance of discipline.

military tribunal a tribunal that is responsible for the trial and punishment of an offence against military law. See COURT MARTIAL.

minority in Scots law, a person under the age of 18. Persons under 16 have no CAPACITY, but those between the two ages have a limited form of capacity. For England, see INFANT.

minority protection rules developed in order to safeguard minority shareholders from possible abuse of power by holders of the majority of shares in a limited company. The remedies that are available include: just and equitable winding up; applying for relief for unfair prejudice; bringing a derivative or representative action; and seeking an inspection and investigation of the company.

misadventure a possible inquest verdict by a coroner that is similar to (but said by some to be different from) accident.

mischief rule in STATUTORY INTERPRETATION, the rule that asks what the law was before an Act and what defects there were that were addressed by the legislation under CONSTRUCTION. The interpretation is favoured that remedies the problem or mischief. Thus, 'no dogs allowed' would not necessarily exclude guide dogs.

misdemeanour a crime that was not punishable by death and forfeiture. See FELONY.

misdescription 1. a provision in a contract in which the subject matter is incorrectly or inaccurately described in some material particular.
  2. there is a specific offence of *property misdescription* where a false or misleading statement about a prescribed matter is made in the

course of an estate agency business otherwise than in providing CONVEYANCING services: Property Misdescriptions Act 1991.

misfeance doing something, essentially legal, wrongly, as opposed to not doing something at all that should have been done (which is called *non-feasance*). A species of the tort is *misfeasance in public office*. Traditionally this was the case of directed malice intended to injure a person – the exercise of public power for an ulterior motive. The House of Lords has recently given new life to the tort by holding that a public officer would be liable for the tort if he acted in the knowledge of or with reckless indifference to the illegality of his acts or with reckless indifference to the probability of causing injury to the particular plaintiff or a class of which the plaintiff was a member. This form of the tort depends upon the absence of an honest belief by the officer that his act was lawful: *Three Rivers DC* v. *Governor and Company of the Bank of Scotland* [2000] TLR 396.

misprision of treason the CRIME of failing to inform the authorities where the accused knows or has reasonable cause to believe that another has committed TREASON.

misrepresentation representing something incorrectly. A misrepresentation is distinct from a statement of opinion. It may have the effect of making an otherwise valid contract void or at least voidable. A distinction is made between innocent, negligent and fraudulent misrepresentations. At best, an *innocent misrepresentation* may affect a contract, a *negligent misrepresentation* may attract in addition liability for negligence, assuming the requirements of that tort can be met, and a *fraudulent misrepresentation* may attract damages for the FRAUD and DECEIT. See also ERROR.

mistake a mental conception divergent from the true position. In law, mistake can be relevant. For a long time a distinction has been made between *mistake of fact* and *mistake of law*. A lenient attitude is taken towards the former, ignorance of the law often being said to be no excuse. In criminal law, many systems may accept the facts honestly believed by the accused to be those upon which he should be judged, but even an honest belief that a course of conduct is not criminal is unlikely to exculpate. In civil law, the general approach is that a mistake that destroys the consent upon which contract is founded can invalidate a contract. *Error calculi*, 'an error in calculation', has often been corrected by courts at their own hand where an error arose in a deed simply through a failure to record the correct computation. This has to be distinguished from cases where the whole basis of the computation was not truly agreed. In English criminal law, mistake can be relevant if it affects one of the essential factual elements of the crime. It seems that a genuine belief that one of the definitional elements of a crime is missing will be sufficient. The belief need not be reasonable: *DPP* v. *Morgan* [1976] AC 182. If in relation to a defence, such as self-defence, the mistake must be reasonable: *Beckford* v. *R* [1988] AC 130.

In relation to mistake of law, a mistake as to the civil law might exculpate; for example, where somebody takes something away genuinely believing it to be his through some application of the civil law. A mistake of criminal law is less likely to succeed, although some statutes may lead to this being available: *Sec. of State* v. *Hart* [1982] 1 WLR 481.

In the Scots criminal law, the word *error* is preferred for the phenomenon under discussion. It is not thought that the law is entirely settled nor internally consistent. It is probably the case that a reasonable mistake as to constitutive element of a crime would exculpate. Erroneous belief as to a defence, such as consent to rape, requires only an honest belief: *Meek* v. *HMA* 1983 SLT 280. So far as *error of law* is concerned, a mistake as to the civil law in principle exculpates (*Roberts* v. *Inverness Local Authority* (1889) 2 White 385), but in one leading case such a defence was not allowed where it was considered that the accused's belief was not founded on rational grounds: *Dewar* v. *HMA* 1945 JC 5. A mistake as to the general criminal law has no effect: *Clark* v. *Syme* 1957 JC 1.

In the English law of contract, if a person completely mistakes the nature of the deed he signs he may be relieved if the restricted doctrine of NON EST FACTUM applies. In other cases mistake may also be operative. A distinction is often made between *common mistake*, where both parties to a contract are both mistaken as to the same thing, and *mutual mistake*, which occurs where both parties are mistaken but make different mistakes. Recognised instances are a case of mistaken identity where the identity of the contracting party is crucial to the contract (*Cunday* v. *Lindsay* (1878) 3 App. Cas. 459) and where the subject matter is mistaken (*Raffles* v. *Wichelhaus* (1864) 2 H&C 906).

In the Scots law of contract, the term *error* is preferred to 'mistake' for the same phenomenon. *Unilateral error uninduced* is seldom successful as a basis for avoiding the contract: *Steel* v. *Bradley Homes (Scotland) Ltd* 1974 SLT 133, but see *Steuart's Trs* v. *Hart* (1875) 3 R

192. The distinction between *common error* and *mutual error* is noticed, and both can be effective: *Stuart & Co.* v. *Kennedy* (1885) 13 R 221. Error in the substantials of a contract renders it void in Scotland. Matters capable of being substantial are the subject matter, the persons involved, the price or consideration, the quality of the thing if essential or the nature of the contract.

In England, in equity, and in Scotland, under the Law Reform Miscellaneous Provisions (Scotland) Act 1986, the court has power to rectify written contracts that do not express the agreement of the parties, a power that in both jurisdictions is subject to detailed rules and qualifications. See MISREPRESENTATION, CONTRACTUAL MISTAKES.

In both England and Scotland, the law of RESTITUTION allows money paid by mistake to be recovered. In England the restitutionary action is called an *action for money had and received*, and in Scotland it will usually be called a *condictio indebiti*. In England a mistake of law has now been held to be a sufficient unjust factor to allow the money to be recovered: *Kleinwort Benson* v. *Lincoln City Council* [1999] 2 AC 349, in this respect catching up with other jurisdictions.

In Australia the rule against recovery based on mistake of law was relaxed: *David Securities Pty Ltd* v. *Commonwealth Bank of Australia* (1992) 175 CLR 353, and it was abandoned in the mixed civilian jurisdiction of South Africa: *Willis Faber Enthoven Pty Ltd* v. *Receiver of Revenue* 1992 (4) SA 202 (A). It had been abandoned in Scotland: *Morgan Guaranty* v. *Lothian Regional Council* 1995 SLT 299.

In New Zealand, under the Contractual Mistakes Act 1977, the law is set out in statutory language and no longer depends upon the distinctions of the common law. Mistake includes mistake of law or of fact, but for most purposes a mistake in the interpretation of a document will be a mistake of law. Three different types of mistake are legislated for – mistake known to the other party, common mistake, and different mistakes about the same matter of fact or law.

misuse of drugs the criminal use of certain specified drugs. The Misuse of Drugs Act 1972 is a complicated measure but essentially it makes it illegal to produce a controlled drug, to supply a controlled drug, to possess a controlled drug, or to possess with intent to supply. It is an offence to cultivate any plant of the genus cannabis. The law extends to make it an offence if an occupier knowingly permits or suffers drug-related activities such as the supply or the smoking of cannabis. The police have extended powers under the Act and may search and detain a person if they have reasonable grounds to suspect a person is in possession of a controlled drug. The particular classification of the drug under the Act is important. It is an offence to use heroin whereas it is not an offence to use cannabis, although it is an offence to possess cannabis or to be ART AND PART in its possession, as where one person holds the cannabis cigarette for another to smoke.

mitigation reduction. It is used in *plea in mitigation* – an attempt to keep the sentence to a minimum, and in *mitigation of damages*, the duty on the victim of a contract-breaker or a delinquent or tortfeasor to keep his losses within reason. Extraordinary measures do not have to be taken to mitigate damages.

mobbing in Scots criminal law, the crime that is committed when people gather together intent on a common purpose that is to be effected illegally, which causes alarm to the public or part of it. A series of unconnected and fortuitous events does not evince a common purpose. Simple presence in the mob can be enough for guilt.

mock action an AUCTION where items are given away or the right to bid is restricted to persons who have bought or agree to buy goods or one where goods are sold to a person lower than his highest bid. It is an offence to organise such an event under the Mock Auctions Act 1961.

modus operandi 'way of doing things'.

moiety (pronounced 'moy-ettee') a half.

money had and received a form of action that lay to recover money paid under MISTAKE or compulsion or for a failed consideration. It also covered cases where the defendant had acquired money from the plaintiff by a tortious act. Many of these cases are now considered to fall within that part of the English law of obligations called RESTITUTION and are not thought to be quasi-contractual in the sense of having anything to do with contract. For Scotland, see CONDICTIO INDEBITI.

money laundering the moving of the proceeds of crime through the financial system so as to conceal its nature. As a result of a European directive, the UK has implemented rules against this practice mainly through the Criminal Justice Act 1993. Aside from controlling the actual criminals, persons can be guilty of offences if they do not report suspicions or information as soon as reasonably practicable where the laundering concerns terrorism or drug money. Assisting another person to retain the benefits of all types of crime is also made an offence.

Monopolies and Merger Commission a now obsolete body that regulated aspects of competition in the UK. See now COMPETITION COMMISSION.

Moorov doctrine in the law of evidence of the law of Scotland, the doctrine that CORROBORATION can be found in cases, especially sexual cases, from the proof of two uncorroborated incidents related closely in time and in their nature. Thus, a man can be convicted on the uncorroborated evidence of two rape victims providing the interval between the two attacks is not excessive: *Moorov* v. *HMA* 1930 JC 68.

moot an old English word for an assembly, but now the word is used only **1.** as a noun to describe a legal argument not in a court of law, usually held for the purpose of legal education based on a tradition established in the English Inns of Court.

2. as an adjective, a point of law is often said to be moot if, raised in a litigation, the point does not any longer affect the decision in the case before the court.

mora delay. In Scots law it is argued that delay, even a delay short of any prescriptive or limitation period, might bar a right.

mortgage a conveyance of land or an assignment of chattels as a security for the payment of a debt or the discharge of some other obligation for which it is given. Every form of property may be mortgaged except the salaries of public functionaries. Mortgages may be *legal*, in which case they must be effected by deed, or *equitable*, in which event they may be effected informally, as, for example, by the deposit of documents of title with the lender. The lender (the *mortgagee*) is accorded certain powers to protect his investment. The principal powers are sale and foreclosure and the right to appoint a receiver – a right that may become exercisable in the event of a default. The borrower (the *mortgagor*) is entitled to redeem in accordance with the terms of the mortgage. On payment of the outstanding balance, together with any interest due, the mortgage is discharged.

In relation to land in England and Wales, a legal mortgage of freehold land is effected by means of a demise subject to a proviso for cesser on redemption; in relation to leaseholds, the mortgage as effected by a sub-demise. An alternative form, provided for by Section 851 of the Law of Property Act 1925, is a charge by deed expressed to be by way of legal mortgage. Since the Law of Property

(Miscellaneous Provisions) Act 1989, the creation of an equitable mortgage requires to be in writing and can, it would seem, no longer be effected merely by deposit of title deeds. To secure protection against bona fide purchasers, equitable mortgagees should ensure that their mortgages are protected by registration as a land charge (where the title is not subject to the Land Registration Acts) or as a charge where the title is so subject.

In Scotland the word is used non-technically to describe the lending relationship in relation to heritage. The legal documentation in Scotland is by way of a STANDARD SECURITY.

mother see PARENTAGE.

motion an application to a court or a meeting.

motive the moving cause or desire that induces action. A person's motive may answer the question: Why did he do it? It may coincide with intention but may differ. The general approach of the law is to ignore motive, however helpful it may be to those who investigate crime. See AEMULATIONEM VICINI, ECONOMIC TORTS.

Motor Insurers Bureau (MIB) a voluntary organisation set up by insurance companies to avoid government interference that makes sure that those injured on the roads by uninsured drivers are compensated. It operates under an agreement with the Secretary of State for the Environment to meet any unsatisfied judgments in respect of a liability against which it was obligatory to insure. There are three types of case:

(1) identified uninsured drivers;

(2) the identified driver with a policy of insurance in force but under which the insurer is not liable, perhaps because of fraud or because of breach of a term of the policy. In this case the agreement between the MIB and its members is called the *domestic agreement*; the insurer deals with the claim as if valid, allowing the injured person to recover damages. The domestic agreement even covers some cases where the insured was not liable at all because the policy did not cover the risk that materialised;

(3) the untraced driver, a type of case covered only since 1968.

moveable property see HERITABLE PROPERTY.

MP abbreviation for MEMBER OF PARLIAMENT.

MR abbreviation for MASTER OF THE ROLLS.

MSP abbreviation for MEMBER OF THE SCOTTISH PARLIAMENT.

mulct to impose a financial penalty, sometimes used of a finding of expenses or costs against a party in a litigation.

multidisciplinary practice (MDP) an organisation that offers a range of professional services such as accountancy and law. Traditionally lawyers have been prevented from entering such arrangements because of the core ethical value of independence and service to the client in hand while at the same time honouring obligations to the court and justice. However, throughout the world pressure from consumers, competition regulators and the large multinational accountancy firms is bringing pressure for change.

multiple poinding (pronounced multiple pinding) a procedure in Scots law whereby all parties who may be claiming an interest in a given fund, called the *fund in medio*, can be convened together so that all pleas may be argued in the one process.

multiplicand the sum that is multiplied by a MULTIPLIER to calculate damages for future loss. The figure represents the plaintiff's net annual wage loss, thus, if he obtains a lower-paid job, this income is deducted. If the injured party is dead, a similar calculation takes place for the surviving spouse and is based upon the money that was received by way of support.

multiplier 1. a number applied by multiplication to a MULTIPLICAND to produce a figure for damages in cases of future loss, which will provide an appropriate annuity equivalent to the loss but which will itself be exhausted at the time of the notional death.

In calculating damages for future loss of earnings, courts are faced with the difficulty that the person is not earning the money and is not going to earn the money, so they have to make a hypothetical calculation. It would be to overcompensate to subtract the plaintiff's age from the retirement and multiply the annual wage loss (as adjusted by various factors to become a multiplicand) by that figure. That would provide a capital sum immediately and would not reflect the fact that the last pound would not have been earned for many years. Secondly, there are the vicissitudes of life. Not everyone lives to retirement age. Accordingly, multipliers are now best found from appropriate use of the actuarial OGDEN TABLES: *Wells* v. *Wells* [1998] 3 All ER 480.

2. an old word for an alchemist, who pretended to increase the quantity of gold or silver.

munus publicum a public office.

murder see HOMICIDE.

murmur (archaic) to defame a judge.

mutual error see ERROR.

mutual wills wills made by two persons who, in pursuance of an antecedent agreement, leave their estates reciprocally to the survivor. In English law, either will may be revoked during the joint lifetimes of the testators, but equity will specifically enforce the mutual wills agreement (thereby effectively making revocation by the survivor impossible) after the death of one of the parties.

mutuum in Roman law, and in Scots law, loan for consumption, the property borrowed being replaced by a similar article. An example would be the 'borrowing' of a pint of milk. See COMMODATUM.

Napoleonic Code the name given to the French Civil Code. It brought together existing rules and implemented many of the new ideas of revolution. The provisions are brief and require judicial interpretation according to its spirit. Its structure is based on its CIVILIAN heritage and very broadly follows Justinian's Institutes (see CORPUS JURIS CIVILIS). The influence of the Code came from its implementation across Napoleon's sphere of influence including parts of Italy and Germany. The Code was a successful export, especially to the Americas. Its influence was weakened only when the German Civil Code (BGB) began to be copied by newer systems.

National Assembly for Wales a devolved council or parliament created by the Government of Wales Act 1998. It is chaired by a Presiding Officer, the equivalent of the Speaker of the House of Commons, who is responsible for the working of the Assembly and relations with the public. The equivalent of council leader is the First Secretary and the equivalent of council convenor or cabinet minister is Assembly Secretary. It has limited powers, mostly those transferred from the Welsh Office. It cannot act beyond its powers or its legislation may be struck down. It has no tax-raising powers.

nationality the legal relationship between a person and a state. Since the British Nationality Act 1981, it is no longer possible to acquire British citizenship by reason only of being born in the UK. Since 1 January 1983, a child will become a British citizen if one of its parents is a British citizen or is settled in the UK.

naturalisation in the CONSTITUTIONAL LAW of the UK, the process by which a person becomes a BRITISH CITIZEN. It is granted at the discretion of the Secretary of State without regard to race, colour or religion. It involves five years' residence, possession of a good character and a knowledge of English, Welsh or Scottish Gaelic, together with an intention to reside in the UK. A spouse of a citizen requires only three years' residence and there is no need to show proficiency in the language. A certificate is required and an oath of allegiance taken.

natural justice in the CONSTITUTIONAL LAW of the UK, used to mean no more than that a decision should be adjudicated by an impartial judge – 'one with no interest in the outcome' – *nemo judex in suo causa*: see *Dimes* v. *Grand Canal* (1852) 3 HLC 759. The other guiding principle is that a decision should not be taken without 'all parties being heard' – *audi alteram parem*: see *Ridge* v. *Baldwin* [1964] AC 40. See also JUDICIAL REVIEW.

natural law a higher law against which human laws can be measured. Articulated by Aristotle and developed by Cicero, the idea of natural law is an old one. St Thomas Aquinas adapted the doctrine to Christianity, thus scriptures could provide content to the natural law. Grotius and Hobbes offered a secular view, which had the natural reason of man as the source of the natural law. The focus was on right reason. Modern HARTIAN JURISPRUDENCE theory allows a minimum content to natural law based on the notion of survival and limited resources. The Natural Law Party, which contested many hundreds of seats in the 1992 UK general election, had nothing to do with jurisprudence but was concerned with transcendental meditation. See POSITIVISM.

natural person a human being, as opposed to an artificial or legal person like a COMPANY.

nautae caupones stabularii an abbreviated form of part of the praetor's edict of the Roman law, which has been accepted as the law of Scotland and provides for the STRICT LIABILITY of the COMMON CARRIER of goods, the stable-keeper and the innkeeper. The position of the common carrier of goods has been altered by statute; the position of the innkeeper has been altered by the Hotel Proprietors Act 1956. Liability is still strict, but it can be severely limited by displaying a notice under the schedule to the Act. The stable-keeper's liability remains in full force.

navigation the right of way of the public over a river to use it as a highway.

nec 'not'; *nec vi, nec clam, nec precario*, 'without force', 'not done secretly' and 'not done with permission'.

necessity a defence in criminal matters that may mitigate but not exculpate, as in the famous case of *R* v. *Dudley and Stevens* (1884) 14 QBD 273, in which a pair of starving survivors of a ship that had recently sunk ate their fellow survivor, the cabin boy. Although convicted of murder, they were not executed. In the English case of *R* v. *Blackshall* [1998] TLR 243, it was held that necessity or duress of circumstances is available as a defence to a case of careless driving where the accused was driving away from a road rage attack. Rea-

sonable perception of a threat is sufficient: *R* v. *Cairns* [1999] TLR
275. In one Scottish case, a driver trying to escape an assault was
acquitted of drink driving: *Tudhope* v. *Grubb* [1983] SCCR 368. The
Scottish High Court of Justiciary has now fully recognised this
concept: *Moss* v. *Howdle* 1997 SLT 782.

In the USA it was held that in a shipwreck the core crew should be
saved first to pilot the ship. After that, supernumerary seamen are
first sacrificed and only then (presumably) the passengers. 'There is,
however, one condition of extremity for which all writers have
prescribed the same rule. When the ship is in danger of sinking, but
all maintenance is exhausted, and a sacrifice of one person is
necessary to appease the hunger of others, the selection is by lot.
This mode is reported to as the fairest mode, and, in some sort, as
an appeal to God, for the selection of the victim': *US* v. *Holmes* 26
Fed. Cas. 360 (1842).

negative clearance the procedure in the COMPETITION POLICY of the
EUROPEAN COMMUNITIES whereby the COMMISSION OF THE EUROPEAN
UNION issues a DECISION at the request of an UNDERTAKING indicating
that it does not consider that a given proposal is prohibited by
Article 81 or Article 82. The Channel Tunnel project was so referred.
The procedure is less common than it once was because of the
increase in block exemptions.

negligence the TORT or DELICT of being careless in breach of a duty to
take care. The distinction to be made is between the act or omission
itself, which is not enough to create legal liability: for this there must
be a breach of pre-existing duty of care. Such a duty can exist on the
basis of precedent, as, for example, a doctor to a patient or a carrier
to a passenger, or can arise through the proximity of the parties. The
categories of negligence are never closed and have been extended to
cover liability for negligent misstatements. For the tort to be
established, the breach of the duty by the act or omission must also
have caused a loss, although if the loss is a pure ECONOMIC LOSS there
are difficulties.

The search for proximity or a suitable relationship between the
parties is aided by the notion of reasonable foreseeability of harm of
the kind that occurs. But this is not enough on its own to establish
liability in every case, although in cases of physical injury or
damage to the plaintiff's property it is likely to carry the plaintiff a
long way.

Negligence in the non-technical sense may well trigger liability under a statute that demands a certain degree of care to be taken. See ECONOMIC LOSS, FAULT, NERVOUS SHOCK.

negotiable instrument an instrument that constitutes an obligation to pay a sum of money and that is transferable by delivery so that the holder for the time being can sue in his own name. Negotiable instruments represent an exception to the general rule that a person cannot give a better title than he has. The categories of negotiable instrument include the BILL OF EXCHANGE, promissory notes and bearer bonds.

negotiate to transfer (used of bills of exchange). The usual method is by endorsing (signing) the back of the document.

negotiorum gestio 'unauthorised administration'. Roman law gave an action, the direct action, against a *negotiorum gestor*, a person who involved himself in the affairs of another without instruction. There was, however, no action if the gestor acted with the care he used in his own affairs, and, indeed, the gestor had a contrary action for the expenses involved in doing the work.

The action, to be found in many civilian jurisdictions, has become the foundation for a wider law of restitution, France being an example. It is known in Scotland but is wholly rejected in England: *Falke* v. *Scottish Imperial Insurance Co.* (1886) 34 Ch. D. 234, but now that English law is beginning to look at questions in terms of restitution for unjust enrichment its future may not be so bleak: *Re Berkeley Applegate (Investment Consultants) Ltd* [1988] 3 WLR 95.

nemo dat quod non habet 'a person cannot grant a better title than he himself has.' This principle (which applies across English property law) is embodied in the Sale of Goods Act 1979 (as amended) applying to the whole of the UK. Thus, a SALE by a non-owner will confer on the purchaser no title to the goods, a rule usually illustrated by reference to a sale by a thief from whom no one can derive title, no matter how innocent his involvement might be. The Act, however, specifically excepts the provisions of the Factors Act 1989 or any enactments enabling an apparent owner to dispose of goods as if he were their true owner. The leading exceptions are:

(1) sale under a VOIDABLE title: when the seller of goods has a voidable title to them, but his title has not been avoided at the time of the sale, the buyer acquires a good title to the goods, provided he buys them in GOOD FAITH and without notice of the seller's defect of title;

(2) sale by a seller in possession after sale, reflecting the provisions of the Factors Act 1889: the Act states that where a person, having sold goods, continues or is in possession of the goods, or of the DOCUMENTS OF TITLE to the goods, the delivery or transfer by that person, or by a MERCANTILE AGENT acting for him, of the goods or documents of title under any sale, PLEDGE or other DISPOSITION thereof, to any person receiving the same in good faith and without notice of the previous sale has the same effect as if the person making the delivery or transfer were expressly authorised by the owner of the goods to make the same;

(3) the buyer in possession after sale: where a person having bought or agreed to buy goods obtains with the consent of the seller possession of the goods or of the documents of title to the goods, the delivery or transfer by that person or by a mercantile agent acting for him of the goods or documents of title, under any sale, or pledge, or other disposition thereof, to any person receiving the sale in good faith and without notice of any lien or other right of the original seller in respect of the goods, has the same effect as if the person making the delivery or transfer were a mercantile agent in possession of the goods or documents of title with the consent of the owner. It is possible for the original seller to become an agent for the buyer 'in possession', so that if the original seller delivers to his buyer's buyer, that third party is a purchaser from a buyer in possession and protected by the section. Specifically excepted from being a buyer in possession after a sale is the buyer under a CONDITIONAL SALE AGREEMENT;

(4) PERSONAL BAR: there is an exception from the nemo dat rule where the owner of goods is by his conduct precluded from denying the seller's authority to sell, implementing the notion of personal bar;

(5) judicial sales: warrant sales and other sales under order of the court are not affected by the rules regarding sale by non-owners;

(6) pledge: the Consumer Credit Act 1974 permits certain pledged goods to be sold on the expiry of the redemption period. Otherwise the pledge would require a power of sale in the contract or a court order;

(7) hire-purchase: hire-purchase, in this context, is a contract where the hire-purchaser agrees to pay a rent and is granted an option to purchase. If the hirer is bound to purchase, that is a sale. In a proper case of hire-purchase, someone who buys from the hire-purchaser, or one deriving title from him, gets no title. The position is different

if the transaction is covered by Part III of the Hire-purchase Act 1964. That provides that where the hirer of a motor vehicle under a hire-purchase agreement or the buyer of such a vehicle under a conditional sale agreement disposes of the vehicle to a private purchaser who purchases in good faith and without notice of the said agreement, the disposition has effect as if the title of the owner or seller to the vehicle had been vested in the hirer or buyer immediately before that disposition.

nemo debet lucupletari ex aliena jactura 'no one may gain from the loss (sacrifice) of another,' a maxim from the Digest in the CORPUS JURIS CIVILIS often encountered in the law of RESTITUTION of civilian systems. It forms the basis of the branch of the law of restitution in Scotland known as RECOMPENSE.

nemo judex in causa sua see NATURAL JUSTICE.

nervous shock a phrase used to describe a certain class of claim, usually in negligence, where the plaintiff is not injured in the sense of a physical injury. It is not strictly speaking a medical term nor is it strictly speaking a legal category. Nervous shock arises when a plaintiff has not suffered direct physical injury, for example, being run down. Instead, the plaintiff claims to have been so affected by the incident in question that he suffers from a recognised condition as a result: 'It is not enough . . . for the pursuers [plaintiffs] in each case to show simply that they got a fright and suffered an emotional reaction, if no visible disability or provable illness or injury followed': *Simpson* v. *ICI* 1983 SLT 601. The FLOODGATES' fear that there would be an army of lying plaintiffs and crooked lawyers and dubious psychiatrists resulted in a strict approach to recovery, demanding that the plaintiff had to be at or about the scene of the incident that caused the shock. The position has now been reached where nervous shock is recoverable subject to three major factors: (1) the relationship of the parties. Plaintiffs should be able to stand the death of strangers, close friends and even relatives as close as siblings. In the case of parents and spouses of the deceased, the necessary relationship is assumed – in other cases it would be for the plaintiff to establish the intimacy of the relationship; (2) the means of perception should be unaided senses; things seen on television are unlikely to trigger recovery, still less a written report; (3) plaintiffs to be successful should be at or near the scene or at least its aftermath. See *McLoughlin* v. *O'Brian* [1983] AC 410 and its interpretation in *Alcock* v. *Chief Constable of Yorkshire Police* [1991] 3 WLR 1057.

However, where a party is considered by the law, unlike the cases above, to be a primary victim then damages are recoverable without any of these qualifications. So it was held in the House of Lords in *Page* v. *Smith* [1996] 1 AC 155 in which the plaintiff's ME flared up after a minor collision in which he was not physically injured.

nexus a tie or connection. The phrase often encountered was *legal nexus*.

nobile officium the 'noble office' or special jurisdiction of the COURT OF SESSION. Claims are made to the nobile officium when some remedy is needed but none is apparent.

no case to answer 1. in procedure, the plea at the end of the plaintiff's case that a prima facie case has not been made out and that the defendant should accordingly win.

2. in Scotland, the name given by the profession to the opportunity given by the Criminal Justice (Scotland) Act 1980 to plead that the Crown case against the accused is insufficient in that it has not established sufficiently the necessary facts legally to constitute a crime of which the accused could be convicted under the complaint in question. A failure to provide corroboration will usually result in the plea being successful.

no-fault a convenient phrase used to describe compensation systems that do not depend upon the claimant establishing the fault of some other person. The most often discussed is the New Zealand ACCIDENT COMPENSATION system. However, even in the UK interstitial reform is bringing about a larger area of no-fault liability, some within the delict/tort system and some of it outside. See ACCIDENT, ANIMALS, PRODUCT LIABILITY.

nolo contendere 'it is not intended to contend', a plea permissible in certain US jurisdictions whereby a person accused of a crime can be disposed of without, however, the accused admitting his guilt. It is not allowed in the UK, and *pleas of convenience* – 'I can't be bothered fighting this and would like to get it over with' – are frowned upon and usually treated as pleas of not guilty, resulting in the case having to proceed to a trial.

nominal damages an award of a (usually) small sum to reflect the fact that a tort has been committed but where no actual damage has been sustained. In the case of negligence, or any other tort where damage is part of the essence of the tort, nominal damages cannot be awarded. In contract cases, nominal damages can be awarded even if there is no loss sustained.

non aedificandi see LIGHT OR PROSPECT.

non-delivery in the law of sale, as it is the seller's duty to DELIVER the goods, DAMAGES are due for failure to do so. Where the seller wrongfully neglects or refuses to deliver the goods to the buyer, the buyer may maintain an action against the seller for damages for non-delivery. The measure of damages is the estimated loss directly and naturally, resulting in the ordinary course of events from the seller's breach of contract. Where there is an available market for the goods in question, the measure of damages is prima facie to be ascertained by the difference between the contract price and the market or current price of the goods at the time or times when they ought to have been delivered or, if no time was fixed, at the time of the refusal to deliver. Other remedies are available, including in both Scotland and England SPECIFIC PERFORMANCE, and in Scotland at common law, the remedy of SPECIFIC IMPLEMENT.

Late delivery gives the buyer the right to retain the price in security for his claim for damages arising there, when the claim is based on either non-delivery within a reasonable time or on delivery delayed beyond the time specified in the contract. Whether or not late delivery will entitle the buyer to rescind the contract and refuse to accept the goods depends on whether, in the particular case, the delay amounts to a material failure on the part of the seller. Whether a stipulation as to time in a particular contract is or is not of the essence of that contract depends on its terms. Where a contract is silent on the question of time, time can be made essential by notice.

Some cases of defective delivery are included in the Sale of Goods Act 1979 (as amended):

(1) where the seller delivers to the buyer a quantity of goods less than he contracted to sell, the buyer may reject them, but if the buyer accepts the goods so delivered, he must pay for them at the contract rate;

(2) where the seller delivers to the buyer a quantity of goods larger than he contracted to sell, the buyer may accept the goods included in the contract and reject the rest, or he may reject the whole;

(3) where the seller delivers to the buyer a quantity of goods larger than he contracted to sell and the buyer accepts the whole of the goods so delivered he must pay for them at the contract rate;

(4) where the seller delivers to the buyer the goods he contracted to sell, mixed with goods of a different description not included in the contract, the buyer may accept the goods that are in accordance with the contract and reject the rest, or he may reject the whole. 'Different description' refers to identification under the contract and will generally not cover goods of the same description that are not of the appropriate QUALITY.

The foregoing rules are subject to any usage of trade, special agreement or course of dealing between the parties, and in a case of the delivery of an incorrect quantity, where the buyer is not a consumer, the right to reject where the variation is so slight that it would be unreasonable to reject.

non-discrimination notice see DISCRIMINATION.

non-entitled spouse see ENTITLED SPOUSE.

non est factum 'it is not the deed,' in English law the plea that what seems to be a person's deed is not. It is usually raised when there has been a mistake as to the nature of the transaction. The courts do not accept it lightly: see *United Dominions Trust* v. *Western* [1976] QB 513. Where old and infirm people sign things thinking they are not legal documents, the plea is more likely to be successful.

non-materialisation in the law of RESTITUTION, a category of unjust factors that compels the defender to disgorge an enrichment. The cases are those when the transfer is with qualified intent and the qualification does not materialise.

non-molestation order an order of the court requiring the object to refrain from molestation or harassment of the applicant.

non officiendi luminibus see LIGHT OR PROSPECT.

non-patrial a person who does not have a right of abode but may live, work and settle in the UK by permission and subject to control of entry into and departure from the UK: Immigration Act 1971.

norm something that ought to happen. Associated primarily in modern times with KELSINIAN JURISPRUDENCE, the dictum 'law is the primary norm that stipulates the sanction' indicates what is meant by a norm. Kelsen's theory of concretisation describes the process of tracing the norm, which makes an official apply the sanction to the ultimate justification for it, the GRUNDNORM.

Norris-La Guardia Act a US statute of 1932 (the Labor Disputes Act) prohibiting federal courts from issuing temporary injunctions against striking employees. It outlawed so-called *yellow-dog contracts* by which workers agreed not to join a labor (trade) union in order to get a job.

Northern Ireland see IRISH LAW.

Northern Ireland Human Rights Commission under Section 69 of the Northern Ireland Act 1998, the Commission has the following duties: to keep under review the adequacy and effectiveness in Northern Ireland of law and practice relating to the protection of HUMAN RIGHTS: to advise the Secretary of State and the Executive Committee of the Northern Ireland Assembly of legislative and other measures that ought to be taken to protect human rights; to advise the Northern Ireland Assembly whether a Bill is compatible with human rights; to promote understanding and awareness of the importance of human rights in Northern Ireland; to provide advice to the Secretary of State on the scope for defining, in Westminster legislation, rights supplementary to those in the EUROPEAN CONVENTION ON HUMAN RIGHTS; to make to the Secretary of State within two years such recommendations as it thinks fit for improving the Commission's effectiveness; to do all that it can to ensure the establishment of a Joint Committee with the (proposed) Human Rights Commission in the Republic of Ireland. The Commission has the power: to give assistance to individuals who apply to it for help in relation to proceedings involving law or practice concerning the protection of human rights; to bring proceedings involving law or practice concerning the protection of human rights; to conduct such investigations as it considers necessary or expedient for the purpose of exercising its other functions and to publish its advice and the outcome of its research and investigations.

noscitur a sociis 'it is known by its companions,' the rule of interpretation that permits the reading of a word in its context. It permits a wider reading than the similar EJUSDEM GENERIS.

notarial execution an ancient procedure whereby a NOTARY PUBLIC signs a will for a person who is blind or otherwise legally capable but physically unable to read the will. The procedure is that the notary reads the will and, noting the assent of the testator, writes a paragraph on it stating that he is signing instead.

notary public an ancient legal and administrative office found all over Western Europe. Generally, the function is to attest deeds, to witness certain documents, to administer oaths and to execute formalities in relation to bills of exchange and other mercantile paper. The office is common in Scotland.

not guilty the verdict of a court that a person is not, in law or in fact, responsible for the crime charged against him. See GUILTY, NOT PROVEN.

not proven the verdict in a Scottish criminal trial that amounts to an acquittal but that is not the same as the verdict of NOT GUILTY. In the 17th century, practice developed such that the jury found facts alleged by the prosecution either proven or not proven, and it was then for the judge to convert this to an appropriate level of guilt. In 1728, however, a jury returned a verdict of not guilty, leaving thereafter three verdicts available. The consensus appears to be that the not proven verdict is available where there is insufficient evidence to convict but suspicion still attaches to the accused. Whether or not this is satisfactory is often debated.

notice of general meetings notice required for a COMPANY general meeting. Not less than 21 days' notice of meetings must be given to those who are entitled to receive notice. The period in any given case will be governed by the articles but must not be less than 21 days.

notice of intended prosecution intimation that must be made to a person of the intention to prosecute him for a road traffic offence. The notice must be given within 14 days of the alleged commission of the offence. It is necessary only for certain offences under the Road Traffic Offenders Act 1988 as amended. Generally, it does not apply to cases where there has been a road accident.

notice of intention to defend in Scottish ORDINARY PROCEDURE, the method by which a DEFENDER lets the PURSUER and the court know that the action is to be defended so that the court may appoint further hearings and procedure.

notour bankruptcy in the Scots law of INSOLVENCY, a term no longer used, having been replaced by APPARENT INSOLVENCY.

nova causa interveniens see CAUSATION.

novation in English law, an agreement between at least three parties allowing an original contracting party to be released and another party to be brought in as obligant. It is a commonly used method of rescheduling loans.

In the law of CONTRACT in Scotland, novation is the discharge of a contract by the substitution of a fresh obligation between the same parties.

novus actus interveniens see CAUSATION.

noxal surrender in ROMAN LAW, the handing over of a beast or a person in power, to make up for their having caused damage to another person.

nudum pactum 'a naked agreement', an agreement where there is no consideration. Unenforceable, generally, in English law and originally so in Roman law. The influence of the CANON LAW and the maxim *pacta sunt servanda* means that such agreements are enforceable in many jurisdictions, notably in Scotland.

nuisance the TORT or DELICT of wrongful interference in another's use of the defendant's land, usually by the plaintiff's use of his land. It also protects the interests of the individual, even temporarily, in the neighbourhood of the property in his life and health (although this is less clear in Scotland).

It is largely a matter of fact and degree, depending upon the circumstances of the case, whether or not a nuisance has been or is being committed: 'Things which are forbidden in a crowded urban community may be permitted in the country. What is prohibited in an enclosed land may be tolerated in the open': *Inglis* v. *Shotts Iron Co.* (1881) 8 R 802 at 810. Injunction or interdict in Scotland will be granted to prevent a nuisance being continued or repeated and damages will be granted in respect of loss caused by it. Here the laws of England and Scotland diverge.

The law of England distinguishes between public and private nuisance. A *public nuisance* is one that affects a particular class or group of citizens. The conduct must be such as materially affects the complainer. No one can complain of a public nuisance if he is not himself able to allege and prove some special or particular damage. Thus, a hole in the road would not be actionable under this head but it would become so if someone fell into it and broke a leg. *Private nuisance*, in its pure form, happens when someone interferes with another's use or enjoyment of land. This is a simple matter of balance, depending on the locality. In modern times, planning legislation has had a tremendous impact on such cases, preventing as it does certain excesses. In English law, nuisance provides the remedy for infringement of a land law servitude. A plaintiff must own or have an interest in the land in question, thus depriving the visitor of a right in private nuisance for personal injury. Generally, in England, it is thought that the standard of care is strict. However, it may well be the case that different considerations apply where the remedy is for injunction as opposed to when it is for damages. When restraining conduct, the court is more likely to take the view that if a plaintiff is suffering more than it is reasonable that he should suffer, that he be entitled to injunction. When seeking damages the courts may want to look for some blameworthy conduct, but the English law has not made this distinction firm, and it is probably still the case that liability is strict. The significance of this is that a plaintiff in England is better served by trying to make out a claim in nuisance instead of negligence, assuming the conduct is of a kind that constitutes a nuisance. In particular, the harm must usually be a continuing one.

In Scotland there is no distinction between public and private nuisance. The case *RHM Bakeries* v. *SRC* 1985 SLT 214 has confirmed that in Scotland there can be no liability without fault, or, to put it in its positive and Latin form, there is liability only for *culpa*. In that case, however, it was accepted that in most cases that we could call nuisance there will be an almost irresistible inference of fault. Scots law remains very similar to the English law where the remedy sought is interdict (the Scots equivalent of injunction). The courts will restrain any use of land that results in unreasonable inconvenience to another, going as far as to contemplate stopping the erection of the grandstand needed for the Edinburgh Military Tattoo at the instance of a young woman who found the noise more than reasonably tolerable: *Webster* v. *L. Adv.* 1984 SLT 13; 1985 SLT 361.

The Latin maxim encountered in this area does not assist in deciding cases but offers a rhetorical focus for the evaluation of the various factors: thus, *sic utere tuum ut alienum non laedas* ('use your own property in such a way that it does not harm another') raises questions about use and harm.

nulla poena sine lege 'no penalty without law'. This principle opposes, among other things, arbitrary punishment and retrospective legislation.

nullity of marriage the avoidance of a marriage, as opposed to its termination by DIVORCE. A marriage may be declared null as a result of some defect existing at the time the marriage was celebrated or because the marriage was never consummated.

nullum temporis occurrit regi 'time does not run against the king.'

nuncupative will see PRIVILEGED WILLS.

oath a solemn or holy statement or promise to tell the truth. The main purpose of oaths in modern times is not as in the past to ensure that a witness actually tells the truth (for fear of God) but now to punish him severely if he lies – for the crime of PERJURY. Accordingly, there is in fact no need for the oath for that purpose, and secular and mixed societies allow evidence and statements to be given by way of AFFIRMATION.

oath of allegiance an oath to be faithful and bear true allegiance to the Crown (see NATURALISATION). See ALLEGIANCE.

obiter dictum something said by a judge in a decision that is not essential to the decision and does not form part of the RATIO DECIDENDI.

objection 1. an intervention by counsel contending that a question by opposing counsel is improper and should be disallowed or that a document or production or label sought to be tendered by another party should not be received.
2. an objection in point of law is a form of pleading by a defendant in his defence that raises an issue of law. When raised, the court may order this to be tried as a preliminary point of law.
3. objection to indictment is a procedure in which the accused objects to the indictment on legal grounds.
4. in planning and licensing matters, applications have to be intimated and advertised, and those entitled to oppose and who do oppose are frequently called *objectors*.

objects clause a clause or clauses in the memorandum of a company setting out the objects of the company. It is important in relation to what the company can and cannot do both as regard to the world and in relation to its shareholders. See ULTRA VIRES.

obligation a legal tie, in ROMAN LAW divided into CONTRACT, DELICT, QUASI-CONTRACT and QUASI-DELICT. In modern Western systems that do not have codes modelled on the old Roman law, the division is into contract, TORT/delict and RESTITUTION. Some commentators have commented upon the need to reserve a fourth miscellaneous category rather than force some obligations into categories to which they are not suited.

obligationes literis for centuries, a category of obligation in Scots law but made obsolete in 1995. See REQUIREMENTS OF WRITING, SELF-PROVING.

obscenity the effect of an article to tend to deprave and corrupt persons likely to come into contact with it, according to the Obscene Publications Act 1959 (as amended). The balance against censorship is sought to be maintained by the inclusion of a defence that the publication is justified as being for the public good on the grounds that it is in the interests of science, literature, art or learning, or other subjects of general interest. Perhaps the most celebrated prosecution was *R* v. *Penguin Books* [1961] Crim. LR 176, the article in question being D. H. Lawrence's novel *Lady Chatterley's Lover*. The defence showed the moral attitude of the legislation and, indeed, showed the prosecution to be rather out of touch with prevailing attitudes to morality, the prosecution asking the jury to decide based upon the following test: 'Is it a book that you would even wish your wife or your servants to read?' Nonetheless, the Act is still used, although with more subtlety.

occupation a mode of original acquisition of property. It is done by taking a thing, intending to be its owner. Property to wild animals is obtained in this way, a hunter becoming the owner of wild animals killed and taken. Goods lost abandoned and ownerless (called *bona vacantia*) fall to the Crown. It is a criminal offence not to take found things to a police station. Land in England is likely to revert to the Crown. In Scotland, land is unlikely to be obtained in this way for most land in Scotland is held feudally and thus is never ownerless.

occupier of premises see OCCUPIERS' LIABILITY.

occupier's liability the liability of the occupier of land, buildings and other premises to those coming on to the premises. The English law has gone through a number of phases resulting in matters now being regulated by the Occupiers' Liability Acts 1957 and 1984. The initial focus is on the nature of the plaintiff. If the plaintiff is a lawful visitor, his rights are governed by the Occupiers' Liability Act 1957. If the plaintiff is a trespasser, his rights are determined by Occupiers' Liability Act 1984. A visitor is someone who has express or implied permission to come on to the premises. Indeed, anyone who enters by virtue of a right given by the law, even if without permission, is entitled to sue under the Act. So, a police officer going to arrest an occupant would be protected. The English law assumes that, generally, a person gives implied permission to people to enter with a view to communicating with the occupier. Visitors are entitled to the common duty of care. The common duty of care is to take such care as in the circumstances is reasonable to see that the visitor will be safe in using the premises for the purposes for which he is invited or permitted to be there. The Act provides some specific guidance. It indicates that an occupier must be prepared for children to be less careful than adults. A person who comes on the premises in pursuance of a calling should appreciate and guard against special risks – so the gas man must be aware of dangers from gas pipes. A warning will not determine liability unless it was enough to enable the visitor to be reasonably safe.

The traditional English law was that there was only liability to a trespasser if there was harm done deliberately or in wilful disregard of the trespasser's safety. The occupier will be liable if he is aware of the danger or has reasonable grounds to believe that it exists; he has reasonable grounds to believe that the defendant is in the vicinity of the danger; and the risk is one against which, in all the circumstances of the case, the occupier may reasonably be expected to offer some protection.

Scotland's native law was restored and enhanced by the Occupiers' Liability (Scotland) Act 1960. It applies a basic standard of reasonable care, which obviously depends upon the circumstances of the case. In particular, a duty is owed to a trespasser like anyone else. The care that an occupier of premises is required, by reason of his occupation or control of premises, to show towards a person entering thereon in respect of dangers that are due to the state of the premises or to anything done or omitted to be done on them and for which the occupier is in law responsible shall, except insofar as he is entitled to and does extend, restrict, modify or exclude by agreement his obligations towards that person, be such care as in all the circumstances of the case is reasonable to see that that person will not suffer injury or damage by reason of any such danger.

In neither Scotland nor England is occupier defined. In both jurisdictions the common law focuses upon the person who has actual physical control over the premises: *Wheat* v. *E. Lacon & Co. Ltd* [1966] AC 552; *Telfer* v. *Glasgow District Council* 1974 SLT (Notes) 51.

offence see CRIME.

offences triable either way in England, offences that can be charged either on indictment or as SUMMARY OFFENCE.

offensive weapon any article made or adapted for use for causing injury to the person or intended by the person having it with him for such use by him. A razor is not an offensive weapon in its own right but could be such if intended by the person to be used as such. Any person who, without lawful authority or reasonable excuse, the proof being on that person, has with him in any public place any offensive weapon is guilty of an offence.

offer an expression of willingness made to another party to form a binding legal contract. It is to be distinguished from an invitation to treat, which is merely an indication that a person is open to offers: see *Pharmaceutical Society of Great Britain* v. *Boots Cash Chemists* [1953] 1 QB 401; *Carlill* v. *Carbolic Smoke Ball Co.* [1893] 1 QB 256.

offer of amends see DEFAMATION.

office or employment the object of income tax under SCHEDULE E. In *GWR* v. *Bater* (1920) 8 TC 231, 'office' was described as 'a subsisting, permanent, substantive position which has an existence independent of the person who filled it and was held in succession by successive holders'.

Official Journal (OJ) the authorised publication of the EUROPEAN COMMUNITIES.

Official Receiver the official appointed by the Secretary of State who acts as interim receiver and manager of the estate of the debtor and presides at the first meeting of creditors. In a company winding up he often becomes provisional liquidator when a winding-up order is made.

official secrets government information that cannot be revealed. The UK has a special statutory regime that protects the free flow of information within government. This is enforced by very serious penalties and operates as something of a major restriction on the freedom of speech and information. Very lowly officials are asked to sign declarations under the Acts, including ordinary postal workers. There is no overriding defence of public interest. See, generally, Official Secrets Acts 1911 to 1989.

offshore a term used to describe vehicles or institutions based in, or regulated by, the laws of a jurisdiction that either has no tax or low tax for non-locals and that specialises in providing services of a financial or legal nature to persons and businesses 'onshore', that is to say, in high-tax jurisdictions. While many such jurisdictions are based on islands, which has brought about the terminology in a literal sense, the littoral location of the investment is irrelevant.

Ogden tables a set of actuarial tables provided to assist in calculating the amount of money payable as damages for loss of future benefits – especially future wage loss. They are named after the chairman of the committee that devised them, Sir Michael Ogden QC. They are now admissible as evidence in England in terms of the Civil Evidence Act 1996. Essentially, they provide more scientific MULTIPLIERS, and they are usually higher multipliers than the courts would have chosen. They have been accepted in the UK by the courts as the proper starting point: *Wells* v. *Wells* [1998] 3 All ER 480.

Oireachtas the parliament of the Republic of Ireland, set up by the 1937 Constitution and comprising the President, a lower house (DAIL EIREANN) and upper house (SEANAD EIREANN).

OJ the abbreviation for OFFICIAL JOURNAL.

Old Bailey see CENTRAL CRIMINAL COURT.

ombudsman a person appointed by parliament to investigate citizens' complaints. The name derives from the first example appointed in Sweden in 1809. There are now many in the UK, both in the public and private sector, and as a result of devolution, e.g. the Welsh Administrative Ombudsman (Ombudsman Gweinyddiaeth Cymru).

omnia praesumuntur rite et solemniter acta see PRESUMPTION.

ope exceptionis 'by way of exception', used to describe pleas that can be taken as a defence to a principal claim.

opening speeches in English criminal practice, the speech made by the prosecution indicating what it is it is trying to establish against the defendant. The defence may do so too if it has witnesses in addition to the defendant. In Scotland, the practice is not followed and is often criticised. It has the benefit that the jury and judge get some idea of what the case is about and puts the evidence that is to be heard into context. On the other hand, a jury might become predisposed against the defendant from the start. Having heard so much detail from the Crown, the jury might confuse allegation with proof of fact.

open-texture in JURISPRUDENCE describes the phenomenon that legal rules, being a function of language, are similarly subject to constant deferral of meaning. For those subscribing to HARTIAN JURISPRUDENCE, this is explained by accepting that words have a core of certainty and a penumbra of uncertainty. This is said to be consonant with (one of) the linguistic philosophy(s) of Wittgenstein.

Modern linguistic philosophers such as Derrida or Barthes probably would find the core of certainty uncertain.

open verdict see VERDICT.

operative words words in a deed or conveyance that have the effect of creating or transferring the interest that is the subject matter of the transaction.

opinion 1. a form of Act of the EUROPEAN COMMUNITIES having no legal effect other than as a necessary part of legislative activity. **2.** sometimes used of the judgment of a law lord in the House of Lords, which is also called a speech. **3.** judgment of a Scottish judge in the Court of Session. **4.** the statement of law offered by a barrister or counsel, viz. *counsel's opinion.*

oral evidence spoken testimony given by witnesses in court, usually under OATH.

order bill a BILL OF EXCHANGE payable to order is a bill payable to a given person, or as such person shall direct by an indorsement he may make on it. Until the bill is so indorsed no other person can maintain an action on it.

Order in Council a form of legislation made by the Queen by and with the advice of the PRIVY COUNCIL. Some are made in virtue of the ROYAL PREROGATIVE and others by ACT OF PARLIAMENT, making it a kind of DELEGATED LEGISLATION.

ordinarily resident the concept of being in an abode in a particular place or country voluntarily or for settled purposes (e.g. education) as part of the normal state of a person's life for the time being. A person can be absent for insignificant periods and still be ordinarily resident so long as he maintains some tie or connection with the UK.

ordinary shares the shares issued to members of a limited company. These represent the equity or risk capital of a company; they carry no prior rights in terms of entitlement to dividend or return of capital on a winding up. Ordinary shares generally carry full voting rights. Different are preference shares, which entitle the holder to a stipulated fixed rate return in the form of a dividend (like the fixed rate return to which holders of loan stock are entitled) whereas the dividend declared in respect of the former is purely a matter for the directors and subject to approval by the shareholders in general meetings. In the event of a winding up, holders of preference shares are entitled to be paid before ordinary shareholders.

ostensible authority authority that appears from the circumstances to exist whatever the reality may be. The manager of a shop has ostensible authority in relation to many transactions, regardless of what authority the owner may actually have given him. See AGENCY, APPARENT AUTHORITY.

ostensible partner a person who allows his credit to be pledged as a partner (e.g. where his name appears in the list of partners on the firm's notepaper, or where he interferes in the management of the business so as to produce in third parties a reasonable belief that he is a partner). In such a case the individual concerned is answerable and liable as if he were a partner to all who deal with the firm without having notice at the time that he is unconnected with it. See PARTNERSHIP.

outgoing partner see PARTNERSHIP.

overdue bill a BILL OF EXCHANGE still in circulation beyond the date specified for payment for an unreasonable length of time. Where an overdue bill is sought to be negotiated, such negotiation can only be effected subject to any defect in title affecting the bill at its maturity; after that no person who acquires it can acquire or give a better title than that which the transferor had.

overrule to set aside the rule of a lower court. When achieved by a superior court in the Anglo-American system, the effect is retrospective. The term can be used of a statute that changes the legal effect of a decision. This is done from the date the statute comes into force. Parliament can, of course, make the statute come into effect retrospectively, but this is something that is generally thought to be a dangerous form of legislation that may go against the rule of law: see *Burmah Oil Co. Ltd* v. *Lord Advocate* [1965] AC 75 and the War Damage Act 1965.

overseas company a company incorporated outside the UK with an established place of business within the UK (see Companies Act 1985, Section 744).

own brander in PRODUCT LIABILITY, one of the persons who can be held liable as a defendant or defender for a DEFECT in a product. In terms of the Act, a person who, by putting his name on the product or using a trademark or other distinguishing mark in relation to the product, can be held liable as a producer.

ownership the full and complete right of dominion over property. It has been said that ownership is either so simple as to need no explanation or so elusive as to defy definition. At its most extreme and absolute, it means the power to enjoy and dispose of things absolutely. In almost every society the power is limited by the general law. Because it is possible under many legal systems for an owner to grant rights over a property, it may be that the owner will be unable to use his property – the owner of a car sold on hire-purchase never drives it, indeed, may never even have seen it. Thus, ownership is often considered to be the ultimate residual right that remains after all other rights over a thing have been extinguished.

In Roman law and in civilian systems, the owner of property is usually able to recover his own property by an action called a *vindicatio*. For practical reasons, civilian systems usually adopt a presumption of ownership from possession and, indeed, such appears in the French and German civil codes and is a rule of law in Scotland: *Pragnell-O'Neill* v. *Lady Skiffington* 1984 SLT 282. In English law, possession itself is protected. See CONVERSION.

Ownership is said to be *original*, where the owner has brought the property into human control for the first time, as by occupying land or capturing a wild animal, or *derivative*, where the owner acquires from the previous owner as in a sale.

So far as the most common transaction – SALE – is concerned, the law is set out by the Sale of Goods Act 1979. The English approach to ownership is adopted in the UK whereby the Act sets out who has property in the goods or who gets a good title to the goods – both concepts being practically equivalent to ownership.

Theoretically, ownership of land in England and Wales is vested in the Crown; the concept of ownership by individuals and companies is expressed through the doctrine of estates. Only two legal estates may exist since 1925, namely the fee simple absolute in possession (FREEHOLD), which is akin to absolute ownership, and the term of years absolute (LEASEHOLD), which confers ownership or possession rights for a temporary period.

In Scotland too, with a few exceptions, land is held feudally under the Crown.

oyer and terminer 'to hear and determine', now obsolete, the commission given to judges of the assize.

oyez 'hear ye'. Listen up. Here comes the judge.

P

PACE abbreviation for POLICE AND CRIMINAL EVIDENCE ACT.

pact promise or agreement, often used of important treaties between states.

pacta illicita in the law of CONTRACT, 'illegal contracts'. If an agreement is unlawful in its aim or its performance, the courts will not enforce the agreement. Recognised categories are:

(1) contracts to commit crimes, torts or delicts;

(2) contracts promoting sexual immorality: see *Pearce* v. *Brooks* (1866) LR 1 Ex 213, a rule that has had the effect of inhibiting cohabitation agreements;

(3) *pacta de quota litis*, or 'agreements to share the proceeds of litigation', a rule that prevents lawyers taking percentage fees;

(4) contracts against justice, such as the purchase of knighthoods other than by subscription to party funds in the usual way;

(5) contracts in restraint of trade. Examples of this type are restrictive covenants, which try to restrain a person from working or trading for a given length of time and over a given territory. They are allowed only if reasonable and in the interests of the parties and the public. They are construed CONTRA PROFERENTEM.

Much more leniency is apparent when the restraint is in a sale of a business selling the goodwill. Again, so-called *solus* agreements have been upheld whereby, when granting a person some right or title, a condition is inserted tying that person to using the transferor's products and those of no other, although this sort of agreement, if widespread, can be struck at by the law on COMPETITION. See, generally, *Fitch* v. *Dewes* [1921] 2 AC 158, *Bluebell Apparel Ltd* v. *Dickinson* 1980 SLT 157, *Nordenfelt* v. *Maxim Nordenfelt Guns and Ammunition Co. Ltd* [1894] AC 535.

In all these cases the rule EX TURPI CAUSA NON ORITUR ACTIO applies: 'an action does not arise out of an illegal cause.' This can be harsh if property or money has been transferred contrary to some obscure and technical statute and the parties are not equally blameworthy: *in pari delicto*. RESTITUTION may be allowed in some such cases. In England the innocent party may enforce if the contract is illegal, but there is a collateral warranty and if there has been fraud there can be damages for the fraud. The restitutionary doctrine of RECOMPENSE in Scots law can operate to compensate an innocent party for work done: *Cuthbertson* v. *Lowes* (1870) 8 M 1073; *Jamieson* v. *Watts Trs* 1950 SC 265.

pacta sunt servanda 'agreements are binding'. This doctrine of the canon law taken into civilian systems is not accepted in English law, which requires CONSIDERATION.

palinode a retraction. In Scots law, when DEFAMATION was a matter for the commissary courts, one remedy was a conclusion for a retraction to be made.

Pandects see CORPUS JURIS CIVILIS.

pander to arrange for prostitution.

panel see ACCUSED.

paralegal a person who assists a fully enrolled or admitted lawyer. The scope of activity varies from place to place but often the paralegal can have substantial client care contact, be heavily involved in drafting standard documents and actively liaise with the professionals in progressing court actions.

paraphernalia in English law, a wife's apparel, jewellery and the like.

parcel a description in a deed of the lands that are the subject matter of the transaction.

pardon see ROYAL PARDON.

parens patriae the jurisdiction of the court to assume responsibility for the welfare of those otherwise unprovided for, such as children or lunatics, regardless of whether there is STATUTORY POWER.

parentage in both England and Scotland it is legally presumed that a child born during marriage is also the child of the husband. The presumption can be rebutted. The court can order DNA or other tests, but if the mother, having control, does not allow samples to be taken then all the court can do is draw such inferences as are appropriate. There are very technical rules as to who is a parent in cases of artificial insemination and the like: Human Fertilisation and Embryology Act 1990. See ILLEGITIMACY.

parental responsibility all the rights, duties, powers and authority that by law a parent has in relation to his child. If a man and woman are married they automatically have parental responsibilities. An unmarried father requires to have them declared. It is possible by legal agreement for an unmarried father to gain parental responsibility. A local authority can be awarded parental responsibilities. See Children Act 1989, Children (Scotland) Act 1995.

pari passu 'share and share alike', a term used in several contexts but especially in relation to the rights and ranking of creditors of an insolvent estate; it denotes an entitlement to payment of their debts in shares proportionate to their respective claims.

Parliament in the CONSTITUTIONAL LAW of the UK, originally a body summoned to assist the monarch in discussing important matters and dispensing justice and hearing grievances. In modern times it is divided into two houses: the HOUSE OF COMMONS, which is democratically elected, and the HOUSE OF LORDS, which is inhabited by hereditary and appointed peers. It sits in Westminster (formerly a royal palace) and is now under the control of the SPEAKER of the House of Commons. Still known as the High Court of Parliament, its functions are not simply legislative, although that is its most important role today. It is summoned by exercise of the ROYAL PREROGATIVE, and this meeting is known as a parliament that lasts until that parliament is dissolved. While convened, it divides into sessions, now two a year, each session being terminated by *prorogation* (again an exercise of the prerogative). The Meeting of Parliament Act 1694 provides (following the Triennial Act 1664) that parliaments must be called at least once every three years. The CONVENTION that requires the important Finance, Army, Air Force and Navy Acts to be re-enacted annually means that parliament sits at least once a year, although having become the modern government of a modern nation it is in almost constant session.

Its pomp and ceremony are legendary. The Gentleman Usher of the Black Rod leads the members of the House of Commons to the House of Lords on the opening of Parliament. The Queen usually attends the opening of a parliament, and, indeed, each session, to give the *Queen's speech* (drafted in fact by the CABINET), setting out the legislative programme. A bill for the Suppression of Clandestine Outlawries is read at the start of every session except the first to show the world that the Commons can initiate bills not in the Queen's speech. In the Lords, the debate on the Queen's speech takes place after a formal reading of the Select Vestries Bill and in the form of a debate on a loyal address.

The Parliament Acts 1911 and 1949 represent the present state of the long-running struggle between Lords and Commons, and reflects the fact that universal suffrage, which began in 1832 with the great Reform Act, has strengthened the hand of the Commons over the Lords. The thrust of the Acts read together is that the Lords can at best delay a bill by sending it back to the Commons, who then have only to bide their time to turn it into law. The 1949 Act was actually passed under the provisions of the 1911 Act, and it was this 1949 provision that effectively made the power a delaying one instead of one that might have allowed a longer period and one in which the electorate has a say in an important matter over which the two houses had disagreed. Its constitutionality is not entirely unquestioned. See also NATIONAL ASSEMBLY FOR WALES, SCOTTISH PARLIAMENT.

Parliamentary Commissioner for Administration in the CONSTITUTIONAL LAW of the UK, an officer who is charged with investigating complaints where officials are charged with having obeyed the law but have not acted in a proper administrative way, examples being bias, delay, perversity and arbitrariness. The immediate model was that of the Scandinavian ombudsman, which had been introduced in New Zealand, and to an extent the idea was not unlike the Comptroller and Auditor General. He can be removed only on an address to both houses and is a member of the COUNCIL ON TRIBUNALS. He oversees most government departments but not the health service, nationalised industries and the like, nor the police. He has considerable power to investigate and to demand documents and papers, there being no Crown privilege. Complaints, however, must still come through a Member of Parliament and not from a member of the public directly. The House of Commons has a select committee on the Parliamentary Commissioner for the Administration to monitor his performance and the exercise of the office generally. Various National Health Service Acts have since set up three Health Service Commissioners for Scotland, Wales and England. There are, since 1974 in England and 1975 in Scotland, three Commissions for Local Administration. See also EUROPEAN PARLIAMENT.

parole the release of a convicted prisoner on licence before the end of his sentence (the term is derived from the French for 'word of honour'). The authority for this comes through the Home Secretary, advised by review committees or by reference to the PAROLE BOARD. The applicable rules change often. See Criminal Justice Act 1991.

parole board essentially an advisory body set up to assist the Home Secretary in granting prisoners early release and in deciding to recall those out on licence. Originating in England in the Criminal Justice Act 1967, the board has a supporting network of local advisory committees. Since the Criminal Justice Act 1991, procedures are more open. There are now Parole Board Rules (1992) governing procedure at hearings. There is a Parole Board for Scotland to advise the Secretary of State.

particulars details of an allegation of fact made in pleadings.

particulars (of sale) that part of a contract for the sale of land in which the details of the property to be sold are set out.

partnership an association of two or more persons carrying on business in common with a view to profit. The main principles of the law of partnership are to be found in the Partnership Act 1890, an Act that, for the most part, applies equally to England and Scotland. The Act did not substantially alter the common law and, indeed, intended to codify the law; accordingly, cases decided before 1890 may be used to illustrate the principles contained in the Act. Except in the case of a LIMITED PARTNERSHIP, formed under the Limited Partnerships Act 1907 or under the Limited Liability Partnerships Act 2000, each partner is liable to the full extent of his property for the whole debts of the partnership firm should the firm be unable to meet them. Every partner must account to the firm for any benefit derived by him without the consent of the other partners from any transaction concerning the partnership or from any use by him of the partnership property, name or business connections. This also applies to transactions after the partnership has been dissolved by the death of a partner and before its affairs have been completely wound up. A partnership is essentially a contract between those involved, and the rights and obligations of the partners are governed by the terms of the agreement between them: see *Pooley* v. *Driver* (1876) LR 5 Ch. D. 458. Under English law, a partnership does not have a legal personality separate from its members. In Scotland it does, so a partnership can own property, although the title to heritable property is usually taken in the name of the partners or some of them as trustees for the firm.

The sharing of profits and losses is usually governed by the ARTICLES OF PARTNERSHIP or *partnership agreements*. In the absence of express or implied agreement, partners contribute equally towards losses, whether of capital or otherwise, sustained by the firm. Where the profits are not shared equally, the losses are, in the absence of agreement, borne in the same proportion as the profits are shared, regardless of whether one partner has put up more capital than others.

An attempt by a partner to pledge the firm's credit for a purpose apparently not connected with its ordinary business will not bind the firm unless he has been especially authorised by the other partners: *Tower Cabinet Co.* v. *Ingram* [1949] 2 KB 397. A partner has no implied authority to execute deeds on behalf of his firm; equally, the implied authority does not extend to acts not usually incidental to the scope of the partnership business.

Partners in a firm are jointly and severally liable for any breach of trust committed by one partner, in which they were implicated.

Persons other than partners may have authority to deal with third parties on behalf of the firm; however, such persons have no implied mandate. Any act or instrument relating to the business of the firm, done or executed in the firm's name, or in any other manner, showing an intention to bind the firm, by any person authorised thereto (whether a partner or not) is binding on the firm and on each and every partner.

Provisions in articles of partnership or deeds of dissolution frequently provide that the partners continuing the firm's activities are to indemnify the outgoing partner against existing partnership liabilities. Often the articles will confer on continuing partners an option to purchase the interest of an outgoing partner; if that option is exercised, the outgoing partner is not entitled to any further share of profits. If there is no such option (or if it has not been exercised), the outgoing partner has the option of taking either interest at 5 per cent per annum on the value of his share or on such share or profit as the court may find attributable to the use of such share. Articles often contain provisions prohibiting an outgoing partner from carrying on a similar trade or profession within specified limits of time and distance, although the limitations must be reasonable to be enforced.

Subject to any agreement in the articles of partnership, the following may cause a partnership to be dissolved: (a) notice; (b) elapse of fixed time as provided for in the partnership articles; (c) where the partnership is formed for a particular purpose or adventure, the fulfilment of that purpose or completion of the adventure; (d) bankruptcy of a partner; (e) expulsion of a partner; (f) by order of the court. See generally, *Chandroutie* v. *Gajadhar* [1987] AC 147.

Proposals for substantial reforms were initiated by the Law Commission and the Scottish Law Commission in 2000.

partnership agreement see ARTICLES OF PARTNERSHIP, PARTNERSHIP.

partnership at will a PARTNERSHIP with no fixed term. It can, as the name suggests, be terminated by any partner giving notice of termination.

passenger any person carried on a ship except: (a) persons employed on the ship; (b) persons on board in pursuance of the obligation laid upon the master to carry shipwrecked, distressed or other persons; and (c) children under the age of one year: Merchant Shipping (Safety Convention) Act 1949.

passim 'here and there'.

passing off the tort or delict of putting up goods in such a way that the goodwill of another trader is harmed. The paradigm case is that of selling goods under the pursuer's name or mark or using his get-up or set-up (i.e. packaging). *Reverse passing off* is where the accusation is that the defender is damaging the pursuer's sales by selling an inferior product that will damage the pursuer's future sales, as opposed to depriving him of actual sales. Passing off is often considered a form of INTELLECTUAL PROPERTY. See *Erven Warnik BV* v. *Townend* [1979] AC 731.

passing of property see PROPERTY.

passing on the defence to a claim for RESTITUTION that the plaintiff, albeit he suffered a loss at the defendant's expense, has passed on that loss to others. Most likely to be encountered in cases of wrongfully demanded taxes – the business making the payment, and seeking repayment, being passed on the liability to its customers. It has been discussed in the UK, *Woolwich* v. *Inland Revenue* [1993] AC 70; it was unsuccessful in the High Court of Australia, *Mason* v. *The State of New South Wales* (1958) 102 CLR 106; unsuccessful in the Supreme Court of the USA, *Hanover Shoe* v. *United Shoe* 392 US 481 (1968); it has been considered and accepted as not necessarily incompatible with European Community law by the European Court of Justice, *Amministrazione delle Finanze dello Stato* v. *San Giorgio SpA* [1985] 2 CMLR 647.

passport a document (for UK citizens issued by the Foreign Office) certifying the holder's nationality and citizenship. It suggests allegiance to the Crown, and thus is important in relation to the crime of TREASON.

pasturage in Scots property law, the SERVITUDE right to feed cattle or sheep on the land of another.

patent open. Used as a verb, *to patent* an invention is to register that invention with the Patent Office, making it open to others but securing the exclusive right to make and sell that invention for a period of years. Used as a noun, the registration itself is called a *patent* and can be bought and sold. See INTELLECTUAL PROPERTY.

pater est quem nuptiae demonstrant see PRESUMPTION.

paternity natural fatherhood. In English law it is possible to obtain a *declaration of paternity* that a man is the father of a child: Civil Evidence Act 1968 (as amended by Family Law Reform Act 1987). See also *Re JS* [1980] 1 All ER 1061.

In Scots family law, by the Law Reform (Parent and Child) (Scotland) Act 1986, a man is presumed to be the father of a child if he was married to the mother at any time during the period beginning with the child's conception and ending with his or her birth. This makes the father liable to ALIMENT the child and gives him PARENTAL RIGHTS automatically. The presumption can be rebutted on BALANCE OF PROBABILITIES. There is rebuttable presumption that registration by a man as the father of a child means that he is the father of the child.

patriality a concept applicable to citizens of the UK and colonies having a right of abode in the UK. Patriality can be acquired in the following ways:

(1) by being born, adopted, naturalised or registered in the UK, Channel Islands or Isle of Man;

(2) by descent from or adoption by a parent who was within (1) above or was himself descended from or adopted by a parent who was within (1) above;

(3) by being settled at any time in the UK and Islands and having been at that time ordinarily resident there for five years or more;

(4) by marriage.

patriation (Canada) the process by which laws made in the UK became accepted by Canada as law for Canada.

pawn see PLEDGE.

PAYE abbreviation for Pay As You Earn, a scheme for the collection of income tax chargeable under SCHEDULE E under which tax is deducted by the employer from payments of salary, etc, to the employee and accounted for to the Inland Revenue.

payment in due course payment made at or after the maturity of a BILL OF EXCHANGE to the holder of the bill by a payer in good faith and without notice that the holder's title might be defective. A bill is discharged by payment in due course by or on behalf of the drawee or acceptor. When a bill is paid by the drawer or indorser it is not discharged and the party paying may have rights on it.

payment into court a payment by a defender in an action for debt or damages in attempted satisfaction of any or all of the plaintiff's claims. Payment into court may not be disclosed during trial except in an action to which a defence of tender before action is raised.

PC abbreviation for PRIVY COUNCIL, PRIVY COUNSELLOR, police constable.

Peace Commissioner in the Irish Republic, a person appointed by the government to an office giving powers and duties such as signing summonses and warrants, administering oaths and taking declarations. They have no judicial functions.

pedlar 'one might say that a pedlar is one who trades as he travels as distinct from one who merely travels to trade.' Per J. Hutchison in *Watson* v. *Malloy* [1988] 1 WLR 1026. The significance is that a pedlar requires a pedlar's certificate (under the Pedlars Act 1871) but not a street trading licence.

peer originally a person with a right to be summoned to Parliament and a hereditary right for his heirs to be so summoned, now created by letters-patent. Disputes as to entitlement are made to the House of Lords on the advice of the Committee for Privileges, one of the best known being the *Wensleydale Peerage Case* (1856) 5 HLC 968. The order of precedence is dukes, marquesses, earls, viscounts and barons.

penal code a code setting out all or at least most of the main principles of the criminal law of a system. The UK has generally not followed this course. In the USA many states have turned the common law into codes or partial codes. Under the influence of the NAPOLEONIC CODE, the Code d'Instruction Criminelle of 1808 and the Code Pénal of 1810, many continental European states have adopted penal codes that require from time to time to be revised.

penalty clauses clauses that impose a liability more extensive than general damages. They are contrary to public policy and accordingly unenforceable. However, the courts will allow parties to agree the amount of damages in advance by way of what is called a *liquidate damages provision*. These often look the same, and the result may be little different. From *Dunlop Tyre Co. Ltd* v. *New Garage Motor Co.* [1915] AC 79, it can be said that the factors in determining what is allowed and what is not are as follows:

(i) the difficulty of calculating the actual loss on breach;

(ii) the reasonableness of the stipulated sum;

(iii) a clause will be presumed penal if it makes the same sum payable for breaches of differing severity;

(iv) a clause will be penal if the principal obligation is to pay money and the stipulated sum is larger.

pendente lite 'while an action is going on'.

pension the payment of a sum of money, usually a periodical payment, for past services. Pensions are taxable under SCHEDULE E.

per annum 'yearly'.

per capita 'by head', one of two common methods of division of a fund, usually an estate. *Per capita* is division by head. Everyone gets an equal share, no matter how close or distant the relationship. *Per stirpes* is 'division by branch' – each branch of the family gets the same. The idea is best represented by the diagram below:

If William dies and then Robert dies, then the estate would per capita be divided equally between Tom, David and Edward, each getting one third (Mike and Harry being excluded by their living father, Edward). If the division is per stirpes, then the William branch and the Edward branch get half each. Edward is alive and gets his half, whereas on this model Tom and David take a per capita division of the amount allocated to the stirpes, i.e. one quarter of the estate.

per curiam 'by the court'.

peremptory challenge the right to challenge jurors without having to give a reason or show cause. It was abolished in England and Wales by the Criminal Justice Act 1988 and in Scotland by the Criminal Justice (Scotland) Act 1995.

per incuriam 'by mistake'. If it is held that a precedent in point and binding was decided per incuriam, then the strict rule of STARE DECISIS does not apply, so the case does not have to be applied. Clearly, the mistake in the earlier case must be very plain: *Morelle* v. *Wakeling* [1955] 2 QB 379.

periodical allowance in Scots family law, the award made to a spouse when a marriage is terminated by DIVORCE or NULLITY. It should not be made unless a capital sum would be inappropriate. It stops when the party to whom it is awarded dies or is remarried. The hope of the Family Law (Scotland) Act 1985 was to provide a 'clean break', so periodical allowance should be out of the ordinary. This is, of course, not to be confused with ALIMENT payable to a former spouse in name of children of the marriage. See PERIODIC PAYMENT ORDER.

periodic payment order an order in DIVORCE proceedings for regular payments of money. If the court is satisfied that the application of the 'CLEAN BREAK' principle is inappropriate, it may instead make an order for the payment of a periodical allowance. For Scotland see PERIODICAL ALLOWANCE.

perjury false swearing. The CRIME of judicial affirmation of falsehood upon oath or affirmation equivalent to oath. There needs to be a denial of what is true or an assertion of what is false. The statements complained of must be pertinent to the issue that was originally being tried.

permanent trustee in the Scots law of INSOLVENCY, the person appointed in a SEQUESTRATION by the court to administer the insolvent estate. This may be done before sequestration is awarded if there is cause when the person is an interim trustee and, indeed, until the first meeting of creditors, the trustee is an interim trustee. Trustees are appointed from a panel of suitable and qualified persons. They must accept appointment although they may apply to resign. The duties of the interim trustee involve preservation of the estate and organising and reporting to the first meeting of creditors. As permanent trustee the property of the bankrupt estate vests in the trustee, and his duty then is to ingather the estate and distribute it according to the rules of ranking. See VESTING. For England, see TRUSTEE IN BANKRUPTCY.

permission in the English law of PRESCRIPTION, at common law any consent or agreement by the servient owners, whether oral or written, rendered the user a precarious possession; it made no difference how long ago the permission was given provided that the user was enjoyed under it and not under a claim to use as of right. Under the Prescription Act, this rule now applies to the shorter periods only (20 years for easements, 30 years for profits) but not to the longer periods (40 years for easements, 60 years for profits) where permission had to be given by deed to be effective.

permutatio see BARTER.

perpetuities see RULE AGAINST PERPETUITIES.

per pro (pp) abbreviation for per procurationem, 'through an agent or procuratory'.

perquisites see BENEFITS IN KIND, EMOLUMENT.

per se 'by itself'.

person the object of legal rights. There are two kinds of legal person: human beings and artificial persons such as corporations. A

PARTNERSHIP in England is not a separate legal person but in Scotland it is said to have *quasi-personality*.

personal bar behaviour by a party that allows a court to hold the party bound to another or as having given up a right. See ESTOPPEL, HOMOLOGATION, REI INTERVENTUS, WAIVER.

personal bond in Scotland, the name given to a formal deed of debt, which, as the name suggests, is personally binding only. Most contain a warrant for execution and can thus be enforced by SUMMARY DILIGENCE.

personal injury an injury to the person. Although it appears a simple phrase to interpret, in some contexts it proves difficult. In Scotland, it was held that a foetus born alive and surviving very briefly could sue for personal injury in the womb (*Hamilton* v. *Fife Health Board* 1993 SLT 624). An action against a solicitor for failing to raise an action for personal injury is not a personal injury action (*MacKenzie* v. *Digby Brown* 1992 GWD 191). In England, it has been held that an unplanned pregnancy was a personal injury (*Watkin* v. *South Manchester Health Authority* [1995] TLR 380).

personal property property that is not REAL PROPERTY. It includes goods and chattels but also leaseholds and land, whether freehold or leasehold, held on trust for sale and conversion into money.

personal representatives executors or administrators of a deceased person's estate.

personal rights rights of personal security, such as life, limb, body, health, reputation and liberty.

persona non grata an unwelcome diplomat who must accordingly leave the host country.

per stirpes see PER CAPITA.

persuasive see STARE DECISIS.

pertinents things pertaining to. The word appears in most transfers of land in Scotland where the ground is purchased with the parts, privileges and pertinents.

perverse verdict see VERDICT.

petition of right originally, the means of proceeding against the Crown in a civil action (e.g. breach of contract). The petition of right procedure was rendered obsolete by the passing of the Crown Proceedings Act 1947.

pettifogger a lawyer of little importance and now impliedly, one who is perhaps dubious and who will make small points more for his own gain or pleasure than that of the client.

picketing from the French for 'pike', this describes the practice of placing strikers between the worker and his place of work to stop him coming off strike or to encourage him to go on strike. Almost a century of oscillating legislation controls the practice in the UK. Generally, it is permitted if carried out peacefully and with a view to communicating information or persuading persons and is carried out at a person's own place of work. This latter phrase prevents picketing outside the target's garden and restrained the *flying picket*, someone who would go anywhere to help out workers in a strike even though he himself might not have any dispute with the target. *Secondary picketing*, where suppliers of the target become themselves targets, is prohibited. While the law generally does not prohibit peaceful picketing, it has not created a right to picket; a picket standing in front of a lorry and obstructing it peacefully to communicate with the driver commits the offence of obstruction: *Broome* v. *DPP* [1974] ICR 84. Picketing also must be in accordance with the GOLDEN FORMULAE. Many pickets are not illegal simply for that reason: a code of practice issued by the Secretary of State indicates that there should be no more than six pickets at any entrance.

piracy 1. the taking of ships or persons or property from ships. Piracy is punishable wherever the pirates are found. It is defined by the 1958 Geneva Convention on the High Seas and the 1982 Convention on the Law of the Sea as any illegal act of violence or depredation that is committed for private ends on the high seas or outside the territorial control of any state.

2. used colloquially to describe the appropriation of the INTELLECTUAL PROPERTY of others, e.g. 'pirate video'.

place of safety order in Scots law, a child may be removed compulsorily from his family home into the care of the local authority under a place of safety order. The child can be detained at the place of safety for up to seven days, during which arrangements can be made for a *children's hearing* to determine whether or not the child is in need of care. The equivalent order in England is an EMERGENCY PROTECTION ORDER.

plaintiff the person bringing an action in court. For Scotland see PURSUER.

planning permission permission to develop land or buildings. The need for such permission is the linchpin of the system for controlling the development of land in the UK; before land can be developed, planning permission for such development must be granted by the local planning authority. There is a whole regime of investigation, advertisement, appeals and legal decision applying to such applications. See BLIGHT NOTICE.

plc abbreviation for PUBLIC LIMITED COMPANY.

plea bargaining the practice by which the prosecutor will alter the indictment in exchange for a guilty plea. In England there are guidelines under Practice Direction (Court of Appeal) [1976] LR 561. It takes place in Scotland too. In the USA, in some states, the judge may be party to the bargain offering the accused a more certain range of sentence.

pleadings the formal written statements of the parties in a civil action developing and ultimately defining the points at issue between them; they contain assertions of fact, which the parties propose to prove, and statements as to the remedies sought.

pleas-in-law in Scottish civil procedure, the part of an INITIAL WRIT or SUMMONS that very concisely sets out the legal support for the CONCLUSIONS or CRAVE based upon the facts alleged in the CONDESCENDENCE.

pledge a security transaction applicable to chattels under which the borrower (*pledgor*) gives possession of the chattel to the lender (the *pledgee*) as security for the payment of a debt or performance of an obligation. The pledgee is entitled to hold the chattel until payment or performance and, upon failure duly to pay or perform at the proper time, to sell it. Until any such sale, however, the pledgor remains entitled to redeem it by payment or performance.

pluries see ALIAS WRIT.

poaching the crime of taking game or other specified beasts and trespassing so to do. It is criminalised by, among other enactments, the Night Poaching Act 1828, the Game Laws (Amendment) Act 1960 and the Deer Act 1980.

poinding (pronounced 'pinding') in the Scots law of DILIGENCE or legal enforcement, after a CHARGE has expired without payment, SHERIFF OFFICERS or MESSENGERS at arms will attend the debtor's premises and make up a schedule listing goods and valuing them to a sum sufficient to cover the debt expenses and the expenses of the poinding. If payment is not made, application is made to the court for a warrant to sell the goods. Certain household goods are excluded, as are tools of a trade and articles for the care and upbringing of children – food, beds and the like. Radical reform is planned by the Scottish Parliament.

poinding of the ground (pronounced 'pinding') in the Scots law of DILIGENCE or legal enforcement, a procedure for attaching MOVABLE PROPERTY. It can be exercised only by a creditor holding a HERITABLE SECURITY.

police the local constabulary. In England, governed by the Police Act 1976 and in Scotland by the Police (Scotland) Act 1967. Police generally have no more powers than ordinary citizens, but there are many additional powers that they are given under legislation and under many other enactments. Thus, police have powers of search, seizure and to obtain information beyond that of the ordinary citizen. It is an offence to obstruct them in the course of their duties as it is to waste their time. The Chief Constable is vicariously liable for the wrongs of his force but answers on financial matters to the local authority. The Metropolitan force answers to the Home Secretary, who himself is responsible to Parliament. They will not generally be liable to a member of the public for a failure to prevent crime: *Hill* v. *Chief Constable* [1988] 2 All ER 238. It is difficult to sue the police for negligence in carrying out their duties, but it is at least now possible to argue such a case since the decision of the European Court of Human Rights in *Osman* v. *UK* [1998] TLR 68.

Police and Criminal Evidence Act (PACE) an Act of Parliament from 1984 setting out for England and Wales the powers of the police to arrest, search and question people. In addition to the principles set out in the Act, it also contains a number of codes intended to give guidance on the operation of these powers.

policy of insurance see INSURANCE.

political asylum refuge granted to a person in order to avoid political persecution or harassment. See ASYLUM.

pollicitatio in the Scots law of contract, not strictly a contract at all but a unilateral gratuitous obligation. Thus, rewards, options and undertakings can all be legally binding in Scotland without the need for an acceptance nor for consideration.

polygamous marriage having more than one lawful spouse. Polygamous marriage cannot be validly contracted in the UK.

position statement see BALANCE SHEET.

positive prescription in Scots law, a period of time that fortifies a defective title. Thus, a person who obtains land from a person who does not own it but has a title that on the face of it is valid and is able to include the property in question will obtain a valid title in ten years if it is possessed openly and peaceably and without interruption.

In English law, title to land may be acquired by ADVERSE POSSESSION, the relevant period being 12 years. Where the land is subject to the Land Registration Acts, adverse possession for the requisite period confers on the squatter a POSSESSORY TITLE. This may mature into an ABSOLUTE TITLE after a further ten years.

positivism as a theory of law, it may be summarised by saying that law may have any content. The law is what is laid down and that is an end to it. It is directly contrary to NATURAL LAW theories, which tend to have some touchstone that a man-made law has to meet for its validity. Positivism faces serious problems in that it opens the way to the use of law as a means of social engineering. It is of value in giving up law's claims to protect higher values. The rule of law and constitutions are only as strong as the individuals working with them and the political realities of the society to which they apply.

posse comitatus 'the power of the county'. The sheriff was able to call together able-bodied men to keep the peace. The institution transplanted to the USA, thence into ordinary parlance: 'round up a posse'.

possession 1. physical control or detention of a thing.

2. legal possession recognised and protected by law; inherent in this is *animus possidendi*, the intention to hold the thing against others.

3. one of the elements of ownership.

postal acceptance rule an offer is accepted when the acceptance is posted: *Entores* v. *Miles Far Eastern Corporation* [1955] 2 QB 327. This means that a binding contract is formed and, accordingly, the person who made the offer cannot sell to another without being liable in damages for breach of contract. The acceptor is bound but may be able to withdraw his acceptance if he can communicate this before the acceptance reaches the person who made the offer. It has been held in England that an acceptance that never actually came out of the other end of the postal system was effective: *Household Fire Insurance* v. *Grant* (1879) 4 Ex D. 216. This extreme position has been questioned in Scotland: *Mason* v. *Benhar Coal Co.* (1882) 9 R 883. There are some decisions against the rule in the USA: *Rhode Island Tool Co.* v. *United States* 130 Ct Ct 698.

post-dating see ANTEDATING.

post diem 'after the day'.

post mortem 'after death', a term applied to the medical examination of a corpse with a view to determining the cause of death. Also known as an *autopsy*. See CORONER.

power of attorney an authority given by one person to another to act in his absence.

pp abbreviation for PER PRO.

practising certificate the document issued to solicitors in England and Wales by the Law Society and in Scotland by the Law Society of Scotland, entitling the solicitor to practise.

praepositura in Scots family law, the doctrine abolished in 1984 that stated that a wife living with her husband had his presumed authority to pledge his credit in relation to certain domestic expenditure.

preamble the preliminary part of a document, legislation, a contract or a treaty, usually setting out what it is all about or why it has been prepared, specially used of an ACT OF PARLIAMENT where Parliament expresses the general purposes of the piece of legislation: *Att. Gen. v. Prince Earnest Augustus of Hanover* [1957] 1 All ER 842. It can be referred to for the purposes of STATUTORY INTERPRETATION.

precario request.

precedent previously decided case. One practical aspect of justice is that like cases be treated alike; lawyers consult the reports of previously decided court cases. How a particular system uses precedent is another matter. Continental systems such as the French and German allow that a series of cases interpreting the code will carry great weight. In the Anglo-American system the rules are far stricter, with courts being *bound* to follow previous decisions. These rules are often considered under STARE DECISIS.

precognition in Scottish legal practice, a statement by a witness taken by a lawyer, his clerk or agent. It is not only taken by a person other than the witness, but it is also framed by the *precognoscer*, so it is never certain that it reflects the precise words of the witness. While there is no obligation to give a precognition, in criminal law matters either the prosecution or the defence or both can apply to the court to have a person precognosed on oath in front of the court.

pre-emption 1. the right of buying before anyone else.

2. in international law, the right of a state to buy the property of another power in transit over its territory (or allow its own nationals to buy it).

3. in the USA, laws passed from 1841 onward allowing settlers to acquire title to public land.

pre-emption clause a clause usually found in the articles of private companies designed to restrict the opportunities of shares being sold outside a prescribed group of people. Essentially, the clause provides that no shares are to be transferred to any person who is not a member of the company, provided that an existing member is prepared to purchase them at a fair price to be determined in accordance with the articles. See PRE-EMPTION.

preference share a special type of share in a company, which has the characteristic that it confers an entitlement to a specified percentage rate of dividend that is payable in priority to the claims of ordinary shareholders. A company's share capital may be split between ordinary shares and preference shares. Ordinary shareholders are entitled to the remaining profits that have been appropriated for the payment of dividends.

preferential debts categories of debts listed in the Insolvency Act 1986 and having priority to any claims to principal or interest under a debenture.

pre-incorporation contract a contract made or purporting to be made by a person acting on behalf of a company that has not yet been formed. Under the Companies Act 1985, such a person is personally liable on such a contract.

preliminary ruling a ruling of the COURT OF JUSTICE in European law. The jurisdiction to make such a ruling arises in cases that have not come before the court itself but have arisen in the court of proceedings in national courts. Because COMMUNITY LAW is law in the MEMBER STATES, it is necessary that it is not distorted across the Community by uneven interpretation by national courts. A study of the earlier judgments of national courts confirms the tendency of the national courts to take a local view of Community law. Under Article 177, a national tribunal may request a ruling each and any time it considers that it requires an answer to the interpretation of Community law. If there is no appeal the court *must* request a ruling. The applicability and interpretation of the conditions for a reference have now been settled in the UK: see *Bulmer* v. *Bollinger* [1974] 1 Ch. 401; *Commissioners of Customs and Excise* v. *Samex* [1983] 1 All ER 1042. The UK courts recognise the existence of the doctrine of *acte claire*, which is the doctrine that allows a national court to apply its own interpretation of Community law rather than request a preliminary ruling. The Court of Justice has made it plain that the interpretation must be so obvious as to leave no scope for any reasonable doubt: see *CILFIT* v. *Ministero della Sanità* [1983] 1 CMLR 472; *Garland* v. *British Rail* [1983] 2 AC 751. In relation to matters of primary law, for example the treaties, the court may rule only on interpretation; in respect of secondary law, like regulations, the court can also rule on validity. Once the court has ruled, the case is returned to the national court to apply as appropriate.

pre-nuptial agreement see ANTE-NUPTIAL AGREEMENT.

prerogative see ROYAL PREROGATIVE.

prescription the process of acquiring rights, immunities or obligations as a result of the passage of time. Prescription is founded on the idea that a person who has enjoyed quiet and uninterrupted possession of something for a long period of years is supposed to have a just right, without which he would not have been allowed to continue in enjoyment of it. In particular, easements and profits may be acquired by prescription if enjoyed without interruption for the appropriate length of time (usually 20 years in the case of easements and 30 years in the case of profits). Prescription may be:

(1) under the common law rules,

(2) under the doctrine of lost modern grant, or

(3) under the provisions of the Prescription Act 1832.

In Scotland the word is used in a similar way in relation to the acquisitions of rights: see the Prescription and Limitation (Scotland) Act 1973 (as amended). The *positive prescription* in Scotland is ten years. It allows a person who has possessed land openly, peaceably and without interruption on the strength of an ex facie valid recorded title covering the land in question, to obtain a good title to it. In cases of the acquisition of servitude rights or rights in the foreshore or salmon fishings, the positive prescription is 20 years. In Scotland the word prescription is used in a negative sense of shutting off stale claims in a way very similar to that sense denoted by the word *limitation* in England. Limitation was not a native Scottish concept. Thus, there is a five-year *short-negative prescription* that cuts off very many claims – the most significant being mostly claims for damages or payment with the exception of claims for personal injuries, which are dealt with by way of limitation. The main difference between prescription and limitation is that limitation must be pled whereas prescription operates by law and can be noticed by the court. There is in addition a *long-negative prescription* of 20 years, which shuts off claims not already closed by the limitation period or the short negative prescription or a category of obligation known as *imprescriptible*, the most significant of which are obligations under solemn deeds and the obligations of a trustee in respect of trust property. See LATENT DAMAGE, LIMITATION, PRODUCT LIABILITY.

presentment presentation. A BILL OF EXCHANGE must be duly presented for payment; if it is not so presented, the drawer and indorsers will be discharged. Where a bill is not payable on demand, presentment must be made on the day it falls due; if it is payable on demand, it must be presented within a reasonable time. In the case of a bill payable after sight, presentment for acceptance (as opposed to payment) is necessary in order to fix its maturity date.

Presiding Officer the equivalent of the SPEAKER in the NATIONAL ASSEMBLY FOR WALES and the SCOTTISH PARLIAMENT.

Press Council established in 1953 by newspaper proprietors and journalists to prevent the government legislating to control the press by showing that it could responsibly self-regulate, it still fundamentally fulfils this role. However, in order to satisfy pressure for press control, it has had to do more. It has issued three declarations on privacy, chequebook journalism and financial journalism. It receives complaints, sending these to the relevant editors. Half the complaints go no further. After that, committees sift the complaints and recommend solutions to the full council. Decisions are published.

presumption in the law of evidence, certain assumptions either of fact, judicial decision or statute that must be rebutted, that is, controverted by evidence, or the assumptions will stand as effective proof. Presumptions in law include: (i) presumption in favour of life;
(ii) presumption of ordinary physical condition; (iii) *pater est quem nuptiae demonstrant,* or 'the husband of the woman who has a child is presumed to be the father'; (iv) presumption of innocence in criminal cases and against wrongful acts in civil matters; *omnia praesumuntur rite et solemniter acta,* or 'a presumption in favour of regularity and validity'; (v) presumption from business, such as *donatio non praesumunitur,* 'that against donation'.

Both England and Scotland presume death in certain cases. In England a person is presumed dead if he has not been heard of for seven years. In Scotland, the Presumption of Death (Scotland) Act

1977 provides that a person may be presumed dead if the court is satisfied that he has died or has not been known to be alive for a period of at least seven years.

Presumptions of fact are really no more than cases where it is reasonable and likely that a court will infer a state of affairs from other facts. Thus, a person in possession of recently stolen property may be presumed to be the thief, but this can be rebutted by showing that he had found them and was taking them to the nearest police station when apprehended. The maxim *res ipsa loquitur* ('the happening speaks for itself'), once treated as a matter of law, is no more than a very strong inference. If an accident happens, caused by something that is under the defender's control and in such a way that, if well operated, it should not have happened, then *res ipsa loquitur*, 'and the incident is eloquent of negligence.'

price in the law of sale, a money consideration that is called the price. In a contract of sale of goods, the price may be fixed by the contract or may be left to be fixed in a manner agreed by the contract or it may be determined by the course of dealing of the parties. Failing any of the foregoing, the buyer must pay a reasonable price. What constitutes a reasonable price is a question of fact dependent on the circumstances of each particular case: see *May & Butcher* v. *Rex* [1934] 2 KB 17 and, in Scotland, *R. and J. Dempster Ltd* v. *Motherwell Bridge and Engineering Co. Ltd* 1964 SLT 353. The price may be left to the decision of arbiters, may be fixed by some public standard or may be left to the decision of one of the parties. Where there is an agreement to sell at valuation by a third party and he cannot or does not make a valuation, the agreement is avoided; but if the goods or any part of them have been delivered and appropriated by the buyer, he must pay a reasonable price for them. Where the third party is prevented from making the valuation by the fault of the seller or buyer, the party not at fault may maintain an action for damages against the party at fault. Unless a different intention appears from the terms of the contract, stipulations as to time of payment are not of the essence of a contract of sale. Various statutes relating to competition or consumer protection affect the price at which goods can be sold or advertised.

prima facie 'on the face of it'.

primary rules see HARTIAN.

Prime Minister in the CONSTITUTIONAL LAW of the UK, the leading minister of the Crown. Technically, *primus inter pares*, or 'first among equals', the position has grown very considerably in stature and power over the latter part of the 20th century, taking on an ever more presidential function and, in some hands, style. The tasks are to form a government and to preside over the CABINET. The Prime Minister holds the offices of First Lord of the Treasury and Minister for the Civil Service. The power of appointment or concurrence in appointments is vast and increases the power of the office. The Prime Minister is chosen by the sovereign, a power that is rarely more than a formal selection of the leader of the opposition or the next most senior minister of the ruling party. The title *Deputy Prime Minister* has no official standing and does not fetter the ROYAL PREROGATIVE in selecting the new Prime Minister. See also TAOISEACH, FIRST MINISTER, FIRST SECRETARY.

primogeniture being first-born. Many legal systems have from time to time and place to place given precedence to the first-born in INHERITANCE. It has the benefit of preserving large hard-won estates. It is not popular with the other children. Concentration of wealth in money as opposed to land has made it much less useful. It no longer applies to ordinary property in the UK.

principal see AGENCY.

priority need in housing law, persons who are entitled to local authority housing ahead of others: pregnant women, persons residing with dependent children, emergency cases, those vulnerable from old age, mental illness or disability.

prison a place where people are held in captivity, either pending trial or serving a sentence of imprisonment. Administration is in the hands of the Home Office and Prison Commissioners. There is an HM Inspector of Prisons. Prisons are run under prison regulations.

prison-breaking in Scots law, the CRIME of breaking out and escaping from a prison (but not a temporary police cell) if held on a lawful warrant. Likewise, a person who breaks into a prison to rescue a prisoner commits the crime. See, for England, ESCAPE.

privacy the tort or delict (unrecognised formally in the UK) of infringing a person's right to be left alone. Although the notion of privacy is protected by law in many systems in the continental Europe and in the USA, there is no recognised tort in English law of *invasion of privacy*. Scotland arguably recognises a verbal injury called CONVICIUM, which makes it a delict to bring a person into public ridicule and hatred, but this in itself would not cover a polite and neutral exposure of personal details. Scots law also recognises interference with liberty. The Human Rights Act 1998 provides a right to respect for a person's private and family life. See DEFAMATION and CONFIDENCE.

private bill in the constitutional law of the UK, a bill that affects a private interest specially and is therefore different from a PUBLIC BILL. They are initiated by petition of persons outside PARLIAMENT, like local authorities or, in the past, railway companies. The main feature of the special standing orders that govern its passage are that the bill is sent to a select committee that will hear objectors providing they have LOCUS STANDI. See HYBRID BILL.

private carrier a carrier who operates under a particular contract in each case and who may choose whether to accept or reject any request to carry. In the absence of a special term in the contract, a private carrier probably has no lien over the goods of a consignor. The Carriers Act 1830 does not apply to private carriers. See COMMON CARRIER.

private company a COMPANY that is not a public company and that, as such, cannot offer its shares to the public.

private international law the rules of a legal system governing which rules are to be applied in cases with an international dimension, as where one party is French and one German and the subject of the transaction is in Africa. It also considers enforcement of judgments obtained. It does consider matters of public law, which are treated under public international law. See FORUM NON CONVENIENS, LEXI LOCII DELICTI, LEX LOCI SITUS, LIS ALIBI PENDENS.

private law the law applying between persons or between a person and a thing insofar as not involving the state.

private nuisance see NUISANCE.

privilege a right or immunity in connection with legal proceedings conferred upon a person by virtue of his position. For example, in the law of evidence a person may generally refuse to answer a question on the grounds that the answer might incriminate him; likewise, a spouse may refuse to answer questions about the other spouse in relation to events occurring during the time of their marriage.

The word has a specialised meaning in the context of the law of DEFAMATION.

privileged wills wills of soldiers on actual military service and of mariners at sea may be valid even although they do not satisfy the requirements of the Wills Act 1837 by virtue of the provisions of that

Act and the Wills (Soldiers and Sailors) Act 1918. A will in these circumstances can be nuncupative (oral). The special circumstances must apply at the time the will is made. Actual military service does not require a war to be in progress: *Re Jones* [1981] Fam. 7. 'Mariner at sea' has been held to include a civilian employee of a merchant ship employed as a typist: *Re Sarah Hale* [1915] 2 IR 362. The words must still be of testamentary intent: *Re Knibbs* [1962] 2 All ER 829. The person need not be 18 years of age.

In Scotland, any oral legacy is valid up to the amount £8.33. The Roman law doctrine of *testamentum militare* (see below) has not been accepted into Scots law but neither has it been authoritatively rejected: see *Stuart* v. *Stuart* 1942 SC 510. Neither the Wills Act 1837 nor the Wills (Soldiers and Sailors) Act 1918 apply to Scotland.

It was the Roman law doctrine of *testamentum militare*, 'military wills', that has been influential in this respect. The privilege attached to soldiers or seamen was eventually limited to actual service with the colours. If allowed, it covered wills made before the service and the will remained valid for a year after the service ended. Some evidence other than that of the claimant was needed.

privity of contract the relationship between the parties privy to the contract, i.e. those who are direct parties to it. Until the passing of the Contracts (Rights of Third Parties) Act 1999, English law did not permit parties not in a relationship of privity to sue on a contract. Thus, a third party benefited by a contract could not sue on it. The effect of the Act has been to substantially relax this rule. Scots law and other civilian systems recognise a JUS QUAESITUM TERTIO.

Privy Council (PC) the great council of state comprising the sovereign and the councillors. Councillors are addressed as 'The Right Honourable'. The CABINET discharges the advice function, and a JUDICIAL COMMITTEE sits as the highest court of appeal for some Commonwealth states such as New Zealand and formerly for Canada and Australia. It now has power to adjudicate on certain aspects of devolution, notably under the Scotland Act 1998 and to declare legislation incompatible with the Human Rights Act 1998.

prize property lawfully appropriated in war.

probate an order of court appointing a person to administer the estate of a deceased person. Where a person dies leaving a will that makes an effective appointment of executors, the executors' title to deal with the deceased's estate is completed by the issue of a *grant of probate*. This is in fact and in law (like a grant of LETTERS OF

ADMINISTRATION) an order of the High Court. Probate may be either in *common form* (where the probity of the will is not in dispute), issued by one of the Probate Registries, or where the will is disputed in *solemn form*. Contentious business is dealt with in the Chancery Division; non-contentious business is assigned to the Family Division.

proclamation (royal) a formal notice given by the Queen of any matter that she sees fit to advertise to her subjects.

procurator a representative of a party.

procurator fiscal a public prosecutor in Scotland. The procurator fiscal prosecutes in the sheriff courts (although proceedings on indictment there run in the name of Her Majesty's Advocate) and the district courts. A decision not to prosecute can probably be reversed by the Crown Office. There are other duties: the fiscal investigates sudden and suspicious deaths and has responsibilities in relation to intestate estates. He also instigates fatal accident inquiries. For England, see CROWN PROSECUTION SERVICE.

Procureur in Guernsey, the senior law officer, equivalent to the ATTORNEY-GENERAL in England and in Jersey.

producer in the law of PRODUCT LIABILITY, in relation to a product, (a) the person who manufactured it; (b) in the case of a substance that has not been manufactured but has been won or abstracted, the person who won or abstracted it; (c) in the case of a product that has not been manufactured, won or abstracted but essential characteristics of which are attributable to an industrial or other process having been carried out (for example, in relation to agricultural produce), the person who carried out that process: Consumer Protection Act 1987.

product in PRODUCT LIABILITY, any goods or electricity including any goods comprised in another product whether by virtue of being a component part or raw material or otherwise. 'Goods' is defined as including substances, growing crops and things comprised in land by virtue of being attached to it, and any ship, aircraft or vehicle: Consumer Protection Act 1987.

product liability liability in TORT or DELICT in respect of produce. Essentially an application of the law of tort although the term can be used to cover liability under sale and supply of goods. Although there is now a Europe-wide regime of strict liability, the foundation of this head of liability in tort or delict was rooted in the case of *Donoghue* v. *Stevenson* 1932 SC (HL) 31, now important for its principled approach to negligence generally. However, the narrow ratio of that case was the issue at the time the case was decided and explained its early importance, extending as it did the liability of manufacturers. The narrow ratio is apparent from Lord Atkin's dictum: 'a manufacturer of products, which he sells in such a form as to show that he intends them to reach the ultimate consumer in the form in which they left him with no reasonable possibility of intermediate examination, and with the knowledge that the absence of reasonable care in the preparation or putting up of the products will result in an injury to the consumer's life or property, owes a duty to the consumer to take that reasonable care.' The maxim RES IPSA LOQUITUR made it much easier for pursuers to recover compensation, but a combination of consumer pressure in the late 20th century and the need for HARMONISATION OF LAWS in the EUROPEAN UNION has resulted in a Europe-wide regime of strict liability that focuses upon defects in products, the liability being primarily upon PRODUCERS of products. In the UK, the directive was implemented by the Consumer Protection Act 1987. The defences limit the general rule considerably. It is crucial to know the defences as they affect the scope of liability significantly. They are:

(1) compliance with any requirement imposed by or under any enactment or with any community obligation;

(2) the defender did not supply;

(3) non-commercial supply does not attract liability, but this does not include a commercial supplier who gives his product away as a trial;

(4) it is a defence if the state of scientific and technical knowledge at the relevant time was not such that a producer of products of the same description as the product in question might be expected to have discovered the defect if it had existed in his products while they were under his control. This is often known as the development risks' defence. The European Union is currently reviewing this defence as part of an overall review;

(5) the component manufacturer is allowed to show that the defect was a defect in a product in which the defender's product is comprised. This is a defence only if the defect is wholly attributable to the design of the subsequent product or to compliance by the defender with instructions given by the final producer;

(6) CONTRIBUTORY NEGLIGENCE is recognised.

production of documents the making available by a party of documents in his possession, custody or power for inspection by the other party or for use as evidence at trial.

profit and loss account an account that shows the revenue and expenditure of a business during a given period, resulting in a net profit or loss, and provides a link between successive balance sheets.

profit a prendre a right to take something from the land of another (for example, a right of pasture or sheepwalk). This can be contrasted with an EASEMENT, which is a right to do something on the land of another.

prohibited degrees the relationships between persons that make it illegal for them to marry. In England the position is regulated by the Matrimonial Causes Act 1971. For a man, the relationships are his mother, daughter, grandmother, granddaughter, sister, aunt, niece, the wife of his father, son, grandfather or grandson. For a woman, the prohibited relationships are her father, son, grandfather, grandson, brother, uncle, nephew, the husband of her mother, daughter, grandmother or granddaughter, her husband's father, son, grandfather or grandson. The general prohibitions were relaxed slightly by the Marriage (Prohibited Degrees of Relationship) Act 1986, which permits marriage between a man and a woman who is the daughter or granddaughter of a former spouse of his if both the parties are over 21 and the younger party had not, before attaining the age of 18, been a child of the family.

In Scotland the law is similar, being set out in the Marriage (Scotland) Act 1977, as amended by later legislation including the 1986 Act (above).

prohibited steps order see SECTION 8 ORDER.

prolixity of pleadings excessive length or repetitiveness.

promissory estoppel see ESTOPPEL.

promissory note promissory notes are one species of NEGOTIABLE INSTRUMENT. Section 83 of the Bills of Exchange Act 1882 refers to 'an unconditional promise in writing made by one person to another, signed by the maker, engaging to pay on demand or at a fixed or determinable future time, a sum certain in money, to or to the order of a specified person or to a bearer.' A promissory note differs from a BILL OF EXCHANGE in that the maker stands in the place of both the drawer and the acceptor.

proof before answer in Scots procedure, the hearing of the facts of the case before legal arguments are disposed of. Such a procedure is common in cases of negligence where, because liability often depends on the facts of a case, the legal question of liability needs to be left until the facts are determined.

proof by writ or oath in Scots law, a mode of proof by the writ or separate testimony on oath of the opponent, which was abolished by the Requirements of Writing (Scotland) Act 1995.

proper law in PRIVATE INTERNATIONAL LAW, that body of law that is most realistically connected with the issue in question. In cases of conflict over which legal system applies to a contract, the proper law of the contract is becoming widely accepted as the appropriate test. An expressed intention by the parties helps determine the proper law but that is not completely binding on a court.

property things and rights that can be owned or that have a money value. Property also signifies a beneficial right to a thing. In English law, property is either *realty*, which comprises freehold land, or *personalty*, which comprises everything else, including leasehold land and land held on trust for sale; *pure personalty* is the term used to denote chattels and other forms of personal property having no connection with land.

In relation to GOODS, because of the Sale of Goods Act 1979, there will be an identifiable instant at which the ownership or right of property in the goods passes from seller to buyer. The importance of ascertaining the precise time lies not only in questions of risk but also in cases of insolvency where the destination of the goods to a trustee in bankruptcy, receiver or liquidator can leave the other party to the transaction only with the right to rank for a dividend as a general creditor. The Act provides that property passes when it is intended to pass, i.e. the *traditio*, or physical transfer, required by the CIVIL LAW is not required. Property does not pass in UNASCERTAINED GOODS. If the parties' intention cannot be determined, certain rules are laid down to resolve the matter.

Rule 1: where there is an unconditional contract for the sale of SPECIFIC GOODS in a DELIVERABLE STATE, the property in the goods passes to the buyer when the contract is made; it is immaterial whether the time of payment or the time of delivery, or both, be postponed. Thus, in the case of a sale in a shop to a customer of an item identified in the shop, property will pass when the contract is formed.

Rule 2: where there is a contract for the sale of specific goods and the seller is bound to do something to the goods for the purpose of putting them into a deliverable state, the property does not pass until the thing is done and the buyer has notice that it has been done. The requirement for notice is important if the rules relating to risk are considered. As risk normally passes with property, this notice would have the effect of transferring property to the buyer, who then should consider insuring the goods, even although they are outwith his possession.

Rule 3: where there is a contract for specific goods in a deliverable state but the seller is bound to weigh, measure, test or do some other act or thing with reference to the goods for the purpose of ascertaining the price, the property does not pass until this has been done and the buyer has notice that it has been done.

It is important to distinguish Rule 3 from Rule 2. Rule 2 refers to goods that are not in a deliverable state whereas Rule 3 refers to goods that are in a deliverable state.

Rule 4: when goods are delivered to the buyer on approval, or on sale or return, or other similar terms, the property in the goods passes to the buyer:

(a) when he signifies his approval or acceptance to the seller or does any other act adopting the transaction;

(b) if he does not signify his approval or acceptance to the seller but retains the goods without giving notice of rejection, then, if a time has been fixed for the return of the goods, on the expiration of that time, and, if no time has been fixed, on the expiration of a reasonable time.

Rule 5: this rule does not apply to specific goods but to goods that at the time the contract was made were unascertained. Where there is a contract for the sale of UNASCERTAINED or FUTURE GOODS by description and goods of that description and in a deliverable state are unconditionally appropriated to the contract, either by the seller with the assent of the buyer or by the buyer with the assent of the seller, the property in the goods then passes to the buyer; the assent may be express or implied, and may be given either before or after the appropriation is made. Where, in pursuance of a contract, the seller delivers the goods to the buyer or to a carrier or other bailee or custodier (whether named by the buyer or not) for the purpose of transmission to the buyer and does not reserve the right of disposal, he will be taken to have unconditionally appropriated the goods to the contract. This complicated rule is illustrated by *Pignataro* v. *Gilroy* [1919] 1 KB 459, in which there was a contract for the sale of

140 bags of rice. A delivery order was given for 125 bags to allow the buyer to collect goods from a wharf. The seller said that the other 15 could be collected at the seller's own warehouse in Long Acre. When the buyer went to collect the 15 bags, it was found that they had been stolen. The court held that the seller had appropriated the goods to the contract with the implied assent of the buyer, so property had passed to the buyer and was at the buyer's risk.

proportionality 1. in English court practice, the new idea that costs of a case should be related to its importance and value. It is expected to have dramatic effects on cost recovery but also upon the conduct of litigation.

2. for European law see SUBSIDIARITY.

proprietary right a right over or in respect of property that can be asserted against others, that is not personal to a given individual but that exists by reason of and as an incident to ownership of other property.

prorogation 1. an agreement to accept the jurisdiction of a given court.

2. the exercise of the PREROGATIVE ending a session of PARLIAMENT.

protected person a head of state or plenipotentiary or representative of a state or international organisation is a protected person under the Internationally Protected Persons Act 1978. The Act makes certain conduct directed at such persons criminal.

protest a procedure under which evidence of the dishonour of a BILL OF EXCHANGE is provided.

protocol an addition or supplement to a treaty.

proving a will see PROBATE.

proving the tenor in Scots law, a procedure for establishing the terms of a lost document, like a will, usually by producing an earlier draft.

provisional order a system for avoiding expensive PRIVATE BILLS. Under an ACT OF PARLIAMENT, certain bodies are given authority to investigate a matter and make orders that then have to be ratified by PARLIAMENT before taking legal effect.

provocation in the criminal law of Scotland, a doctrine that will mitigate the offence, reducing murder to culpable HOMICIDE or attempted murder to ASSAULT. In the civil law in Scotland, provocation can reduce the damages payable for an assault in delict: *Ross* v. *Bryce* 1972 SLT (Sh. Ct) 76, but not in England for tort: *Lane* v. *Holloway* [1968] 1 QB 379.

proxy 1. a person appointed by a COMPANY member to attend and vote in place of the member at a company meeting.

2. the instrument appointing a person to act as proxy.

prudence concept the principle of commercial accounting that profits may not be anticipated in the books of a business; on the other hand, it is perfectly acceptable to make provision for losses as soon as they are foreseen. The term 'prudence', which is used to denote this style of accounting, developed during the 1970s; prior to that it had been known as 'conservative' accounting. See, generally, *BSC Footwear* v. *Ridgeway* [1972] AC 544.

public company a registered company that can offer its shares to the public. Its memorandum of association must state that it is a public company, that its authorised capital is at least the authorised minimum (£50,000) and that its name ends with *plc* (or public limited company).

public defender a lawyer provided by the state to represent a person accused of a crime. Clearly, where there is respect for the human right of a FAIR TRIAL, there has to be a separation of powers between the public defender and the prosecution – something that is difficult where there may be a similar 'civil service' type of career structure and movement of individuals between divisions. They are well known in the USA and the system is the subject of an experiment in Scotland. It is now provided for in English legislation and the precise system is a matter of consultation. See CRIMINAL DEFENCE SERVICE.

public domain 1. (USA) land owned by the government.

2. property rights not attached by anyone. In the UK so far as heritable or real property is concerned, almost anything that is not owned by someone is owned by the Crown or inherited by the Crown. The main practical use of the phrase in contemporary UK law is to denote INTELLECTUAL PROPERTY rights that are either still open or have been let out to the public in such a way that they are not protected by copyright patent, trademark or by obligations of confidence.

public good see OBSCENITY.

public law that area of law that deals with the state and the relations of the state with the public.

public nuisance see NUISANCE.

public rights rights enjoyed by persons as members of the public, as distinct from private rights attached to the personality of the individual or deriving from property owned by him. Public rights may derive from the common law (such as the right of members of the public to pass and repass along the highway) or from statute. In either case, the remedy for infringement is by indictment or in a relator action for an injunction.

puff an exaggerated statement or advertisement.

puffer a person who attends an auction on behalf of the seller and tries to put the price up. Restricted by the Sales of Land by Auction Act 1867 and the Sales of Goods Act 1979. See WHITE BONNET.

puisne (pronounced 'puny') junior. A *puisne mortgage* is not as important as a simple mortgage, but, curiously, High Court judges, who are quite senior, are called *puisne judges*.

pupillage see ADVOCATE.

pupil master see ADVOCATE.

pure theory of law see KELSINIAN JURISPRUDENCE.

putative father the alleged father of an illegitimate child.

Q

QB abbreviation for Queen's Bench.

QC abbreviation for Queen's counsel. See BARRISTER.

qua 'as'.

qualified acceptance see OFFER.

qualified privilege see DEFAMATION.

qualified title a registered title to land that is subject to some exception or qualification specified in the register. See LAND REGISTRATION.

quality an implied term in contracts of sale and supply. The Sale of Goods Act 1979, as amended by the Sale and Supply of Goods Act 1994, provides for certain IMPLIED TERMS in contracts for sale of goods and other supply of goods such as hire-purchase, hire and barter. The importance of the implication of these terms is that if they are not complied with, the purchaser has a right to sue; this allows it to be said that the Act gives buyer's rights.

The general rule is *caveat emptor*, 'let the buyer beware'. Thus, except for the implied terms in the Act, there are no implied terms. Thus, a sale between two private individuals for private purposes will not be subject to any implied quality terms. Terms are implied where there is a sale in the course of a business. Goods must be of satisfactory quality. Goods are satisfactory only if they meet the standard that a reasonable person would regard as satisfactory, taking account of the description of the goods, the price and the other circumstances. Statutory examples of that are that the goods be fit for all common purposes for which the goods in question are commonly supplied; that their appearance and finish be satisfactory; that the goods be free from minor defects; that they be safe; and that they should be durable. These do not apply, however, where the goods have been examined or the defects pointed out. It should also be appreciated that if there is a breach in a consumer contract, the buyer is allowed to reject the goods; in other sales the breach will have to be material. Goods must be reasonably fit for any specified purpose. So even satisfactory goods may still be supplied in breach of contract if a more stringent standard was clearly intended.

quantitative restrictions usually known as *quotas*, these measures, being non-pecuniary measures, are significant in that they are controlled by the law of the EUROPEAN UNION. These prohibitions are designed to bolster up the rules against CUSTOMS DUTIES and CHARGES HAVING EQUIVALENT EFFECT. The law also applies to MEASURES HAVING EQUIVALENT EFFECT to quantitative restrictions.

quantum 'how much', the amount.

quantum lucratus 'insofar as made richer', associated with RECOMPENSE. See QUANTUM MERUIT. See also RESTITUTION.

quantum meruit 'as much as deserved', an award to a party on the basis of an implied contract. In England it is also used to describe payments made on the basis of unjust enrichment. See QUANTUM LUCRATUS, RESTITUTION.

quarter day any of four days in the year when certain payments become due. In England, they are Lady Day (25 March), Midsummer Day (24 June), Michaelmas Day (29 September) and Christmas Day (25 December). For Scotland the days are Candlemas (28 February), Whitsunday (28 May), Lammas (28 August) and Martinmas (28 November).

quash to annul.

quasi 'as if'.

quasi-contract 'like' contract. A very contentious term at present, it describes cases where parties have an obligation that resembles contract but where there is actually no contract at all. In England it was (and still is) predominantly used for cases involving MONEY HAD AND RECEIVED, and in Scotland was (and still is) used to describe cases under the various actions for recovery of mistaken payments and for work done without contract. Modern theorists have demonstrated that quasi-contractual actions have nothing to do with contract at all but rather describe, mostly, claims in RESTITUTION for unjust enrichment. Accordingly, the term is becoming used by fewer and fewer commentators.

quasi ex contractu see QUASI-CONTRACT.

quasi-judicial proceedings that seem judicial but that are conducted by a person other than a judge.

Quebec see CONSTITUTION.

Quebec Civil Code (Canada) the code of law applying in civil matters in the Canadian province of Quebec. The British conquest of Nouvelle-France in 1760 marked the beginning of the difficulty of running two different legal systems together. Even immediately after conquest, it was accepted in the capitulation of Montreal that the French civil law should apply until altered fully in compliance with the accepted view in the English system in relation to its colonies. The French law was subordinated by the proclamation of 1763, but the Quebec Act 1774 reinstated French civil law (but maintained English criminal law). The Civil Code of Lower Canada became law in 1866 and was closely modelled on the NAPOLEONIC CODE.

Queen's counsel see BARRISTER.

Queen's evidence the evidence of someone who decides to give evidence incriminating his accomplice. He may be given immunity from prosecution for doing this. In England the jury will be warned that it is dangerous to convict on such evidence unless corroborated. In Scotland, this notice is no longer required.

Queen's proctor a solicitor representing the Crown who may intervene in English divorce proceedings. Generally, his interference is on the basis of new information received and occurs at the stage between decree nisi and absolute. See, generally, Matrimonial Causes Act 1973.

quia emptores 'whereas purchasers', the first words of a statute of 1290 that allowed freemen to alienate their lands without the consent of their feudal lord. It abolished SUBINFEUDATION.

quia timet see INJUNCTION.

quid pro quo 'something in exchange for something else'. See CONSIDERATION.

quiet enjoyment an obligation of a landlord under a lease or of a seller under a conveyance entitling the tenant or purchaser to possess and enjoy the land free from lawful interference and claims of others, except those claiming by title paramount.

qui facit per alium facit per se see VICARIOUS LIABILITY.

quinquennial taking five years. In Scots law the five-year prescriptive period is known as the *quinquennium* despite the fact that the present legislation does not use that term. It applies to most claims for money other than those arising from personal injuries.

quit see NOTICE TO QUIT.

qui tam action an action by an informer that in the event of success results in the state and the informer sharing the penalty.

quoad ultra 'so far as the rest is concerned', a phrase used in nearly all Scots written pleadings where, unless statements of facts are denied, they are held to be admitted. So pleaders, after making admissions, will say '*quoad ultra* denied'.

quod nullius est fit domini regis 'anything that has no ownership falls to the Crown.'

quorate used to describe a meeting at which a QUORUM is present.

quorum 'of whom', used to denote the number of people required to constitute a meeting legally.

quo warranto 'by what authority', the name of an obsolete writ issued by the King's Bench to demand to know the authority by which a person held a public office.

R

R abbreviation for *rex* or *regina*, 'king' or 'queen'. The initial letter is used in proceedings, especially English criminal proceedings, to indicate that the Crown is the plaintiff or, more usually, prosecutor: *R* v. *Haddock*. In Scotland, prosecutions run in the name of Her (or His) Majesty's Advocate, hence cases are cited *HMA* v. *McFable*.

race discrimination adverse treatment on grounds of race. The employment law of the UK provides protection against racial discrimination in addition to the rights of employers under the law on UNFAIR DISMISSAL provided by the Race Relations Act 1976. Racial discrimination occurs if a person treats a person less favourably than he treats others on racial grounds. Anti-avoidance measures abound so that the imposition of a condition that only a very small proportion of persons of the complainer's racial group could fulfil is struck at unless justifiable on other grounds and is detrimental to the complainer. Segregation, colour and nationality of ethnic origin can be the focus for such discrimination. It is against these rules to offer different conditions of employment or different promotion possibilities. It strikes at the offering of employment in the first place so that employers cannot discriminate by not offering jobs on racial grounds. The law applies to many bodies other than employers in the private sector. A person may complain to the EMPLOYMENT TRIBUNALS. The House of Lords has held that subconscious discrimination can be unlawful: *Nagarajan* v. *London Regional Transport* [1999] TLR 538.

racially aggravated crime in terms of the Crime and Disorder Act 1998, a period of up to two years' imprisonment can be added to a sentence where the crime involves a racial element. It has been suggested that the factors to be considered include the nature of the racial hostility, whether the location was public or private, the location, e.g. a mosque or synagogue, but that a discount might be considered for genuine remorse coupled with a guilty plea and previous good conduct: *R* v. *Saunders* [2000] TLR 52. There is a particular and new offence of *racially aggravated conduct*, which amounts to harassment either intended or which would appear to a reasonable person to amount to harassment causing alarm and distress. Racial aggravation is shown by racial hostility at the time of the offence or immediately before or after.

rape in English criminal law, unlawful sexual intercourse with a woman who at the time of the intercourse does not consent to it and where, at the time, the man knows that the woman does not consent to the intercourse or he is reckless as to whether she consents to it. The word 'unlawful', which had been thought by many to mean 'outwith marriage', was held not to prevent a husband being held to be able to commit rape against his wife, and indeed the House of Lords held that the rule laid down for over 150 years that a man could not be guilty of raping his wife no longer applied: *R* v. *R*. [1991] 3 WLR 767.

In Scots criminal law, intercourse with a woman by force and against her will. The consent of the woman is a defence, and as a result of the difficult case of *Meek* v. *HMA* 1983 SLT 280, an erroneous belief that the woman was consenting need not be reasonable to exculpate although it must be an honest belief. In Scots law a husband can be guilty of raping his wife: *S.* v. *HMA* 1989 SLT 469.

The state of Victoria (Australia) in the Crimes (Sexual Offences Act 1990) expanded rape to include continued intercourse contrary to an instruction to desist. This reflected the law in New Zealand, which had been upheld by the Privy Council in *Kaitamaki* v. *R* [1984] 2 All ER 435.

ratification affirmation of a previous and unauthorised Act; ratification has the effect of putting the Act in the same position as if it had been originally authorised. For example, the confirmation or ratification by a principal of an unauthorised contract entered into by his agent: see *Firth* v. *Staines* [1897] 2 QB 70.

ratio decidendi 'the rule in a decision'. This is a crucial part of the understanding of the way in which the common law works. Once a system has adopted of binding PRECEDENT, it has to be discovered what it is in the previous decision that binds the court later in time. While it is sometimes possible to peruse the opinion of the judge to find the rule, this is not by any means a reliable way of discovering the rule in the case. The soundest general method is to discover the material facts of the case, determine what the decision was and then to draw the proposition that most closely marries the material facts to the actual decision. It is difficult enough to do this with a single opinion but very much harder with multiple opinions such as come from the Court of Appeal, the Inner House and the House of Lords. Sometimes it is said to be impossible to form a *ratio* of general application. Anything that is said that is not part of the *ratio* is said to be an OBITER DICTUM.

re 'in the matter of, concerning'.

real evidence in the law of evidence, a nebulous category that broadly describes anything, other than a document, that is examined as a means of proof. Examples include clothing and fibres, weapons, fingerprints and dental impressions, blood samples, tape recordings, film and video recordings. Its importance is that the jury or other fact-finder does what it will from the sight of the evidence and inspection of it. Real evidence does not exclude oral evidence, as is the case frequently with written evidence. Usually oral evidence is required to connect and make relevant the real evidence. Generally, the real evidence should be produced in court, an oral description being generally inadmissible.

realised profits and losses for accounting purposes, a transaction is normally treated as being effected at the point at which the invoice in respect of the goods or services supplied is issued; at this point the profit or loss made on the transaction is regarded as being realised.

realism a theme in JURISPRUDENCE often considered to divide into two schools, the *American* and the *Scandinavian*. Oliver Wendell Holmes is perhaps the most famous figure on the American side. Famous dictums like 'the life of the law has not been logic; it has been experience' and 'the prophecies of what the courts will do in fact, and nothing more pretentious, are what I mean by the law' epitomise the approach. The Scandinavians, such as Olivercrona and Ross, produce a theoretical critique that to the ordinary lawyer seems not terribly reflective of reality: 'a rule can be valid law to a greater or lesser degree varying with the degree of probability with which it can be predicted that the rule will be applied.'

real property tangible landed property or incorporeal hereditament. See PROPERTY.

real right a proprietary right enforceable against the whole world.

reasonable doubt see BEYOND A REASONABLE DOUBT.

reasonable man a judicial standard of conduct used to determine liability, especially in relation to negligence. The need to charge juries has brought forth many folksy definitions, the most famous being the man on the Clapham omnibus (or the omnibus of whichever city the court sits in). See *Glasgow Corporation* v. *Muir* [1943] AC 448.

rebus sic stantibus 'in these circumstance', in public international law the doctrine that considers a treaty as being no longer obligatory if there is a material change in circumstances. See Fisheries Jurisdiction case *UK* v. *Iceland* 1973 ICJ Rep. 3 and Article 62 of the Vienna Convention on the Law of Treaties.

rebut to contradict.

rebuttable presumption see PRESUMPTION.

rebuttal evidence evidence adduced to rebut a presumption of fact or law.

recaption in English law, the taking back of goods or a person wrongly detained so long as this is carried out without RIOT or BREACH OF THE PEACE.

receipt a written acknowledgement of the payment of money; a receipt for the purchase price of land should be embodied in the conveyance.

receiver 1. a person appointed by the court to receive the rents and profits of real property and to collect personal property affected by the proceedings and to do any act stated in the court's order. The object of the appointment is to protect the property until the rights of the parties have been ascertained. In such a case the receiver is an officer of the court and generally has to give security for the due performance of the duties of his office. In bankruptcy proceedings, the Official Receiver may be appointed as interim receiver at any time after the presentation of the petition if that course is necessary for the preservation of the estate; it is his duty so to act after adjudication until a trustee is appointed.

2. a mortgagee may appoint a receiver, being the agent of the mortgagor in law, without having to apply to the court where he is empowered to do so by the mortgage instrument, or in any event by virtue of Section 101 of the Law of Property Act 1925 if the mortgage is contained in a deed.

reckless driving see DANGEROUS DRIVING.

reckless endangerment (USA) the crime recognised in some jurisdictions of behaving indifferently to the consequences in such a way as to create a substantial risk of serious physical injury or death to another person.

recognisance a bond given by an offender to obey a judgment or keep the peace.

recommendation a form of Act of the EUROPEAN UNION that has no binding force. It has been held that recommendations should still be taken into account by the national courts, especially if the recommendation assists with interpretation of some European law: *Grimaldi* v. *Fonds de maladies professionnelles* (1989) 322/88. Nonetheless, it is not possible to have them reviewed nor to seek a PRELIMINARY RULING upon them. A recommendation in the ECSC is more like an EEC DIRECTIVE.

recompense the Scots term for the obligation to pay for services in the absence of contract or, indeed, an as yet unrecognised general enrichment action. An aspect of the law of RESTITUTION and founded upon the civil law, the remedy is to make the recipient of the work done or services rendered disgorge the value to the recipient of the work (in *quantum lucratus*). This can be, and usually will be, less than the contract price and indeed may be less than would be due under an implied contract, which would allow recovery *quantum meruit* – for the market value of the services. The service must usually be done without an intention to donate. If rendered in error, then recovery is assisted, but it is unlikely that error is required. See *Edinburgh Trams* v. *Courteney* 1909 SC 99; *Varney (Scotland) Ltd* v. *Lanarkshire* 1974 SC 245; *Lawrence Building Co.* v. *Lanark Co. Co.* 1978 SC 30.

reconvention the doctrine in PRIVATE INTERNATIONAL LAW that allows a party sued in one jurisdiction to establish jurisdiction against the party suing him, even if, leaving aside the instant action, the party sued could not have founded jurisdiction against the party suing him.

recovery of money see FIERI FACIAS, GARNISHEE.

rectification in English law, the power in the courts to correct a document that has been drawn in such a way that it incorrectly reflects the intention of the parties: *Craddock* v. *Hunt* [1923] 2 Ch. 136. Scots law had to await the Law Reform (Miscellaneous Provisions) (Scotland) Act 1985 for a similar measure.

reddendum that which requires to be paid, a clause in English leases and formerly a clause, the *reddendo clause*, in Scottish dispositions of land.

redemption, right of see ADJUDICATION.

redemption of feu duty see FEU DUTIES.

reduction in the Scots law of civil remedies, the remedy to have a writing annulled. In lower courts it can only be done OPE EXCEPTIONIS.

reduction of capital a company's capital may be lawfully reduced in two ways:

(1) by extinguishing or reducing the liability of its members on any uncalled capital; or

(2) by repaying to them the nominal value of their shares.

Where a company has suffered losses, it can cancel paid-up shares on the ground that they are unrepresented by available assets. A reduction requires a special resolution; it must be authorised by the articles and confirmed by the courts.

redundancy termination of employment because of the disappearance of the need for a job. In the employment law of the UK, certain rights accrue to someone who is made redundant, i.e. if his dismissal is the result wholly or mainly of the cessation of the employer's business or to the cessation or diminution of demands for particular work. Redundancy can be a potentially fair reason for dismissal, preventing a claim for UNFAIR DISMISSAL, but it might be unfair if the particular employee has been unfairly selected, as where he is perhaps the longest-serving employee but is the first to be made redundant. In any event, an employee who has served two years of CONTINUOUS EMPLOYMENT will be entitled to a redundancy payment based upon the years of service and the employee's age.

re-engagement see UNFAIR DISMISSAL.

re-examination subsequent examination. After cross-examination, counsel calling a witness may wish to re-examine him, being limited to clearing up points left in doubt; if re-examination discloses some new matter, the court may permit further cross-examination.

reference to oath see PROOF BY WRIT OR OATH.

refugees for the purposes of the United Nations, refugees are persons who, having left their country, be determined to have a well-founded fear of persecution on certain specific grounds or are unable to avail themselves of the protection of the government of their state or origin.

regalia minora in Scots law, rights adhering to the Crown but which can be alienated. Included are the rights of ferry, port and harbour. Ferry includes the right to prevent others from ferrying. Precious metals, forestry and highways are included. Highway is a right to pass – the *solum* is still owned by the proprietor but naturally many of these are now owned by local authorities. Salmon fishings are included, but the mode of fishing is restricted. Even if the banks are not owned, the owner of the salmon fishings is allowed access.

There are many statutory provisions regulating such rights. The foreshore itself (that part of the shore between the high and low water mark) is part of the regalia minor; this, however, does not include a right to exclude the public.

regional policy in the law of the EUROPEAN UNION, a body of rules that seeks to redress inequalities among the regions (which need not be states) within the community. The idea is to balance the effect of the other rules of the community in favouring certain regions at the expense of others. The SINGLE EUROPEAN ACT (SEA) formally incorporated the policy into Community law although it had been recognised for some time. It operates through the EUROPEAN REGIONAL DEVELOPMENT FUND. The SEA attempts to coordinate various Community schemes to be more effective in assisting less developed areas of the community. It seeks to assist where economic development is very retarded against the Community average, deals with industrial decline and assists the long-term unemployed as well as assisting rural areas.

register an official list recording names, events or transactions.

registered design a form of INTELLECTUAL PROPERTY and now governed by the Copyright, Designs and Patents Act 1988. A design right covers any part of the design of a product and does not require registration, but it must be original and have been expressed tangibly. Registered designs must have eye-appeal, and the protection is attracted to aesthetic concepts rather than artistic works, which tend to attract COPYRIGHT. The design must be new before it can be registered.

registered office the official address of a company. A company must at all times have a registered office. It must be notified to the Registrar of Companies before registration; it must appear on the company's letter-heads and order forms. Various registers and records may be inspected at the company's registered office; documents and writs may be served there.

Register of Charges a record kept by the Registrar of Companies that provides a record of all fixed and floating charges granted by a company. As 21 days are allowed for it to be registered, there is always the danger that one will appear after settlement of a transaction.

Register of Inhibitions and Adjudication the Scottish public record showing whether a person's property is subject to INHIBITION or ADJUDICATION.

Register of Sasines a Scottish public record. Created by the Registration Act 1617, this register is still the most important property register in Scotland. It is a register of deeds rather than land and is entirely feudal in nature. It is being replaced by a modern system of LAND REGISTRATION as quickly as finance and the profession can manage.

registrar an official in charge of keeping a register.

registration a method of becoming a BRITISH CITIZEN by administrative grant.

registration of births a compulsory procedure under which births must be officially recorded. The parents are issued with a birth certificate showing details of the date of the child's birth, sex and name, and the names and occupations of the parents.

Clergymen must cause to be registered particulars of all baptisms, marriages and burials conducted by them.

registration of company the standard method of setting up a company at the present day. After delivering various documents (e.g. the memorandum of association signed by at least two members, a statutory declaration that the requirements of the Companies Acts have been complied with) to the Registrar of Companies, the Registrar will then enter the name of the company in the company's register and issue a certificate of incorporation.

registration of title to land see TITLE.

regrating the offence of buying a commodity in a market with a view to selling it in the same market at a better price. In Scotland it was outlawed in Acts of 1449 and 1592 and thereafter and included an area within a four-mile radius of the market. It ceased to be an offence in England in 1847. See FORESTALLING.

regulation 1. a form of Act of the EUROPEAN UNION that has general application. A regulation, unlike a decision, applies to more than an identifiable or defined limited number of persons. It is binding in its entirety, unlike a DIRECTIVE, which simply sets out the aim to be achieved. It is DIRECTLY APPLICABLE and does not require to be subsequently enacted in a MEMBER STATE. It can also have DIRECT EFFECT. Much of the implementation of the COMMON AGRICULTURAL POLICY is done in this way, and regulations are frequently very detailed, dealing with technical matters.

2. a form of delegated legislation in the UK.

rehabilitation of offenders the principle of allowing people to 'write off' their conviction if they stay out of trouble: Rehabilitation of

Offenders Act 1974. The period required for rehabilitation varies with the seriousness of the original offence, and some cannot be extinguished. After the time has elapsed, the conviction becomes *spent* and the offender rehabilitated. The effect is that the conviction need not be revealed in various applications, although there are some exceptions that can be made by order. The spent conviction is not a good ground for dismissal from employment. Special rules apply where a spent conviction is the subject of defamation proceedings.

rei interventus in Scots law, a doctrine of PERSONAL BAR that prevents a person who does not want to adhere to a formally defective agreement being allowed to do so by the party who wants the bargain to succeed. There must be important actings by the party wanting to rely on the agreement, known to and permitted by the other party. It prevents *locus poenitentiae*, which is said to exist between informal agreement and formal execution. Its practical importance has been eclipsed by the regime provided by the Requirements of Writing (Scotland) Act 1995, which provides an equivalent protection for parties affected by a lack of required writing. See SELF-PROVING.

reinstatement see UNFAIR DISMISSAL.

rejection of goods the return by the buyer of the GOODS and the recovery of the PRICE. Often it will be the best remedy, certainly better than the alternative, which is to allow damages to be recovered. This right is lost once the goods have been accepted. See ACCEPTANCE OF GOODS.

release 1. a document or act discharging rights or claims.
2. to give up or discharge rights or claims.

relevance a key concept in the law of evidence that considers the link between a piece of evidence and the enquiry itself. 'Facts relevant in relation to each other if according to the common course of events one either taken by itself or in connection with other facts proves or renders liable to proof the past, present, or future or non-existence of the other'. Compare ADMISSIBILITY.

relevant claim in the Scots law of PRESCRIPTION, a claim that will interrupt the running of the prescriptive period. Generally, for NEGATIVE PRESCRIPTION, the claim must be by a court action served on the part, albeit a sketchy one. The rules are more complex for POSITIVE PRESCRIPTION.

reliability in the law of evidence, the aspect of evidence that the fact-finder feels able to rely upon in coming to a decision. Before the evidence can be relied upon, it must usually also be credible. It is at this stage that a court may believe a witness because he says he saw the accused stab the victim, but the court may or may not rely upon that evidence depending upon the circumstances, such as the prevailing light or weather conditions or state of mind of the witness. See CREDIBILITY.

relief I. an allowance from total income for income tax purposes.

2. the obligation to redress the unjust enrichment gained by A when B pays a decree under which A was also jointly or proportionately liable. In the UK there is statutory provision for relief in very many cases.

3. the opportunity to avoid the forfeiture of a lease. Forfeiture of a lease may follow upon a breach by a tenant of a fundamental term (the procedure is contained in the Law of Property Act 1925); relief may be available if the default is capable of being remedied and the tenant is willing to remedy it (e.g. payment of arrears of rent due). For Scotland, see IRRITANCY.

remand the disposal of an accused person during further process of law. A person may be remanded on BAIL or in custody.

remoteness of damage I. in contract law, the concept that protects the contract-breaker from having to pay for all the consequences of his breach. Since one of the principal aims of the law of contract is certainty, the rules are well settled. The leading case is *Hadley* v. *Baxendale* (1854) 23 LJ Ex 179, in which it is generally accepted that two rules were laid down (although many prefer, with justification, to describe the case as having set out two branches of a single rule). Alderson, B., stated the law as follows: 'where two parties have made a contract which one of them has broken, the damages which the other party ought to receive in respect of such breach of contract should be, either, such as may fairly and reasonably be considered arising naturally, i.e. according to the usual course of things, from such breach of contract itself, or such as may reasonably be supposed to have been in the contemplation of both parties at the time they made the contract, as the probable result of the breach of it'. Following this case and the fuller restatement in *Victoria Laundry (Windsor) Ltd* v. *Newman Industries Ltd* [1949] 1 All ER 997, cases can be split into those where the contract-breaker knew no more than any other person in his position and those where he was possessed of (or could be held to have been possessed of) special knowledge.

A recent authoritative restatement is that 'the crucial question is whether, on the information available to the defendant when the contract was made, he should, or the reasonable man in his position would, have realised that such loss was sufficiently likely to result from the breach of contract to make it proper to hold that the loss flowed naturally from the breach or that loss of that kind should have been within his contemplation': *Koufos* v. *Czarnikow Ltd* [1967] 3 All ER 686. The position is the same in Scotland, although it has been argued that there is an independent line of Scottish authority supporting the same rules. For the USA, see *Krauss* v. *Greenbarg* 137 F 2d 569 (3rd Cir. 1943).

2. in tort or delict different rules apply because the obligation is imposed by the law and not by the consent of the parties. English law has settled on a test of reasonable foreseeability: *Overseas Tankship (UK) Ltd* v. *Morts Dock & Engineering Co.* (known as the Wagon Mound No. 1) [1961] AC 388, rejecting the test of direct and natural consequences laid down in the earlier case in *Re Polemis* [1921] 3 KB 560. The law of Scotland is not authoritatively settled: *McKillen* v. *Barclay Curle & Co. Ltd* 1967 SLT 41.

removing in Scots law, the remedy for recovering possession that has been lost. Many cases now take place as summary cause actions for recovery of heritable property.

rent the sum or amount agreed in the lease or tenancy agreement to be paid by the tenant to the landlord for exclusive possession of the property leased for the period of the lease.

renvoi to send back, the doctrine in PRIVATE INTERNATIONAL LAW that remits a question of choice of law back to the system from which the cause arose in the first place. The doctrine can result in a 'magic roundabout' because a double renvoi theory can apply where a court tries to place itself in the place of the foreign court and to decide it like the foreign court. The Contracts (Applicable Law) Act 1990 applying the European Rome Convention excludes the doctrine of renvoi. The Private International Law (Miscellaneous Provisions) Act 1995 excludes the doctrine in delict. In relation to wills, renvoi is excluded as to formal validity by the Wills Act 1963.

repatriation a person's return, voluntary or otherwise, to the country of which he is a national.

replevin the remedy by which a person recovered goods if the goods were seized by DISTRESS. It was extended to cover wrongful detention generally. See now the County Courts Act 1984 and the

Torts (Interference with Goods) Act 1977.

replication in reply. Evidence in replication is evidence allowed after the other side has said something but when the party seeking to lead in replication has already had its proper say, an example being where something new emerges in re-examination that was not covered in CROSS-EXAMINATION.

reply 1. a speech by counsel for the plaintiff in a civil case, or for the prosecution in a criminal case, in answer to the points raised by the defence.

2. a pleading served by the plaintiff in a civil action in answer to the defence. Where there is a counterclaim it is often contained in the same document.

reporter see CHILDREN'S HEARING.

representation 1. a statement of fact. A representation should be distinguished from a statement of opinion for many legal purposes, especially in relation to contractual obligations.

2. in the law of succession, the concept by which issue of predeceasing issue of the deceased are entitled to take their deceased ancestor's share. For England, see Administration of Estates Act 1925; for Scotland, see Succession (Scotland) Act 1964.

reprobate see ELECTION.

repugnancy the making of a bequest by a testator that also tries to prevent the beneficiaries' rights of ownership. It is generally not allowed.

requirements of writing see SELF-PROVING.

resale the legitimate selling of goods despite the fact that they have already been sold to another. Where an unpaid seller who has exercised his right of LIEN or RETENTION or STOPPAGE IN TRANSIT resells the goods, the buyer acquires a good title to them as against the original buyer. The Act provides for two instances of resale. First, where the goods are of a perishable nature or where the UNPAID SELLER gives notice to the buyer of his intention to resell and the buyer does not within a reasonable time pay or tender the price, the unpaid seller may resell the goods and recover from the original buyer damages for any loss occasioned by his BREACH OF CONTRACT. Secondly, where the seller expressly reserves the right of resale in case the buyer should make default, and on the buyer making default resells the goods, the original contract of sale is rescinded but WITHOUT PREJUDICE to any claim the seller may have for DAMAGES.

rescission revocation of a contract. In the event of a breach of a contract, rescission is the remedy sought to bring the contract to an end, allowing the innocent party to perform no further, recover any part performance and seek damages. It is an equitable remedy and will not be granted unless *restitutio in integrum* can be made – 'restoration of the parties' pre-contractual state': *Buckland* v. *Farmer and Moodey* [1978] 3 All ER 929.

The Misrepresentation Act 1967 allows a court to award damages in place of rescission if equitable in relation to the position of the parties if rescission were granted, in cases of innocent misrepresentation.

In Scots law the position is not so clear that a definite answer can always be given. This is because the trigger is the notion of material breach, which can mean either breach of a very significant term or a breach that has great effects. The most general accepted version is to determine whether the stipulation breached is one that goes to the root of the contract: *Wade* v. *Waldon* 1909 SC 571.

Applying to the whole of the UK, under the Sale of Goods Act 1994, a consumer has a statutory right of rejection for breach of the major implied conditions no matter how trivial the result; for non-consumers the breach must be material.

reservation of title see ROMALPA CLAUSE.

reserved matter a subject upon which the NATIONAL ASSEMBLY FOR WALES and the SCOTTISH PARLIAMENT may not legislate as set out in the legislation. For example, defence is outwith their scope. The Scottish Parliament has limited tax-raising powers; the Welsh Assembly does not.

reset in Scots criminal law, the possession of property dishonestly appropriated by another, for example by theft, knowing it to have been so obtained and intending that the owner should be deprived of it. It may be committed by being privy to the retention of the property from the true owner. A wife, in Scotland, cannot be charged in respect of goods brought in by her husband unless she has taken an active part in trading in the goods.

res gestae see HEARSAY.

residence order see SECTION 8 ORDER.

Resident Magistrate (RM) in Northern Ireland, full-time legally qualified judges who sit in the magistrates' courts trying less serious criminal cases without a jury and conducting committal proceedings in more serious cases. They also have limited jurisdiction in civil matters. The office was created in Ireland in the

19th century when it was considered that in some areas lay justices could not be relied on.

residue in the law of succession, the part of an estate left over after legacies and bequests have been met.

res inter alios acta nocere non debet 'a transaction between parties should not affect another party.'

res ipsa loquitur see PRESUMPTIONS.

res merae facultatis in the Scots law of property, rights that can be exercised at will and do not prescribe if they are not used, such as the ordinary uses of property.

resolutions of a company a decision of a company in general meeting. Members may debate and pass (or otherwise) ordinary, extraordinary or special resolutions; an *extraordinary resolution* requires to be passed by a three-quarter's majority; a *special resolution* requires likewise and in addition it has to be passed by a majority of such members as may be present at a subsequent meeting of which not less than 21 days' notice has been given.

res perit domino see RISK.

respondeat superior see VICARIOUS LIABILITY.

respondent the other party to a petition or an appeal.

respondentia a contract in the maritime law, recognised by many nations, concluded in a foreign port for prepayment of advances made to supply a ship with necessaries secured over the cargo and recorded in a *bond of respondentia*. See also BOTTOMRY, HYPOTHEC.

restatements the publications of the private American Law Institute, which is made up of law professors, judges and practising lawyers. The project is to state the precedents of the US jurisdictions, like a continental code, so that it is manageable and so that some degree of principle can be abstracted from the many decided cases. They are not authoritative but carry much weight.

restitutio in integrum 'putting things back the way they were', originally a remedy in Roman law allowing a party to be restored against his own deed. It has now come to be part of the process of RESCISSION of contract in English law and in Scots law. Generally, a party will be allowed to rescind only if he can effect *restitutio in integrum*.

restitution the branch of the law of obligations that deals with the redressing of unjust enrichment subtracted from the plaintiff. In a wider sense it also covers restitution in respect of wrongs done to the plaintiff. It can be expressed by saying that a defendant must disgorge an unjust enrichment made at the expense of the plaintiff. Restitution for unjust enrichment is now a recognised basis of obligation in English law as a result of the decisions in *Lipkin Gorman* v. *Karpnale* [1991] 2 AC 548 and *Woolwich* v. *Inland Revenue* [1993] AC 70. There is a search for an 'unjust factor'. In Scotland, in some cases restitution must be made where there has been a transfer for no legal cause (hence the use of 'unjustified' in Scotland and other civilian jurisdictions) and it is inequitable for the defender to retain the enrichment. It has been recognised in Canada and Australia for some time. An analytical vocabulary has grown up in the Anglo-American world that makes it easier to analyse problems and find principled solutions: see NON-MATERIALISATION, FREE ACCEPTANCE, PASSING ON, CHANGE OF POSITION. The former categorisation QUASI-CONTRACT is now less frequently encountered.

Both the English and Scottish legal systems have well-known heads of liability, the most important of the English heads being the action for MONEY HAD AND RECEIVED and in Scotland RECOMPENSE, the CONDICTIO INDEBITI, the CONDICTIO CAUSA DATA CAUSA NON SECUTA and NEGOTIORUM GESTIO. The Scots law is based upon developments in the civil law, but it has taken its own path in many instances.

Other obligations like RELIEF, SALVAGE and SUBROGATION can be seen to have restitutionary features. The *constructive trust* is increasingly being seen as a form of remedial obligation that has the effect of making restitution for unjust enrichment. The term restitution is also used narrowly in Scots law to denote the obligation on a defender to return the pursuer's specific property still in the pursuer's ownership.

rest period see WORKING TIME.

restrictive covenant a legal promise restricting the granter's freedom. It is used in relation to an undertaking, restrictive in nature, enforceable in equity against a purchaser of land with notice of the existence of the undertaking by an owner of benefited land in the neighbourhood.

It is also used in relation to agreements not to set up in business against a former employer or partner or the like. Such agreements are prima facie unenforceable as being in restraint of trade but will be allowed if they are fair in relation to the public interest in free competition and as between the parties.

retention in the Scots law of contract, the right for A not to pay money due to B under a contract until damages due by B to A under the same contract are ascertained. Thus, a claim for freight may be opposed by a claim for damage done to the goods in transit. In bankruptcy or liquidation, a party who is facing an illiquid claim may retain in respect of an illiquid sum owed to him by the bankrupt and it is not necessary that the debts should arise out of the same contract.

In the law of Sale of Goods 1979, where the property in goods has not passed to the buyer, the UNPAID SELLER has a right to withhold delivery similar to and co-extensive with his rights of LIEN or RETENTION and STOPPAGE IN TRANSIT where the property has passed to the buyer.

retention of title see PASSING OF PROPERTY IN SALE, ROMALPA CLAUSE.

revocation the nullification of an act or transaction or the withdrawal of authority formerly given.

In the relationship of principal and agent, the general rule is that in the absence of any contractual rule to the contrary, the principal is free to revoke his agent's authority at any time provided that the agent has not already fulfilled his obligations. See AGENCY, OFFER.

revolving credit facility an arrangement (usually with a bank) that requires the borrower to undertake to make regular periodic payments into a designated account in return for the facility to borrow on that account up to a specified sum, the amount of which is usually expressed as a multiple of each contractual payment into the account. See FIXED CREDIT.

right of abode the right freely to live in and come and go from the UK without let or hindrance. See BRITISH CITIZEN, CERTIFICATE OF ENTITLEMENT.

right of support the right of a landowner to have his buildings supported by his neighbour's house or other structure. Equally, every landowner is entitled to have his land in its natural state supported by the adjoining land of his neighbour, against whom an action will lie if, by digging or other excavation on his own land, he removes that support. This right of support is not an easement but rather a right of property passing with the soil.

right of way a right enjoyed by one person (either for himself or as a member of the public) to pass over another's land subject to such restrictions and conditions as are specified in the grant or sanctioned by custom, by virtue of which the right exists.

rights issue an issuing of extra shares. A company may raise additional capital from its members as opposed to from the public at large by issuing extra shares; this is called a rights issue. See PREEMPTION RIGHTS.

right to silence the idea that a person should not be able to incriminate himself simply by saying nothing at all.

In England and Wales the right has been known for some time, even although there is no constitutional provision. The history is not as might be expected. Originally all witnesses could be interrogated, and although this was stopped in the 17th century the accused was denied the right to give evidence in his own defence. This was changed by the Criminal Evidence Act 1898. In the 20th century the position was arrived at first under the Judges' Rules of 1912 and latterly under the Police and Criminal Evidence Act 1984 that a suspect had to be cautioned that he need not answer any questions put to him (see *R* v. *Sang* (1979) 69 Cr. App. R 282). However, in terms of the Criminal Justice and Public Order Act 1994 (similar to the Criminal Evidence (Northern Ireland) Order 1988), courts are permitted to comment on a failure to give evidence. As a result, the caution given to suspects has been changed to warn the suspect of this fact. It has been held that the Northern Ireland rules do not infringe the EUROPEAN CONVENTION ON HUMAN RIGHTS (*Murray* v. *UK* 9.2.1996) albeit the Convention has been interpreted in the past to the effect that the right to silence is an inherent part of the protection available under Article 6 of the Convention.

In Scotland, the history is similar, and the principle has been described as sacred and inviolable: *HMA* v. *Von* 1979 SLT (Notes) 62. There are no statutory measures such as exist in England, but the common law caution administered warns suspects of their right and a detained person must be warned that he need only give his name and address. So far as comment is concerned, the Scots courts have always been able to comment but subject to restraint and only in special and appropriate circumstances: *Scott* v. *HMA* 1946 JC 90. Under the Criminal Justice (Scotland) Act 1995, the prosecutor may now also comment, and it is expected that in practice this will be subject to restraint and special circumstances. The right has been further reinforced in the UK by the Human Rights Act 1998.

In the USA, the use of the Fifth and Fourteenth Amendments have long given constitutional protection to citizens – a person does not have to answer a question if, truly answered, it would tend to incriminate him. Being a constitutional provision, the right is more general and of wide influence in matters outside the actual courtroom. Suspects have to be cautioned and informed of their right.

See also EXCLUSIONARY RULE.

riot a criminal offence in England under the Public Order Act 1986 if 12 or more persons use or threaten to use unlawful violence for a common purpose, causing people to fear for their safety. For Scotland, see MOBBING, RIOTING.

riparian pertaining to the bank of a river.

risk 1. the possibility of loss or harm occurring. Normally, the risk of accidental destruction lies with the owner.

In respect of GOODS, the position is regulated by the Sale of Goods Act 1979. Unless otherwise agreed, the goods remain at the seller's risk until the property in them is transferred to the buyer, but when the property in them is transferred to the buyer the goods are at the buyer's risk whether delivery has been made or not. This section expresses the maxim *res perit domino* ('ownership is lost with the thing'), and the 1893 Act represented a change in the common law of Scotland, which was that risk passed as soon as the contract was formed regardless of the fact that property might not have passed by TRADITIO. In respect of generic sales, the rule does not apply. The applicable maxim in such cases is *genus nunquam perit*: i.e. 'no commodity ceases to exist.' This principle applies even if the seller's stock from which he had intended to fulfil his bargain is accidentally destroyed. Goods may be treated as having perished when they are so damaged that they no longer answer to the description under which they were sold: *Nickoll & Knight* v. *Ashton, Edridge & Co.* [1901] 2 KB 126. It is however, open to the parties to make their own agreement as to risk. The time of destruction of the goods is important. Where there is a contract for the sale of SPECIFIC GOODS, and the goods, without the knowledge of the seller, have perished at the time when the contract is made, the contract is VOID. Where there is an AGREEMENT TO SELL SPECIFIC GOODS and subsequently the goods, without any fault on the part of the seller or buyer, perish before the risk passes to the buyer, the agreement is avoided. Where delivery has been delayed through the fault of either buyer or seller, the goods are at risk of the party at fault as regards any loss that might not have occurred but for such fault. Fault for these purposes is defined as a wrongful act or default. 'Default' means a lack of reasonable care in the circumstances.

2. in the law of insurance, the danger, peril or event insured against.

RM abbreviation for RESIDENT MAGISTRATE.

robbery the crime of using force or fear of force to commit a theft. The force may be before, during or after the robbery. Technically, the force must be against the person and not the property, making 'bag-snatching' problematic.

In Scots criminal law, robbery is theft committed by way of personal violence or intimidation. Violence to the person after the theft is not robbery, as where something is stolen and the attempts of the owner to recover the property are resisted.

rolled-up plea in an action of libel, a form of DEFAMATION, this plea indicates a defence on the basis that so far as a statement is a statement of fact, the statement is true and so far as it is one of comment, the defence of fair comment applies.

Romalpa clause a clause in a contract modelled on the clause that was upheld in the English Court of Appeal in the case *Aluminium Industrie Vassen BV* v. *Romalpa Aluminium* [1976] 1 WLR 676. There are two main elements:

(1) retention of title. Because of the rules on PASSING OF PROPERTY IN SALE, it is possible for parties to stipulate that property shall not pass until the seller has been paid. The controversial idea was to say that property should not pass until all sums that might be due to the seller have been paid. This could mean that the actual price of the actual goods delivered has been paid but because of an unpaid debt in relation to some other transaction (even a transaction by another company in the same group) the property has not passed. The importance of this commercially is that if the buyer becomes INSOLVENT then the seller has a right to reclaim the property in question and it does not fall into the hands of the creditors. This is frequently much better than simply RANKING for a dividend. The concept has now been recognised in the Scots law, which had previously refused to recognise such clauses as constituting security without possession: *Armour* v. *Thyssen* 1991 SCLR 139;

(2) the other main component of the clause involves a TRUST provision. This is to cover the situation where the buyer uses the goods and sells them on. Because of the retention, the property the buyer used to sell on was truly that of the seller and the trust provision seeks to make the buyer hold the money on trust for the seller. Because of the TANTUM ET TALE rule, should the buyer become insolvent the sums so collected have to be accounted for to the seller and do not form part of the insolvent estate. See *Re Bond Worth Ltd*

[1980] Ch. 228, *Re Andrabell Ltd* [1984] Ch. 131.

Roman law the law of ancient Rome; also the legal system and science built upon it and adopted in various ways in various places at various times up to the present. The classical period ran from roughly 27 BC to the middle of the third century AD. The first phase of the law then concluded with the codification of all the law by Justinian (AD 527–565) in the CORPUS JURIS CIVILIS. The Roman law survived in watered-down form in Constantinople until its fall in 1453. Its real 'second life' began in the West when Justinian's Digest was discovered and used as the heart of a revived study of Irnerius (1050–1130) at the University of Bologna. While England developed its own system, other states looked to Roman law for inspiration. The NAPOLEONIC CODE began a process of the adoption of Roman and Romantic legal thought throughout Europe. Often the term civil law or civilian is used for the post-Justinian period.

The importance of the Roman tradition lies in the fact that the law was set out in a systematic way – obligations, property and persons being separated yet related. This meant there was less danger of haphazard, incongruous organic development where the reports of decided cases are simply collected.

roup a word used in Scotland for an AUCTION.

royal assent the agreement of the monarch to a bill becoming an ACT OF PARLIAMENT. It is a CONVENTION that the monarch shall so assent. For public bills, the Clerk of the Parliaments communicates the assent by the words 'La reine le veult,' different forms being used for money bills and private bills.

Royal Court the main court in each of the Bailiwicks of Jersey and Guernsey, having both civil and criminal jurisdiction.

royal prerogative in the CONSTITUTIONAL LAW of the UK, the powers of the Crown exercised under the common law. New prerogatives cannot be assumed and old ones can be legislated away. Recognised instances are the rule that the king never dies, there is no interregnum, the king is never an infant and the king can do no wrong, albeit this particular prerogative has been severely curtailed by the Crown Proceedings Act. The more important prerogatives relate to domestic affairs and foreign affairs. In domestic affairs, certain appointments are made in virtue of prerogative affairs. The control of the armed forces and the civil service is a matter of prerogative act. Control of remaining colonies and of the Crown estates is also carried through under the prerogative. The Queen is governor of the Church of England (but has no such position in relation to the equally established Church of Scotland) and is the fountain of honour in relation to the creation of peers and the like, although this is exercised on the recommendation of the PRIME MINISTER. Some honours are in the personal gift of the monarch. The Crown may use reasonable force to put down riots. The Crown has the duty of defending the nation, although the way in which it does so is restricted by the Bill of Rights 1688. The House of Lords held in *Burmah Oil Co. Ltd* v. *Lord Advocate* [1965] AC 75 that compensation was payable for damage caused by the lawful exercise of the prerogative, but this decision was reversed and with retroactive effect so as to deny the successful pursuers their compensation by the War Damage Act 1965. The prerogative in relation to legislation includes the right to summon and dissolve parliament and that the Crown is not bound by statute save expressly. Of prerogatives relating to foreign affairs, the most significant is Act of State, that is, an act done to another state or person not owing allegiance to the Crown. The courts will generally treat such as non-justiciable. Examples of Act of State are the making of war and peace and the conclusion of treaties. An alien cannot sue in respect of loss sustained as an Act of State: see *Buron* v. *Denman* (1848) 2 Ex 167, in which the actual deed was ratified after it had been carried out.

rubric 1. the headnote of a law report setting out the main facts and the point of law decided in the case.

2. the long title of an ACT OF PARLIAMENT.

Both usages derive from the fact that these parts used to be printed in red.

rule against perpetuities a rule developed by the common law designed to prevent the vesting of future interests in property at a time too remote in the future. As the rule matured, it came to be required that a contingent interest under a settlement or trust, to be valid, was required to vest, if it vested at all, within 'the perpetuity period'. The *perpetuity period* at common law was a period of a *life* or *lives in being* at the date the instrument creating the instrument came into effect plus 21 years. *Lives in being* could be, and frequently were, expressly nominated in the instrument; if none was so nominated, the period would be measured by reference to *implied lives*; these were the lives of persons whose existence had an effect on the vesting of the interests under the settlement or trust. Where no such implied lives were to be found, the perpetuity period at common law was 21 years from the date of the coming into effect of the instrument. Under the Perpetuities and Accumulations Act 1964, a new statutory period of up to 80 years could be employed if expressly provided for in the instrument.

rule of law everyone acts under the law. A phrase as old as Aristotle, it has a special meaning in the CONSTITUTIONAL LAW of the UK and in relation to discussions of law and politics everywhere. Perhaps the most practically useful sense in which the doctrine is applied is to demand that the executive must be acting under the law. But even then this authority need not be explicit in a state where everyone is free to do anything unless it is prohibited. In another sense it reflects the view that there is a higher law than that of the government. In the UK no parliament can bind its successor, and it is difficult to see the doctrine operating in this sense, although the supremacy of the law of the EUROPEAN UNION has given such a view renewed prominence. The significance of the doctrine in modern times is probably because of the writings of Dicey, who considered that the rule of law involved three issues:

(1) the absence of arbitrary power;

(2) equality before the law; and

(3) liberties and constitutional law generally are the result of law and law made in the courts.

The phrase still has a rhetorical significance, but it is arguable that its technical significance has been overshadowed by the notion of fundamental law or HUMAN RIGHTS.

rule of recognition see HARTIAN JURISPRUDENCE.

running account credit a facility under a personal credit agreement whereby the debtor is enabled to receive from time to time (whether in his own person or by another person) from the creditor or a third party cash, goods and services (or any of them) to an amount in value such that, taking into account payments made by or to the credit of the debtor, the credit limit (if any) is not at any time exceeded: Consumer Credit Act 1974.

runrig in Scotland, lands that were alternate or mixed and owned by different owners. The Runrig Lands Act 1695 permitted division of such lands.

S

S. abbreviation for section, as of an Act. If there is more than one then the abbreviation is **SS.**

sacrilege the offence of breaking into a place of divine worship: Theft Act 1968.

safe system of work see EMPLOYERS' LIABILITY.

safety see PRODUCT LIABILITY.

sale a transaction involving the transfer of property from one person to another for a consideration. In the case of goods, a money consideration called the price. If money is not exchanged then the contract may be one of BARTER. In the UK a common code (with some important differences reflect the civilian origin of the Scottish legal system) exists for GOODS in the Sale of Goods Act 1979. The original Act of 1893 became something of a model for many Commonwealth jurisdictions. Sale of HERITAGE or REAL PROPERTY rules are different because of the general attitude of respect for landed property rights. Both in England and in Scotland, the buyer of land must satisfy himself that the property meets his expectations in regard to quality, title and description. See CIF, DESCRIPTION, FAS, F.O.B., NEMO DAT QUOD NON HABET, QUALITY, RISK, SAMPLE, SPECIFIC GOODS, STOPPAGE IN TRANSIT, TITLE, UNPAID SELLER.

sale and leaseback a transaction whereby a business (whether incorporated or not) sells a property (often its factory or offices) to raise capital and then leases it back at a rent from the purchaser.

salmon fishing see REGALIA MINORA.

salus reipublicae suprema lex 'the welfare of the people is the supreme law.'

salvage a sum payable to a person who saves a ship or its cargo from certain loss. It is not due by contract and, indeed, agreement excludes salvage. It resembles RESTITUTION in that the recipient of the *salved goods* is enriched by the effort of the *salvor*. It does not precisely fit the scheme of restitution, seen as redressing unjust enrichment, because salvage awards are usually much higher than the expense involved in the rescue.

sample (sale by, implied term) a contract of sale is a sale by sample where there is an express or implied term to that effect in the contract. Where there is a sale by sample there is an implied condition: (a) that the bulk will correspond with the sample in quality; (b) that the buyer will have a reasonable opportunity of comparing the bulk with the sample; (c) that the goods will be free from any defect, rendering them unacceptable, which would not be apparent on reasonable examination of the sample. If a sale is by sample as well as by DESCRIPTION, it is not sufficient that the bulk corresponds with the sample if the goods do not also correspond with the description. It is the duty of the seller to make the sample available to the buyer for comparison. See *Godley* v. *Perry* [1960] 1 WLR 9, *E. & S. Ruben* v. *Faire Bros & Co. Ltd* [1949] 1 All ER 215.

sanctions see COMMAND THEORY, KELSINIAN JURISPRUDENCE.

sasine feudal possession of land in Scotland. Where this is not recorded in the LAND REGISTER, it is achieved by recording in the REGISTER OF SASINES.

satisfactory quality see QUALITY.

schedule a small scroll; an appendage; most commonly encountered as a part of an ACT OF PARLIAMENT. Modern legislation often has numerous schedules that include details that would detract from the overall sense of the provision (an example being the Dangerous Wild Animals Act 1976) or that lists other enactments affected by the Act to which the schedule is attached. The schedule is as authoritative as the text of the Act itself: *Shepherd* v. *Pearson Engineering Services (Dundee) Ltd* 1980 SC 268.

Schedule A the provision under which the Inland Revenue taxes the annual profits or gains arising in respect of rents or similar payments arising from ownership of land or an interest therein in the UK.

Schedule B the provision under which the Inland Revenue taxed income from woodlands in the UK. It was abolished as from 6 April 1988.

Schedule C the provision under which the Inland Revenue taxes public revenue dividends (i.e. interest payments on government stock) payable in the UK. The stock need not be that of the UK government; however, if the stock is of a foreign government, the payments must be made via a paying agent (e.g. the Bank of England) in the UK.

Schedule D the provision under which the Inland Revenue taxes annual profits or gains that fall under one or other of six cases. Case I deals with profits from a trade or an adventure in the nature of a trade; Case II deals with profits from a profession or vocation (the rules as to the computation of profits under Case I and II are the same); Case III covers interest, annuities and other annual payments and certain public revenue dividends (e.g. in respect of securities issued by UK local authorities) not covered by SCHEDULE C; Case IV covers profits or gains from securities outside the UK; Case V covers profits or gains from possessions outside the UK; Case VI taxes any annual profits or gains not falling under any other case or schedule.

Schedule E the provision under which the Inland Revenue taxes emoluments from OFFICE OR EMPLOYMENT; tax is levied on a current year basis and is usually collected via the PAYE system. Schedule E has three cases according to the location of the employment: Case I covers the earnings of a person resident and ordinarily resident in the UK, subject to deductions for foreign emoluments and for earnings in respect of duties performed abroad; Case II applies to the earnings of a person who is not resident, or one who is resident but is not ordinarily resident in the UK where the earnings are in respect of duties performed in the UK; Case III applies to foreign earnings of a UK resident that are received in the UK; i.e. it is charged on a remittance basis.

Schedule F the provision under which the Inland Revenue taxes distributions by companies resident in the UK; the tax is due on the dividend in the year of assessment and is in effect deducted at source (see ADVANCE CORPORATION TAX).

schedule of poinding see POINDING.

Schengen Agreement an extension of the policy of the EUROPEAN COMMUNITIES on FREE MOVEMENT OF PERSONS whereby the governments of Belgium, Netherlands, Luxembourg, Germany and France agreed to eliminate (as at 1 January 1993) all border controls against persons.

scienter see ANIMALS.

Scottish Administration the 'civil service' of the SCOTTISH PARLIAMENT.

Scottish Criminal Cases Review Commission a body set up by the Crime and Punishment (Scotland) Act 1992 with power to investigate miscarriages of justice and refer them to the Appeal Court. It has no power to quash convictions itself.

Scottish Conveyancing and Executry Services Board the body, newly activated, that regulates conveyancers and executry practitioners who are not solicitors.

Scottish Executive the 'cabinet' of the SCOTTISH PARLIAMENT.

Scottish Law Commission the body that reviews Scots law with a view to its systematic development and reform, including the codification of law, the elimination of anomalies, the repeal of obsolete and unnecessary enactments and the modernisation of the law. The Commission comprises a chairman and four other commissioners, appointed by the Scottish Minister.

Scottish Legal Aid Board see LEGAL AID.

Scottish Parliament by virtue of the Scotland Act 1998, there is a devolved Scottish Parliament as of 1 July 1999. It has all the powers of a big local authority and all the pomp, officials and expense of a sovereign parliament.

scrip dividend the issue of a certificate entitling the holder to acquire shares in a company; frequently used in connection with bonus issues, such scrip has in some instances been issued as a stock dividend instead of cash.

SEA abbreviation for SINGLE EUROPEAN ACT.

seal a formal mark impressed by a person on deeds. Originally, all documents executed by a company had to have the company seal attached; this is no longer necessary since the Companies Act 1989.

Before the Law of Property (Miscellaneous Provisions) Act 1989, deeds in English law were validly executed only if they were 'signed, sealed and delivered'. Sealing is no longer a requirement.

Seanad Eireann the upper house of the parliament, or OIREACHTAS, of the Republic of Ireland, which is composed of 60 members of whom 11 are nominated by the TAOISEACH, or prime minister, and 49 are elected. Of the elected members, six represent Dublin University and the National University of Ireland. The other 43 are elected by an electorate comprising members of the new dail, the outgoing senators and members of county and borough councils from various panels representing agriculture, the arts, industry, commerce and professions and public administration.

search examination of records or registers, especially by or on behalf of purchasers, to ascertain the existence of encumbrances. Whether title to land is or is not subject to the Land Registration Acts, a purchaser should search the Local Land Charges Register maintained by the local authority for details of public local charges and burdens. Where title is subject to the Land Registration Acts, a search should be made of the land registry to discover the existence of charges, restrictive covenants, etc, affecting the land. Where the title is not subject to the Land Registration Acts, searches should be made in the General Register of Land Charges in connection with these matters.

In Scottish conveyancing practice there must be searches showing no advance encumbrances in the appropriate registers – the Property Register for cases where the land is registered – in the Register of Sasines and the Register of Inhibitions and Adjudications where the land is held feudally. In the case of land to be first registered, a form 10 report is required, and in respect of land already registered, a form 12 report.

secondary agents commercial agents whose activities are insufficiently active to fall within the protection of the regulations.

secondary evidence evidence that is not of the best and most direct character which may be excluded if that better evidence is available.

secondary rules see HARTIAN.

second reading see ACT OF PARLIAMENT.

secret profit profit made by an agent that is not revealed to the principal. An agent, being in a fiduciary position as against the principal, is not permitted to make a profit out of the performance of his duties as an agent unknown to the principal. It is his duty to account for all such profit; failure to do so will render him liable to dismissal and give the principal a ground for refusing to pay him his commission. The secret profit itself must be disgorged under the law of RESTITUTION.

Section 8 Order an order made under Section 8 of the Children Act 1989. The Act provides (among other things) the following:

(1) a *contact order*: an order requiring the person with whom a child lives, or is to live, to allow the child to visit or stay with the person named in the order, or for that person and the child otherwise to have contact with each other;

(2) a *prohibited steps order*: an order that no step which could be taken by a parent in meeting his parental responsibility for a child and which is of a kind specified in the order, shall be taken by any person without the consent of the court;

(3) a *residence order*: an order settling the arrangements to be made as to the person with whom a child is to live;

(4) a *specific issue order*: an order giving direction for the purpose of determining a specific question that has arisen or that may arise in connection with any aspect of parent responsibility for the child.

Most of this terminology is now applicable in Scotland but as an independent civilian system they are called Section 11 Orders: Children (Scotland) Act 1995.

Section 11 Order see SECTION 8 ORDER.

securities stock and shares. In relation to a company not limited by shares (whether or not it has a share capital), the interest of a member of the company as such; thus, debentures and loan stocks are securities.

security in connection with the granting of a loan facility, the obtaining by the lender of rights additional to those deriving from the borrower to pay the interest due and to repay the principal debt in accordance with the provisions of the loan agreement; it confers a right to look to some identified fund or property, or to some other person, for payment. Those forms of security conferring recourse to particular funds or property are MORTGAGE, CHARGE, PLEDGE, HYPOTHEC and LIEN. The forms of security permitting a creditor to look to a third party for satisfaction are GUARANTEE and INDEMNITY. See STANDARD SECURITY.

security of tenure statutory protection conferred on tenants restricting the rights of landlords to obtain possession of the premises let. In the case of residential tenancies, a court order is required before possession can be enforced.

sedition acts, deeds, writing or speeches that can, even if not intended, stir up the peace of the state or that move the people to dislike, resist or subvert the government of the day. See DISQUALIFICATION.

seisin feudal possession of freehold land.

seizure of goods the process of taking possession of GOODS for the purpose of satisfying the claims of a judgment creditor. By the seizure the goods are placed under the custody of the law, albeit that the general property in the goods remains in the judgment/execution debtor.

Select Vestries Bill see PARLIAMENT.

self-defence DEFENCE of one's person (or depending on the context, other persons or property) against criminal charges or tortious or delictual claims.

In English law a self-defence is a defence to criminal charges. The defence can be of persons other than oneself: *R* v. *Williams* (1984) Cr. App. R 276. Defence of property is also sufficient: *R* v. *Hussey* (1924) 18 Cr. App. R 160. Only such force as is necessary may be used.

In the criminal law of Scotland, a special defence of which notice

must be given that can justify HOMICIDE or ASSAULT. There must be
fear to life or a fear of rape. There should be no possibility of escape,
and the defence must not itself amount to cruel excess, as where a
punch is answered with a dagger blow. The concept has recently
been applied in relation to BREACH OF THE PEACE.

In the law of tort and delict, self-defence is a defence against a civil
action for assault. See PROVOCATION.

self-incrimination the giving of evidence, by testimony or otherwise,
by a witness that incriminates him. In many systems a person does
not have to answer a question that, if truly answered, would tend to
incriminate. See RIGHT TO SILENCE.

self-proving in Scots law, a document that meets the requisite
formalities to be treated as signed by the grantor without the need
for proof. This is a new idea, replacing many well-established and
ancient rules. The rules applicable are all found in one modern Act
– the Requirements of Writing (Scotland) Act 1995. The essential
requirement is that the deed be signed by the grantor and witnessed
by one witness whose name and address must be stated. The
document is not self-proving if the signature purporting to be that
of a witness is false, if the witness is also the grantor, if he did not
know the grantor, is under 16 years of age, is mentally incapable or
does not witness the signature or its acknowledgement. Documents
need only be signed on the last page unless they are wills. Where
there is not statutory presumption of self-proving status, the court
can be petitioned to declare it so. Alterations made prior to
execution are valid if the deed itself is signed and they are
presumed as valid if mentioned in the testing clause. Only certain
contracts need to be in writing and of these only some require to be
self-proving. Writing is required for the creation transfer or
variation of an interest in land and for the making of wills. It is
required for a TRUST where a person is making himself sole trustee
of his own property. Where there is a need for writing *under the Act*
and there is none, special provisions exist to allow the contract to be
upheld, notwithstanding the absence of writing, reflecting the
common law doctrines of REI INTERVENTUS and HOMOLOGATION,
which both still exist albeit they may not be used in cases where the
Act applies. The special provisions focus on reliance by the parties
and whether such reliance has been with the knowledge and
acquiescence of the other party to a material extent and take into
account whether there would be an adverse effect if the contract

were allowed to be ignored. Thus, if A buys a house from B but the requirements of writing are not met, then A will still get the house and B cannot escape if A had been allowed by B to build a conservatory attached to it and had sold his own house.

seller in possession, sale by see NEMO DAT QUOD NON HABET.

seller, unpaid see UNPAID SELLER.

semble 'it seems', seen in law reports to indicate doubt.

Senior Counsel see BARRISTER.

SEPA abbreviation for Scottish Environmental Protection Agency. See ENVIRONMENTAL LAW.

separation in family law in both England and Scotland, a court order ordaining and permitting the parties to live apart. The grounds are the same as those required to show irretrievable breakdown in DIVORCE. The courts have the same powers in relation to financial orders and children as they do when making a decree of divorce. Judicial separation does not actually terminate the marriage and is therefore an appropriate course to take if there are religious objections to divorce or if the parties have not finally agreed to divorce. The term separation is also used to describe the state arising when parties agree to live apart – frequently under the terms of a legally binding agreement that provides for the payment of money and the welfare of children. The term is used non-technically to describe people who are *de facto* living apart.

separation of powers the doctrine, derived from Locke and Montesquieu, that power should not be concentrated but separated. The traditional separation is between the LEGISLATURE, the EXECUTIVE and the JUDICIARY. A complete separation is unwieldy. In the UK it is nothing like complete, with the Lord Chancellor, the highest judicial officer, and the Lord Advocate, the highest judicial officer in Scotland, sitting in Parliament. Indeed, the Lord Chancellor sits in Cabinet. Members of Parliament sit in the government, and 'the government' in the sense of appointed members of the government extends usually to a very large number of Members of Parliament.

In the USA, the theory was carried to its most practically perfect. Executive power lies in the President, legislative power in the Congress and judicial power is in the Supreme Court. However, the need to function and coordinate is achieved by a series of checks and balances that also serve to prevent either of the three organs gaining the ascendancy. The Supreme Court can strike down legislation, but its members can be impeached or its membership extended with presidential appointments while these appointments themselves may not be confirmed by the Senate.

A similar situation can be seen in the EUROPEAN COMMUNITIES, where the Council, the Commission and the Parliament are linked in a series of relationships that are even more sophisticated than the system in the USA because they have flexibility built into their structure, for example, to allow the Parliament to acquire more and more power as it becomes ever more representative of the peoples of Europe.

sequester the practice, prevalent in the USA, of keeping juries sealed up during sensational trials. In this way they do not have access to prejudicial materials or contacts.

sequestration 1. an order of the court to commissioners directing them to seize property belonging to a person or body, usually applied where that person or body is in contempt of court.

2. in Scotland, the technical name for BANKRUPTCY proceedings.

sequestration, writ of the writ of sequestration is a process of contempt by proceeding against the property of the contemnor and is a means of enforcing judgments or orders only where the person in contempt has disobeyed an order of the court. Accordingly, before a writ of sequestration will be allowed to issue, the court must be satisfied that a contempt of court has been committed. Thus, the writ of sequestration is a writ of last resort to enforce a judgment or order that requires a person to do an act within a specified time or to abstain from doing a specified act.

sequestrator an officer of the court responsible for effecting a SEQUESTRATION.

seriatim 'one after another', as listed in a series or list.

serious arrestable offence see ARRESTABLE OFFENCE.

Serious Fraud Office an agency established by the Criminal Justice Act 1987 having a director and charged with instituting and conducting proceedings involving serious or complex fraud. It may take over cases run by others. It was given much more sweeping powers to obtain information than the police had to obtain documents and other papers. The suspect has to answer questions, and these answers may be put to him in later proceedings.

serious professional misconduct the offence committed by certain professionals within their own code that justifies sanctions, including striking from their professional register. The most frequently encountered usage is in connection with the discipline of medical doctors by the GENERAL MEDICAL COUNCIL. The concept is also used by, among others, dentists and pharmacists.

servant see EMPLOYMENT.

services see FREE MOVEMENT OF SERVICES.

servient owner see EASEMENT.

servitude see EASEMENTS. See ALTIUS NON TOLENDI, FUEL FEAL DIVOT, LIGHT OR PROSPECT, STILLICIDE.

set-off the plea that there exists a debt owed to the debtor by the creditor so that the creditor's claim against the debtor should be extinguished or reduced to the extent of that debt. Set-off is limited to money claims and is a ground of defence rather than a substantive claim.

settled property for capital gains tax and inheritance tax purposes, property is property held on trust for persons in succession, or upon a contingency (e.g. the attainment by a beneficiary of a specified age) or where the income or capital is payable at the discretion of the trustees (or some other specified person). Not all property held in trust is settled property. For example, property held under a *bare trust* (that is, where the beneficiaries are absolutely entitled to the trust property as against the trustees and as a result must hold or transfer the property to the order of the beneficiaries). The definition employed by the tax legislation derives from (but is not identical to) that found in the Settled Land Act 1925.

settlement 1. an instrument by which property is limited to persons in succession or is to vest on the occurrence of specified contingencies. Settlements in England or Scotland are invariably made through the medium of the trust. In English law it is not competent for a settlement, whether of realty or personalty, to be made otherwise. Technically, in other jurisdictions (e.g. Australia and New Zealand and, indeed, Scotland) it is possible to create a simple settlement without a trust but, in practice, such settlements are rarely, if ever, encountered.

In English law, settlements of land developed to a high degree of sophistication. In the 1925 reforms it was provided that land might be settled either by way of strict settlement or by way of trust for sale, but not otherwise.

2. in Scottish CONVEYANCING practice, the day when the title is exchanged for the money.

3. settlement in the sense of living in the UK gives a person a right to permanent residence in the UK provided he continues living here; such a person is subject to deportation if he commits a serious crime or if his presence is no longer conducive to the public good. Having a right of settlement may lead to the right to register or to be naturalised as a British citizen. Once settled, a person may call for members of his family and other dependants to join him in the UK provided their maintenance and accommodation does not require recourse to public funds.

severability the rule of construction of contracts that allows a court to ignore a part of a contract that would render it in some way defective and to read instead what is left. It has been applied to RESTRICTIVE COVENANTS where, if the words are capable of being so read, the court will ignore a severe restriction and allow a lesser restriction. It also applies in cases involving ROMALPA CLAUSES where certain words might render the clause wholly inoperative, the court can, again only if the words are capable of sustaining such a reading, allow the plaintiff some lesser power to trace the goods or their proceeds.

sex discrimination in the employment law of the UK, a body of rules designed to prevent and remedy discrimination on the basis of a person's sex. An *equality clause* is incorporated by law in every contract of employment by the Equal Pay Act 1970. It is even included in contracts for services. The equality clause has the effect in the contract of stating that men and women are employed on *like work* or employed on *work rated as equivalent*, the terms and conditions of employment will not be more favourable for one sex as against the other in any relevant respect.

Like work is work of a broadly similar nature. An employee may claim his or her work is of equal value and such a question may be remitted to an independent assessor. The value of the job on the employment market cannot determine matters, for the purpose of the legislation is to change the market: *Rainey* v. *Greater Glasgow Health Board*, 1987 SLT 146. A party can take the matter to an EMPLOYMENT TRIBUNAL or, if it is not reasonably to be expected that a person will raise the matter, the Secretary of State can lay the matter before a tribunal. A complainant must have been working for six months before the proceedings.

The Sex Discrimination Act 1972, 1986 along with Article 119 of the European Economic Community Treaty, provides a range of control over discrimination based on sex. *Direct discrimination*, treating a member of one sex better than another, is restrained but so too is *indirect discrimination* through some gender-based criterion. The Act also applies to protect married persons. An indirect case is that a criterion is set whereby the proportion of the people who can apply differs between the sexes: *Pearce* v. *City of Bradford* [1988] IRLR 379. Justification is possible. The Act controls discrimination in selection for employment and promotion within employment. A person's sex may be a genuine occupational qualification, as where a producer is casting the role of Desdemona. There are other exceptions, including national security. *Sexual harassment* has been described as a form of sex discrimination: *Porcelli* v. *SRC* [1986] ICR 564. An Equal Opportunities Commission has responsibility for monitoring the Act and can issue non-discrimination notices and support litigants by way of test cases.

The European law may subvert UK measures where they fail to meet European requirements.

Sex Offender Order by virtue of the Crime and Disorder Act 1998 the police can apply for a civil order against a person with a previous conviction for a sexual offence, ordering him to refrain from that conduct. Breach of that order becomes a criminal offence.

Sex Offenders Register a (UK) register of persons convicted of certain sexual offences kept under the authority of the Sex Offenders Act 1997. Depending on the length of sentence, the offender must keep the police advised of his whereabouts. For sentences of over 30 months, the offender is under a lifelong obligation. There are arguments being put forward to extend the Act to cover offences committed abroad and for pan-European cooperation in tracking certain offenders. It is not presently a public register, no doubt for fear of vigilante action.

shareholder see SHARES.

share premium the excess of the issue price of a share over its nominal value. A company's share premium account exists for certain defined purposes, namely: (i) to issue fully paid bonus shares; (ii) to write off preliminary expenses; (iii) to write off the expenses of, or any discount allowed on, any issue of shares or debentures; (iv) to provide for any premium payable on the redemption of debentures.

shares a stake in the ownership of a company. Shares may be ORDINARY SHARES or PREFERENCE SHARES. Ordinary shares confer an entitlement by way of dividend to those profits appropriated to the payment of a dividend after payment of dividend on preference shares. On a winding up, ordinary shareholders are entitled to what remains after payment of creditors and preference shareholders.

sharia see ISLAMIC LAW.

Shepherdise see CITATOR.

sheriff the shire reeve. In England, the sheriff is the chief officer of the county. The sheriff is the official to whom judgments of the High Court are sent for enforcement although in practice enforcement is carried out by the *under-sheriff*. In cases where the sheriff cannot act, writs are sent to the CORONER and then passed to the under-sheriff to act for the coroner. In Scotland, the sheriff is a judge who sits in the *sheriff court* with powers to deal with many civil actions, including many of unlimited value, and a criminal jurisdiction to sentence for up to three years if sitting with a jury.

Sherman Act a US statute that was the first to regulation competition there. It controls contracts, combinations and conspiracies in restraint of trade and agreements and the like designed to bring about monopolies in any part of commerce.

SI abbreviation for STATUTORY INSTRUMENT.

sic utere tuo ut alienum non laedas 'use your own property in such a way that it does not harm others.' See NUISANCE.

sidebar (USA) a discussion between the judge and the lawyers outwith the hearing of the jury in the court itself. In the UK, the love of form and ceremonial means that the jury have to trek out to the jury room from time to time – usually much to their bafflement as to what is going on when they are not there.

signature the name of a person written by himself, either in full or by the initials of the forename with the surname in full.

silk a name for the gown worn by Queen's (or King's) counsel (see BARRISTER), hence *to take silk,* to become such a counsel.

simplex commendatio non obligat 'a simple recommendation does not impose liability.' This old maxim hardly states the law today, particularly if the recommendation engenders reliance or shows an assumption of responsibility in respect of the matter.

simpliciter 'simply', without reservation.

sine die 'without day, indefinitely'.

Single European Act a foundation treaty in the law of the EUROPEAN COMMUNITIES. It became effective as at 1 July 1987 and provided for a timetable for the completion of the free market, an extension of the use of qualified majority voting and foreshadowed the existence of a treaty on ECONOMIC AND MONETARY UNION. It also made provision for inclusion in the Communities' treaties of sections dealing with the environment and economic and social cohesion. It also provided for the EUROPEAN COURT OF FIRST INSTANCE and formally recognised the PARLIAMENT and the COUNCIL OF THE EUROPEAN COMMUNITIES. See EUROPEAN UNION.

single member private limited companies see COMPANY.

sist in Scottish civil procedure, a suspension of proceedings.

skeleton defence in Scottish civil procedure, an informal name used for DEFENCES that simply deny everything without further elaboration. Sometimes such defences will be sufficient but on other occasions they may lack SPECIFICATION and have to be repelled, allowing the PURSUER to succeed.

SLAB abbreviation for Scottish Legal Aid Board. See LEGAL AID.

sleeping partner a partner who takes no active part in the administration of the firm. As far as liabilities of the firm are concerned, however, he is as much a partner and responsible as such just as much as if he took an equally active part in the administration of the PARTNERSHIP business as the partners who actually carry it on.

small claim in England the phrase is applied to cases decided under the arbitration procedure in the County Court which deals with cases involving up to £5,000 unless they involve personal injuries when the limit is £1,000.

In Scotland, an informal procedure for cases worth less than £750, introduced in 1988. In defended actions, no expenses are awarded against the unsuccessful party if the claim is for less than £200 and only £75 if more than that. However, there is no protection from expenses when cases are appealed. Pleadings are kept to a minimum and there is an early meeting with the sheriff to focus the key issues. The procedure is continually under review and revised rules are expected during 2001. It has had an unpleasant knock-on effect in that insurers are often now unwilling to reimburse solicitors' costs in negotiated settlements as they would not have had to do so had the case been taken by the party to court.

There are also small claims procedures in Ireland. In Northern Ireland a scheme was established in 1979 and can now deal with many claims for up to £1,000 (soon to be increased to £3,000), although not those involving personal injury or defamation. In the Republic of Ireland a scheme was started in 1992 that can deal with consumer claims for up to £500.

Social Chapter see EUROPEAN UNION.

Social Fund an instrument of the social policy of the EUROPEAN COMMUNITIES. The Social Fund assists in the task of promoting working conditions and aspirations towards an improved standard of living.

socius criminis 'an associate or accomplice in the crime', specially used when discussing a person who is not a co-accused.

sodomy the crime of having sex by insertion of the male member into the rectum of another person. It is a crime if committed by two men unless they are over 18 and acting in private. The 'private' requirement is being reviewed so as to protect a human right to indulge in homosexual group sex. See BUGGERY.

solatium in Scots law, the sum of money claimed by way of damages for pain and suffering in delictual claims. Similar sums can be recovered in contract if, but only if, one of the expectations engendered by the contract was a freedom from pain and suffering: *Jarvis* v. *Swan Tours Ltd* [1973] QB 233.

solicitor a legal practitioner in the UK. The positions and the rights, duties, obligations and privileges are now regulated by statute. The UK still has a distinction on the one hand between the ordinary lawyer who is a man of affairs and a generalist who (in England especially) does not essentially appear in courts, and on the other hand the BARRISTER or ADVOCATE. However, the distinction is becoming blurred with the creation of the SOLICITOR ADVOCATE. See LAW SOCIETY, LAW SOCIETY OF SCOTLAND.

solicitor advocate a SOLICITOR in England having rights of audience before the higher courts. The extension was authorised by the Courts and Criminal Evidence Act 1990. A solicitor in Scotland having the right of audience before any of the higher courts previously the exclusive domain of the ADVOCATE. The new role was made possible by the Law Reform (Miscellaneous Provisions) (Scotland) Act 1990.

Solicitors follow a course of study and attendance laid down by the LAW SOCIETY or the LAW SOCIETY OF SCOTLAND under rules for rights of audience. They do not wear wigs, and the working relationship with the Faculty of Advocates is ongoing. The new arrangements allow clients to obtain a full legal service at lower cost – paying for one lawyer instead of two or three. It allows a client to be sure that the lawyer he has instructed will see his case through. However, if the solicitor advocate is not isolated in his office, the responsibilities of running a business, carrying out the investigative phase and presenting the case with due detachment could prove to be most difficult.

Solicitor General law officer for England and Wales in the Westminster Parliament, deputy to the ATTORNEY GENERAL. There is a Solicitor General for Scotland who is junior to the LORD ADVOCATE. In the USA a law officer who assists an attorney general and the official who represents the federal government in court.

solus agreement a contract under which a party is bound to buy his supplies from a single source. See RESTRAINT OF TRADE.

sovereignty in UK CONSTITUTIONAL LAW, the doctrine that the monarch in PARLIAMENT is competent to make or unmake any law whatsoever and cannot be challenged in any court. The doctrine developed historically, its first major enunciation being in the BILL OF RIGHTS. Possible limitations are: (i) the ACTS OF UNION; (ii) the inability of Parliament to bind its successors; (iii) territorial competence, being a practical limitation rather than a legal one.

By far the most significant restraint is found in the law of the EUROPEAN UNION, which asserts its supremacy in matters subject to the Treaties. Enforcement of an Act of Parliament has been enjoined on the basis of conflict with European law: *Factortame Ltd* v. *Secretary of State for Transport* (No. 2) [1991] 1 All ER 70.

Speaker in the CONSTITUTIONAL LAW of the UK, an office as old, or older, than the 14th century, the main duty of which is to preside over the HOUSE OF COMMONS. Now, the Speaker of the House of Commons is elected by the Commons but on the nomination of the party leaders after wide consultation with ordinary members. It is a CONVENTION that the sovereign's consent is sought and given. The Speaker is usually re-elected in subsequent parliaments. The Speaker liaises with the Queen and between the Commons and the Lords. See LORD CHANCELLOR.

special damages see GENERAL DAMAGES.

special destination in Scots law, a clause in a deed other than a will that grants property but specifies to whom it should next transmit. It is a very technical area of law. In some cases the destination may be revoked or evacuated during life, but some factors, like a contractual link between the parties who took title, may make it impossible.

special relationship see NEGLIGENT MISSTATEMENTS.

specificatio in the law of Scotland, following Roman law, the doctrine whereby the creator of a new thing takes property in it if the materials are incapable of separation as a result of the creation. The painter owns the cloth on which he paints, contrary to the doctrine of ACCESSIO. A sculptor would not own the rock he sculpted unless this was considered a new species – a work of art instead of a rock. There is a personal claim by the owner against the creator for the price of the materials. The doctrine does not apply if the worker steals the materials.

specific goods GOODS identified and agreed on at the time a contract of sale is made are *ascertained goods*. *Unascertained goods* can become ascertained goods, which occurs when goods of the description and in a deliverable state are unconditionally appropriated to the contract, either by the seller with the consent of the buyer or the buyer with consent of the seller.

specific implement the primary remedy for breach of contract in Scotland, differing in this respect from England where it is damages. It is enforced by interdict for negative obligations and a decree *ad factum praestandum* for positive obligations, both of which orders, if not complied with, can result in imprisonment. However, it will be refused in a number of cases, including: (i) where the obligation is to pay a sum of money; (ii) contracts like service or partnership where the compelled performance would be useless; (iii) where performance is impossible; (iv) where the court cannot enforce the decree, as in the case of a person outwith the jurisdiction; (v) generic sales where there is no pretium affectionis, i.e. there is nothing special about the item or items sold. See also SPECIFIC PERFORMANCE.

specific issue order see SECTION 8 ORDER.

specific performance an equitable remedy for BREACH OF CONTRACT where damages are felt to be an inadequate remedy. It is available in respect of all contracts except positive contracts of a personal nature (e.g. to give a theatrical performance in a theatre). It is most often encountered in the context of contracts for the sale and purchase of land. In any action for a breach of contract to DELIVER SPECIFIC or ASCERTAINED GOODS, the court may, if it thinks fit, direct that the contract shall be performed specifically, without giving the defendant the option of retaining the goods on payment of damages. Further, it is expressly stated that the provisions of the section are supplementary to, and not in derogation of, the right of SPECIFIC IMPLEMENT in Scotland.

speculative fee see CONTINGENCY FEE.

Speluncean explorers' case a fictitious case written by a Harvard law professor to illustrate various arguments current in JURISPRUDENCE in a practical context. The facts of the case are that four men are trapped underground and in order to survive they have to eat one of their number. The original plan was to draw lots. The man whose idea it was ultimately changed his mind, rejecting chance. However, he became the ultimate meal. The fictitious case is the appeal on the conviction and death sentence of the three survivors. The judgments illustrate POSITIVISM, NATURAL LAW and LEGAL REALISM as well as illustrating the operation of the judicial process. See also NECESSITY.

spent see REHABILITATION OF OFFENDERS.

spes successionis an expectation of succeeding to property. It is not a title, but adventurous lenders may see it as a form of comfort. A person whose hope did not come to fruition because the testator's intentions were not legally effected by a negligent solicitor was compensated to the amount of the succession from the solicitor's insurers rather than the estate, which went to someone else: *Ross* v. *Caunters* [1980] 1 Ch. 297. See also *White* v. *Jones* [1995] 2 AC 507.

sponsiones ludicrae in the law of CONTRACT, promises relating to gaming. The courts consider them too trivial to be given legal effect: see *Lipkin Gorman* v. *Karpnale* [1991] 2 AC 548.

sports law the application of law to the practice of sport as well as the study of laws relating to sport. It is generally not considered to be a separate branch of legal science but conveniently describes a new area of activity. The best claim it has is that there is a developing international jurisprudence arising out of the activities of the COURT OF ARBITRATION FOR SPORT.

spousal support see ALIMONY.

spouse a party to a marriage; i.e. a husband or a wife.

spuilzie (pronounced 'spooly') **1.** the Scots word for the taking away of another's property.
2. in Scots law, a remedy that seeks RESTITUTION of property taken and violent profits being the most that could have been made with the thing.

STABEX see LOMÉ CONVENTION.

Staff of Government Division effectively the COURT OF APPEAL for the Isle of Man.

stale see CHEQUE, LACHES.

stamp duty a tax imposed on written instruments (e.g. conveyances). Stamp duties are either AD VALOREM, where the amount of duty payable varies according to the value of the transaction effected by the instrument, or fixed in amount, whatever the effected value. Where a stamp is essential to the legal validity of an instrument, that instrument cannot be used as evidence in civil proceedings unless the conditions required by the Stamp Act 1891 are met and the penalties set out there paid.

standard form contract a contract that is not specially set out for the transaction in question but is drawn up in advance and applied to numerous transactions. Such contracts are not defined in the UNFAIR CONTRACT TERMS Act 1977 but controlled by it. See *McCrone* v. *Boots Farm Sales* 1981 SLT 103; *Border Harvesters* v. *Edwards Engineering (Perth) Ltd* 1985 SLT 128. The concept is that one party is only willing to trade on a set of terms that have been thought out in advance and usually favour the party putting them forward. The other party is usually offered the terms on a 'take it or leave it' basis. A term that is not individually negotiated is more likely to be an unfair contract term by virtue of the Unfair Terms in Consumer Contract Regulations 1999.

standard of proof in criminal cases this denotes BEYOND REASONABLE DOUBT; in civil cases, the BALANCE OF PROBABILITIES.

standard security the only competent way to obtain a SECURITY over HERITABLE PROPERTY in Scotland or, more accurately, over an interest in land. Since 29 November 1970, as a result of the Conveyancing and Feudal Reform (Scotland) Act 1970, this has been the case. Two standard forms are provided – *Form A* has the Personal Bond as its first part, but *Form B* merely refers to some other source. Standard terms are included and those in relation to the power of sale and foreclosure cannot be varied although others can. Preliminary procedures to sale include calling up and notice of default. Apart from sale, the creditor can on default enter into possession and also has powers to effect repairs. For England, see MORTGAGE.

Star Chamber a tribunal abolished in 1641. It was effectively the king in council exercising criminal jurisdiction. It was inquisitorial, and torture is believed to have been used.

stare decisis 'let the decision stand'. The Anglo-American system of dealing with PRECEDENTS depends on a COURT's position in the hierarchy of courts. A court will be compelled to follow the previous decision where the decision is in *point*, i.e. where the facts are sufficiently similar to require the application of the same law, e.g. in England the Court of Appeal must follow the House of Lords, and the High Court, the Court of Appeal. The House of Lords, to allow some flexibility in 1966, allowed itself to depart from its own previous decisions. In recent years when such a step is contemplated a larger court is convened; see, for example, *Murphy* v. *Brentwood* [1990] 3 WLR 414. It is the RATIO DECIDENDI of the case that must be followed. The system is a good one, providing certainty and predictability, which is of value for the many thousands of cases that go nowhere near a court. Its main drawback is inflexibility.

state aids part of the COMPETITION POLICY of the EUROPEAN UNION that prohibits MEMBER STATES granting aid in such a way that it affects trade between member states. Member states must notify such aid, and it may be permitted as being in the general interest of the economy without distorting trade.

state for settlement in Scots CONVEYANCING practice, the account of charges, fees and outlays presented to the buyer showing how much must be paid. Once paid, it is receipted and at the same time the title deed is handed over.

state immunity the general principle that one state does not impose civil or criminal liability on another. Thus the head of state or former head of state of a country is normally free from prosecution in another country. However, where a crime is internationally recognised as such and is one which at the time did not fall within the function of a head of state, there may be no immunity: *R. V. Bow Street Magistrate, ex parte Pinochet Ugarte* (No. 3) [1999] TLR 222.

statement of affairs a debtor's statement in bankruptcy proceedings listing relevant information: see Insolvency Act 1986, Section 288.

States of Deliberation the legislative body for the Bailiwick of Guernsey.

States of Jersey the legislative body for the Bailiwick of Jersey.

statute an enactment of a legislative body expressed in a formal document.

Statute of Westminster 1. the Statute of Westminster 1931 distinguished dominions from colonies and legislation applicable to colonies. Dominions were permitted to pass extraterritorial legislation and no UK legislation was to extend to the dominions unless expressly stated to be by dominion consent. The statute has featured in the development of the CONSTITUTIONS of Canada, Australia, New Zealand.

2. the Statute of Westminster 1275 was the foundation of the English law of LIMITATION OF ACTIONS.

An important Act in the constitutional law of the UK but also in many other states' constitutions. Britain's empire changed its nature in the latter part of the 19th century into the first half of the 20th century. Granting of dominion status to Canada was the start, and the British North America Act 1867 was replicated in relation to Australia, New Zealand, Newfoundland, the Irish Free State and South Africa. The Balfour Declaration of 1926 referred to freely associated nations within a British Commonwealth of Nations of equal status. Common Crown allegiance was the unifying factor.

statutory prescribed, authorised or recognised by a STATUTE.

statutory authority in the law of TORT or DELICT, a defence to a claim that the defendant is acting under statutory authority. It is a defence even to NUISANCE, which is seen in England as a form of STRICT LIABILITY. If, however, an act could be carried out under statutory authority without creating a nuisance as well as by creating a nuisance, the plea will be unsuccessful if the nuisance-avoiding method is not taken.

statutory company a company formed under a private Act of Parliament.

statutory instrument a form of delegated legislation regulated by the Statutory Instruments Act 1946. They are cited by the year they are passed and by their number in the year. Non-publication is a defence. They are often accompanied by a useful but unofficial explanatory note.

statutory interpretation a generic title for the practice of reading statutes. Certain rules have grown up both in interpretation generally and for statutes in particular. A major aid in the Interpretation Act 1989, which lists a number of deemed interpretations. See EIUSDEM GENERIS, EXPRESSIO UNIUS, GOLDEN RULE, LITERAL RULE, MISCHIEF RULE, NUSCITUR A SOCIIS.

stay of action the putting to an end of proceedings in an action by a summary order of the court.

stay of execution an order that operates to prevent the judgment creditor from putting in operation the legal process of execution; it does not affect rights acquired independently of the process stayed. Unlike the position with regard to STAY OF PROCEEDINGS, the court has no inherent power to order a stay of execution of a judgment or order requiring the payment of money, which goes to the question of enforceability of the judgment rather than its validity or correctness.

stay of proceedings a court order suspending proceedings or sanctioning a total discontinuance where an action has been compromised or because of some other misconduct by the plaintiff.

stillicide in Scots property law, the urban SERVITUDE that allows a proprietor of grounds, otherwise contrary to the law, to build so as to throw rainwater falling on his own land on to his neighbour.

stipendiary magistrate see MAGISTRATE.

stipulatio in ROMAN LAW, the formal contract whereby a party was bound absolutely by using the special words. One party would say 'spondesne transfer your copy of Aristotle for 20 sesterces', and the other would say 'spondeo'. It mattered not in the early law that the party asking the question was applying force or intimidation to the promissor. As the law developed, the prestations became ever more subtle and the defence became wider and consensual contracts based upon the will of the parties took over.

stipulation an agreement or a term in an agreement.

stock 1. borrowing (usually other than short-term) by government or local authorities. In the case of corporate borrowing, the term *loan stock* is commonly used.

2. shares in a company that have been converted into a single holding with a nominal value equal to that of the total of the shares; accordingly, after conversion a shareholder formerly holding a thousand shares of £1 each will have a holding of £1,000 stock.

stock exchange an investment exchange where company and other securities are bought and sold. In particular in the UK the London Stock Exchange. See YELLOW BOOK.

stop notice 1. a remedy available to a person claiming to be beneficially entitled to securities enabling him to be notified of any proposed transfer of those securities.

2. an order preventing development issued by a planning authority: Town and Country Planning Act 1990.

stoppage in transit stopping goods in the course of their delivery at a distance. When the buyer of goods becomes insolvent, an UNPAID SELLER who has parted with the possession of the goods has the right of stopping them in transit, that is to say, he may resume possession of the goods as long as they are in the course of transit and may retain them until payment or tender of the price. By stopping the goods in the course of their transit, the seller puts the CARRIER under an obligation to redeliver the goods to him and thereby re-acquires the right of possession of the goods. The exercise of the right of stoppage in transit does not in itself terminate the contract of sale; it merely prevents the buyer from obtaining possession of the goods and puts the seller in a position in which he can effectively exercise his statutory power of RESALE. Goods are deemed to be in the course of transit from the time when they are delivered to a carrier or other BAILEE or custodier for the purpose of transmission to the buyer until the buyer or his agent in that behalf takes delivery of them from the carrier or other bailee or custodier.

If the goods are subject to REJECTION by the buyer and the carrier or other bailee or custodier continues in possession of them, the transit is not deemed to be at an end, even if the seller has refused to receive them back.

Stormont see IRISH LAW.

street trading the selling, or exposing for sale, of articles on certain streets. It is an offence in both England and Scotland although under different legislation. A pedlar holding a certificate is exempted provided he is behaving as a pedlar and not as a street trader.

strict liability 1. in TORT and DELICT, liability without proof of fault, i.e. that the mere happening of a proscribed event incurs liability but always subject to certain defence. The defence recognised in common law cases are: (i) act of the Queen's enemies; (ii) ACT OF GOD, or in Scotland *damnum fatale*; (iii) the intervention of a third party.

English law has historically supported many instances of strict liability, as did (and still, to an extent, does) Scots law. Some UK legislation imposes forms of strict liability that sometimes, because of the absence of defence, goes as far as to be appropriately described as ABSOLUTE LIABILITY. In English law the main instances are liability for NUISANCE, non-natural user of land under the doctrine established in *Rylands* v. *Fletcher*, the escape of fire and, at common law, for wild animals (FERAE NATURAE). In Scotland it has recently been established that neither nuisance nor non-natural user are instances of strict liability but are instead governed by the concept of FAULT, with the exception, until the matter comes up for decision, of the diversion of the course of a natural stream: *RHM Bakeries* v. *SRC* 1985 SLT 214. Liability is still strict in matters covered by the Praetorian edict in respect of innkeepers, carriers and stable-keepers, although both in Scotland and in England the hotel proprietor, as defined, is given some exemptions from the rigours of strict liability, as indeed is the carrier. The UK has two main schemes of strict liability – for ANIMALS and for DEFECTIVE PRODUCTS. There are three others, less commonly invoked:

(1) in respect of nuclear occurrences under the Nuclear Installations Act 1965;

(2) oil pollution under the Merchant Shipping (Oil Pollution) Act 1971;

(3) regular pollution under the Control of Pollution Act 1974.

2. in CONTRACT. Generally, liability in contract is to perform to the letter of the contract, so liability is often said to be strict. However, the parties may expressly or by implication have agreed that, for example, only reasonable care ought to be exercised. The doctrine of FRUSTRATION operates to free a party in certain cases from the obligation.

3. in criminal law, strict liability is an exception to the general rule of liability, which usually demands that it is essential to show MENS REA. However, many statutory crimes and offences do not require this, particularly those under the Road Traffic Acts. Again, some of these offences in the absence of defence or provisions amount to absolute liability.

striking out the treating by the court as deleted any pleading or part thereof that discloses no ground of claim or defence or that is frivolous or scandalous.

sua sponte 'of its own accord', where the court does something without a motion from any of the parties. See EX PROPRIA MOTU.

subcontract the CONTRACT between a party and a main contractor who himself is contracted to another, often called the employer, albeit the contract is not one of employment in the contemporary colloquial sense. Subcontracts are very commonly found in building contracts. The employer contracts with the main contractor, who himself contracts for work to be done, like windows or floors, by others who can do so better or cheaper. A subcontractor may be nominated by the employer. There are effectively and legally only two contracts, the subcontractor not being contractually bound to the employer. Standard forms govern many of the relationships between the parties. In one case it was held that a subcontractor could be held liable to an employer in tort or delict where the relationship was proximate, indeed, very like contract: *Junior Books* v. *The Veitchi Company* 1982 SLT 492, a decision that although doubted has not been overruled and has been followed elsewhere in the Commonwealth. In the case of CARRIAGE BY AIR, the provisions of the Warsaw Convention are extended to situations where the carrier has subcontracted business to another carrier to perform the whole or part of a carriage so that the goods are being carried by a carrier who has no direct contractual relationship with the owner.

subinfeudation the process whereby a freehold estate was created out of another freehold estate to be held by the grantee of the grantor in return for specified services or amounts of produce or money. The grant created a tenurial relationship between the parties. Subinfeudations (except those made by the Crown) were forbidden by the statute QUIA EMPTORES 1290.

sub judice 'under judicial consideration'. The Contempt of Court Act 1981 controls publication of such matters.

subordinate legislation see DELEGATED LEGISLATION.

subornation procuring a person to commit an offence, the most common being subornation of PERJURY.

subpoena a term no longer in use in England and Wales for an order to a person to appear in court on a certain day to give evidence or produce a document.

sub rosa 'under the rose'; confidential.

subsequente copula in Scots family law, a form of IRREGULAR MARRIAGE that took place as at the date of sexual intercourse if a promise to marry had been made fore it and the act took place on the faith of it. Clearly, this helped avoid the stigma of children being ILLEGITIMATE.

subscription 'writing below'. This usually means a signature. The sovereign writes her name at the top.

subsidiarity the idea that functions that can be exercised at a lower level of organisation should be rather than being taken over by a higher level organisation. The idea appears within the Roman Catholic Church in the encyclicals *Rerum Novarum* (1891) and the *Quadragesimo Anno* (1931). Its present importance, however, is as a new principle within the legal system of the EUROPEAN UNION. The Treaty on European Union embodies the concept in various places, most notably in the Preamble, where the parties intend to create an ever closer union in which decisions are taken as closely as possible to the citizen in accordance with the principle of subsidiarity. It has been described as the Euro-concept that all can admire by giving it the meaning they want. It has been questioned whether, save in the narrow area of cooperation on justice and home affairs, the concept is sufficiently 'legal' to be subject of decisions by the courts. Rather, it may be a political directive or at most an aid to interpretation. The applicability of the doctrine is made more difficult by the fact that the precise role of the European Union is not specifically defined, and it acquires and has acquired functions over time. Finally, if the superior body is to exercise a function it should be proportionate – appropriate to the scale of the problem addressed.

subsidiary a company is a subsidiary of another company if the second company (the *parent*) owns more than 50 per cent of the ordinary share capital of the first company or otherwise has voting control over it.

succession following another, used in relation to the taking over of a body corporate including the Crown. Succession to the Crown is governed by law but can be upset by ABDICATION. Technically, the area of law regulating the passing of property from a deceased person. See INTESTACY, TESTATE.

sufficiency the question in the law of evidence as to whether a party has produced enough evidence that supports his case. In criminal cases in England and in Scotland, a failure to produce a sufficiency can result in a case being dismissed on a plea of NO CASE TO ANSWER. See CORROBORATION.

suicide a killing of the self, a *felo de se*, and not a crime in England since the Suicide Act 1961. Aiding and abetting a suicide is an offence under the Act. It is a possible verdict in an inquest where it be established beyond a reasonable doubt. It is not a crime in Scotland.

sui generis 'of its own kind'.

sui juris 'subject to his own law', an independent legal person.

summary short and free from the complexities and delays of a full trial.

summary cause a form of small debt action in Scotland. It replaced the small debt action and predates the SMALL CLAIM with which it overlaps. It was intended to be useful for laymen but is more like a stripped-down ordinary action convenient for debt collection. The rules have been interpreted rather strictly even in relation to points of pleadings, and it might be asked whether there is any real need for this intermediate tier of procedure. As from some time in 2001 it is likely that it may be used only in cases under £5,000.

summary diligence in Scots law, a procedure whereby certain constituted obligations can be enforced without the need to apply to a court. To be able to exercise this right it is necessary that the deed contains a clause containing the debtor's comments to registration for execution. Once registered, the debt can be enforced in much the same way as a court decree.

summary judgment a judgment in a SUMMARY CAUSE.

summary trial in CRIMINAL PROCEDURE, a trial without a jury decided upon both on the facts and the law by a judge who may be legally qualified or may be a magistrate (who has legal advice if required). Maximum sentences are usually lower than cases prosecuted on INDICTMENT. A summary trial, depending on the jurisdiction, usually involves a swifter procedure and a lessening of the procedural requirements associated with serious cases. Thus, it is unlikely that the requirements of notice and lodging of documents will be so strict and the presence of shorthand writers is unlikely to be a requirement or indeed an option. In England an offence that may be charged whither on indictment or in a summary court.

summing up the last part of a speech or the judge's statement of a case to the jurors before they retire to consider their verdict.

superior in feudal law, the person from whom a person lower in the feudal chain holds his land.

supranational greater than a state. More specially, a supranational organisation is different from a superstate or a federation. While it is bigger than a nation, the supranational organisation is limited in the functions for which it is responsible. Its first legal appearance was in the EUROPEAN COAL AND STEEL COMMUNITY (ECSC) Treaty in which the high authority of that Community, the precursor of the COMMISSION. The treaty obliged the members to refrain from action incompatible with the supranational character of their duties. The MEMBER STATES were enjoined to respect this supranational character.

supremacy see EUROPEAN COMMUNITY LAW.

supremacy clause the part of the sixth Article of the Constitution of the USA that provides that federal law is superior to state law. See CONSTITUTIONAL LAW.

Supreme Court 1. the highest federal court in the USA. It comprises nine justices appointed by the President with the two-thirds majority consent of Senate. The court deals with federal law mainly on appeal but also at first instance. It was Chief Justice Marshall in *Marbury* v. *Madison* 1 Cranch 137 (1803) who arrogated to the court the power to strike down federal law as well as state laws. Its superiority even to the President has emerged from *Youngstoun*

Sheet & Tube Co. v. *Sawyer* 343 US 579 (1952) and *United States* v. *Nixon* 418 US 683 (1974).

2. Supreme Court of Judicature is the Court of Appeal and the High Court.

3. in Scotland the Court of Session, which is subject to an appeal to the House of Lords and comprises a first instance Outer House and appellate Inner House, is sometimes described as the supreme court.

4. in Ireland, the court of final appeal, created by Article 34 of the constitution, consisting of a Chief Justice and other judges of whom five must sit on constitutional cases and three on others. It deals with appeals from the High Court on civil matters and from the Central Criminal Court as well as giving its opinion on the constitutionality of legislation passed by the OIREACHTAS when the President so requests.

surety a guarantor of another's obligation.

surrender 1. to give up a right.

2. the bringing to an end of a lease by the tenant's giving up his interest to his landlord. Surrender may be express or implied; *express surrender* should be effected by deed whereas *implied surrender* can be gleaned from the behaviour of the parties indicating that they both regard the lease as at an end.

surrogacy the role of a woman who is paid to bear a child by a married couple unable to have children themselves. The Surrogacy Arrangements Act 1985 prohibits commercial agencies from engaging women to act as surrogate mothers.

suspended sentence a sentence of imprisonment that is not put into effect but held over the convicted person on condition he behaves. If he does not, the sentence takes effect. For Scotland, see DEFERRED SENTENCE.

symbolic delivery see DELIVERY.

synallagmatic contract a bilateral contract creating reciprocal obligations. Sale is an example.

SYSMIN see LOMÉ CONVENTION.

Table A see ARTICLES OF ASSOCIATION.

tack in Scots property law, another word for LEASE.

Taft-Hartley Act a US statute (the Labor Management Relations Act) in the field of labour law that deals with unfair union practices like the secondary boycott. States were permitted to prohibit the closed shop by right-to-work legislation. If strikes affect national health or security, a court can order a cooling-off period of 80 days.

tailzie see ENTAIL.

takeover bid an offer made by one company to the shareholders of another company to acquire sufficient shares in that other company to give it control. See MERGER.

talaq in ISLAMIC LAW, the repudiation of a wife by her husband, achieved by a triple declaration: *Fatima* v. *Home Secretary* [1986] AC 527.

Talmud the ancient law of the Jews, originally oral but later written down. It is now codified and is influential in dispute resolution among Jews. See DIN TORAH; BETH DIN.

Tanaiste under the constitution of the Republic of Ireland, the deputy prime minister who acts for the TAOISEACH during his absence, permanent incapacity or on his death.

tantum et tale 'to the same extent and of the same kind'.

Taoiseach in the Republic of Ireland, the prime minister and head of government appointed by the President on the nomination of DAIL EIREANN.

tax a levy made by national or local government to pay for services provided by public bodies. There is no inherent power in the Crown to raise money in this way; express provision must be made by statute. Changes to tax law are made annually in the Finance Act(s); periodically the law is consolidated, as for example in the Income and Corporation Taxes Act 1988 or the Taxation of Chargeable Gains Act 1992. See TAXATION.

taxable income see TOTAL INCOME.

taxation 1. tax

2. the process of checking a lawyer's bill by an independent accountant.

tax avoidance legally reducing tax liability. Tax planning is the activity by which a taxpayer seeks to arrange his affairs so that his tax liability is minimised; avoidance of tax within the limits of tax law is perfectly legitimate; *tax evasion* is the illegal activity of seeking not to pay tax (e.g. by failing to declare income).

Taxes Management Act 1970 the statute that makes provision for the administrative and judicial machinery required for the effective collection of taxes. See, for example, *Hitch and Others* v. *Stone (Inspector)* [1999] TLR 276.

tax evasion see TAX AVOIDANCE.

Teachta Dala (TD) a member of DAIL EIREANN, the lower house of the Irish parliament.

tenant one who holds land under a LEASE or tenancy agreement.

tenant for life a person entitled under a TRUST to the use of or income from property for the duration of his life.

tender an offer. In Scotland, a *judicial tender* is an offer to settle a court action.

tenement 1. property held on tenure.
2. a multi-storeyed building in Scotland.

tenure the holding or occupying of property, especially realty, in return for services rendered, etc. See, for example FEUDAL SYSTEM.

terce in Scotland, an obsolete term for a one-third LIFE RENT in her husband's property given to a wife.

territorial sea see HIGH SEAS.

test case see CLASS ACTION.

testamentum militare see PRIVILEGED WILL.

testate having made a WILL. See INTESTACY.

testator the person who makes a WILL.

testatum that part of a deed that introduces the operative part, usually with the words 'Now this deed witnesseth.'

testimony a statement of a WITNESS in court, usually on oath, offered as evidence of the truth of what is alleged.

testing clause in Scotland, the clause in which the names of the witnesses, their designations and date of execution are recorded.

theft in English law, now defined in statutory terms by the Theft Act 1968 as the dishonest appropriation of property belonging to another with the intention of permanently depriving the other of it. The law has however been complicated by semantic arguments, leading the Court of Appeal to say that the law is in urgent need of reform to make cases understandable to juries: *R* v. *Hallam*; *R* v.

Blackburn [1994] TLR 306. Wheel-clamping is not theft in England (contrary to the position in Scotland) because there is not the intention to permanently deprive: *Arthur and Another* v. *Anker* [1995] TLR 632.

In Scots criminal law, the felonious taking or appropriation of the property of another without his consent and (in most cases) with the intention to deprive him of it permanently. The felonious taking is sometimes known as *amotio*. It has been held that temporary deprivation is sufficient in some cases. A nefarious purpose in the taking may be enough. Wheel-clamping has been held to be theft, even although the vehicle is not moved by the clamper: *Black* v. *Carmichael* 1992 SLT 897.

third party a party who is a stranger to a transaction or proceeding between two other persons.

third party beneficiary contract in US law a contract that allows a party to whom the parties in a main contract intend to receive a benefit to enforce a duty created by the main contract, irrespective of an issue of CONSIDERATION: *Lawrence* v. *Fox* 20 NY 268 (1859).

English law has only recently adopted a similar position. See JUS QUAESITUM TERTIO, PRIVITY.

third reading see ACT OF PARLIAMENT.

threshold price see COMMON AGRICULTURAL POLICY.

ticket cases a convenient name given to cases that relate to the effect of writing on tickets, such as those given by railway companies, deck-chair attendants or parking companies. The cases arise from a reluctance of courts to enforce the letter of contracts where the party issuing the ticket is escaping liability on the basis of a term included on a ticket. In theory, the ticket is treated as an OFFER and it is up to the customer to reject it. These cases arose before the UK Parliament intervened to pass the UNFAIR CONTRACT TERMS Act 1977. The limitation clause must be contained in a document having contractual effect. *Parker* v. *SE Rly Co.* (1877) 2 CPD 416; *Chapelton* v. *Barry Urban District Council* [1940] 1 All ER 356; *McCutcheon* v. *David MacBrayne Ltd* 1964 SC (HL) 28. The ticket cannot include conditions if the contract has already been formed. *Olley* v. *Marlborough Court Ltd* [1949] 1 KB 532, *Thornton* v. *Shoe Lane Parking Ltd* [1971] 1 All ER 686.

time immemorial 1189. See ACQUISITIVE PRESCRIPTION.

time off an employee is entitled to time off for public service, jury service, to carry out duties as safety officer and during pregnancy.

timeshare consecutive sharing of accommodation with concurrent ownership. An agreement by which a person pays a capital sum to the promoter of a timeshare resort and in consequence acquires a right to use accommodation and facilities in that resort for a defined period each year for a defined number of years. They can be bought and sold and inherited. Some may be swapped on informal exchanges, allowing the 'investment' to be used as a right to obtain a different holiday. This fine business idea for a 'product' for the leisure industry has been successful. There have been many difficulties because the concept is not one recognised in the law in its own right – it is an amalgam of legal rights and duties. There have been many complaints from purchasers throughout all of Europe. The UK passed the Timeshare Act 1992 to allow people a cooling-off period of 14 days to prevent them being pressured into purchase when on holiday. As the problem is international, the European Union acted by promulgating a DIRECTIVE on the topic (given effect in the UK by amendment of the 1992 Act) – it affects any contract or group of contracts concluded for at least three years under which directly or indirectly, for payment or a certain price, a real property right or other right relating to the use of the property for a specified period of the year, which may not be less than one week, is established or is the subject of a transfer or an undertaking to transfer. Try as one might, it is difficult to see the benefit for the purchaser. Perhaps the main one is cost when compared to the full cost incurred in taking families on package holidays – the timeshare, depending on annual charges, can appear cheaper. If there is a resale market, the economics appear even more favourable. However, like all markets, the value of a timeshare can go down as well as up.

title in general terms a title to an asset relates both to a person's right to enjoyment of that asset and the means by which that right has accrued and by which it is evidenced. Thus, for example, a stock or share certificate is evidence of the right of the person named therein to ownership of the specified amount of stock or shares. In relation to land, titles may be either REGISTERED or UNREGISTERED. The Land Registration Act 1925 provides for four types of registered title, each backed up by a state guarantee; the different types of title correspond to the extent of that guarantee. These are an *absolute title*, a *good leasehold title*, a *possessory title* and a *qualified title*. Registration with an absolute freehold or leasehold title confers a full guarantee against claims arising before or after first registration; registration with a good leasehold guarantees that the lease is valid but does not guarantee that the freehold or other superior interest out of which the grant was made is valid; registration with a qualified title guarantees against all claims except those deriving from a specified instrument or specified circumstances.

In the case of land subject to the Land Registration Acts, a proprietor's title is constituted by the entry of his name on the register; the LAND CERTIFICATE that is issued constitutes evidence of that title.

In the case of land not subject to the Land Registration Acts (see UNREGISTERED TITLE), title is shown by tracing transactions affecting the land from deeds that constitute a *good root of title*, ending with the deeds transferring the land to the current owner. The deeds relating to each of these transactions are referred to as *links* in what is known as the *chain of title*; the last link, obviously, is the conveyance to the current owner. For a deed to qualify as a good root, it must:

(1) deal with the whole legal and beneficial interest in the land;

(2) cast no doubt on the validity of the title;

(3) relate to a transaction for valuable consideration; and

(4) relate to a transaction effected at least 15 years before the date of the transaction sought to be effected.

In relation to GOODS, an inaccurate summary of the detailed legal rule that follows would be to say that a seller or supplier in relation to other suppliers of goods promises the buyer that the buyer will be the owner of the goods and be able to enjoy the fruits of that ownership. In a CONTRACT of sale of goods other than one in which there appears from the contract or is to be inferred from its circumstances an intention that the seller should transfer only such title as he or a third person may have, there is an IMPLIED CONDITION on the part of the seller that in the case of a sale he has a right to sell the goods and in the case of an agreement to sell he will have such a right at the time the property is to pass. There is also an implied warranty that:

(1) the goods are free, and will remain free until the time when the property is to pass, from any charge or encumbrance not disclosed or known to the buyer before the contract is made, and

(2) the buyer will enjoy quiet possession of the goods except so far as it may be disturbed by the owner or other person entitled to the

benefit of any charge or encumbrance so disclosed or known.

In a contract where it appears from the contract or is to be inferred from its circumstances that there is an intention that the seller should transfer only such title as a third person may have, there is an implied WARRANTY that all charges or encumbrances known to the seller have been disclosed to the buyer before the contract is made. In such a contract there is also an implied warranty that none of the following will disturb the buyer's quiet possession of the goods, namely: (a) the seller; (b) in a case where the parties to the contract intend that the seller should transfer only such title as a third person may have, that person; (c) anyone claiming through the seller or that third person otherwise than under a charge or encumbrance disclosed or known buyer before the contract is made (see *Rowland* v. *Divall* [1923] All ER 270; *Niblett* v. *Confectioners Materials* [1921] All ER 459).

title financing a form of lending over goods. One of the defects of the law governing the creation of security rights over goods and chattels is the requirement that for the security to be validly constituted, either the cumbersome registration procedures must be complied with or, alternatively, possession of the goods and chattels must be transferred to the lender. To overcome the inconveniences associated with these rules, techniques were devised to develop alternative transaction forms that in commercial substance were very similar to the conferring of security in return for a loan but that in law were treated differently; these transaction forms have become known generically as 'title financing'. These forms exploit the dichotomy between vendor (or lessor) credit and lender credit and involve the retention of title to the goods or chattels by the vendor or financier with possession being granted to the debtor. The principal transactions in which these techniques are used (and which achieve a similar commercial result to that achieved by a mortgage) are leasing, sale and leaseback, sale and repurchase, factoring and TITLE RETENTION.

title retention the holding of title by a seller after possession has been given to the buyer. In the law of sale, property on goods and chattels passes on delivery and, in the absence of specific terms in the contract to the contrary, does so even where the purchase price has not been paid or has not been paid in full. Title retention is intended to secure the vendor's position (especially against the possibility of the purchaser's creating mortgages or charges over the goods that would take priority over the rights of the unpaid vendor) by postponing the moment when property passes to the purchaser until such time as the purchaser's outstanding debt to the vendor has been paid off. In modern law there are two principal title retention techniques: HIRE-PURCHASE and CONDITIONAL SALE, and ROMALPA CLAUSES.

tontine a scheme for raising money by which the lenders receive an annuity for life that increases as the other investors die until the last survivor receives the total of all the annuities.

top order a remedy available to a mortgagee or chargee prohibiting the sale or transfer by the mortgagor of the mortgaged property or the income therefrom.

Torrens system a system of LAND REGISTRATION adopted in Australia by Sir Robert Torrens, the prime minister in 1858, and modelled on the Shipping Acts. Canada began operating a similar system in 1860 and England in 1875 with the Land Transfer Act. Scotland began a gradual change over to a land registration system by the Land Registration (Scotland) Act 1979.

tort tortious liability arises from the breach of a duty fixed by law; this duty is towards persons generally and its breach is redressable by an action for unliquidated damages (Winfield). It is part of the English law of obligations along with CONTRACT and RESTITUTION. See also ANIMALS, CONVERSION, DUTY, ECONOMIC LOSS, ECONOMIC TORTS, EMPLOYERS' LIABILITY, FAULT, NEGLIGENCE, NUISANCE, OCCUPIERS' LIABILITY, PRODUCT LIABILITY, STRICT LIABILITY, TRESPASS, TROVER.

tortfeasor one who commits a TORT.

Total Allowable Catch (TAC) see FISHERIES POLICY.

total income the aggregate of a taxpayer's income from all sources calculated in accordance with the provisions of the Income and Corporation Taxes Acts. From this figure must be deducted certain sums (e.g. loss relief, interest relief ranking as a charge on income, capital allowances) to obtain the taxpayer's taxable income.

totting up in road traffic law, the scheme whereby courts endorse points on the driving licences of offenders; if offenders accumulate 12 points in three years they become liable to be disqualified for at least six months unless there are mitigating circumstances or special reasons for not endorsing or disqualifying. Hardship is not sufficient unless it is exceptional, so the loss of a job is seldom considered to be exceptional as it is the very kind of thing that happens. However, hardship to others may be enough to give the court a discretion.

trade and adventure in the nature of a trade profits from trade are the subject matter of taxation under Case I of SCHEDULE D. It has been variously described by judges although no universally accepted definition has been produced. Essentially, 'trading' connotes operations of a commercial character involving the provision to customers of goods or services for reward; an adventure in the nature of a trade connotes a single such operation.

trade description an indication, direct or indirect and by whatever means, given of a range of matters relating to goods, such as their quality, size, fitness for purpose, and history. Such have been controlled for some time but most notably by the Trade Descriptions Act 1968 (as amended by the Consumer Protection Act 1987). *False trade description*, making one that is false to a material degree, constitutes an offence. A *misleading trade description* is deemed to be a false trade description. It is defence to show that the commission of the defence was due to another person and that all reasonable precautions were taken to prevent the offence. The Act protects consumers by utilising the criminal law in support of the civil law.

trade dispute see GOLDEN FORMULAE.

trademark a particular name or design used to identify a particular product. Registration of such a name or design as a trademark has the consequence that it cannot be used by other manufacturers in respect of their own products.

trade union an organisation (whether permanent or temporary) that consists wholly or mainly of workers all in an organisation whose principal purposes include the regulation of relations between workers and employers. It is not to be treated as a body corporate but it may sue or be sued in its own name. Special rights and privileges accrue to a union that is certified as independent by the Certification Officer, who must also maintain a list of unions. The main legal benefit a union has over other bodies is the immunity that it and its members and official have against many tort actions. However, aside from the GOLDEN FORMULAE, which must be satisfied, recent restrictions require action that is sought to be immune to be founded upon open and fair balloting of members.

traditio in ROMAN LAW (and in such areas of Scots law as are not affected by the Sale of Goods Act), the conveyance of moveable property by handing it over.

traditionibus non nudis pactis dominium transferuntur 'delivery, not a simple agreement, transfers ownership'. This is the basic rule of the civilian systems, but it no longer applies in Scotland to goods where the Sale of Goods Act 1893 allowed property to pass by agreement. In relation to non-'goods', mainly land, the common law rule applies.

transfer to make over to another rights in or interests over property; sometimes the term is used as a noun to denote the instrument by which this is effected.

transfer of shares the conveyance of a member's share(s) to another person. Shares are transferable in such manner as may be prescribed in the articles. The transfer is achieved by the execution of a transfer form by the transferor and its being lodged, together with the share certificate, with the registrar of the company so that the entry in the company's register of shareholders can be amended. Actual transfer of the legal title to the shares is effected when the charge is made in the company's register.

transfer of value a disposition made by a person (the transferor) as a result of which the value of his estate immediately after the disposition is less than it would be but for the disposition, and the amount by which it is less is the value transferred. This definition is for inheritance tax purposes where tax is charged on the loss to an estate resulting from a transfer of value. The definition is found in the Inheritance Tax Act 1984.

The value transferred is usually the value of the property transferred, but this is not always so; for example, where A owned 51 per cent of the shares in a company and gave away 5 per cent, the loss to his estate would be greater (because of the consequent loss of control of the company) than the value of the 5 per cent transferred.

transport policy one of the foundations of the EUROPEAN COMMUNITIES to provide a uniform system of transport by road, rail and waterway to prevent distortion of the market. Progress was slow until PARLIAMENT raised action against the COUNCIL OF THE EUROPEAN COMMUNITIES: *Parliament v. Council* [1985] ECR 1513. The Council was held to be in breach of its obligation.

travaux preparatoires see STATUTORY INTERPRETATION.

traverse the formal denial of a fact alleged in the opposite party's pleading.

treason a breach of the allegiance owed to the Crown. It cannot be committed unless the person concerned is a child of a British father or is under the protection of the Crown as by having a British passport. Naturalisation as a citizen of another state is not sufficient to elide liability. The location of the traitor is not relevant as where Lord Haw Haw broadcast demoralising propaganda from Germany to the UK: *R* v. *Casement* [1917] 1 KB 98. A wider offence of treachery under the Treachery Act 1940 applied for the Second World War and a good time thereafter. By the Treason Act 1708 the English law was applied to Scotland.

treason-felony ancient crimes that could be applied to acts, deeds, writing or speaking that have as their aim the deposition of the sovereign, levying war or intimidating parliament.

treasure in Scotland, treasure found hidden in the ground belongs to the Crown and not to the finder nor the owner of the land. See TREASURE TROVE.

treasure trove in England, valuables found hidden without anyone knowing to whom they belong, belong to the Crown. See TREASURE.

Treasury the government department responsible for the administration of the nation's finances. Certain transaction (e.g. especially those involving non-resident companies controlled by UK residents) require Treasury consent before they can be lawfully effected.

treaty an agreement. The word is usually used of an agreement between states in international law but also used of in the phrase *private treaty* in the sale of property between individuals.

trespass in relation to property, a tort of wrongful interference. *Trespass de bonis asportatis* was the earliest form and consisted in removing or damaging the goods. It is essentially a wrong against possession – it was not necessary that the defendant should have appropriated the goods. The remedy was not accordingly available where the plaintiff had voluntarily given possession of his goods to the defendant. *Trespass to goods* remains and consists in any wrongful interference with them, e.g. removing a car from a garage (*Wilson* v. *Lombank Ltd* [1963] 1 WLR 1294), killing an animal (*Sheldrick* v. *Abery* (1793) 1 Esp. 55) or has been held recently, wheel-clamping a motor car (*Vine* v. *Waltham Forest CBC* [2000] TCR 288). The rise of negligence has caused it to be doubted whether, at least in unintentional cases, there is any need to prove damage (*Letang* v. *Cooper* [1965] 1 QB 232), and, because it has been held that in cases of unintentional *trespass to the person*, negligence must be proved, it might well be the case that the same will be held to apply in relation to trespass to goods: see *Fowler* v. *Lanning* [1959] 1 QB 426. However, if the act is intentional towards the goods, then that is sufficient even if the defendant is mistaken. The plaintiff must be in possession at the time of the alleged interference.

In relation to the person, it is the tort of touching another person's body or invading his land. In Scotland it is not recognised in any form other than in discussion of temporary intrusion on heritage and even then in a non-technical sense. It is not, in Scotland, a ground of action unless damage is done, although it may be restrained by INTERDICT. The Trespass (Scotland) Act 1865 (as amended) applies to Scotland, so it is of technical importance in that respect, creating a criminal offence in some special examples of intrusion upon property. In the UK some terms of trespass have been criminalised. See COLLECTIVE TRESPASS.

tribunal in the constitutional law of the UK, an alternative forum for the resolution of disputes instead of the ordinary courts. They are most miscellaneous and are set up by statutes for various purposes. They quite often have entirely different rules of evidence and procedure from ordinary courts. They are generally supposed to be more flexible, more expert and speedier than the normal courts. They operate in many fields, including taxation, immigration and landlord and tenant. The lives of many are affected by the social security tribunals and the EMPLOYMENT TRIBUNALS appear to have been so much of a success that they are busy, respected and are given new jurisdictions from time to time. Some form of appeal usually lies from a tribunal, at least on law, to the ordinary courts, and there is a supervisory jurisdiction in the COUNCIL ON TRIBUNALS.

trover an action on the case that became a distinct species of case requiring allegations that: (i) the plaintiff had possession of goods; (ii) that he lost them by accident; (iii) the defendant found them; and (iv) the defendant converted them to his own use.

It was assumed that any dealing with the goods was a denial of the owner's title. DETINUE, another possibility, became unpopular for the procedural reason that the defendant was allowed to proceed by trial by wager of law. It is a form of WRONGFUL INTERFERENCE WITH GOODS covered now by the Torts (Interference with Goods) Act 1977.

trust an institution, developed in England by the Court of Chancery, whereby ownership of property is vested in one person (called a TRUSTEE) in order that the property be held for the benefit of another person (called a BENEFICIARY). Any property, real or personal, may be held in trust, although in English law, if the trust is other than a simple trust, if land is to be so held the form of trust is required by statute to be either a *strict settlement* or a *trust for sale and conversion*. Trusts for sale are now rare since all trusts of land are united in a single regime under the Trusts of Land and Appointment of Trustees Act 1996. Trusts may be classified in a number of ways: they may be *express trusts*, created by act of the settlor, to give effect to his intentions as expressed in the trust instrument; they may be *implied* or *resulting trusts*, where the law implies a trust to give effect to the intentions of the settlor that are not explicitly expressed; or they may be *constructive trusts*, where the court imposes a trust on the legal owner of property where it feels, in the interests of equity and good conscience, that the beneficial interest should be enjoyed by someone else.

Express trusts may be public trusts or private trusts. *Public trusts* are trusts established for the satisfaction of some purpose for the benefit of the public or a section of the public; under English law, such purpose trusts are void unless they are CHARITABLE (although this is not the case with some trust systems – mainly *offshore trusts*). Trusts may also be classified as to whether they are *simple trusts* (where the trustees have no active duties to perform, their sole function being to hold the legal title for the beneficiaries) or *special trusts*, where the trustees manage the trust property for the benefit of the beneficiaries and the satisfaction of their beneficial interests. *Special trusts* may be either fixed trusts or discretionary trusts; a *fixed trust* is one in which each beneficiary has a fixed and certain interest under the trust, which interest gives rise to rights that may be enforced against the trustees; an example of a fixed trust is where property is limited to X and Y on trust for A for life with remainder to B absolutely. Both A and B, because of their particular interests, have rights to income and capital respectively that are exercisable against the trustees. In contrast, a *discretionary trust* is one where the trustees have a discretion to exercise in deciding whether the beneficiaries shall receive what, if any, part of the trust property. Such trusts are usually coupled with a POWER so that the beneficiaries have no interest under the trust unless and until the discretion or power is exercised in their favour. An example would be where property is limited to X and Y on trust for such of the children of Z as X and Y should in their absolute discretion appoint. See also VARIATION OF TRUSTS.

trust corporation a company that has as its main or subsidiary sphere of operations the administration of TRUSTS, with itself as

TRUSTEE. The company should have an issued capital of at least £250,000 of which at least £100,000 should have been paid up. It is empowered to charge fees for it services at a level not higher than those charged by the public trustee.

The *public trustee*, set up under the Public Trustee Act 1906, is in effect the nationalised trust corporation. Its fees may be altered from time to time by statutory instrument.

trustee a person appointed to hold trust property and, in the case of an active TRUST, to administer it for the benefit of the beneficiaries. In the ordinary case, trusteeship will be 'full' in the sense that the trustees will have vested in them the property subject to the trust together with the powers of management enabling them to discharge their functions. However, under the Public Trustee Act 1906, provision was made for trust corporations to act as custodian trustees holding the legal title to the trust property and being responsible for its safekeeping but without any powers of management.

A *judicial trustee* is a special trustee appointed by and under the control of the court under the Judicial Trustees Act 1896. The court will not appoint a judicial trustee in the absence of special circumstances warranting it; an example of a case where such an appointment might be warranted would be where a trustee was also a BENEFICIARY and where there was a conflict of interest between his duties as a trustee and his position as a beneficiary.

A trustee may be removed either under an express power conferred in the trust instrument or by the court under the provisions of Section 36 of the Trustee Act 1925 where he has become unfit to act (through physical or mental incapacity) or has been abroad for more than 12 months.

The office of trustee is a gratuitous one, with the consequence that, in general, while trustees may be reimbursed for expenses properly incurred, they may not receive remuneration. To this general rule there are a number of exceptions, the most important of which is where the trust instrument expressly empowers trustees to charge for their services. Additionally, the court may, if it considers it in the interests of the trust, authorise charges to be made or to be increased: see *Re Duke of Norfolk's Sett. Trusts* [1981] 3 All ER 220.

A trustee is personally liable for any loss to the trust estate caused by or resulting from any breach of trust committed by him, whether that breach was deliberate (i.e. fraudulent) or negligent. However,

Section 61 of the Trustee Act 1925 provides that the court may absolve a trustee from such liability if he can demonstrate that he had acted honestly and reasonably and that he ought fairly to be excused.

Tynwald the legislature of the Isle of Man.

uberrima fides 'the utmost good faith'. Both in England and in Scotland, certain contracts are such that the parties are obliged to observe the utmost good faith. Indeed, parties who are about to enter such a contract are held to be under an obligation to disclose all relevant matters before the contract. Recognised instances are insurance, fidelity guarantees for officials and probably partnership. The effect of this is to allow a party, quite often an insurer, to avoid liability as the contract will be treated as voidable if there has not been disclosure.

ubi jus ibi remedium 'where there is a right there is a remedy.'

ultimus haeres 'the final inheritor'. In the UK, any property not disposed of by WILL goes to the Crown.

ultra vires 'beyond the power'. An act is *ultra vires* if it is beyond the legal powers of the person doing it; thus an act by a company not expressly or impliedly permitted by its memorandum or articles is *ultra vires*. In the UK, the *ultra vires* doctrine has been radically changed by the Companies Act 1989 to the extent that persons doing business with companies without notice of the problem have little to fear. The doctrine still applies in relation to other bodies such as local authorities: *Hazell* v. *Hammersmith & Fulham LBC* [1991] 1 All ER 545.

UN abbreviation for UNITED NATIONS.

unascertained goods see ASCERTAINED GOODS.

unconscionable morally abhorrent. In the legal context, from time to time and place to place the law insofar as not already incorporating moral issues allows exceptions to allow parties some degree of relief from being imposed upon. The modern legal conception tends to be discussed around the more practical and objective concept of inequality of bargaining position, which can help consumers as much as the more traditional beneficiary of protection the small debtor pressed for excessive interest or repossession.

undated instrument a BILL OF EXCHANGE is not invalid by reason only that it is undated.

undertaking in the law of the EUROPEAN UNION, one of the subjects of the law. It covers companies, partnerships and sole traders and is particularly the focus of the COMPETITION POLICY.

undischarged bankrupt a person against whom a BANKRUPTCY order has been made but who has not yet been discharged.

undisclosed principal a person of whose existence a third party is unaware so that the third party does not know that the person with whom he is dealing is an agent. So far as he is concerned, the agent is really a principal dealing on his own behalf and in his own name. There is no duty on a third party to enquire whether there is an undisclosed principal.

undue influence in the law of CONTRACT, the doctrine that will render a contract at least VOIDABLE if a person is reasonably considered to be in a position of trust (used non-technically) in relation to another person and abuses that trust. *National Westminster Bank* v. *Morgan* [1985] AC 686. This doctrine or a variety of it has allowed courts in the UK to prevent banks exercising mortgage powers against spouses who have been taken advantage of by the customer spouse: *Barclays Bank* v. *O'Brien* [1994] 1 AC 180; *Smith* v. *Bank of Scotland* 1997 SLT 1061.

unenforceable (of a CONTRACT) unable to be enforced by either party or unenforceable by one. In the former case, the contract is for practical purposes VOID, but in the latter case the other party may enforce. This question arises most often in relation to ILLEGAL contracts.

unfair contract terms certain provisions in CONTRACTS (and in some non-contractual provisions) that are controlled by legislation because they are unfair (as defined). In UK law, provision is now made to regulate unfair contract (and other) terms by the Unfair Contract Terms Act of 1977. The provisions differ as between Scotland and the rest of the UK. At common law, contract theory is such that men are free to make their own bargains, although the common law has always exercised some restraint on the freedom of contract. The Act generalises this protection. Although primarily directed towards contracts, it also covers other unfair writings such as non-contractual notices, and since the Law Reform (Miscellaneous Provisions) (Scotland) Act 1990 does so also in Scotland. It excludes certain contracts from its ambit, notably INSURANCE contracts, and does not apply in Scotland to unilateral gratuitous obligations. Terms that seek to exclude or limit or disclaim liability in respect of breach of duty, as through NEGLIGENCE, are VOID so far as personal injury is concerned, otherwise they have to be fair and reasonable. Terms in a standard form contract (which term is not defined in the Act) are also controlled. Any term that attempts to exclude the implied terms under the Sale of Goods Act 1979 is void in a consumer contract but must also be fair and reasonable in other contracts. In England the focus is upon parties who deal as a consumer. A party deals as a consumer in relation to another if:

(a) he neither makes the contract in the course of a business nor holds himself out as doing so;

(b) the other party does make the contract in the course of a business;

(c) in sale and other similar transactions the goods are of a type ordinarily supplied for private use or consumption.

In a sale by auction or competitive tender, the buyer is not in any circumstances to be regarded as dealing as a consumer. In Scotland, a consumer contract is a contract (not being a contract of sale by auction or competitive tender) in which one party to the contract deals, and the other party to the contract (the consumer) does not deal or hold himself out as dealing, in the course of a business, and where the contract involves goods, the goods are of a type normally supplied for private use or consumption. The time for judging the fairness and reasonableness of a contract is the time of contracting, not once the consequences of a breach are known. For the purposes of the provisions relating to the exclusion of the implied terms, certain matters are specifically included within the inquiry (so long as they appear to be relevant) as to whether terms are fair and reasonable both in England and in Scotland:

(1) the strength of the bargaining positions of the parties relative to each other, taking into account (among other things) alternative means by which the customer's requirements could have been met;

(2) whether the customer received an inducement to agree to the term, or in accepting it had an opportunity of entering into a similar contract with other persons but without having to accept a similar term;

(3) whether the customer knew or ought reasonably to have known of the existence and extent of the term (having regard, among other things, to any custom of the trade and any previous course of dealing between the parties);

(4) where the term excludes or restricts any relevant liability if some condition is not complied with, whether it was reasonable at the time of the contract to expect that compliance with that condition

would be practicable;

(5) whether the goods were manufactured, processed or adapted to the special order of the customer. See *Denholm Fishselling* v. *Anderson* 1991 SLT (Sh. Ct) 24.

Other additional controls affect consumer contracts under the Terms in Consumer Contract Regulations 1999. A term that has not been individually negotiated is unfair if, contrary to the requirements of good faith, it causes a significant imbalance in the parties' rights and obligation under the contract to the detriment of the consumer. Written terms have to be drafted in plain intelligible language and since the 1999 Regulations the Office of Fair Trading and some other bodies can enforce the law and require business to remove unfair terms.

unfair dismissal in the employment law of the UK, a termination of the employment of a worker for a reason that is not permitted under statute. This area of law is statutory and is superimposed on the common law of employment. An employee is 'dismissed' if the employment is terminated without notice or where a fixed term contract expires without notice. There are 'constructive' dismissals, where the employee terminates because of the employer's conduct. FRUSTRATION, as by a long illness, might not be a dismissal. As to 'unfair', the law deems a dismissal as a result of trade union membership or activity or non-membership of a trade union as unfair. Pregnancy is deemed to be an unfair reason. Making a person redundant can be unfair if the employee was wrongly selected. The general rule as to fairness depends upon two factors: (1) whether the reason for dismissal related to the employee's capability, qualification or conduct or was that the employee was redundant or that his continued employment would itself be a breach of the law or whether there was some other substantial reason of a kind such as to justify dismissal; and

(2) whether having regard to the reason shown, the employer acted reasonably or unreasonably in the circumstances in treating that reason as sufficient reason for dismissal. The employer must show the reason for the dismissal. There is no burden of proof either way in relation to the proof of the reasonableness of the dismissal. The test applied is the test of the reasonable employer.

The remedies available for unfair dismissal are of considerable practical importance in that the remedies are of a special nature. The cases are dealt with not by the ordinary courts but by the

EMPLOYMENT TRIBUNALS. The principal remedy is *reinstatement*, which gives the employee his job back just as if he had never been unfairly dismissed in the first place, with the same rights and seniority as he had before. *Re-engagement* is a lesser remedy, the employee being re-hired in a job similar to the one he lost but not with the same continuity and seniority. Various factors are considered in making such an order, and it may not be granted, either because the employee does not want to go back or because the employer offers to demonstrate that it would be impractical to have the employee back again. The alternative remedy is a payment comprising a basic award resembling a REDUNDANCY PAYMENT, and a compensatory award that is to be just and reasonable. The award may be reduced insofar as the employee has contributed to his own dismissal. There are limits on the maximum that can be paid (£50,000 at the time of writing) in ordinary cases but no limits in some others, like SEX DISCRIMINATION cases. If an employer is ordered to reinstate or re-engage and does not do so, the tribunal may award a further 13–26 weeks' pay (26–52 in cases of sex discrimination or RACIAL DISCRIMINATION).

unfair prejudice see MINORITY PROTECTION.

unicameral 'having one chamber'. The term is found in reference to parliaments. Thus, the UK has a *bicameral* PARLIAMENT consisting of the HOUSE OF COMMONS and the HOUSE OF LORDS, whereas the New Zealand parliament has a unicameral structure.

Uniform Commercial Code a code of rules, proposed in the 1950s, adopted by almost all the states in the USA, albeit with variations. It applies to almost all sales of goods.

unilateral 'one way'.

unilateral error ERROR of one party. If induced by the other party, the unilateral error may amount to an operative MISREPRESENTATION. If it is uninduced, then it is very likely that it will have no effect on a contract whatsoever. In Scots law, it is treated as being a weighty factor in relieving a party who has granted a unilateral gratuitous obligation.

unincorporated company an association that has no legal personality, as distinct from that of its members (e.g. a partnership or club).

unintentional defamation see DEFAMATION.

United Nations (UN) an international organisation founded by charter in 1945 after the Second World War. Leaving aside its enormous political influence, its charter obliges it, among other things, to reaffirm faith in fundamental human rights, to establish conditions under which justice and respect for the obligations arising from treaties and other sources of international law can be maintained, which founding objects clearly establish law as an important aspect of its work. It comprises six main bodies: the General Assembly, Security Council, Economic and Social Council, Trusteeship Council, International Court of Justice, and Secretariat. So far as narrow legal analysis is concerned, the United Nations most resembles a legal state when it applies sanctions. The Security Council may require members of the United Nations to apply sanctions against any state found guilty of threatening the peace, creating a breach of the peace, engaging in an act of aggression, or failing to perform the obligations incumbent upon it under a judgment of the International Court of Justice. In this way there is the appearance of a full legal system operating under the rule of law. The only problem is that it is a practically restricted system with, for example, the permanent unelected members of the Security Council being able to veto any action they dislike.

unjust enrichment see RESTITUTION.

unlawful assembly a meeting of three or more people with the intent of carrying out any unlawful purpose. See EUROPEAN CONVENTION ON HUMAN RIGHTS.

unlimited company a species of registered company whose members have an unlimited liability for the debts of the company so that the personal fortune of members are at risk. This is balanced by certain advantages in that such companies do not have to deliver their accounts to the Registrar of Companies and have more freedom to deal with their capital than limited companies.

unpaid seller a seller of goods is an unpaid seller within the meaning of the Sale of Goods Act 1979 when the whole price has not been paid or tendered or when a BILL OF EXCHANGE or other negotiable instrument has been received as conditional payment and the condition on which it was received has not been fulfilled by reason of the dishonour of the instrument or otherwise. Such a seller is entitled to the remedies provided in the Act LIEN, a RIGHT OF RETENTION and if the buyer is INSOLVENT the right of STOPPAGE IN TRANSIT.

unregistered company a company incorporated otherwise than by registration under the Companies Acts. This class of companies includes statutory companies and foreign companies; such companies are subject to some provisions of the Companies Act 1985.

unregistered land land the title to which is not subject to the Land Registration Acts; in such a case the title is manifested by deeds covering transactions affecting the land over the period of title (since 1969, 15 years).

usucaption acquisition of ownership by uninterrupted possession.

usufruct the right of enjoying the fruits of property of another person, e.g. the wife of a deceased person living in an estate house until her death.

usury the lending of money at very high rates. For centuries the law has controlled such lending and for centuries lenders and borrowers have conspired to transact with each other. Controls still exist in most jurisdictions. It may be treated as a crime and/or a ground for making the deal unenforceable to the detriment of the lender.

usus modernus Pandectarum 'the modern use of the Digest' of the CORPUS JURIS CIVILIS.

uttering in the criminal law of Scotland, the crime of using as genuine a fabricated writ intended to pass for that of someone else. It does not matter that the document was forged by someone else. FORGERY, unless criminalised by statute, is not a crime in Scotland.

v. abbreviation for *versus*, 'against'.

vacant possession land not subject to any lease or other adverse interest that would prevent the purchaser taking possession.

validity see HARTIAN, KELSINIAN.

value-added tax (VAT) a tax levied on the supply of goods or services in the UK and on the importation of goods into the UK. The imposition of VAT was required as a condition of the UK's entry into the European Community, and the original provisions were contained in the Finance Act 1972; the basic statutory provisions are now consolidated in the Value Added Tax Act 1983. Corresponding taxes exist in all other EC member states, and a similar (although not identical) Goods and Services Tax is levied in New Zealand and Canada.

vandalism destruction of, or damage to, property, usually but not necessarily maliciously. Scots law has a statutory offence that criminalises this syndrome.

variation of trust change in the operation of a TRUST. It is the duty of a TRUSTEE faithfully to carry out the terms of the trust and to give effect to the beneficial interest thereunder. It is possible, however, for the trusts to be varied either by the beneficiaries themselves under the rule in *Saunders* v. *Vautier* (1841) Cr. & Ph. 240 or pursuant to an application to the court under the Variation of Trusts Act 1958. For a variation under the rule in *Saunders* v. *Vautier* to be possible, there must be an agreement to that end by all the beneficiaries, and those beneficiaries must all be of full age and capacity and their entitlements must in aggregate amount to the entire beneficial interest under the trust. It follows from this that where a beneficiary, by reason of infancy or other incapacity, is unable to assent to the proposed arrangement, the rule cannot apply. In such a case an application may be made to the court under the Variation of Trusts Act. The court may approve the arrangement if it is of the opinion that it is for the benefit of the beneficiaries who lack the capacity to assent.

VAT abbreviation for VALUE-ADDED TAX.

VC abbreviation for VICE-CHANCELLOR.

veil see LIFTING THE (CORPORATE) VEIL.

venditioni exponas a writ. Where it appears upon the return of a writ of FIERI FACIAS that the sheriff has seized goods of the judgment debtor that he has not sold or that he has been unable to sell for want of buyers, the judgment creditor may apply for a writ of *venditioni exponas*, directing the sheriff to 'sell for the best price obtainable'.

verbal injury in Scots law, a generic term for delicts that cause harm by words, although this does not normally include negligent misstatements where it is the negligence that causes the harm, the words being merely the mode. Comprised within the category is DEFAMATION, CONVICIUM and MALICIOUS FALSEHOOD.

verbatim 'word for word'.

verdict vere dictum, 'truly said'. The decision of a jury based on its interpretation of the factual evidence led and the law as stated to it by the judge. A verdict of guilty means that the jury is satisfied BEYOND A REASONABLE DOUBT that the accused did the things required to constitute the crime as legally defined. Any other verdict (including in Scotland NOT PROVEN) is an acquittal and on the basis of the presumption of innocence, the accused can, indeed must, be described as innocent of the charge. In Scotland a bare majority (eight out of fifteen) is required for conviction. In England there must be ten out of 12 for the verdict. The Scottish system has in its favour that it would be more expensive to bribe or terrify the jury and there would be more witnesses to speak to failed attempts.

vergens ad inopiam 'on the brink of INSOLVENCY', of significance in relation to DILIGENCE and now to a lesser extent in insolvency.

vertical direct effect see DIRECT EFFECT.

veritas see DEFAMATION.

vesting the process whereby a right to or interest in property becomes the subject of entitlement by someone. If an interest *vests in possession*, the holder will become entitled to the immediate possession thereof; if it *vests in interest*, this signifies the existence of a prior interest that requires to be satisfied before possession can be assumed.

In Scotland, *vesting subject to defeasance* refers to conditional bequests where the condition is resolutive and not suspensive: see generally *Taylor* v. *Gilbert's Trs* (1878) 5 R (HL) 217. It is most commonly encountered where a testator makes a bequest that is conditional only upon the possible birth of a child, in which case, if the doctrine applies, the condition is ignored but may later be defeated by the happening of the event.

vexatious litigant a person who brings actions with no reasonable chance of success with the object of causing annoyance to opponents; such actions may be struck out, and the court may order, on application of the ATTORNEY GENERAL, that no further legal proceedings may be begun by the vexatious litigant without the leave of the court: *Re Wilson* [1973] 1 WLR 314.

A similar procedure has existed in Scotland at least since the Vexatious Actions (Scotland) Act 1898 whereby the LORD ADVOCATE may apply to the Inner House preventing a party raising an action without the permission of a LORD ORDINARY: *Lord Advocate* v. *Cooney* 1984 SLT 434.

vi 'force'.

vicarious liability liability where one person, himself blameless, is held liable for another person's conduct. The rule is often justified by reference to two Latin maxims: *respondeat superior* ('let the master answer') and *qui facit per alium facit per se* ('he who acts through another acts himself'). It is now accepted in modern times as a matter of policy, shifting the burden of the cost of accidents upon someone more likely to be able to pay. The most widely used example is the employer's liability for his employee. There is, however, generally no liability for an independent contractor like a taxi driver or removal firm: *Salsbury* v. *Woodland* [1970] 1 QB 324. For there to be vicarious liability in respect of an employee, the acts must be 'in the course of his employment', which does not rule out negligent or even deliberate wrongs by the employee but excludes cases where the employee has gone off 'on a frolic of his own. See *Rose* v. *Plenty* CA [1976] 1 WLR 141. For there to be liability in respect of an agent, the relationship will be examined to see whether the wrongdoer is acting on the other's business or for his instructed purposes: *Ormrod* v. *Crosville Motor Services* [1953] 1 WLR 1120. However, there is not in the UK any concept of a family car that would, without more, make one spouse liable for the other spouse's driving: *Morgans* v. *Launchberry* [1973] AC 127.

Vice-Chancellor an English judge. Since 1970 appointed by the Lord Chancellor, the Vice-Chancellor is responsible for the organisation of the business of the Chancery division and is *ex officio* a member of the COURT OF APPEAL.

victim impact statement information given to a criminal court when it is considering sentence as to the views of the victim. Such statements are contrary to the basic principle for criminal justice, which is the state's response to the offender. They are not used in Scotland but, subject to guidance, are in use in England and Wales. The guidance there requires the statement to be in proper form, and great caution is to be exercised where the defence cannot check out what is in the statement. On the other hand, it can be used to help the offender, for example where sentencing the offender would distress the victim: *R* v. *Perks* [2000] TLR 351.

Vienna Convention a term given to international conventions concluded in Vienna, e.g. Vienna Convention on the Law of Treaties 1969, Vienna Convention on Diplomatic Relations 1961 and Vienna Convention on Consular Relations 1963.

vigilantibus non dormientibus subvenium SEE LACHES.

vindicatio in Roman law, the action for enforcement of the right of ownership in a thing (including land), strictly only brought against another claiming full ownership as opposed to a possessor. In Scots law the term is often used in a loose sense to mean an enforcement of the right of ownership by recovering possession.

visa a form of certificate of entrance that is taken as evidence of a person's eligibility (other than as a British citizen) to enter the UK. A visa does not guarantee entry but refusal may only be given on specific grounds.

visitor a person seeking entry to the UK as a visitor will be admitted if he satisfies the immigration officer that:
(1) he is genuinely seeking entry for the period of the visit stated by him;
(2) for that period he will maintain and accommodate himself and any dependants, or will, with any dependants, be maintained and accommodated adequately by friends or relatives without working or having recourse to public funds; and
(3) he can meet the cost of his return or onward journey.
See also OCCUPIERS' LIABILITY.

void having no legal effect. In the law of CONTRACT, certain agreements may be treated as void, and if so they are treated as void *ab initio*, or 'from their inception' – i.e. they cannot ever have created legal consequences. Examples are SPONSIONES LUDICRAE, some, but not all, contracts entered into under ERROR or MISTAKE. The UNFAIR CONTRACT TERMS Act 1977 renders certain terms in contracts void, an example being one that tries to exclude liability for a breach of duty arising in the course of a business that causes death or personal injury.

voidable capable of being made VOID.

voidable marriage where a marriage has not been consummated owing to the impotency of one of the parties, the marriage subsists until an order of the court is obtained declaring it to be null. The process of obtaining such an order is referred to as *annulment*.

void marriage where an impediment exists to a lawful marriage (such as the fact that one of the parties is under age or is already married) that marriage is VOID and of no legal effect whatever. There is no need for the other party to obtain a court order declaring the marriage a nullity.

voir dire 'to speak the truth', a trial within a trial or initial inquisition to see if a confession is voluntary. In some US states it is used in the process of empanelling jurors.

volenti non fit injura see ASSUMPTION OF RISK.

voluntary winding up a winding up of a company initiated by a special or extraordinary resolution of the company rather than by a petition to the court.

wager of law an ancient mode of proof that became unpopular because the defendant could call people as witnesses just to testify to his general oath-worthiness, even if they knew nothing of the facts of the case. It may have accounted for the ascendancy of TROVER over DETINUE. Wager of law was well recognised in Scotland. Professor Walker indicates that, although unknown to the Romans, it was 'probably indigenous in Scotland and anterior to the Norman importation of the duel'.

Wagner Act a US statute of 1935 called properly the National Labor Relations Act. It established a board that supervised elections deciding upon acceptance of a union as a collective bargaining agent and it dealt with employee complaints regarding unfair practices by employers.

Waitangi Tribunal (New Zealand) a body set up in 1975 to deal with claims under the Treaty of Waitangi 1840. It was restructured in 1985. For the Maoris, it is said to be more than a simple consensual contract, having as it does the additional force of the obligation to venerate ancestors' promises. The treaty had three articles. It gave the British Crown sovereignty over New Zealand; it assured Maori New Zealanders that the Crown would protect all cultural and property rights. The third article gave Maoris full rights of British citizenship. The 1985 Amendment Act allowed the tribunal to look into violations that had taken place right back to the original treaty. The 1988 Amendment Act was required to help process a large backlog of claims, many complaining of conduct in imperial times. The tribunal's remit is to consider claims relating to the practical application of the treaty. The tribunal considers whether the claimant was one judicially affected. The claimant must be Maori or of Maori descent. Since 1988 the tribunal can make decisions that bind state enterprises. The tribunal is investigative rather than adversarial, and its proceedings could be described as casual and permit cases to be argued in Maori.

waiver the act of abandoning or refraining from asserting or exercising a right. A waiver may be express or implied from conduct (i.e. doing nothing or acting in a manner inconsistent with the existence or exercise of the right).

waiver of tort in English law a plaintiff can, instead of seeking damages for a wrong done, seek RESTITUTION of the gains made by the defendant. Some torts can be waived, like TRESPASS and deceit, and others cannot.

The defendant, on authority, has to have received a specific sum of money. The value of use and occupation of land cannot be recovered from a trespasser, but this is a narrow rather than a principled exclusion, a fee being recoverable in the case of conversion of a chattel: *Strand Electric & Engineering Co.* v. *Brisford Entertainments* [1952] 2 QB 246. In the USA, the concept has been extended to cover even the tort of interference in contract: *Federal Sugar Refining Co.* v. *US Equalization Board* 268 F 575 (1920).

war crime a concept of international law that denotes prohibited activities even during the carnage of war. It includes crimes against humanity, genocide and mistreatment of civilians and captured combatants. The problem has been that familiar in international law of enforcement. The high point of recognition was in the Nuremberg trials of German politicians soldiers and others after the Second World War. In more recent times, the establishment of a war crimes tribunal, which has tried individuals during a state of conflict, has lent the concept a stronger core. It will be a successful legal construct when a soldier can disobey an order instructing a war crime without fear of penalty.

wardship the condition and relationship between a guardian and his ward. In England, a child may be made a *ward of the court*.

warranty a promise or undertaking by one party to a contract to secure the other party in the enjoyment of anything agreed between them. In particular, warranty is used in connection with a contract of sale whereby the vendor warrants that the thing sold is the vendor's to sell and is good and fit for use, or at least such use as the purchaser wishes to make of it (see Sale of Goods Act 1979). A warranty may be express or implied. In marine insurance, an *express warranty* is an agreement expressed in the policy whereby the assured stipulates that certain facts are or that certain acts shall be done relative to the risk. It may relate to an existing or past fact, or it may be promissory and relate to the future. An *implied warranty* is such as necessarily results from the nature of the contract. In a colloquial sense, it applies to promises by manufacturers to consumers to repair or replace goods.

warranty of authority a promise that one is an authorised agent. Where an agent has contracted as an agent (rather than personally) the agent cannot be made personally liable to the third party who has contracted with him. If, however, the agent had no authority to contract and the contract was entered into on the strength of representation of authority made by the agent, he will be so personally liable. See AGENCY.

wayleave a right of way, usually in the nature of an express easement and granted by deed or by reservation in consideration of a rent or other charge being exacted.

weight of evidence the degree of reliance that a court places on a piece of evidence.

Welsh Assembly the common name for the NATIONAL ASSEMBLY FOR WALES.

Welsh mortgage a special kind of mortgage, which has been used quite commonly in Ireland, under which the mortgagee takes possession of land as security for a loan. The mortgagee takes the rents and profits from the land in place of interest. The mortgagor has no obligation to pay the principal but may redeem it at any time on doing so.

Westlaw one of the world's biggest online legal research tools. Originally a leader in the USA, Westlaw UK now provides an increasing service to the English and Scots jurisdictions.

wheel-clamping the practice of immobilising a motor vehicle for illegal parking. The lawful authorities now have this power in many legal systems. Without such powers the practice can infringe the criminal law depending on the circumstances and the legal system applying: see e.g. TRESPASS, THEFT, EXTORTION.

whistleblower a person, usually an employee, who reveals information, which he is contractually obliged to keep secret, because of an overriding public interest. The principle was recently introduced into the UK by the Public Interest Disclosure Act 1998, which has, for example, resulted in an accountant who was dismissed for exposing financial irregularities of his manager to the company headquarters in the USA being awarded not that much short of £300,000.

white bonnet in Scotland, the term used for a person bidding on behalf of the owner to raise the price at an auction, now restricted by statute. See PUFFER.

Whitsunday see QUARTER DAY.

will a legal document in which a person (the TESTATOR) directs how his property is to be distributed after his death. Such documents must be executed in due form (i.e. in England, in accordance with the provisions of Section 9 of the Wills Act 1837) and must be duly witnessed.

winding up an alternative term for the LIQUIDATION of a company, the process of bringing to an end the existence and affairs of the company. Companies may be wound up either voluntarily at the motion of either members or creditors or by the court or under the supervision of the court. The winding up is conducted by a LIQUIDATOR appointed by the court.

without prejudice a phrase written on letters to indicate that the letter is not to be founded upon in a court, particularly as an admission of liability. It is given effect in both England and Scotland but subject to some subtle exceptions.

witness a person who gives evidence; in court such evidence must be given on oath or by affirmation.

Woodhouse Report (New Zealand) the report issued in December 1967 that gave birth to the much discussed ACCIDENT COMPENSATION Act of 1982.

Woolf Reforms the reforms to the civil justice system in England and Wales that followed the review of the civil justice system undertaken by Lord Woolf. He produced an interim report and a final report entitled Access to Justice. Many of his recommendations are reflected in the civil procedure rules that now govern civil litigation. A central feature of the reforms is that cases should be allocated to an appropriate 'track'. These are: the *small claims track* for simpler cases of low value; the *fast track* for cases involving £5-15,000; and the *multi-track* for complex cases. Also important is the idea that once a case is allocated to a track judges should manage its progress rather than, as in the past, that the parties and their lawyers should be in control of the speed at which the case progresses. Costs are strictly controlled and are expected to reflect the value of the cause.

worker the beneficiary of much modern legislation, sometimes in capacity as an employee under a contract of employment but also under separate regimes such as the Wages Act 1986. In the law of the EUROPEAN COMMUNITIES, the worker is the subject of many legal provisions. See FREE MOVEMENT OF PERSONS.

working time in the law of the EU as applied by MEMBER STATES, any period during which the worker is working, at the employer's disposal and carrying out his activities or duties, in accordance with national laws and/or practices. The average working time for each seven-day period, including overtime, generally must not exceed 48 hours. The UK government managed to secure an opt-out provision by which for the first seven years of the directive coming into force, workers can voluntarily continue to work more than 48 hours a week but not under compulsion. The directive requires that every worker is entitled to a minimum daily rest period of 11 consecutive hours per 24-hour period (Article 3). The directive also requires that member states take the measures necessary to ensure that per each seven-day period, every worker is entitled to a minimum uninterrupted rest period of 24 hours plus the 11 hours' daily rest. A rest period is any period that is not working time, e.g. the lunch hour. Workers are generally entitled to four weeks' annual leave and at least a week of it in one block. The employer can decide, subject to detailed rules, when the leave can be taken.

work permit a document, issued by the Department of Employment, allowing visitors to the UK for a limited period (not exceeding 12 months) to work while in the UK. The permit controls the place and duration of the work, which must be with a specific employer.

World Court see INTERNATIONAL COURT OF JUSTICE.

writ something in writing. More specially, a document under SEAL, issued in the name of the Crown or a court, commanding the person to whom it is addressed to do or refrain from doing some specified act. See, for example, CERTIORARI, MANDAMUS, INITIAL WRIT.

Writer to the Signet a member of the oldest society of SOLICITORS in Scotland. Members utilise the initials **WS** after their names. Some firms use an alternative appellation, **CS** (Clerk to the Signet). The signet in this context is the royal seal. Actions raised in the Court of Session had to pass the signet and hence members of the society were involved in the early stages of litigation. Now there is no special procedure in initiating an action and no real need for a separate society.

writ of execution one of the series of writes (e.g. FIERI FACIAS) by which judgments or orders of the court are enforced.

writ of restitution a writ of restitution may issue after the reversal or setting aside of a judgment for possession or where the defendant wrongfully resumes possession of land after entry by the sheriff.

wrongful dismissal dismissal in breach of contract. This is an ordinary common law claim for damages and is not to be confused with the special statutory regime for cases of UNFAIR DISMISSAL, although it is now possible to bring such claims before an EMPLOYMENT TRIBUNAL.

wrongful execution an execution is wrongful where it is neither authorised nor justified by the WRIT OF EXECUTION or by the judgment under which it is issued.

wrongful interference with goods a generic heading in terms of the Torts (Interference with Goods) Act 1977 for CONVERSION, TROVER, TRESPASS to goods and NEGLIGENCE so far as it results in damage to goods. See also DETINUE.

wrongful trading see FRAUDULENT TRADING.

WS abbreviation for WRITER TO THE SIGNET.

WTO abbreviation for World Trade Organisation. See GATT.

yellow book a publication of the London Stock Exchange setting out the requirements to be met for the admission of securities to listing. Since the Financial Services Act 1986, its provisions had official legislative status in that they are 'listing rules' for the purposes of the Act. This will continue to be the case under the Financial Services and Markets Act 2000. See FINANCIAL SERVICES LAW.

yellow dog see NORRIS-LA GUARDIA ACT.

York-Antwerp rules voluntary rules implementing, for those who choose to accept them, a common regime in respect of GENERAL AVERAGE. The names derive from the first two international conferences which settle the rules – York in 1864 and Antwerp in 1877. The most recent edition was prepared in 1974.

young defendant as a result of a decision of the European Court of Human Rights, the English courts now adhere to a practice direction by which children and young persons are to be called young defendants in the County Court and provision is made for making the court process fairer and 'friendlier' for such persons and to avoid treating them along with 'harder' adult offenders: Practice Direction, [2000] TLR 111.

young offender institution a place of detention for persons under 21 years of age. The idea is to keep the younger offender away from the older and more experienced criminals in the adult prisons that would otherwise become 'academies of crime'.

youth court the court in England and Wales that hears criminal cases against those under 18.

TABLE OF CASES

TABLE OF STATUTES